# The Trial o
# Random de berenger

Sir Thomas Cochrane, commonly called Lord Cochrane, The Hon. Andrew Cochrane Johnstone, Richard Gathorne Butt, Ralph Sandom, Alexander M'Rae, John Peter Holloway, and Henry Lyte for A Conspiracy In the Court of King's Bench, Guildhall, On Wednesday the 8th, and Thursday the 9th of June, 1814

(Transcriber: William Brodie Gurney)

Alpha Editions

This edition published in 2024

ISBN : 9789362090805

Design and Setting By
**Alpha Editions**
www.alphaedis.com
Email - info@alphaedis.com

As per information held with us this book is in Public Domain.
This book is a reproduction of an important historical work. Alpha Editions uses the best technology to reproduce historical work in the same manner it was first published to preserve its original nature. Any marks or number seen are left intentionally to preserve its true form.

# THE TRIAL OF CHARLES RANDOM DE BERENGER, AND OTHERS.

On the 20th of April, 1814, the Grand Jury for the City of London, at the Sessions-House, in the Old Bailey, returned a True Bill, which set forth:

[*First Count.*]—That at the times of committing the several offences in this Indictment mentioned, there was, and for a long time before, to wit, two years and upwards, had been an open and public war between our Lord the King and his Allies, and the then ruler of France, to wit, Napoleon Bonaparte, and the people of France:

And that *Charles Random de Berenger, Sir Thomas Cochrane*, commonly called *Lord Cochrane, Andrew Cochrane Johnstone, Richard Gathorne Butt, Ralph Sandom, Alexander M'Rae, John Peter Holloway*, and *Henry Lyte*, supposing and believing, that false reports and rumours of the death of said Napoleon Bonaparte, and of disasters and losses having recently occurred and happened to the said people of France, would induce the subjects of our said Lord the King to suppose and believe, that a peace between our said Lord the King and his subjects, and the said people of France would soon be made, and that an increase and rise in the Government Funds and Government Securities of this Kingdom, would be occasioned thereby. And unlawfully, &c. intending to injure and aggrieve the subjects of our said Lord the King, who should make purchases of and in said Funds, &c. on the 19th February, in Fifty-fourth year of the Reign of our said Lord the King, at the parish of St. Bartholomew, by the Exchange, in the Ward of Broad-street, in London aforesaid, unlawfully, &c. did conspire, &c. to make and propagate, and to cause, &c. to be made and propagated, a false report and rumour, that the French had been then lately beaten in battle, and that said Napoleon Bonaparte was killed, and that the Allies of our said Lord the King were in Paris.

And that they, the *Defendants*, would thereby induce the subjects of our said Lord the King to suppose and believe, that a peace would soon be made between our said Lord the King and the said people of France, and occasion an increase, &c. of the prices of the Government Funds, &c.

And that *Defendants, Sir Thomas Cochrane Johnstone, Richard Gathorne Butt, and John Peter Holloway*, respectively, should then sell, and cause, &c. to be sold for them, to divers liege subjects, &c. divers large parts, and shares in said Funds, &c. at higher and greater prices than said parts and shares of and in said Funds, &c. would otherwise sell for, with a wicked and fraudulent intention to thereby cheat, &c. the said subjects, &c. of divers large sums of money.

And that afterwards, to wit, on the 21st February, in the year aforesaid, at the parish and ward aforesaid, in London aforesaid, to wit, at Dover, in the county of Kent, the said *Charles Random de Berenger*, in pursuance, &c. of said conspiracy, did unlawfully, &c. write a certain false and counterfeit letter, containing divers false matters, which said false and counterfeit letter is directed as follows:

"To the Honorable J. Foley, Port Admiral, Deal, &c. &c. &c.

*Dover, One o'Clock, A. M.*
*February 21, 1814.*

SIR,

I have the honor to acquaint you that the L'Aigle from Calais, Pierre Duquin, Master, has this moment landed me near Dover, to proceed to the Capital with dispatches of the happiest nature. I have pledged my honor that no harm shall come to the crew of the L'Aigle; even with a flag of truce they immediately stood for sea. Should they be taken, I have to entreat you immediately to liberate them. My anxiety will not allow me to say more for your gratification, than that the Allies obtained a final victory; that Bonaparte was overtaken by a party of Sachen's Cossacks, who immediately slaid him, and divided his body between them.—General Platoff, saved Paris from being reduced to ashes. The Allied Sovereigns are there, and the white cockade is universal; an immediate peace is certain. In the utmost haste, I entreat your consideration, and have the honor to be,

Sir,
Your most obedient humble Servant,
R. DU BOURG,
*Lieutenant Colonel and Aid de Camp to Lord Cathcart.*

"To the Honorable J. Foley,
Port Admiral, Deal, &c. &c. &c."

And did then and there send, and cause and procure to be sent, the said false and counterfeit letter to Thomas Foley, Esquire, at Deal; he, the said Thomas Foley, then being the Commander in Chief of His Majesty's Ships &c. employed on the Downs Station, with intention that the said T. Foley, should, by Telegraph, communicate the false matters in the said false letter, to the Commissioners of our said Lord the King, for executing the office of Lord High Admiral, &c. and that such false matters should be promulgated &c. to the liege subjects of our said Lord the King.

And that said *Charles Random De Berenger*, did also then and there unlawfully &c. assert and report to Timothy Wright, and other persons, that he, the said *Charles Random De Berenger*, had just then landed and arrived from France, and that the French were beaten, and that said Napoleon Bonaparte was killed, and that the Allies of our said Lord the King, were then in Paris; and the said *Charles Random De Berenger*, on same day &c. did travel from Dover towards London, and did unlawfully &c. falsely assert and report at Dartford in the County of Kent, and at other places on his way between Dover and London, the several false matters and things last mentioned, to divers other of the liege subjects of our said Lord the King with intention that the said last mentioned false matters &c. should be believed to be true, and should be generally reported, &c. by the said liege subjects, &c. to whom he asserted the same to divers other of the liege subjects, &c.

And more especially, with intention that the said false assertions &c. should reach London, to be reported and rumoured and believed there. And that on the said 21st February, at the parish &c. aforesaid, at London aforesaid, to wit, at Dartford aforesaid, the said *Ralph Sandom*, *Alexander M'Rae* and *Henry Lyte*, in pursuance &c. of the aforesaid conspiracy did unlawfully &c. hire and take a post chaise to go from Dartford, and did go from thence, the said *Alexander M'Rae* and *Henry Lyte*, then and there having white cockades in certain cocked hats, which they wore; and the horses drawing the said post-chaise then and there being decorated with branches of laurel, to and over London Bridge, and through the City of London, unto and over Blackfriars Bridge, and unto a certain place called the Marsh Gate, in the Parish of St. Mary Lambeth, in the County of Surry, with intention thereby to induce the liege subjects, &c. whom they should pass, and who should see them in their route and way from Dartford to near the Marsh Gate, to suppose and believe, and to report and rumour to divers other of the liege subjects, that they the said *Ralph Sandom*, *Alexander M'Rae*, and *Henry Lyte*, were the bearers to the Government of this kingdom, of great and important foreign news, highly favorable to the interests of our said Lord the King, and his subjects, and thereby to occasion an increase and rise in the prices of the said public Government Funds, &c. in order and for the purpose that the said *Sir Thomas Cochrane, Andrew Cochrane Johnstone, Richard Gathorne Butt*, and *John Peter Holloway*, respectively should then sell and cause and procure to be sold for them respectively to divers subjects, &c. divers large parts and shares of and in the said public Government Funds &c. at higher and greater prices than they would otherwise sell for, with a wicked and fraudulent intention, to thereby cheat and defraud the said last mentioned liege subjects, of divers large sums of money.

And that the said *Defendants*, in pursuance and further prosecution of said conspiracy, afterwards, to wit, on the said 21st February, did, by means of the premises aforesaid, unlawfully &c. cause and occasion a temporary increase and rise in the prices of said Funds, &c.

And the said *Sir Thomas Cochrane, Andrew Cochrane Johnstone, Richard Gathorne Butt* and *John Peter Holloway*, in pursuance and further prosecution of the aforesaid conspiracy, did on the said 21st of February, unlawfully, &c. respectively sell, and cause and procure to be sold for them respectively, unto divers subjects, &c. divers great parts and shares of and in the said public Government Funds and other Government Securities, (that is to say,) the said

| *Sir Thomas Cochrane* | £139,000 Omnium. |
| *Andrew Cochrane Johnstone* | £141,000 Omnium, and £100,000 Consols |
| *Richard Gathorne Butt* | £224,000 Omnium, and £168,000 Consols |
| *John Peter Holloway* | £20,000 Omnium, and £34,000 Consols |

at and for greater and larger prices than such parts and shares of and in the said public and Government Funds, &c. would otherwise have sold for, with a wicked and fraudulent intention, then and there to cheat and defraud the said subjects respectively, of divers large sums of money, of the respective monies of the said last mentioned liege subjects, to the damage of the said last mentioned liege subjects, to the evil example &c. in contempt of our said Lord the King and his Laws, and against the peace of our said Lord the King, his crown and dignity.

[*Second Count.*]—That the *Defendants* on the said 19th February, unlawfully &c. to induce the subjects &c. to believe that a peace between our said Lord the King and his Subjects and the people of France, would soon be made, and thereby to occasion an increase and rise in the prices of the public Government Funds, and other Government Securities, and to greatly injure and aggrieve the subjects of our said Lord the King, who should on the 21st February, purchase and buy a part or parts and share or shares of and in the said public Government Funds, &c. on said 19th February, with force and arms, &c. unlawfully &c. did conspire &c. together to make and propagate, and to cause and procure to be made and propagated, a false report and rumour, that the French had then lately been beaten in battle, and that said Napoleon Bonaparte was killed, and that the Allies of our said Lord the King were then in Paris.

And that they, the *Defendants*, would by such last mentioned false report and rumour induce the subjects, &c. to suppose and believe that a peace would soon be made, and occasion an increase and rise in the prices of the public government funds, &c.

And that *Sir Thomas Cochrane, Andrew Cochrane Johnstone, Richard Gathorne Butt*, and *John Peter Holloway*, respectively, should then sell and cause, &c. to be sold for them respectively, to divers of the liege subjects of our said Lord the King, divers other large parts and shares of and in the said government funds, &c. at higher and greater prices than said parts and shares would otherwise sell for, with a wicked and fraudulent intention to thereby cheat and defraud the said liege subjects, &c. of divers large sums of money.

And that on the said 21st of February the *Defendants*, in pursuance of said conspiracy, &c. unlawfully, &c. did cause and procure divers false reports and rumours to be made, spread, and circulated unto and amongst many of the liege subjects, &c. in certain parts of the counties of Kent and Surry, to wit at Dover in the said county of Kent, and in and along and near unto the King's common highway leading from Dover aforesaid to the said City of London, and also in the said City of London and parts adjacent thereto, that the French had then lately been beaten in battle, and that the said Napoleon Bonaparte was killed, and that the Allies of our said Lord the King were then in Paris. And that a peace between our said Lord the King and his subjects, and the said people of France would soon be made, with intention thereby to occasion an increase and rise in the said funds, &c. in order and for the purpose that the said *Sir Thomas Cochrane, Andrew Cochrane Johnstone, Richard Gathorne Butt*, and *John Peter Holloway*, respectively, should then sell and cause and procure to be sold for them respectively to divers liege subjects, &c. divers other large parts and shares of and in the said public government funds, &c. at higher and greater prices than they would otherwise sell for, with a wicked and fraudulent intention to thereby cheat and defraud the said subjects of divers large sum of money, &c.

[*Third Count*.]—That the *Defendants* on the said 19th of February unlawfully, &c. by false reports, rumors, *arts and contrivances* to induce the subjects of our said Lord the King to believe that a peace would soon be made between our said Lord the King and his subjects, and the said people of France, and thereby to occasion *without any just or true cause a great increase and rise of the public government funds, &c. and to injure, &c. the subjects of our said Lord the King who should* on the said 21st of February *purchase and buy any part or parts and share or shares of and in the said public government funds, &c.* then and there, to wit, on the said 21st of February, unlawfully, &c. did conspire, &c. to make and propagate, and cause and procure to be made and propagated unto and amongst divers of the liege subjects, &c. in the county of Kent, to wit at Dover, Deal, and Dartford, and other places in that county, and also unto and amongst divers of the liege subjects, &c. at London aforesaid, and places adjacent thereto divers false reports and rumours that the said Napoleon Bonaparte was killed, and that a peace would soon be made between our said Lord the King and his subjects and the people of France.

And that the said *Defendants* would by such false reports and rumours as far as in them lay, occasion an increase and rise in the prices of the public government funds and other government securities, with a wicked intention to thereby greatly injure and aggrieve all the liege subjects of our said Lord the King who should, on the said 21st of February, purchase or buy any part or parts and share or shares of and in said public government funds, &c. To the great damage of all the last mentioned liege subjects, &c. To the evil example, &c. and against the peace, &c.

[*Fourth Count.*]—That the said *Defendants* unlawfully contriving, &c. to injure and aggrieve divers of the liege subjects, &c. on the 19th February unlawfully, &c. did conspire, &c. to write and cause to be written *a certain other false and counterfeit letter* containing therein divers false matters of and concerning the Allies of our said Lord the King, and the said Napoleon Bonaparte and the French people, and to send and cause and procure the said last mentioned letter to be sent to the aforesaid Thomas Foley at Deal, the said Thomas Foley then and there being the Commander in Chief of His Majesty's ships and vessels employed on the Downs' station, with a wicked intention to impose upon and deceive the said Thomas Foley, and to induce and cause the said Thomas Foley to communicate the false matters contained in the said last mentioned false and counterfeit letter to the said Commissioners for executing the office of Lord High Admiral of Great Britain. And also with a wicked intention, that by the means in this Count mentioned the said false matters contained in said last mentioned false and counterfeit letter, should be promulgated and publicly made known to the liege subjects, &c. and thereby to occasion *a temporary* rise and increase in the prices of the public government funds, &c. and to injure and aggrieve all His Majesty's liege subjects who should *contract for*, and also, all the subjects, &c. who should *purchase* any part or parts, share or shares of, and in the said public government funds, &c. *during such temporary rise and increase* in the prices thereof, to the evil example, &c. in contempt, &c. and against the peace, &c.

[*Fifth Count.*]—That the Defendants unlawfully contriving, &c. to injure and aggrieve divers of the liege subjects of our said Lord the King, afterwards to wit, on the said 19th February, at the parish and ward aforesaid, &c. unlawfully, &c. did conspire together, to make and propagate, and to cause and procure to be made and propagated unto, and amongst divers of the liege subjects of our said Lord the King, divers false reports and rumours *of and concerning the said Napoleon Bonaparte and the French people*, and thereby to occasion a temporary rise and increase in the prices of the public Government Funds, &c. and to injure and aggrieve all his Majesty's liege subjects who should *contract for*, and also all the liege subjects of our said Lord the King who should *purchase* any part or parts, share or shares of, and in the said public Government Funds, &c. during such last mentioned temporary rise and increase in the prices thereof, to the evil example, &c. &c.

[*Sixth Count.*]—That the *Defendants*, on the said 19th February unlawfully, &c. did conspire, &c. to make and propagate, and cause, and procure to be made and propagated unto and amongst divers subjects, &c. a certain false report and rumour, *that a Peace would then be soon made* between our said Lord the King, his subjects, and the people of France, and thereby to occasion a temporary rise and increase in the prices of the public Government Funds, &c. and to injure and aggrieve all his Majesty's subjects who should contract for, and also all the liege subjects, &c. who should purchase any part or parts, or share or shares of and in the said public Government Funds, &c. during such last mentioned temporary rise and increase in the prices thereof, to the evil example, &c.

[*Seventh Count.*]—That the *Defendants*, unlawfully contriving, &c. *for their own lucre and gain*, to injure and aggrieve divers of the liege subjects of our said Lord the King, on the said 19th February, unlawfully, &c. did conspire, &c. by divers *false and subtle arts, devices, contrivances, representations, reports, and rumours*, to occasion without just and true cause, a rise and increase in the prices of the public Government Funds, &c. and thereby to injure and aggrieve all his Majesty's liege subjects who should contract for, and also all his Majesty's liege subjects who should purchase any part or parts, share or shares of and in the said public Government funds, &c. during such last mentioned rise and increase in the prices thereof, to the evil example, &c.

[*Eighth Count.*]—That the *Defendants* unlawfully, &c. contriving to injure and aggrieve divers of the liege subjects of our said Lord the King, on the 19th February unlawfully, &c. did conspire, &c. by divers *false and subtle arts, devices, contrivances, representations, reports and rumours*, to induce, cause and occasion, divers and very many of the liege subjects of our said Lord the King, *to suppose and believe, without true and just cause, that a peace would soon be made between our said Lord the King and his subjects, and the people of France*, to the great and manifest injury of divers and very many of the liege subjects of our said Lord the King, to the evil example, &c.

*Plea*—NOT GUILTY.

The Indictment was removed into the Court of King's Bench, at the instance of the Prosecutors, in Easter Term.

---

COURT OF KING'S BENCH, GUILDHALL,

*Wednesday, 8th June, 1814.*

Before the Right Hon. LORD ELLENBOROUGH.

*Counsel for the Prosecution.*
Mr. GURNEY,
Mr. BOLLAND,
Mr. ADOLPHUS.

*Solicitors.*
Messrs. CROWDER, LAVIE, and GARTH.

*Counsel for C. R. De Berenger.*
Mr. PARK,
Mr. RICHARDSON.

*Solicitor.*
Mr. GABRIEL TAHOURDIN.

*Counsel for Lord Cochrane, The Hon. A. C. Johnstone, and R. G. Butt.*
Mr. Serjeant BEST,
Mr. TOPPING,
Mr. SCARLETT,
Mr. BROUGHAM.

*Solicitors for Lord Cochrane.*
Messrs. FARRER and ATKINSON.

*Solicitors for the Hon. A. C. Johnstone, and R. G. Butt.*
Messrs. BRUNDRETT, WAINWRIGHT, and SPINKS.

*Counsel for R. Sandom, J. P. Holloway, and Henry Lyte.*
Mr. Serjeant PELL,
Mr. C. F. WILLIAMS,
Mr. DENMAN.

*Solicitor.*
Mr. YOUNG.

*Counsel for Alexander M'Rae.*
Mr. ALLEY.

*Solicitor.*
Mr. TWYNAM.

## THE JURY.

| | |
|---|---|
| Thomas Brown, Church-row, Aldgate.<br>Henry Septimus Wollaston, Devonshire-street.<br>George Spedding, Upper Thames-street.<br>George Miles, Gracechurch-street.<br>John Parker, Broad-street.<br>Lewis Loyd, Lothbury.<br>John Peter Robinson, Austin Friars.<br>John Hodgson, New Broad-street.<br>Thomas Wilson Hetherington, Nicholas-lane.<br>Richard Hall, Lawrence-lane.<br>Richard Cheesewright, King-street.<br>John Green, Suffolk-lane. | Merchants. |

*The Indictment was opened by Mr.* ADOLPHUS.

Mr. GURNEY.

May it please your Lordship.

Gentlemen of the Jury.

It is my duty, as Counsel for this Prosecution, to state to you the facts which I shall have to lay before you, and to apply those facts to the several Defendants, and to the Charges contained in the Indictment, which has been opened by my learned Friend; and, Gentlemen, I am sure that it is unnecessary for me to request that you will dismiss from your minds every thing that you may have heard upon this subject before you entered that Box. It is one of the circumstances which necessarily attends a free press, that many cases which come under the consideration of a Court of Justice, shall previously have undergone some public discussion; without blame to any one, that will sometimes occur from the nature and publicity of the case itself. It does also sometimes occur, that they who are accused, industriously circulate matters which they consider as useful to their defence; and even on the very eve of trial, force them into public notice. If any thing has fallen under your observation, either on the one side or the other, I intreat you to lay it totally aside; to come to the consideration of this subject with cool, dispassionate, unprejudiced, unprepossessed minds, to attend to the evidence that will be laid before you, and to that evidence alone—by that evidence let the Defendants stand or fall.

Gentlemen, it would be very extraordinary indeed, if it could ever have been supposed by any person, even the most ignorant, that this was not a crime. It would be a disgrace to any civilized country, if its laws were so defective. If that which has been done by these Defendants *in conspiracy*, had been done by any one of them *singly*, it would have been unquestionably a crime; but when done *by conspiracy*, it is a crime of a more aggravated nature—*To circulate false news*, much more *to conspire to circulate false news* with intent to raise the price of any commodity whatever, is, by the Law of England, a crime, and its direct and immediate tendency is to the injury of the public. If it be with intent to raise the price of the public funds of the country, considering the immense magnitude of those funds, and, consequently, the vast extent of the injury which may be produced, the offence is of a higher description. The persons who must be necessarily injured in a case of that kind, are various; the common *bona fide* purchaser who invests his money—the public, through the commissioners for the redemption of the national debt—the persons whose affairs are under the care of the Court of Chancery, and whose money is laid out by the Accountant General, all these may be injured by a temporary rise of the public funds, growing out of a conspiracy of this kind; and, Gentlemen, this is no imaginary statement of mine, for it will appear to you to-day, that all these persons were in fact injured by the temporary rise produced by this conspiracy. Undoubtedly the public funds will be affected by rumours, which may be considered as accidental; in proportion as they are liable to that, it becomes more important to protect them against fraud.

If this had been a conspiracy to circulate false rumours, merely to abuse public credulity, it would not have been a trivial offence; but if the object of the conspiracy be not merely to abuse public credulity, but to raise the funds, in order that the conspirators may sell out of those funds for their own advantage, and, consequently, to the injury of others, in that case the offence assumes its most malignant character—it is cold blooded fraud, and nothing else. It is then susceptible of but one possible aggravation, and that is, if the conspirators shall have endeavoured to poison the sources of official intelligence, and to have made the officers of government the tools and instruments of effectuating their fraud—Gentlemen, this offence, thus aggravated, I charge upon the several Defendants upon this Record, and I undertake to prove every one of them to be guilty.

Gentlemen, when I undertake to prove them to be guilty, you will not expect that I shall give you proof by *direct evidence*, because, in the nature of things, *direct evidence* is absolutely impossible—they who conspire do not admit into the chamber in which they form their plan, any persons but those who participate in it; and, therefore, except where they are betrayed by accomplices, in no such case can positive and direct evidence be given. If there are any who imagine, that positive and direct evidence is absolutely necessary to conviction, they are much mistaken; it is a mistake, I believe, very common with those who commit offences: they fancy that they are secure because they are not seen at the moment; but you may prove their guilt as conclusively, perhaps even more satisfactorily, by *circumstantial evidence*, as by any *direct evidence* that can possibly be given.

If direct and positive evidence were requisite to convict persons of crimes, what security should we have for our lives against the *murderer by poison?*—no man sees him mix the deadly draught, avowing his purpose. No, he mixes it in secret, and administers it to his unconscious victim as the draught of health; but yet he may be reached by *circumstances*—he may be proved to have bought, or to have made the poison; to have rinsed the bottle at a suspicious moment; to have given false and contradictory accounts; and to have a deep interest in the attainment of the object. What security should we have for our habitations against the *midnight burglar*, who breaks into your house and steals your property, without disturbing your rest or that of your family, but whom you reach by proving him, shortly afterwards, in the possession of your plate? What security should we have against the *incendiary*, who is never seen in the act by any human eye, but whose guilt, by a combination of circumstances over which he may have had no controul, or part of which he may have contrived for his own security, is as clearly established as if deposed to by the testimony of eye-witnesses.

Gentlemen, by the same sort of evidence by which in these, and various other cases, the lives of individuals are affected, I undertake to bring home this case to the Defendants upon this Record. I undertake to shew, that such a conspiracy did exist as this Indictment charges; and I undertake to prove every one of these Defendants acting in furtherance and execution of the conspiracy, so as to leave no more doubt upon your minds, when you have heard the evidence, that they were all parties to this conspiracy, than if you had witnesses before you who were present with them in consultation, and heard them assign to each man the part which he was to act.

Gentlemen, in the security in which we now repose, in the triumph in which we are now indulging, it is difficult to carry back our minds to the state of agonizing suspense in which we were at the critical time at which this conspiracy took place. At that time the empire of him for whom Europe itself appeared too small, was not confined within the narrow limits of the Isle of Elba; he had been driven back, it is true, from the extremity of Europe into France.—France itself was invaded, and our illustrious Allies had made considerable progress towards Paris, but they had been more than once repulsed, and one army had, by almost super-human efforts, preserved itself from destruction; but the fortune of war was uncertain; in this age of miracles, no man could tell what would be the final event; and every one was waiting in breathless expectation for the destruction of him (or at least of his power) who had been so long the destroyer of his species. Gentlemen, at that most critical moment, when the funds were so liable to be affected by every event of the war, when they were liable to be affected still more by the Negotiations at Chatillon, which were then pending—at that moment this conspiracy with respect to the Funds took place; and you will bear this in mind, Gentlemen, that if the false news were believed but for a single hour, the mischief to the public would be done—the object of the conspirators would be accomplished.

Gentlemen, the first person whom I shall have to present to you, as bearing a principal part in this conspiracy; the main agent in its execution, will be proved to be the Defendant, Charles Random de Berenger;—he was a fit person to be selected for the purpose;—he was a foreigner by birth; he had resided long in this country; he would pass very well for an officer; he had been for fourteen or fifteen months a prisoner for debt in the King's Bench, or rather within the Rules of the King's Bench; he would be a convenient man afterwards to convey away; as he would prefer a residence in any other country, because his creditors resided in this.

You will find that he made his appearance a little after midnight of Sunday, the 20th of February—the morning of Monday, the 21st of February; at Dover; he was first seen in the street, enquiring for the Ship Hotel; he was shewn to it, he knocked loudly at the door, and obtained admittance; he was dressed in a grey military great coat, a scarlet uniform, richly embroidered with gold lace, (the uniform of a Staff Officer) a star on his breast, a silver medal suspended from his neck, a dark fur cap with a broad gold lace, and he had a small portmanteau; he announced himself as an Aid de Camp to Lord Cathcart, just arrived from Paris; that he was the bearer of glorious news, that a decisive battle had taken place, that Bonaparte was pursued and killed by the Cossacks, that the Allied Sovereigns were actually in Paris, and that now (that most welcome news to the Inhabitants of Dover) an immediate Peace was certain. He desired to have a sheet of paper, that he might write a letter to the Port-Admiral at Deal, Admiral Foley; paper was furnished, and he sat down to write, and soon afterwards the letter was dispatched to the Port-Admiral at Deal. Upon persons coming round him and importuning him with questions, he pretended to be extremely fatigued. He said he had travelled two or three nights. "Do not pester me with questions, you will know it to-morrow from the Port-Admiral." He ordered a post-chaise and four for London, and he offered to pay with some gold Napoleons; the landlord of the inn did not know exactly the value of a

Napoleon, and scrupled to take them, upon which this gentleman, rather inconsiderately, produced from his pocket some one pound Bank of England notes, with those notes he paid for his chaise, and he set off for London in the post-chaise and four. When he arrived at Canterbury he rewarded his post-boys very liberally; he gave each of them a Napoleon. A Napoleon, I dare say you know, is worth eighteen or twenty shillings; he ordered horses on to Sittingbourn; the same chaise brought him from Canterbury to London, and he gave Napoleons to all his post-boys. It was difficult to say which was first upon the road, this Colonel Du Bourg or other expresses which had been sent off from Dover with this happy news, for as soon as this news was announced all Dover was in agitation. Post-horses were ordered out, and I believe some of the expresses reached London half an hour before this person himself.

Gentlemen, it will be necessary that I should read to you the letter to Admiral Foley, it is dated Dover, one o'clock A. M. February 21, 1814, addressed to the Honorable J. Foley, Port-Admiral, Deal, &c. &c. &c. signed R. Du Bourg, Lieutenant-Colonel and Aid de Camp to Lord Cathcart. "SIR, I have the honor to acquaint you, that the L'Aigle from Calais, Pierre Duquin, Master, has this moment landed me near Dover, to proceed to the Capital with dispatches of the happiest nature. I have pledged my honor that no harm shall come to the crew of L'Aigle; even with a flag of truce they immediately stood for sea: should they be taken, I have to intreat you immediately to liberate them, my anxiety will not allow me to say more for your gratification, than that the Allies obtained a final victory, that Bonaparte was overtaken by a party of Sachen's Cossacks, who immediately slaid him, and divided his body between them. General Platoff saved Paris from being reduced to ashes, the Allied Sovereigns are there, and the white cockade is universal, an immediate peace is certain; in the utmost haste, I entreat your consideration, and have the honor to be, Sir, your most obedient humble Servant, R. Du Bourg."

A post boy was sent over with this letter to Admiral Foley; he delivered it to the Admiral between three and four o'clock, I think, and nothing but the haziness of the morning which obstructed the working of the telegraph, prevented the news reaching the Admiralty, in which case the conspiracy in question, which was effectual to a great degree, would have been complete, and all the expectations of the conspirators fully realized.

Gentlemen, when Colonel Du Bourg, alias Mr. De Berenger, arrived at Rochester, he saw the landlord Mr. Wright, he conversed with him a considerable time, and to him he repeated this news. He ordered horses on for Dartford, and gave Napoleons to the post boys, and when he arrived at Dartford, he there repeated his news to the landlord and the waiter, partly in the hearing of the post boys. When he set off from Dartford he desired the post boys to drive as fast as possible; they did so for the first three miles; when they arrived at Bexley Heath, the road being within sight of the telegraph, he spoke to the post boys, and told them they need not drive so fast, that his business was not so pressing, as the telegraphs could not work; they told him they were sure they could not work, that they knew the telegraphs all along the road. In coming up Shooter's Hill, the post boys alighted from their horses and walked by the side of the chaise. They were naturally very desirous to know distinctly what the news was, and one of them said, "Pray Sir, what is the news?—Oh it is all over—Bonaparte is killed—the Cossacks fought for a share of his body; he was literally torn to pieces by the Cossacks,"—he said, "I landed last night within two miles of Dover, and the French boat immediately put to sea; I went to the Ship at Dover. I wrote a letter to Admiral Foley, in order that he might forward the news by the telegraph; I was obliged to do that—it was my duty;" and then still more to put them in good humour, he handed out to them some wine, which he had brought from Dover.—He said to them, do not talk of this news as you go along—as soon as you have parted with me you may tell who you please; by and by he said, Pray where can I get a hackney coach? the first stand, the boy told him, was at the Bricklayer's Arms—"No, I will not take one there;" then the Marsh Gate—"Very well, I will get one there". When they crossed Saint George's Fields, the post boy, who every now and then turned round for the gratification of looking at this generous bearer of good news, observed that he pulled up the blind, and seemed to avoid observation. He did not know what his reason might be for that, and it did not strike him till afterwards. They tried to get a hackney coach at the Three Stags, they could not, and they went on to the Marsh Gate, there they found one coach, and one coach only; Colonel Du Bourg stepped out of the post chaise into the hackney coach. He gave each of the boys a gold Napoleon; he drove off, and away they went, as happy as they could be, to spread every where this very glorious news. This you will find to have been at about nine o'clock in the morning.

Gentlemen, you may very readily suppose that very soon after ten o'clock, this news reached the Stock Exchange; whether through the post boys or by the expresses sent up from Dover, it did reach the Stock Exchange at a little after ten o'clock. Probably you know that business commences at ten. At ten business commenced as it had left off on Saturday; the price of Omnium for some time was 27-1/2. It began extremely flat at 27-1/2—it went on 27-1/2—but in about a quarter of an hour, accounts came that an officer from Paris had arrived at Dover, and had come up in a post chaise and four to Government with this news, which was recited in detail. The Funds immediately rose to 28—28-1/2—29 and 30, and on it went till about twelve o'clock, when no letter coming from the Secretary of State to the Lord Mayor, people began to doubt its truth, and from 30 Omnium fell to 29, and was getting down, when between twelve and one o'clock there came the amplest confirmation. This, Gentlemen, you will find to be auxiliary to the main plot, and a very important auxiliary. In itself it would have been absolutely nothing. There drove through the City, a post chaise and four, with three persons in it, two of them dressed like French Officers, in blue great coats, with white linings; they wore white cockades, and their horses were decorated with laurel. As they went along they dispersed little billets announcing this news. After a kind of triumphal progress through the City, they turned to the left at Bridge Street, went over Blackfriars Bridge, quitted the main road for the New Cut, and when they had arrived near the Marsh Gate, within a hundred yards of the spot at which Colonel Du Bourg had alighted, these three gentlemen got out of their chaise, folded up their cocked hats, put on round hats, and walked off.

Gentlemen, this you may suppose, indeed we all know, produced an emotion in the City not to be described. There is nothing so contagious as popular feeling, especially on a subject of great public interest. This stamped certainty upon the news; this reached the Stock Exchange, and the funds, which had begun to droop, revived; Omnium rose to 30, 31, 32 and 32-1/2. Thus it went on for a short time, till persons having been sent to the West End of the Town, and it being found that no Messenger had arrived at the Office of the Secretary of State with this intelligence, it was discovered that this had been a gross and wicked deception; and the Funds returned to very nearly their former level. But there were very large sales made, and of course there were many persons defrauded. The members of the Stock Exchange felt it, and felt it deeply; and they appointed a Committee to investigate this business, and to ascertain who were the parties to this fraud. That Committee pursued the investigation with great industry, and they discovered that which I shall lay before you in evidence. As the underplot is the shortest, I may as well dispose of that first.—They ascertained that this second post chaise had come from Northfleet, which is, you know, near Gravesend. That Mr. Ralph Sandom, who is a Spirit Merchant, living at Northfleet, but who was at that time also like Mr. De Berenger, a prisoner within the rules of the King's Bench, and who kept within the rules just as faithfully as Mr. De Berenger did, had sent, early in the morning, to Dartford, for a post chaise and four, to be sent to him at Northfleet, and for four horses to be ready to take him on to town; and that Mr. Sandom; a Mr. Alexander M'Rae, a person in most desperate circumstances; and Mr. Lyte, who is, I believe, a little Navy Agent, and a very poor man, were the persons who had come in this post chaise; and that M'Rae and Lyte were the two persons who were dressed in the uniform of French Officers.

Gentlemen, they ascertained further, that Mr. M'Rae resided at a lodging in Fetter Lane; that on Saturday the 19th of February, he had brought into his lodgings a couple of great coats, blue lined with white, to resemble the coats of French Officers; that he had white cockades made up by his wife in the lodging, and upon enquiry being made by his hostess what all this could mean, said, that it was *to take in the flats*. He quitted his lodging in the afternoon of Sunday, stating that he was going down to Gravesend by water; and he returned about two on Monday, after having, as I stated, quitted the chaise at the Marsh Gate. The great coat was speedily altered, by the white lining being taken out and another lining put in its place, and the white cockades were burnt: and Mr. M'Rae, who had been in the greatest distress for money, was, in the course of that week, exulting in his success, boasting of the money he had earned by that which he had done; and on being expostulated with on the impropriety of that mode of getting money, said, "If I had not somebody else would."

Gentlemen, the Committee discovered that Mr. M'Rae was a party to this business at a still earlier period, and that it had been for some time in preparation, that he had on the 14th (the Monday preceding) written a letter to a person of the name of Vinn, appointing a meeting at the Carolina Coffee-House for the next day. On the Tuesday Vinn met him. Mr. Vinn speaks French very well, and Mr. M'Rae explained the business on which he wished to converse with him; the funds were then in a critical situation, it would be a very good thing if he would but personate a French officer, and bring some good news to Town, and that a hundred pounds were at his service. Mr. Vinn felt a little indignant at this proposal being made to him, saying that he hoped what Mr. M'Rae knew of him would have given him a different opinion of him; but Mr. M'Rae would not let Mr. Vinn go without giving him some French phrases, which you will find were the very phrases in these billets thrown out when they passed through the City. It was therefore completely ascertained that M'Rae was not only concerned as an actor in this under plot, carried on by the chaise from Northfleet to London, but that he had so long before as the Tuesday preceding, proposed to Vinn to do that which De Berenger in fact did.

The Committee afterwards ascertained, that the immediate employer of the persons in the Chaise was Mr. Holloway, a wine merchant, another defendant, who independently of his concerns with those persons, chose to have a little dealing in the funds himself, he had a small milkscore of about forty-thousand pounds omnium, which he disposed of on that 21st day of February, at a handsome profit.

Gentlemen, you will not fail to observe that this part of the plot could have had no effect but for the foundation laid by the appearance of the pretended officer at Dover and his journey to London; for a post-chaise coming through the City with white cockades and laurel branches would have had no effect except to excite laughter and derision, but for the preparation made by De Berenger in the character of Du Bourg; and when you find for the purpose of producing the same effect, such a coincidence of plan, and such a coincidence of time, the one the basis and the other the superstructure, although I shall not be able to prove all the parties meeting together, conferring together, consulting together, still it will be impossible to doubt that these are two parts of one whole; that this is, in short, not two conspiracies, but one and the same conspiracy.

Gentlemen, the enquiry respecting the chaise from Dover led to much more important results. It was the first business of the Committee to learn to what place this pretended Du Bourg went in the Hackney-coach from the Marsh-gate. They found out the Hackney-coachman, and he informed them that he was directed by Du Bourg to drive, and he did drive straight and direct to No. 13, Green-street, the house of Lord Cochrane, and it is not an immaterial consideration in this matter, a house in which Lord Cochrane had resided but three days, a ready-furnished house which he had taken of Mr. Durand, and a person must have been on intimate terms with Lord Cochrane to know where he resided on Monday, Lord Cochrane having gone into the house only on the Thursday evening preceding.

The Coachman further informed the Committee that when he stopped at this house Du Bourg enquired for some person by the description, as he thought, of Captain or Colonel, and that the answer given by the servant was, that he was gone to breakfast in Cumberland-street.

Having proceeded thus far, the next thing for the Committee to discover was whether Lord Cochrane was a person who could have any possible interest in the success of this fraud. They pursued their enquiries upon that subject, and they discovered, to their utter astonishment, that this nobleman—this officer highly distinguished in the navy, then lately appointed to an important command, and one should have supposed his whole soul ingrossed in preparation for the active and important service on which he was going—this Representative in Parliament for the City of Westminster, bound by the most sacred of all duties, not to involve himself in any situation by which his honest judgment could be warped, and his parliamentary conduct influenced—they found Lord Cochrane to have been a deep speculator in omnium; that he had been so for one week only; that on that Monday morning he had a large balance on hand, and that on that Monday morning he had sold out the whole of that balance, and sold it at a profit.

When the Committee had learned thus much, they could not but feel that it was impossible that it could be an accidental coincidence, that this impostor,

Du Bourg, should have alighted at the house of a person thus deeply interested in the success of the imposition which he had practised. But their enquiries and discoveries did not end there; they found that Lord Cochrane had not acted alone in these stock proceedings; that he was connected with two other persons, who were still more deep in them, the one his uncle, Mr. Cochrane Johnstone (also a member of parliament), and the other a Mr. Richard Gathorne Butt, formerly a clerk in the Navy Office. They discovered that these persons were engaged together in speculations of a magnitude perfectly astonishing. I have the statement in my hand; but I do not think it requisite, in my address to you, to go through all the particulars. Mr. Cochrane Johnstone and Mr. Butt, who had commenced their stock speculations on the 8th of February, a week earlier than Lord Cochrane, had dealt much more largely even than he had. Their purchases were the same, their sales the same; they seemed in these stock speculations to have but one soul. If one bought twenty thousand, the other bought twenty thousand; if one bought ninety-five thousand, the other bought ninety-five thousand; you will find the act of one the act of the other; and you will find these three persons, Lord Cochrane, Mr. Cochrane Johnstone, and Mr. Butt, having on the Saturday preceding this Monday, a balance amounting in consols and omnium to very nearly a million—reduced to consols, you will find it amount to sixteen hundred thousand pounds; and on the morning of Monday, on the arrival of this news, they all three sold—they sold all that they had, every shilling of it; and, by a little accident in the hurry of this great business, they sold rather more.

Gentlemen, it was discovered still further, that the principal agent in these purchases and sales, was a Mr. Fearn, a stock broker; that Mr. Butt was the active manager; that the directions for Lord Cochrane's purchases and sales were made mostly by Mr. Butt, and were recognized by his Lordship; that the payment for any loss (sustained by either of the three) was made by Mr. Butt, and the receipt of any profit was by the hand of Mr. Butt. They discovered that Mr. Cochrane Johnstone and Mr. Butt, were in the habit of coming every morning at an early hour to visit their broker, Mr. Fearn; that on the morning in question, they had come at an early hour, in a hackney coach, and that Lord Cochrane, after having breakfasted in Cumberland-street with Mr. Cochrane Johnstone and Mr. Butt, came in the same hackney coach, at least as far as Snow-hill, if he did not afterwards go on to the Stock Exchange. They discovered, too, that Mr. Fearn was not the only broker they employed; they employed a Mr. Smallbone, a Mr. Hichens, and a Mr. Richardson; they may have employed twenty others that we know not of, because it has been only by accident that the Committee learned their employment of Mr. Richardson, for Mr. Richardson not being a member of the Stock Exchange, the Committee had no controul over him to exact information from him. Mr. Butt had employed Mr. Richardson on the

Saturday preceding, to purchase fifty thousand omnium, of which he the same day sold thirty; and so anxious was Mr. Butt on that Saturday to be possessed of as much stock as possible, that he endeavoured to persuade Mr. Richardson to purchase one hundred and fifty thousand, but Mr. Richardson trembled at the idea of making so large a speculation, and refused to go beyond the fifty thousand.

You have these persons, then, linked together in such manner, as will render them perfectly inseparable in these various stock transactions; having dealt for some little time; having bought and having sold; having this tremendous balance, this world of Stock, under which they were, on the Saturday evening, bending and groaning, on the Monday morning they had disburthened themselves completely of this with a profit of a little more than ten thousand pounds. If the telegraph had worked, that ten thousand would have been nearer a hundred thousand—that the telegraph did not work, was not to be ascribed either to them or to their agent.

Gentlemen, when all this was ascertained, the Committee apprised those who had appointed them of the result of their labours; they printed an account for the information of the members of the Stock Exchange; they then had some private information, that Du Bourg really was De Berenger; but on enquiry for Mr. De Berenger, they found he was gone off; they had not, therefore, any positive proof, and on that account they very prudently said nothing upon the subject. When they had printed this information, for the use of their own members only; it did get out, and there were published in the newspapers some accounts of their reports, some of them correct, and some of them incorrect, but sufficient undoubtedly to direct the eyes of all men to these three individuals, Lord Cochrane, Mr. Cochrane Johnstone, and Mr. Butt.

Lord Cochrane, Mr. Cochrane Johnstone, and Mr. Butt, felt that it was requisite for them to give some explanation upon this subject. Mr. Butt was extremely indignant at suspicions being thrown out respecting him, he abused those who had libelled and slandered him, and threatened prosecution, a threat which he has not executed, nor ever will. Mr. Cochrane Johnstone, too, equally threatened prosecution, and he has equally failed in the execution of his threat; but one fact stated by the Committee, roused the indignation of Mr. Cochrane Johnstone. It had been stated by the Committee, that whereas Mr. Cochrane Johnstone and Mr. Butt, had been satisfied before the 21st of February with doing business at the office of their agent, that on that morning they commenced business at an office, taken by Mr. Cochrane Johnstone for the use of Mr. Fearn, in Shorter's Court, Throgmorton-street, an office most conveniently situated, just by the side door of the Stock Exchange itself. This office consisted of three rooms, in one of which rooms were Mr. Cochrane Johnstone and Mr. Butt; in a second

Mr. Fearn, and in the third a Mr. Lance, a person also employed by them; and the Committee stated, from Mr. Fearn's information, that Mr. Cochrane Johnstone had taken this office for Mr. Fearn, even without his (Mr. Fearn's) knowledge.

Mr. Cochrane Johnstone was extremely angry at this; he declared it to be a most unqualified falsehood, and that he was ready to swear positively, that he never had done any such thing; that the office was Mr. Butt's, and that Mr. Butt had given it up to Mr. Fearn; now that would not signify much, for I will shew, that Mr. Butt and Mr. Cochrane Johnstone are one and the same. Gentlemen, I am sorry to say, that after what I have seen of Mr. Cochrane Johnstone's conduct in this transaction, I am not surprised at his denying this, merely because his denial is in contradiction to the fact, but I am surprised that he should dare to deny it, when I have a contradiction not only by a witness, but by a letter under his own hand. I will prove to you, by the owner of the house, that Mr. Cochrane Johnstone did take this office; he not only took this office, but he was desirous of taking the whole house; he had taken the office before the 17th of February, and on the 17th of February he called on Mr. Addis, who had the letting of the house, and he wrote and left on his desk this letter: "Sir, I called again upon you to know if you have power to sell the house, part of which I have taken." This is Mr. Cochrane Johnstone, who is ready to swear that he never took any office at all—"*part of which I have taken.*" Gentlemen, mark the remainder, and apply it to the morning of the 21st of February.—"*As I find there are several persons in the house at present, which is rather awkward, and makes it too public*—WALLS HAVE EARS." Mr. Cochrane Johnstone and Mr. Butt did not like that their consultations should be liable to be overheard—their guilt might then be proved by other than circumstantial evidence. "If you have powers to sell, I will immediately treat with you; have the goodness, therefore, to leave the terms with your clerk, or send them to me at No. 18, Great Cumberland-street. I will however call again this day, before I return to the West end of the Town."

Gentlemen, that is the letter of Mr. Cochrane Johnstone, and so much for Mr. Cochrane Johnstone's denial of his having taken the office in Shorter's Court.

Gentlemen, besides this denial of the fact, and this offer to swear to it, these Gentlemen chose to make some criticisms on the report printed by the Committee of the Stock Exchange, and the first criticism was one of great importance.—One person had said, that Colonel Du Bourg got out of the post chaise into the hackney coach, and another person said, he got into the hackney coach having just alighted from the post chaise, and it was supposed that that was a material contradiction. You will find the fact to be, that he stepped from the one into the other.

Another was, that one person called the great coat, a *mixture*, and another called it *brown*. In truth it was a greyish mixture, a military great coat.

Another was, that one person had called the lace on the cap *gold*, and another called it *silver*. It happens to be a pale gold, which according to the light in which you view it, will appear like either gold or silver. I will produce to you a fac simile of both coat and cap.

But it was felt that these criticisms would not suffice. Lord Cochrane must account for his visitor, and Lord Cochrane came forward with a declaration upon this subject, in a manner, which, I confess, appears to me most degrading. If a person of his rank thought fit to give any declaration, I should have thought that the mode of giving it would have been under the sanction of his honor. Lord Cochrane thought otherwise, and he chose to give it under the half and half sanction of a *voluntary affidavit*. I call it so, Gentlemen, for this reason, that although he who makes a voluntary affidavit attests his God to its truth, he renders himself amenable to no human tribunal for its falsehood, for no indictment for perjury can be maintained upon a voluntary affidavit. I wish that none of these voluntary affidavits were made; I wish that Magistrates would not lend their respectable names to the use, or rather to the abuse, which is made of these affidavits; for whether they are employed to puff a quack medicine or a suspected character, they are I believe, always used for the purpose of imposition.

Gentlemen, this affidavit I have before me, and I will prove the publication of it upon Lord Cochrane, it is thus prefaced:

"Having obtained leave of absence to come to Town, in consequence of scandalous paragraphs in the public papers, and in consequence of having learnt that hand bills had been affixed in the streets, in which (I have since seen) it is asserted, that a person came to my house, No. 13, Green-street, on the 21st day of February, in open day, and in the dress in which he had committed a fraud, I feel it due to myself to make the following deposition, that the public may know the truth relative to the only person seen by me in military uniform at my house on that day.

COCHRANE."

"Dated 13, Green-street, March 11th, 1814."

Now comes the Affidavit:

"I Sir Thomas Cochrane, commonly called Lord Cochrane, having been appointed by the Lords Commissioners of the Admiralty to active service (at the request I believe of Sir Alexander Cochrane) when I had no expectation of being called on, I obtained leave of absence to settle my private affairs previous to quitting this country, and chiefly with a view to lodge a specification to a patent, relative to a discovery for increasing the intensity of light. That in pursuance of my daily practice of superintending work that was executing for me, and knowing that my uncle, Mr. Cochrane Johnstone, went to the City every morning in a coach, I do swear on the morning of the 21st of February, (which day was impressed on my mind by circumstances which afterwards occurred) I breakfasted with him, at his residence in Cumberland-street, about half past eight o'clock, and I was put down by him (and Mr. Butt was in the coach) on Snow-hill about ten o'clock; that I had been about three quarters of an hour at Mr. King's manufactory, at No. 1, Cock-lane, when I received a few lines on a small bit of paper, requesting me to come immediately to my house; the name affixed from being written close to the bottom, I could not read; the servant told me it was from an army officer, and concluding that he might be an officer from Spain, and that some accident had befallen to my brother, I hastened back, and found Captain Berenger, who, in great seeming uneasiness, made many apologies for the freedom he had used, which nothing but the distressed state of his mind, arising from difficulties, could have induced him to do; all his prospects he said had failed, and his last hope had vanished of obtaining an appointment in America, he was unpleasantly circumstanced on account of a sum which he could not pay, and if he could that others would fall upon him, for full £8000. He had no hope of benefitting his creditors in his present situation, or of assisting himself, that if I would take him with me, he would immediately go on board and exercise the Sharp Shooters (which plan Sir Alexander Cochrane I knew had approved of;) that he had left his lodgings and prepared himself in the best way his means allowed. He had brought the sword with him which had been his father's, and to that and to Sir Alexander he would trust for obtaining an honorable appointment. I felt very uneasy at the distress he was in, and knowing him to be a man of great talent and science, I told him I would do every thing in my power to relieve him, but as to his going immediately to the Tonnant with any comfort to himself, it was quite impossible; my cabin was without furniture, I had not even a servant on board. He said he would willingly mess any where; I told him that the ward-room was already crouded, and besides, I could not, with propriety, take him, he being a foreigner, without leave from the Admiralty. He seemed greatly hurt at this, and recalled to my recollection certificates which he had formerly shewn me from persons in official situations: Lord Yarmouth, General Jenkinson, and Mr. Reeves, I think, were amongst the number. I recommended him to use his endeavour to get them or any other friends to exert their influence, for I had none, adding that when the Tonnant went to Portsmouth, I should be happy to receive him, and I knew from Sir Alexander Cochrane that he would be pleased if he accomplished that object.

Captain Berenger said, that not anticipating any objection on my part from the conversation he had formerly had with me, he had come away with intention to go on board and make himself useful in his military capacity. He could not go to Lord Yarmouth or to any other of his friends in this dress, (alluding to that which he had on) or return to his lodgings, where it would excite suspicion (as he was at that time in the rules of the King's Bench) but that if I refused to let him join the ship now, he would do so at Portsmouth. Under present circumstances however he must use a great liberty, and request the favor of me to lend him a hat to wear instead of his military cap. I gave him one which was in a back room with some things that had not been packed up, and having tried it on, his uniform appeared under his great coat, I therefore offered him a black coat that was laying on a chair, and which I did not intend to take with me; he put up his uniform in a towel, and shortly afterwards went away, in great apparent uneasiness of mind, and having asked my leave he took the coach I came in, and which I had forgotten to discharge, in the haste I was in. I do further depose, that the above conversation is the substance of all that passed with Captain Berenger, which from the circumstances attending it, was strongly impressed upon my mind; that no other person in uniform was seen by me at my house on Monday, the 21st of February, though possibly other officers may have called, (as many have done since my appointment;) of this however I cannot speak of my own knowledge, having been almost constantly from home, arranging my private affairs. I have understood that many persons have called under the above circumstances, and have written notes in the parlour, and others have waited there, in expectation of seeing me, and then gone away; but I most positively swear that I never saw any person at my house resembling the description and in the dress stated in the printed advertisement of the Members of the Stock Exchange. I further aver, that I had no concern, directly or indirectly, in the late imposition, and that the above is all that I know relative to any person who came to my house in uniform on the 21st day of February, before alluded to. Captain Berenger wore a grey great coat, a green uniform, and a military cap. From the manner in which my character has been attempted to be defamed, it is indispensibly necessary to state that my connection in any way with the funds arose from an impression that in the present favorable aspect of affairs, it was only necessary to hold stock in order to become a gainer, without prejudice to any body; that I did so openly, considering it in no degree improper, far less dishonorable; that I had no secret information, of any kind, and that had my expectation of the success of affairs been disappointed, I should have been the only sufferer. Further I do most solemnly swear, that the whole of the omnium on account which I possessed on the 21st day of February, 1814, amounted to £139,000, which I bought by Mr. Fearn (I think) on the 12th ultimo, at a premium of 28-1/4; that I did not hold on that day any other sum on account, in any other stock, directly or indirectly, and that I had given orders when it was bought to dispose of it on a rise of one per cent. and it actually was sold on an average at 29-1/2 premium, though on the day of the fraud it might have been disposed of at 33-1/2. I further swear, that the above is the only stock which I sold, of any kind, on the 21st day of February, except £2000 in money, which I had occasion for, the profit of which was about £10. Further I do solemnly depose, that I had no connection or dealing with any one, save the above mentioned, and that I did not at any time, directly or indirectly, by myself or by any other, take or procure any office or apartment for any broker or other person for the transaction of stock affairs."

Gentlemen, Lord Cochrane has complained that he was not called upon by the Committee of the Stock Exchange to give his explanation personally. It appears to me that he has no reason to complain that they did not so call upon him—would that he had been so called upon: what would any man have given to be present to see whether any human countenance was equal to the grave relation of this extraordinary story. Let us examine it, Lord Cochrane tells us that being at this manufactory of Mr. King's he received a note, the name of the writer of which he cannot read, yet, that he hastens home directly; engaged as he is in the superintending the making of a Lamp for which he had a patent—engaged too in this tremendous stock account, which is at this very moment, under the guardian care of Mr. Cochrane Johnstone and Mr. Butt, abruptly closing, he instantly quits the City, and hastens home to see a person whose signature he cannot decypher, and when he comes there he finds Mr. De Berenger to be the writer of the note, and he has all this extraordinary conversation with him about going on board the Tonnant to instruct the crew in sharp-shooting, and then when a negative is put upon Mr. De Berenger's application at least for the present, Mr. De Berenger tells him he *cannot* forsooth "*go to Lord Yarmouth or to any other of his friends in this dress.*" Why, I beg to know, cannot Mr. De Berenger go to Lord Yarmouth or any other nobleman or gentleman in the dress in which he waits upon Lord Cochrane? if he was dressed as Lord Cochrane describes, there could be no impropriety; but still more, "*or return to his lodging, where it would excite suspicion,*" *coming out* of his lodging in this dress might to be sure excite suspicion, for persons who saw him might imagine that a gentleman thus dressed was going a little beyond the rules of the King's Bench, but how could his *return* excite suspicion? If he was returning to his lodgings why would he want any other dress? except that he was afraid to return to his lodgings in that dress because it would afford the means of tracing and detecting him. "If I refused to let him join the ship now, he would join it at Portsmouth, *under present circumstances however, he must use a great liberty, and request the favor of me to lend him a hat to wear instead of his military cap. I gave him one which was in a back room with some things which had not been packed up.*" Then we are to suppose that De Berenger was satisfied; he had got rid of this cap with the gold border which might excite suspicion, and he was content to go. No says Lord Cochrane that will not do. "*Having tried it*," that is the hat, "*on, his uniform appeared under his great coat, I therefore offered him a black coat that was laying on a chair and which I did not intend to take with me.*" We are, I presume then, to understand that he put on the black coat, though that is not expressly stated, "he put up his uniform *in a towel and shortly afterwards went away.*" Then he was to go off entirely, was he? Gentlemen, I am sorry to find that my Lord Cochrane, filling the high situation that he does, sees nothing wrong in assisting a person within the rules of the King's Bench to abscond, for whose stay within those rules sureties have entered into a bond; either Lord Cochrane's mind has confounded all right and wrong, or what is more probable, he confesses this smaller delinquency to conceal the greater, for I say he would not have made this acknowledgment unless he had to conceal that he lent the dress for another purpose, for which purpose I say De Berenger resorted to him, and which purpose was answered by Lord Cochrane's assistance.

Another part of this affidavit is very important, "*Captain Berenger wore a grey great coat, a green uniform, and a military cap.*" I will prove to you that the uniform was scarlet; that it was embroidered with gold, and that there was a star on the breast. I will prove that by many persons who saw it, and I will produce it to you to-day.

A circumstance is resorted to by Lord Cochrane, and indeed by his associates, as a defence which affords another proof of the infatuation of guilt. They have thought it a favorable circumstance for them that they sold out their stock early in the day at a small profit; in my mind it is one of the strongest circumstances against them. If they had believed the news would they have sold out early, and at that small profit? why did they so sell out? but because they knew that belief in the news would last but a very short time, and that they must take advantage of it without delay, for when I have stated that ten thousand or ten thousand five hundred pounds was the amount of their profit I have very much understated it, their profit vastly exceeded that, their profit was all they had been saved from losing, they had been that which is well known in the language of the Stock Exchange, they had been *Bulls* and they had been invariably *Bulls*, they had been raising the price by their purchases, their purchases had vastly exceeded their sales, as appears by the amount of the balance, they had gone on plunging deeper and deeper till they were completely out of their depth; the market was flat, if they had sold at 27-1/2 they would have been losers to a small amount, but unless they had made all mankind as hungry for stock as they were for profit, they could not have got rid of their million of omnium and stock, without an immense loss; and when they tell me they sold at once, I say yes, so you did, that is my argument against you: I say you did not wait half an hour when the news came, that as fast as you found the news operate, the telegraphic communication from Shorter's Court to the Stock Exchange took place, Mr. Fearn was set to work—he was ordered to sell, and he did sell by twenties, thirties, forties, and fifties of Thousands, and in the hurry and confusion they were in, one sold Ten Thousand Consols less than he had, and the other Twenty-four Thousand omnium more than he had; I think therefore this selling early, and selling at a small profit will not much avail them, but very much the contrary.

But, Gentlemen, it was felt that if the case rested there, they had done very little indeed, because no man could be so infatuated as to suppose that this story of De Berenger and his Sharp Shooters would go down, unless they shewed that De Berenger was not Du Bourg: for, if De Berenger was Du Bourg, it was very easily seen through, and therefore they set up for De Berenger, (who was not forth coming to set it up for himself) that best of all defences if true, which is sometimes resorted to in Courts of Criminal Judicature, and is commonly known by the name of an ALIBI.—It is, I say, the best of all defences if a man is innocent, but if it turns out to be untrue, it is conclusive against those who resort to it. Lord Cochrane, Mr. Cochrane Johnstone, and Mr. Butt, published two affidavits of a man and woman of the name of Smith, who were the servants of De Berenger; the affidavits are of the same manufacture with the others. Affidavits are commonly in the third person, "A. B. maketh oath and saith," but I observe all these affidavits, as well Lord Cochrane's as the rest, begin I A. B. do swear, these Affidavits I will read to you, "I William Smith, servant to Baron De Berenger, do swear, that my Master slept at home on Sunday the 20th of February, 1814, as I let him in about eleven o'clock at night; that he went out early next morning, as I went into his room between eight and nine o'clock, and found him gone out. I went about nine o'clock, and did not return till three o'clock, being that day at my mothers cleaning some Pictures for her, and when I returned, I then found my Master at home, and I went to him to ask if he wanted any thing, he desired me to get him some ale and a mutton chop, which I did; I saw his grey military great coat and his green drill dress, and a black coat which I knew was not his, lying upon a chair in the room; he went out that day to dine between five and six o'clock, and came home about eleven that night; he slept regularly at home all that week, until Sunday the 27th, when he went away in the evening, and desired me to carry a box of clothes with him to the Angel Inn, which I did, and I there left him and have never seen him since, and this is all I know about my Master." This, Gentlemen, we have too upon the sanction of a *voluntary affidavit*. Then comes his wife, "I Ann Smith, female servant to Baron De Berenger, do swear, that my Master came home about twelve o'clock on Monday the 21st day of February, in a Hackney Coach,—that I believe he did, he had on a black coat, he had a bundle with him, which to its appearance, contained his grey military greatcoat, and green uniform, he went out the same morning before breakfast without my seeing him; and I do further swear, that I made his bed and cleaned his room as usual, on the 21st day of February, which had been slept in: he always slept at home regularly until Sunday the 27th of February, and he went away that day, and I never have seen him since." Now, Gentlemen, if this be true, to be sure it is idle to talk of Mr. De Berenger having been at Dover on that night; he could not have been at Dover, and at the same time sleeping in his bed within the rules of the King's Bench Prison. These affidavits were put out as complete and conclusive evidence, that all the surmises of Du Bourg and De Berenger being the same person were absolutely mistaken, that the visitor of Lord Cochrane, Mr. De Berenger was not, and could not be the impostor Colonel Du Bourg.

Gentlemen, at that time it was supposed Mr. De Berenger, was safe out of the kingdom, and that no contradiction of these affidavits could ever take place; and that being supposed to be the case, these parties grew very bold and there was a good deal of vapouring. Mr. Butt wanted his money. The Stock Exchange Committee came to this resolution, and it appears to me to be most honorable conduct, they resolved, not that the agreements of that day should be cancelled, but that an account should be taken of the profit made by those persons, who, in these extraordinary circumstances, had attracted suspicion to themselves. That that money should be paid into the hands of trustees, to await the result of the investigation, and if the suspicions were cleared up, they should have it, if not, that it should be disposed of, in a way that could attach no motive of interest whatever to the Stock Exchange or to their Committee. Upon this resolution, £10,500, the profit made by Lord Cochrane, Mr. Cochrane Johnstone, and Mr. Butt, were paid into the hands of trustees, to wait the event. Mr. Butt was not satisfied with this arrangement, and he was clamorous for his money. They said, "wait a little, Mr. Butt, you shall have it presently, if you are entitled to it."—"No," he says, "give me my money."—"It is perfectly safe, Mr. Butt, for your own honor and character's sake wait a little."—No reply, but "the money—give me the money."

———*Populus me sibilat; at mihi plaudoIpse domi, simul ac nummos contemplor in arcâ.*

Gentlemen, that was the consolation to which Mr. Butt looked, for the contempt to which he found his conduct had exposed him;—that consolation he will not have—he will have conviction and shame, but he will not get the money.

Gentlemen, the complete developement of this business, however, now approached. In the beginning of April, Mr. De Berenger was heard of at Sunderland, endeavouring to get out of the kingdom. A warrant had some time before issued from the Secretary of State for his apprehension; and most fitly had it been issued, for though Mr. De Berenger, as an alien, had a licence to live in any part of Great Britain he had no licence to go out of it; and he had abused the privileges of an alien, by having attempted a gross imposition on a high Naval Officer of the country: and information being given to the officer, who had had that warrant in his possession for three weeks, he set off to Sunderland after him. He found he had gone from thence to Newcastle, from thence to Glasgow, and from thence to Leith; and at Leith, on the 8th of April, he apprehended him. He was brought to London, and arrived in London on the 12th, and then on being shewn to various persons who had seen him in the course of his journey, he was identified by every one of them as Du Bourg;—by persons at Dover,—by persons at Dartford,—by the drivers,—by the coachman,—and above all by a very important person in this transaction, he was identified by a Mr. Solomon.—And I will tell you who Mr. Solomon is.—An account of the dress of Colonel Du Bourg having been published, the public attention was drawn to that circumstance, and in the latter end of March a fisherman in dredging in the Thames a little above London Bridge brought up from the bottom a bundle (which had been sunk by pieces of lead) containing a scarlet Aid de Camp's uniform cut in pieces, and a star and badge which identified it beyond contradiction, and upon this being advertised, a Mr. Solomon, an Army Accoutrement Maker, who has one shop at Charing Cross and another in New-Street Covent Garden, came forward and identified these as the cloaths which, together with the grey coat and the military cap, he had sold to a gentleman on Saturday the 19th of February; the gentleman was very liberal in his purchases and said that all these things were to be sent into the country for a person to perform the part of a Foreign Officer. Mr. Solomon said perhaps Sir you had better take them on hire. No. He was not disposed to do that, he would rather purchase them, and he did purchase them, and he paid for them in one pound notes and took them away in a Hackney Coach. On Mr. Solomon being taken to see Mr. De Berenger he recognized his person as the person who had so bought the clothes and paid for them.

Gentlemen, what now becomes of these affidavits and of those who made them? what becomes of this alibi for Mr. De Berenger? what becomes of the affidavits of his servants Smith and his wife? what becomes of Lord Cochrane swearing as he does to his green coat? why do persons resort to falsehood, but because truth convicts them? If any person who is found in suspicious circumstances, and is accused of the highest offence known to the law, resorts to lies to excuse himself, his life pays the forfeit, for no man resorts to lies unless he knows that the truth is absolute conviction: why have these persons thus involved themselves deeper, but because, when they found detection approaching them, they wished to ward it off, careless what were the means, careless who was the instrument, careless too who was the victim.

Gentlemen, suppose I were to rest my case here, and were to call upon my learned friends to answer this case, I beg to know what answer they could give? what are they to say for this impostor Du Bourg, this real De Berenger, resorting to the house of Lord Cochrane thus deeply interested in the success of this fraud? thus linked inseparably with two other persons equally interested in the success of the fraud, who, if a different kind of news had arrived that day, would have been absolutely ruined: for if on the 21st of February that news had arrived, which just a month after did arrive of the rupture of the negociation at Chatillon, there would have been such a fall in the price of the funds that these three persons would have been losers to the amount of upwards of one hundred and sixty thousand pounds. What will my learned friends say for persons thus circumstanced, thus involved in suspicion, thus by falsehood and by moral perjury, though not legal, endeavouring to defend themselves? Will my learned friends to day call these Smiths? will they put these persons whom they have made commit this moral perjury into that box and expose them to the charge of legal perjury? if they do not put them there they "die and make no sign;" and, if they do I think I shall be able to shew you who manufactured these affidavits, and how these servants, the Smiths, have been dealt with. I will undertake to prove out of their own mouths that their master was from home that night instead of being as they pretend, in his bed.

But, Gentlemen, when my learned friends find it impossible to stand upon the ground which their clients have before taken, perhaps they may say, for in the distress of their case I do not know what may not be said;—well, admitting that De Berenger was Du Bourg, are we to infer from his visit to Green-Street that Lord Cochrane and he were thus criminally connected?—why you must infer the contrary; it is a proof of innocence, for if they had been so connected, De Berenger would not have been such a fool as to pay his first visit to Lord Cochrane, he would have gone to any other house rather than to Lord Cochrane's. Gentlemen, that argument will not assist my learned friends, for it is too much to ask credit for rational conduct in those who cannot act criminally without acting irrationally. They who contrive schemes of fraud cannot always provide for all possible events. No, Gentlemen, it is the order of Providence, in mercy to mankind, that wickedness should be defeated by its own folly. When the mind is in disorder the course is not straight and even, but irregular and wavering, it is detected by its obliquity: it is by the winding of the course that you discover you are in the path of the serpent "*Quem Deus vult perdere prius dementat,*" is a maxim which comes down to us sanctioned by the experience of all ages; and no man who has not slept for the last two years, can hesitate to set his seal to its truth. Gentlemen, it is as true of Stock-jobbing conspirators as it is of those who have lately been entrusted with the destinies of empires. There is always something omitted, the omission here was this; in settling their plan of operations they had forgotten to provide where De Berenger should resort on his arrival in Town, and on his way his heart failed him, as to going to his own lodgings; he dared not enter into his own lodgings in a dress, which dress would lead to detection, and he therefore drove to Lord Cochrane's to get rid of his dress; and there he, by Lord Cochrane's assistance, did get rid of it; he procured a round hat and a black coat, and then went confidently and safely home to his lodgings, exempt from observation and suspicion.

But, Gentlemen, I have to tell my learned friends, that if they could dispose of all this, their task would be but just beginning. You will naturally ask, was De Berenger a person known to the Cochranes?—Can it be shewn from any other source, that they had ever been together before? Gentlemen, I will shew you that De Berenger was extremely well acquainted with them; that he was a visitor at Lord Cochrane's, and a visitor at Mr. Cochrane Johnstones; that he made it his boast that he was on very familiar terms with them, and that he had given them important assistance in stock-jobbing transactions, and that he expected to be handsomely rewarded for his services, for that by his means they would get a great deal of money by these stock-jobbing transactions. I will prove this to you by more than one witness. I will prove their acquaintance, if necessary, by persons even of Mr. Cochrane Johnstones family.

Gentlemen, my proof does not end there. If Mr. De Berenger was the hired agent of these persons, for the purpose of committing this fraud, what would you expect?—why that after they had used him they would pay him and send him away.—I will prove to you, that they did so pay him, and that they did send him away.

You have learned from these affidavits of the Smiths, (which so far are true,) that on the evening of Sunday the 27th, (which was the Sunday after he was at Dover,) he quitted his lodgings, and was seen no more. Who do you think was his visitor on Saturday the 26th?—Mr. Cochrane Johnstone. On Saturday the 26th Mr. Cochrane Johnstone came to his lodgings, and left a letter for him; that letter, no doubt, hastened his departure, and off he went. He was taken at Leith, and there were found in his possession certain books and papers and bank notes; these bank notes Mr. De Berenger has desired to have returned to him. The prosecutors thought that one bank note for one pound was as good as another bank note for one pound; and in order that Mr. De Berenger might not complain of being cramped in pecuniary matters, they gave over to him notes of corresponding value. But that does not satisfy

Mr. De Berenger; he wants the very identical notes taken from him; he has contracted an affection for them I suppose, on account of their having been his travelling companions. They were his solace in a long journey, and the support to which he looked in future in a foreign land. What harm can these notes do to Mr. De Berenger?—He is much too deeply implicated in this to make the presence or the absence of these notes of the least consequence to him. Who can be so blind as not to see, in the *pretended anxiety* of Mr. De Berenger for these notes, the *real anxiety* of his fellow conspirators; who having made him their instrument in the fraud, wish to make him their instrument in the destruction of the evidence.

Gentlemen, there have been differences of opinion on the subject of Bank Notes as a circulating medium, but there can be no difference of opinion as to their being most admirable detectors of fraud. I have these Bank Notes here, and you will find that the fears of these Defendants are well founded, for they furnish conclusive proofs of their guilt. I will read to you first, however, a memorandum of Mr. De Berenger's, in a little book, which was found in his letter-case; from this he appears to have written on the 1st of March, a letter to "C. J." which I take to be Cochrane Johnstone; there are other initials mentioned in the same page, as "W. S." which I take to be his servant, William Smith; and "G. T." which I presume to be Gabriel Tahourdin, his attorney.

The name of Mr. Tahourdin reminds me of something which I had forgotten to mention. The sureties for Mr. De Berenger keeping within the Rules of the Bench, were a Mr. Cochrane, and Mr. Gabriel Tahourdin, his attorney, and also the attorney of Mr. Cochrane Johnstone, they were bound in a penalty of four hundred pounds for Mr. De Berenger keeping within the Rules of the King's Bench, Mr. De Berenger absconded and left them liable to the penalty of their bond; and I cannot sufficiently admire the good nature of Mr. Gabriel Tahourdin, who not only has forgiven him for leaving him in the lurch, but actually defends him to-day, and is also one of his bail on this indictment.

Gentlemen, there are some parts of this memorandum which I cannot interpret; perhaps Mr. Cochrane Johnstone will give us the letter, and that will supply the explanation. It begins, "To C. J. by March 1st, 1814, £350, £4 to 5000, assign one share of patent, and £1000 worth shares of Mr. De Beaufain, at Messrs. H. to their care." Now comes the important part; I should tell you, Gentlemen, that Lord Cochrane, Mr. Cochrane Johnstone, and Mr. Butt, allege that their gains were not quite so great as the Committee of the Stock Exchange estimate them to have been. They say, that the gains of the three were but £6500, of which Lord Cochrane's share was £1700, and Mr. Cochrane Johnstone's and Mr. Butt's were £4800. Mr. Butt was the person who transacted the business, being more a man of figures than the other two, and acting as their agent, he had rendered his account to Mr. Cochrane Johnstone; and it should seem as if Mr. De Berenger's compensation was a per centage upon their gains, for he writes thus: "Believe, from my informant, £18,000, instead of £4800;" he thinks their profit was four times as much as they say; "Suspicious that Mr. B." who can that be except Mr. Butt? "does not account correctly to him as well as me—determined not to be duped—no restrictions as to secrecy, requesting early answer."

These are evidently the heads of a letter which he has written to Mr. Cochrane Johnstone. There are other notes of letters to Mr. Tahourdin and William Smith, giving directions, which plainly indicate that he was a man quitting this country never to return.

Gentlemen, there were found I have told you, certain bank notes, and a memorandum book, and you will find in this memorandum book there are the figures 450 and 90 summed up together, making £540. You will find that he must have received about that sum from Lord Cochrane, Mr. Cochrane Johnstone, and Mr. Butt, he accounts here for the expenditure of a considerable part of it, and as you go along with me, you shall be able to account for it: so here is W. S. that is William Smith, £50, W. S. again, £20 and so on, with names and sums altogether amounting to £163, and then there is a statement of expences on his journey: he appears from both to have had in his hands £540. From whom do you think he had it? From his associates in this transaction, Lord Cochrane, Mr. Cochrane Johnstone, and Mr. Butt; we have traced the notes up to every one of them. I shall be enabled to shew these persons actually paying him this very money, and when? Between the time of his transaction and his absconding. I will shew you that Mr. Fearn on the 10th of February, drew a check on Bond and Company for £56 5s. payable to Mr. Butt, that that was paid partly in a fifty pound bank note, that bank note was found in the possession of Mr. De Berenger when he was taken at Leith. On the 16th of February, Mr. Smallbone drew a check on Jones, Loyd, and Company for £470. 14s. 4d. made payable to a number, but actually given by him to Lord Cochrane, that was paid in a two hundred pound note, two one hundred pounds, a fifty pound, some small notes, and the fraction in cash. The two hundred pound note was by order of Mr. Butt, exchanged by Christmas (a Clerk of Fearn's) at Bond's, on the 24th of February.—Mark the day, Gentlemen, the Thursday after this fraud, for two £100 notes, those two £100 notes this same Clerk of Mr. Fearn's carried to the Bank, exchanged them for two hundred notes of one pound each, brought them back and gave them to Mr. Fearn, who put them into the hands of Mr. Butt; and, as if these persons had been anxious to link themselves to each other inseparably, Mr. Butt, in Mr. Fearn's presence, handed them over to Mr. Cochrane Johnstone. Gentlemen, of these two hundred notes, I will shew you that eleven were passed at Hull, Mr. De Berenger having been at Hull at that time; that seven were paid by him at Hull, that seven more have come into the bank from that country, marked with De Berenger's name, and that sixty-seven of them were found in Mr. De Berenger's writing desk at Leith.

Gentlemen, I told you that there were two other notes for £100 each. At the same time that Christmas went to the Bank on the 24th, Mr. Lance, who was another of their Agents, went to the Bank, and immediately after Christmas (for the numbers follow each other in the Bank Books) for the other two notes of £100 each, he got two hundred notes also of one pound each, and he gave them to Mr. Butt. Gentlemen, of those two hundred notes, forty-seven have come into the Bank with De Berenger's name upon them, and forty-nine more of them were found in Mr. De Berenger's writing desk. I mentioned to you that another note given in payment of this check to Lord Cochrane, was one for fifty pounds,—that Bank note of fifty pounds, I will prove Lord Cochrane himself paid away to his own coal merchant.

Then, Gentlemen, there is another check paid the 25th of February, 1814, on Prescott and Company by Lance, for £98. 2s. 6d. made payable to Mr. Butt, this was paid in a Bank note for fifty pounds, another for forty pounds, and the remainder in small notes. In the memorandum book, there is an entry to S. £50 importing that he had given to Smith £50. I will prove that Smith paid to Mr. Seeks that same note for fifty pounds, and the forty pound note I will prove that De Berenger paid at Sunderland to Mr. Bray, the rest we are not able to trace: add these sums together, they amount to the £450, and the £90, the very figures entered in Mr. De Berenger's memorandum book, which memorandum book was found in his writing desk when he was taken. Gentlemen, when I thus shew De Berenger, who quitted London on Sunday the 27th of February, having accomplished this fraud on Monday the 21st, thus possessed of notes of this large value, in this great number, which were in the hands of these Defendants on Thursday the 24th; are you not just as certain that he received those notes from these Defendants as a reward of his criminal service, as if you had been yourselves by, seen the notes paid, and heard the reason assigned for which they were paid.

It was stated in the Newspapers, that some of the notes found on De Berenger, had been in the hands of Mr. Butt, upon which Mr. Butt directly addressed this letter to the Morning Chronicle, which appeared on the 18th of April. "Sir, Having read in several papers, a paragraph mentioning that Bank notes were found in the trunk of Captain De Berenger, which were in my possession, and were paid to me by Mr. Fearn, one of my Stock brokers, I think it proper in answer thereto, to say, that as the circumstances will be more fully discussed at a proper period, your astonishment will cease to exist when you see in what manner Captain De Berenger became possessed of the notes in question." Then Mr. Butt knows in what manner De Berenger became possessed of these notes, I call upon Mr. Butt to tell you how they came into De Berenger's possession; my learned Friends will hereafter have to inform you. And, Gentlemen, you will require something more than my Friend's statement, for the statement of Counsel you know, is from the instructions of the Client, and the instructions of the Client may deserve no more credit than a *voluntary affidavit*. I call upon Mr. Butt to shew that by evidence, and if he does not shew you that those notes came into the hands of De Berenger from some other quarter, for some other reason as a reward for some other service, it is impossible for you to resist the conclusion that they were the reward of De Berenger, for the guilty services which he rendered in this fraud; and if so, it was a reward from Lord Cochrane, it was a reward from Mr. Cochrane Johnstone, it was a reward from Mr. Butt, they are one and the same, there is an identity between these three persons that hardly ever existed, they have but one mind, they are inseparably connected.

Gentlemen, I have to apologize to you for having in this large mass of matter omitted one thing, I stated that I should prove to you that Mr. Cochrane Johnstone had called at the house of De Berenger the day before he finally went off, I shall prove that by Mrs. Davidson, with whom De Berenger lodged, and I shall, by her evidence and that of her husband, falsify the Smith's affidavits, for I will shew by them that on the night in question De Berenger slept out, and that the fact of his sleeping out was known to Smith and his wife, who have made the affidavits.

Now, Gentlemen, it appears to me that I have done a great deal more than sufficient to prove these persons guilty, but they are never contented with giving evidence against themselves; upon the arrival of De Berenger in London they began to apprehend that the hour of detection drew near, and that they must strike a bold stroke to ward off the blow, and on the 12th of April, Mr. Cochrane Johnstone writes a letter to the Chairman of the Committee of the Stock Exchange which I will read to you—"Sir, I have this moment received a letter, of which the inclosed is a copy, and lose no time in transmitting it to you, for the information of the Gentlemen composing the Stock Exchange Committee; from the bearer of the letter I am given to understand that Mr. Macrae is willing to disclose the names of the principals concerned in the late hoax, on being paid the sum of £10,000, to be deposited in some banker's hands in the names of two persons to be nominated by himself, and to be paid to him on the conviction of the offenders. I am happy to say that there seems now a reasonable prospect of discovering the author of the late hoax, and I cannot evince my anxious wish to promote such discovery more than by assuring you that I am ready to contribute liberally towards the above sum of £10,000 and I rest assured that you will eagerly avail yourselves of this opportunity to effect the proposed discovery, and an object you profess to have so much at heart, by concurring with me in such contribution, I have the honor to be, Sir, your obedient humble Servant, A. Cochrane Johnstone." And then there is Mr. M'Rae's letter inclosed, addressed to Mr. Cochrane Johnstone. "Sir, I authorize the bearer of this note to state to you that I am prepared to lay before the public the names of the persons who planned and carried into effect the late hoax practised at the Stock Exchange the 21st of February, provided you accede to the terms which my friend will lay before you, I am, Sir, your obedient servant, A. M'Rae." Mr. M'Rae's friend must have been the bearer of some message, for you observe that Mr. Cochrane Johnstone's letter states more than Mr. M'Rae's letter offers, Mr. Cochrane Johnstone does not receive an answer, and that he considered as very ill treatment. Six days afterwards he writes another letter, "Sir, I have to request that you will be so good as to inform me what are the intentions of the Stock Exchange on the subject of the letter which I addressed to you, relative to the proposal of Mr. M'Rae; Lord Cochrane, Mr. Butt, and myself are willing to subscribe £1,000 each, in aid of the £10,000 required by Mr. M'Rae."

Gentlemen, these letters call for more than one observation; I cannot forbear to make one upon the term which Mr. Cochrane Johnstone employs to describe this transaction—"A HOAX," a mere joke, a matter of pleasantry. Gentlemen, a young, a giddy, an unthinking and careless man, who had no concern in the transaction, and who had never been suspected to have had any, might perhaps, in conversation, make use of that term; but Mr. Cochrane Johnstone is not young, he is not giddy, he is not unthinking, he is not inexperienced, he has seen much of the world, he is a cautious man, he is a man of high and noble family, he knows that he is suspected of having been a party in this transaction, and yet he calls it a HOAX! I beg to know what word in Mr. Cochrane Johnstone's vocabulary is to be found to express FRAUD? I presume he would call obtaining money by false pretences, an indulgence of the imagination, and playing with loaded dice, a mere exercise of ingenuity. Is it possible for any innocent man, situated as Mr. Cochrane Johnstone then was, to describe this foul fraud by the name by which Mr. Cochrane Johnstone here describes it? But, Gentlemen, look at the proposal itself; what must Mr. Cochrane Johnstone have thought of the Stock Exchange Committee? surely he must have thought that they were selected for their extraordinary gullibility, when he made this proposal to them. Undoubtedly they would have had no objection to the assistance of an accomplice, but it must not be an accomplice chosen by his associates. No, Gentlemen, an accomplice chosen by his associates is not chosen to divulge, but to suppress the truth. I should have thought that Mr. M'Rae, knowing that they had complete proof against him—which had been obtained at a cheaper rate than £10,000 might have made a more moderate proposal. I should have thought that impunity for himself, which is the common price of an accomplice, would have been sufficient to have had the evidence of Mr. M'Rae, but Mr. M'Rae's price is ten thousand pounds; his worthy companions are willing to contribute three—that is, they will give him three thousand, and will obtain for him seven thousand more; and I have no doubt, that if the offer had been accepted, Mr. M'Rae would very honestly have earned the whole, and have duly recollected to whom he was obliged for it.

Gentlemen, when Lord Cochrane, a few years ago, was preparing for an attack upon the French fleet in Basque Roads, suppose the French admiral had sent this letter to him:—Sir, You are preparing to attack me to-morrow, the bearer is the best pilot on our coast, I should be sorry that you should run upon a rock, he will pilot you safely, do but accept his services; but as his skill is great his price is high—he requires ten thousand pounds; but so anxious am I for the success of your enterprize, that I will give him three if you will but give the other seven.

Gentlemen, this is the modest proposal which Mr. Cochrane Johnstone makes to the Committee of the Stock Exchange; and when he has so done he affects to be extremely angry that the Committee do not accept it.—Gentlemen what can be said more; what men would have resorted to this expedient but men who felt that they were on the eve of detection, and who tried this desperate expedient to see whether they could ward it off.

Gentlemen,—I believe I have now arrived at the end of my long trespass upon your attention. Survey the whole of these transactions. You find that the principals,—those who were to benefit above all others, were the Cochranes and Butt; Holloway in a smaller degree, but still not slightly;—De Berenger the principal agent;—the others, subordinate agents, who could have done nothing unless the foundation had been previously laid by De Berenger, in the character of the officer from Dover; his news had had its effect upon the funds even before the second arrived. Though it cannot be shewn, as in many cases it cannot, that these parties met and conferred and assigned to each his respective part, yet if you find a coincidence in object, and a coincidence in time; if you find the mode of execution precisely the same, is it possible to doubt that these underplotters were the agents of the great conspirators;—That the great conspirators were the authors of the plan, and that the others were executing their subordinate part?

Gentlemen, I have given you the best assistance in my power to understand and apply the evidence which will be laid before you. They whom I represent, have no wish but that justice should be done; they have investigated this subject with great care, with great assiduity, with great diligence, with great anxiety. They have had no personal difference with any of these defendants; they have never come in collision with them, to have the smallest possible difference; they have no wish but justice, and I am sure that at your hands they will attain that justice; and your verdict to day, (which I am sure after you shall have heard the whole of this case, will be a verdict of guilty,) will be a most salutary verdict:—It will shew the world that as there is no man beneath the law, so there is no man above it. It will teach evil minded persons, the absurdity of expecting that schemes of fraud can be so formed as to provide for all events. It will teach them that no caution can insure safety: that there is no contrivance, that there is no device, no stratagem, which can shield them from detection, from punishment, and from infamy.

## EVIDENCE FOR THE PROSECUTION.

*John Marsh sworn.*

*Examined by Mr. Bolland.*

*Q.* I believe you keep the Packet Boat public house at Dover?

*A.* I do.

*Q.* Was your attention called to any thing early on the morning of the 21st of February?

*A.* No more than a gentleman was knocking at Mr. Wright's door of the Ship Inn, at Mr. Wright's fore door.

*Q.* What time?

*A.* Some time about one, or a little after one, between one and a quarter after one.

*Q.* Did you go out upon hearing that?

*A.* I did.

*Q.* Did you take any light with you, or did you go without one?

*A.* I went without a light.

*Q.* Upon going out whom did you find at Mr. Wright's door?

*A.* Some gentleman there.

*Q.* What was his appearance?

*A.* He appeared to be a gentleman.

*Q.* What was the appearance of his dress?

*A.* He had on a grey greatcoat and a uniform coat under it.

*Lord Ellenborough.* Was there light enough by the moon or the stars for you to see this?

*A.* After I got to the door, I called to a gentleman in my house to bring two lights across, when I had the two lights, the gentleman was in the passage.

*Mr. Bolland.* Do you mean the gentleman you had seen at the door?

*A.* Yes; he had a star on his red coat.

*Lord Ellenborough.* That coat you describe as a uniform coat, was a red coat?

*A.* Yes it was.

*Mr. Bolland.* That was under the great coat?

*A.* Yes.

*Q.* Will you look at this star, (*shewing it to the witness,*) and tell me whether it was like that?

*A.* That I cannot tell, it was something similar to that.

*Q.* Had he any other ornament?

*A.* Not to my knowledge.

*Q.* Did you say any thing to him or he to you?

*A.* He was very anxious for a post chaise and four.

*Q.* Did he apply to you for that?

*A.* No not to me in particular.

*Q.* Who had come down to him?

*A.* The porter at the Ship.

*Q.* Had you any conversation with him?

*A.* He wanted an express horse and a man to send to the Admiral at Deal.

*Q.* Did all this pass in the passage, or had you proceeded further?

*A.* It passed in the passage.

*Q.* Did he proceed into the house?

*A.* I asked him where he came from, and he told me he was the bearer of the most important dispatches that had been brought to this country for these twenty years; I asked him where he came from; he told me from France. I asked him where he landed, he told me on the Beach, and he begged of me to get a post chaise and four for him; and then I went and called Mr. Wright of the Ship Inn; after I came down from calling Mr. Wright, he wanted pen, ink, and paper.

*Lord Ellenborough.* He went into the Ship Inn, did he?

*A.* I shewed him into a room of the Ship Inn. As soon as Mr. Wright came down stairs, Mr. Wright gave me a sheet of paper, and pen and ink, which I carried into the room. I gave it to him, and he began to write upon it.

*Q.* You saw him write upon it?

*A.* I did. He called for a bottle of Madeira, and something to eat. I asked him whether I should call the collector of the port; I told him that it was his business to see such people when they landed; he made answer to me, that his business did not lie with the collectors; then Mr. Wright came to him, and I had no more conversation with him.

*Mr. Bolland.* You say two candles were brought to you?

*A.* Yes.

*Q.* Where were those candles placed?

*A.* On the table where he was writing, one on each side of him.

*Q.* Had you an opportunity from the situation of them of observing his person and face?

*A.* Yes, I think that is the person, (*pointing out Mr. De Berenger.*)

*Mr. Gurney.* I will thank Mr. De Berenger to stand up.

*Mr. Park.* Not unless his Lordship desires it he need not stand up.

*Lord Ellenborough.* He will make his election whether he will stand up or not.

*Mr. Park.* He is not to be shewn about like a wild beast as he has been.

*Mr. Bolland.* Who else was there?

*A.* A gentleman of the name of Gourley, and another of the name of Edis.

*Q.* Did you see another person there of the name of St. John?

*A.* I did not know him, they say there was such a person there.

*Q.* Was there another gentleman in the house?

*A.* Yes there was.

*Q.* Did you go away or remain with him?

*A.* I went to get the horses ready for him with all possible dispatch.

*Q.* Did you see him get into the chaise?

*A.* I saw him after he was in.

*Q.* Did any thing more pass in your presence?

*A.* No more than that he told the two postboys he would give them a Napoleon each.

*Q.* Did you observe how his head was dressed?

*A.* He had a German cap on with a gold fringe on it or silver; I did not pay that attention to it to say which, it had gold lace round the bottom part of it.

*Q.* Was it such a coat as that, (*shewing a grey coat to the witness.*)

*A.* Yes, such a color as that.

*Q.* And such a cap as that, (*shewing a fur cap to the witness?*)

*A.* Such a cap; but whether that was the cap I did not pay attention.

*Q.* Have you told his Lordship all that you saw and heard?

*A.* Yes.

*Q.* Did he tell you how he got to the beach?

*A.* No, he told me he landed on the beach.

*Cross-examined by Mr. Park.*

*Q.* What are you to this Ship Inn, I do not quite understand?

*A.* I live opposite.

*Q.* Are you any way connected with the Ship Inn?

*A.* Not in the least.

*Q.* How came you, hearing a knocking at Mr. Wright's Ship Inn, particularly to get up?

*A.* I was up.

*Q.* What had you to do with the Ship Inn, that because a man is knocking at the Ship Inn door you light candles at your house and carry over?

*A.* I went across to see who the gentleman was.

*Q.* Merely curiosity?

*A.* Mere curiosity.

*Q.* And from the same spirit of curiosity you lit two candles and brought them over to the Ship Inn?

*A.* I told a person to bring them over.

*Q.* Was it very beautiful moonlight that night?

*A.* No it was not moonlight.

*Q.* Was there any moon that night; had there been that night at all?

*A.* I did not pay that attention to the night to say.

*Q.* It was beautifully starlight I suppose.

*A.* I do not know, I did not pay that attention.

*Q.* Was it a foggy night?

*A.* That I did not look after.

*Q.* You will see by the Almanack it was new moon the night before; you did not observe whether it was moonlight, starlight, or foggy?

*A.* No.

*Q.* You found he had got into the passage of the house when you got the candles?

*A.* Yes.

*Q.* Who let him in?

*A.* The boots.

*Q.* Did you see him?

*A.* Yes in the passage.

*Q.* How long did you converse with him about the news that you say he said was greater than had ever been heard of for these twenty years from France? All that passed in the passage?

*A.* Yes.

*Q.* How long a time might you be in the passage?

*A.* Not longer than five minutes before I went to call Mr. Wright.

*Q.* Do you mean you were with him only five minutes before you went up stairs to call Mr. Wright, or altogether?

*A.* Altogether I suppose about that, I cannot speak to a minute; but he was in great haste to get away.

*Q.* How long do you think this person was altogether at Mr. Wright's?

*A.* I should think not more than twenty minutes.

*Q.* Where were the candles all this time you were in the passage with him?

*A.* I had them in my hand.

*Q.* What did you do with them when you went up to Mr. Wright?

*A.* I left them with him in the parlour; boots got me a candle.

*Q.* You held the candles in your own hand while you remained in the passage?

*A.* Yes, while the boots unlocked the parlour door, and I went and put them on the table.

*Q.* Before you went up stairs?

*A.* Yes.

*Q.* Had the person who you say was this gentleman gone into the parlour before you went up stairs?

*A.* Yes he had.

*Q.* I take for granted when you came down stairs and Mr. Wright got the paper you did not go in again?

*A.* No; he wished me gone, and I did not go in again.

*Q.* Then altogether, except for seeing him for five minutes in the passage, and you going into the parlour for the short time you did, and afterwards when you saw him in the post chaise, and when he offered the postboys a Napoleon each you did not see him?

*A.* No.

*Q.* You had nothing to do personally with this inn called the Ship?

*A.* No, I keep the Packet Boat opposite.

*Q.* Do you know whether there had been a large company at the Ship Inn that day?

*A.* I do not know.

*Q.* You had not seen Mr. Wright the innkeeper late in the evening of that day, had you?

*A.* No.

*Q.* Had you ever seen this person who you say is the gentleman sitting before me before that time?

*A.* Not before, nor yet since, till to-day.

*Q.* And from this slight observation of him, which you have described, you take upon you confidently to swear that this person sitting before me is the man?

*A.* Yes.

*Q.* Never having seen him before nor again till this day?

*A.* I am very well satisfied.

*Q.* You are very easily satisfied I see; were you ever examined upon this subject before?

*A.* Mr. Stowe, the collector—

*Q.* I do not ask as to Mr. Stowe, but were you ever examined in London before?

*A.* No, never.

*Q.* Mr. Stowe is the only person who has examined you upon this subject till my learned friend has done it now, and I cross-examine you?

*A.* Yes.

*Re-examined by Mr. Bolland.*

*Q.* Before you sent for the lights, had the gentleman told you what his business was, and that he had landed from the Beach?

*A.* He told me before I sent for the lights; I was in the passage with him at the time till the lights came.

*Q.* Was your attention particularly called to him as a stranger of some importance?

*A.* Undoubtedly.

*Q.* You have said you had not seen the person before whom you have pointed out?

*A.* No.

*Q.* Did any body suggest to you that that was the person when you saw him?

*A.* No, it was by myself in the hall.

*Q.* Did you know him when you saw him?

*A.* The instant I saw him.

*Q.* Had you the least doubt upon your mind of his being the man?

*A.* Not the least.

*Thomas Worthington Gourley sworn.*

*Examined by Mr. Bolland.*

*Q.* You are a hatter at Dover I believe?

*A.* I am.

*Q.* Were you at Mr. Marsh's, the Packet Boat, on the morning of the 21st of February?

*A.* I was.

*Q.* Was your attention called to any thing in particular on that morning?

*A.* Yes it was, after Mr. Marsh went out first and called for lights, I took two candles and went across with him to the Ship.

*Q.* On getting to the inn what did you perceive?

*A.* I perceived a gentleman in a grey coat, a pepper and salt coloured coat, more properly speaking.

*Q.* Look at that coat, and tell me whether it was like that?

*A.* Something similar to that.

*Q.* Did you remark any other part of his dress?

*A.* Not at that time.

*Q.* Tell us what passed when you went over?

*A.* Mr. Marsh asked me to go and call the ostler up, and tell him to get a post chaise and four immediately.

*Q.* Had the stranger said any thing in your presence?

*A.* Not at that time.

*Q.* Did you do so?

*A.* I did.

*Q.* Did you return back again?

*A.* After some considerable time—I was sometime in getting the ostler up.

*Q.* Where did you find the stranger on your return?

*A.* I found him in the parlour.

*Q.* Were there any lights in the room?

*A.* There were.

*Q.* How were the lights placed with reference to him, and what was he doing?

*A.* There were two candles on the table, the gentleman was walking about, he had got a uniform dress on I perceived then.

*Q.* What was the colour of that dress?

*A.* Red, trimmed with gold lace, with a star upon his breast.

*Q.* Did you perceive any other ornament?

*A.* No I did not, to notice it.

*Q.* Did you make any remark upon the dress of his head?

*A.* He had got a cap on.

*Q.* Was it like that cap?

*A.* Something similar to that.

Mr. Park. Does your Lordship think they ought to be exhibiting these paraphernalia; it appears to me something like a novelty exhibiting such things in a Court of Justice till the proof has gone further?

Lord Ellenborough. The witness has said he had a cap on, and so on.

Mr. Park. If they had asked was it that cap I should not object to it if they were prepared to prove that was the cap, but they might send to Covent Garden wardrobe and fetch all these things?

Mr. Gurney. I undertake to prove by the person who made the dress for De Berenger, that these are fac similes of the articles of dress made for him.

Mr. Park. You stated that very expressly and very clearly.

Lord Ellenborough. Unless his recollection goes to their being such things, I think it would not go far; it is a thing that occurs every day, I have seen it twenty times at the Old Bailey.

Mr. Park. It assists the recollection of the witness, which I say my learned friends are not entitled to do.

Lord Ellenborough. When the witness has given a previous description of the dress, it is very usual to ask wherein does it differ, or what sort of a thing is it—they must first lay the foundation for the production which I think they have done in this case.

Mr. Bolland. Had he a cap upon his head similar to that?

*A.* Yes he had.

*Q.* Had that gold lace on?

*A.* It had.

*Q.* You say the gentleman was walking up and down the room?

*A.* Yes.

*Q.* Did he say any thing in your presence?

*A.* I asked him what the news was.

*Lord Ellenborough.* How came you to ask that?

*A.* Because I had heard Mr. Marsh say he was a Messenger come over.

*Mr. Bolland.* Did he reply to that?

*A.* He told me that Messengers were sworn to secrecy, but that he had got glorious news he had brought over to England, the best that ever was known for this country.

*Q.* Had you any further conversation with him?

*A.* He rung the bell and called for a pen, ink and paper, to write a letter to send off to the Admiral at Deal.

*Q.* Was that brought to him?

*A.* It was, and he was writing the letter some little time while I was there, and I bid him good night after that.

*Q.* Did you take leave of him before he had finished the letter?

*A.* I did.

*Q.* Where were the candles during the time that he was writing the letter?

*A.* On the table.

*Q.* Were they sufficiently near him to enable you to observe him?

*A.* Yes they were.

*Q.* Can you point out to the Court that person who wrote that letter on that night?

*A.* Yes.

*Q.* Will you point him out?

*A.* Yes, that is the gentleman (*pointing to De Berenger.*)

*Q.* Have you any doubt upon your mind of that?

*A.* None in the least.

*Cross-examined by Mr. Richardson.*

*Q.* You did not come over until you were called for by Mr. Marsh to bring candles?

*A.* No I did not.

*Q.* You were immediately sent to order horses, were you not?

*A.* Yes, I went and called the ostler up.

*Q.* I think you state that you were absent some time in performing that service?

*A.* Yes, I was some little time before I could wake the ostler.

*Q.* You left the candles in the passage with Mr. Marsh?

*A.* Yes.

*Q.* You handed the candles to him, and went immediately to call the ostler?

*A.* Yes.

*Q.* It was not till after you returned, having been absent some little time that he rung the bell and ordered pen, ink, and paper.

*A.* Yes.

*Q.* That order was given in the parlour, not in the passage?

*A.* Yes.

*Q.* Did you see him write upon the paper?

*A.* Yes, I did.

*Q.* You are a hatter?

*A.* Yes.

*Q.* There is a hatter's club at Dover, is there not?

*A.* Not that I know of.

*Q.* Were you up at this time when this transaction took place, or did you get up for the purpose?

*A.* I was up at the time.

*Q.* Had you any particular meeting on that day?

*A.* No, nothing particular, only I was smoking a pipe with Mr. Marsh.

*Q.* At one o'clock?

*A.* Yes, a little after one, it was between one and two o'clock I stopped there after two o'clock, I stopped some considerable time after the gentleman was gone away.

*Q.* He was not there above a quarter of an hour, or twenty minutes, was he?

*A.* I cannot tell, it might be a quarter of an hour or it might not.

*Q.* He was in a great hurry to get off, and went off as soon as the horses were ready?

*A.* He did.

*Q.* Had you dined at the Packet Boat, or at the Ship on that day?

*A.* No, I had not.

*Q.* Have you seen that gentleman from that time till to-day?

*A.* No, not from the time I saw him at Dover till to-day.

*Q.* Have you not been at London to be examined?

*A.* No.

*Q.* You have heard a great deal about this transaction?

*A.* Yes, it has been in every body's mouth.

*Q.* I take for granted you talk about these things as we do in London?

*A.* Yes we do.

*Q.* And read the newspapers that have been full of this thing for a long time?

*A.* I frequently read the newspapers.

*Re-examined by Mr. Bolland.*

*Q.* How long had you an opportunity of observing him?

*A.* Perhaps I might be in the room three or four minutes.

*Q.* During that time, was your attention called to him?

*A.* Yes, on account of the glorious news he said he had brought.

*Q.* It was a welcome face at Dover?

*A.* Yes, it was indeed, and that made me take more notice than I should have done.

*A Juryman.* Had he a cap on all the time you saw him?

*A.* No, he had not.

*Mr. Park.* It was only three or four minutes altogether?

*A.* I beg your pardon; I did not say it was only three or four minutes, I was asked whether it was three or four minutes, and I said I had no doubt it was.

*A Juryman.* Are you sure that is the man?

*A.* That is the gentleman that I saw there.

*Lord Ellenborough.* You have no doubt whatever?

*A.* No, I have none in the least.

*Eliott Edis sworn.*

*Examined by Mr. Bolland.*

*Q.* You are a cooper in the victualling yard at Dover, are you not?

*A.* Yes.

*Q.* Were you, on the morning of the 21st of February, at the Packet Boat?

*A.* Yes, I was.

*Q.* Was Mr. Gourley there with you?

*A.* Yes.

*Q.* Was your attention called to any thing particular on that morning?

*A.* Yes, a messenger arrived.

*Q.* Did you see the messenger?

*A.* Yes.

*Q.* Where did you first see him?

*A.* At the Ship.

*Q.* Was he in a room, or in the passage of the Ship, at the time?

*A.* In a room.

*Q.* At the time you first saw him, how was he occupied, what was he doing?

*A.* He was walking up and down the room.

*Q.* Did you make any observation on his dress?

*A.* He had a grey coat—his great coat.

*Q.* Did you observe the other coat that he had on?

*A.* He had regimentals; scarlet, trimmed with gold.

*Q.* Had they any other ornament on them?

*A.* I did not particularly take notice.

*Q.* Do you recollect how his head was dressed?

*A.* A cap, with a gold band about it.

*Q.* Will you look at that coat which lies there?

*A.* That is the color of it.

*Q.* How was the cap made?

*A.* A slouch cap.

*Q.* Where was the band?

*A.* Round it.

*Q.* Of what did the cap appear to be made?

*A.* It appeared to be made of a kind of rough beaver; I do not know whether it was black or brown.

*Q.* It had the appearance of rough beaver?

*A.* Yes.

*Mr. Bolland.* Will you now shew him the cap?

*Mr. Park.* I think it should be more described before it is shewn to him; this is a totally different description; this may be very material.

*Mr. Bolland.* Then I will not shew him the cap at all.—Had the cap any flap to it?

*A.* Rather a flap round, as I thought—all round.

*Q.* I ask you, whether the cap was cut off without any rim to it, or had it a rim like a hat?

*A.* No, it had not a rim like a hat by any means.

*Q.* Had you any conversation with him?

*A.* No.

*Q.* You say that at first he was walking about the room?

*A.* Yes.

*Q.* Did he employ himself in any other way while you were there?

*A.* I saw him before I went away sit down to write.

*Q.* Did you hear him order a pen, ink, and paper?

*A.* No, I did not.

*Q.* Did he, in your presence, say any thing as to whom he was writing to?

*A.* No, I could hear him talk, but not to understand him.

*Q.* That was owing to your deafness?

*A.* Yes.

*Q.* Did he keep his cap on the whole time you were there, or did he take it off?

*A.* His cap was on while I was there.

*Q.* From the observation you made upon his person, can you point out who that person was whom you saw on that night; have you seen him? look round and see whether you see him here to-day.

*(The witness looked round the Court for some time.)*

*A.* That is the gentleman *(pointing to De Berenger.)*

*Q.* Have you any doubt upon your mind about it.

*A.* No.

*Cross-examined by Mr. Park.*

*Q.* Had you ever seen him before that night?

*A.* No.

*Q.* Have you ever seen him since?

*A.* No.

*Q.* How long did you see him?

*A.* I did not minute the time.

*Q.* Upon the whole, how many minutes do you think you can now say you saw him that night?

*A.* I might see him perhaps five or six minutes, or more. I was in the room twice.

*Q.* Were you there before Mr. Gourley, or after him?

*A.* I was in the room with him.

*Q.* Did you go over before Mr. Gourley, or after him?

*A.* After him—I followed him.

*Q.* Immediately?

*A.* Yes.

*Q.* Did you come away as soon as he did, or did you remain there after him?

*A.* I did not take particular notice of that; the door was open, and we went in and out as we liked.

*Q.* Will you tell us whether the word you used before was, that he had a flat cap, or a flap cap—had it not a flap to it?

*A.* It was a cap rather slouched down, no brim to it.

*Q.* How could it slouch down, if it had no brim to it? I do not understand that; if it had merely a crown to it that would go round the head, it would not slouch down.

*A.* It was drawn over his forehead.

*Q.* The round part of it was drawn down over his forehead?

*A.* Yes.

*Q.* Where have you been all the time that gentleman has been speaking?

*A.* What gentleman?

*Q.* Were you out of Court?

*A.* No, I was not out of Court.

*Q.* You have been behind?

*A.* Yes.

*Q.* Have you been in view of his Lordship all the time?

*A.* No.


*Q.* When did you come into Court; did you come in when Mr. Gourley was examining, or when Marsh, the former witness, was examining?

*A.* No, I was out of Court at that time.

*Q.* Had you left the Ship Inn before this gentleman, as you say it was, had left the Ship Inn and gone back to the Packet Boat?

*A.* No, I saw him start off.

*Re-examined by Mr. Bolland.*

*Q.* Did you come into Court before you were called?

*A.* No.

*Mr. Park.* No, I give that up.

*Lord Ellenborough.* A deaf man is rather an awkward man to be an eaves dropper.

*Mr. Park.* I could not put so silly a question as that.

*Lord Ellenborough.* He is the very last man that one should suspect; he could not hear if he was in Court.

*Mr. Park.* If he had been as deaf as deaf could be, if he had seen a person point at the Defendant, that would have been sufficient for his purpose.

*Lord Ellenborough.* But you saw how he searched round the Court before he found him.

*Mr. Park.* But when I have a case presented to me I must do my duty, however painful it may be.

*Lord Ellenborough.* Certainly, it is my wish you should.

*The Cap was shewn to the witness.*

*Mr. Bolland.* Was the cap like that?

*A.* It was in the same form as that.

*Q.* Was the lace like that?

*A.* It was like that; I cannot say that was the cap.

*Mr. William St. John sworn.*

*Examined by Mr. Bolland.*

*Q.* Where do you reside?

*A.* In Little Brook street.

*Q.* Were you at the Ship Inn at Dover, on the morning of the 21st of February?

*A.* I was.

*Q.* You were there as a guest—as a traveller?

*A.* I was.

*Q.* Was your attention called to any thing on that morning?

*A.* Yes, it was.

*Q.* Were you up in the morning, or had you retired to rest?

*A.* I had retired to rest.

*Q.* State to the Court what it was which excited your attention.

*A.* I think at a quarter past one, or somewhere thereabouts, I heard a violent knocking at the gate or door, and a person calling out for a post-chaise and four immediately. I got up and dressed myself as quickly as possible, and went down stairs. I met Mr. Wright, the landlord, and asked him——

*Q.* Do not state any thing that passed between you and Wright, unless the stranger was there.

*A.* I went into the coffee-room, I think it is called.

*Q.* Did you observe any body there?

*A.* I saw a gentleman in a military uniform.

*Q.* Will you state, if you recollect it, what his dress was?

*A.* He wore a scarlet coat, with long skirts, buttoned across, with a red silk sash, grey pantaloons, and a grey military great coat, and a seal-skin cap, I think it was a seal-skin cap, on his head, of a fawn colour.

*Lord Ellenborough.* You did not touch it to feel it, did you?

*A.* No; it had a gold band round it.

*Mr. Bolland.* Had he any ornament on his uniform?

*A.* There were some ornaments but I do not know what they were, something of a star on his military dress.

*Q.* How was he engaged at the time you first saw him?

*A.* He was walking up and down the room in a very good pace.

*Q.* Did any thing pass between you and him?

*A.* I asked a question.

*Q.* What question did you ask him?

*A.* I asked him about the arrival of a messenger, and he said, he knew nothing at all about it.

*Q.* What were the terms in which you asked him?

*A.* I asked him if he knew any thing of the arrival of Mr. Johnson, who was the Messenger expected.—He said, he knew nothing at all about him, and begged I would leave him to himself, as he was extremely ill. On my leaving the room, he requested that I would send in paper and pen and ink. I immediately retired, and met the landlord, Mr. Wright, coming into the room, I believe with the paper, pens and ink.

*Q.* Did you return into the room?

*A.* In a few minutes, I believe a few seconds afterwards, I did.

*Q.* How was he then occupied?

*A.* He was writing.

*Q.* Did he say any thing of what he was writing?

*A.* No.

*Q.* Did you afterwards hear him say any thing, or see him do any thing with the paper upon which he was writing?

*A.* No, I did not.

*Q.* Did you hear him say any thing to Mr. Wright?

*A.* No, I did not,—not in the room.

*Q.* Did you continue in the room during the whole time he was writing, or leave it?

*A.* I left it immediately.

*Q.* Did you again see him, and where?

*A.* At the door in the street, stepping into the carriage.

*Q.* Did you hear him say any thing there, or see him do any thing?

*A.* I asked him what the news was,—he told me it was as good as I could possibly wish.

*Q.* Did any thing more pass between you and him?

*A.* Nothing more.

*Q.* Did you see what he did with the paper upon which he was writing?

*A.* No, I did not.

*Q.* Did you hear any thing pass between him and any other persons?

*A.* No, I did not.

*Q.* Did you leave the place or did he go away first?

*A.* He went away first.

*Q.* Did any thing pass from that stranger or to him respecting the letter.

*A.* No, not that I heard.

*Q.* From the observation that you made upon that person, could you point him out?

*A.* Certainly.

*Q.* Look round the Court, and see whether he is here?

*A.* The gentleman is below me, (*pointing to De Berenger,*) this Gentlemen, who is writing here.

*Q.* Have you any doubt of it?

*A.* Not in the least.

*Q.* Had you seen him before that day?

*A.* This is the third time I ever saw him.—I saw him by accident in Westminster Hall, passing through the Hall.

*Lord Ellenborough.* Did you recollect him when you saw him there?

*A.* Immediately.


*Mr. Bolland.* By what accident was it that you saw him there?

*A.* I went down there.

*Q.* And there by chance saw him?

*A.* Yes.

*Q.* Were you desired by any body to go down?

*A.* A friend of mine asked me to go down. The fact is we were going to Newgate; having heard that he was gone to Westminster Hall, I went down there.

*Q.* Was he walking about the Hall, or where was he when you saw him?

*A.* I first saw him in the court.

*Q.* Was he alone, or were there other persons about him?

*A.* There were many persons about him.

*Q.* You have no doubt of the person?

*A.* I have no doubt.

*Q.* You recollect nothing of any letter?

*A.* No, I do not.

*Cross examined by Mr. Richardson.*

*Q.* You told my learned friend you had seen this person three times;—once at Dover, and to day, and another time; by accident that was so—was it?

*A.* It was.

*Q.* Did you go to Newgate by accident?

*A.* No, I did not, I went there accompanied by a friend to see him; it was mere by chance that I went down to Westminster Hall.

*Q.* Do you call that an accident in your vocabulary?

*A.* I had no intention of going there ten minutes before.

*Q.* You did not go with your friend for the purpose of looking at him?

*A.* I went alone, I went with a friend to Newgate.

*Q.* You did not go to Westminster Hall for the purpose of looking at him?

*A.* I did.

*Q.* Do you call that an accident?

*A.* No.

*Q.* Did you not follow him to Westminster Hall for the purpose of looking at him?

*A.* Yes.

*Q.* Who was the friend who went with you to Newgate?

*A.* Mr. Oakes of the Stock Exchange.

*Q.* That was the day you knew he was to come to Westminster Hall for the purpose of pleading to this indictment?

*A.* I did not know any such thing.

*Q.* Were not you so informed when you got to Newgate?

*A.* I was.

*Q.* And then you followed him to Westminster Hall, and saw him pleading to this indictment?

*A.* I saw him in Westminster Hall.

*Q.* Did you not hear the officer read the indictment to him?

*A.* I was not in the Court, I think I just had my head in the inside of the curtain.

*Q.* Did you not hear the officer read something to him, and ask him whether he was guilty or not guilty?

*A.* I heard the Officer read something.

*Q.* And ask De Berenger whether he was guilty or not?

*A.* I heard him ask some question, but not what it was.

*Q.* That person was standing up in Court, under the Officer?

*A.* He was.

*Q.* You were not resident at Dover, I think?

*A.* No, I was not.

*Q.* What is your business in London?

*A.* I have a situation in a public charity.

*Q.* What is that?

*A.* The Irish Charitable Society.

*Q.* Are you Secretary to that?

*A.* No, Accountant.

*Q.* Is that your only line of business?

*A.* Yes.

*Q.* Have you nothing to do with the Stock Exchange?

*A.* No.

*Q.* You never had?

*A.* I do not understand that question.

*Q.* Have you ever had any thing to do with the Stock Exchange?

*A.* I have had some transactions in the Stocks.

*Q.* Have you ever acted as a Broker?

*A.* No, never.

*Q.* Your transactions in the Stocks have been entirely on your own account?

*A.* Yes.

*Q.* Buying and selling Stock upon your own account?

*A.* The fact is, I held some Omnium.

*Q.* And sold it again?

*A.* Yes.

*Q.* About what time?

*A.* I bought it before that time.

*Q.* When was it sold?

*A.* Some days after this transaction.

*Q.* You were in this room twice, I think you said?

*A.* Yes.

*Q.* When you first went down, you did not find your company acceptable?

*A.* The gentleman begged I would leave him, and I did so.

*Q.* Upon your oath, how long were you in the room at that time?

*A.* Not more than a minute.

*Q.* It might be less; you went immediately on his requesting you?

*A.* Yes, as soon as possible.

*Q.* The second time, you stated to my learned friend, you left the room immediately after you went in,—how long were you then?

*A.* I suppose a minute; I went up to the table and back again.

*Q.* You did not see him do any thing, but write a letter?

*A.* No.

*Q.* Had he his great coat and cap on, all the time you were with him?

*A.* Yes, I did not see him without them.

*Q.* It was a slouch cap we have heard it described?

*A.* No, it was not; it was a cap without any leaf at all to it.

*Q.* Coming over the forehead?

*A.* No, it fitted the head tight, but had neither a leaf or any thing else to it.

*Q.* What might be your business at Dover at that time?

*A.* I went down for the purpose of getting information.

*Q.* Was that for the benefit of the Irish Charitable Society?

*A.* No, certainly not.

*Q.* If it is not impertinent, for whose benefit was it?

*A.* One purpose was to send information to a newspaper.

*Q.* Another purpose, to send information to whom?

*A.* If any thing happened, such as the arrival of the preliminaries of a treaty of peace, which was expected, I should have come to London immediately.

*Q.* You would have gone to the Stock Exchange with it?

*A.* No, I should not, I have no connexion with the Stock Exchange.

*Q.* Upon your oath, you would not have communicated it to the Stock Exchange?

*A.* I should not.

*Q.* It was by Mr. Oakes's desire, you say, that you went to Newgate,—was it by his desire you went to Dover?

*A.* It was not.

*Q.* Did he know of your going to Dover?

*A.* He did not.

*Q.* By whose desire did you go down?

*A.* By desire of a friend of a mine.

*Q.* Who was that person?

*A.* He was a friend of mine.

*Q.* What was his name?

*Lord Ellenborough.* There is no objection to your telling it.

*Mr. Richardson.* Have you any doubt of it in your memory?

*A.* No.

*Q.* At whose desire did you go down?

*A.* Mr. Farrell.

*Q.* Who is Mr. Farrell?

*A.* He is a Merchant.

*Q.* A Merchant in the City of London?

*A.* Yes he is.

*Q.* Has he any thing to do with the newspaper you have spoken of?

*A.* Yes he has, he is a proprietor of it.

*Q.* What is the name of it?

*A.* The Traveller.

*Q.* Where does Mr. Farrell live?

*A.* In Austin Friars.

*Q.* What day did you go to Dover?

*A.* I went on the Saturday.

*Q.* That was the very day before?

*A.* Yes.

*Q.* For the purpose of getting any intelligence that might arrive and to communicate it immediately to Mr. Farrell?

*A.* Yes, or Mr. Quin, the other proprietor of the newspaper.

*Q.* You told me just now, your object was to get information, partly for the newspaper;—what was the other object?

*A.* I do not recollect having said partly.

*Q.* I am in the recollection of the gentlemen of the Jury, whether you did not say so.

*A Juryman.* You said one object was that.

*Mr. Richardson.* What other object had you?

*A.* That was the only distinct object I had.

*Q.* Then you meant that you had no other object but that?

*A.* If there had been a preliminary Treaty of Peace arrived, I should have returned to London, and of course I would have made what I possibly could of the little Omnium I held.

*Q.* That was the other object?

*A.* Yes.

*Q.* All information of slighter importance you would have communicated to Mr. Farrell, who sent you; if it had been very important, you would have come to London and sold your omnium?

*A.* Certainly.

*Re-examined by Mr. Bolland.*

*Q.* At the time you saw that person in Westminster Hall, I think you told me he was standing with a number of others?

*A.* He was.

*Q.* Did any person point out that person to you?

*A.* No.

*Q.* Was it from the recollection of your own mind, that you discovered him?

*A.* It was.

*Q.* Do you know a boy of the name of Ions?

*A.* No. I do not know him by name.

*William Ions was called into Court.*

*Mr. Bolland (to St. John.)* Do you know that boy?

*A.* Yes.

*Q.* He is one of Wright's boys?

*A.* He is.

*Q.* Did you see him on that night.

*A.* I did.

*Q.* Upon what occasion?

*A.* He was sent as an express, there were two expresses that night, he went with one of them.

*Q.* To whom was that lad sent?

*A.* I think to the Port Admiral at Deal.

*Q.* Whose express was that?

*A.* It was an express I believe that Mr. Wright gave him from the gentleman who was there.

*Q.* Do you mean from that gentleman?

*A.* Yes.

### William Ions sworn.

### Examined by Mr. Gurney.

*Q.* In the month of February last were you in the service of Mr. Wright of Dover.

*A.* Yes.

*Q.* Were you up when the officer arrived there, or were you called up?

*A.* I was called up.

*Q.* Were you sent off with an express to Admiral Foley?

*A.* Yes.

*Q.* Did you take to the Admiral's the letter you received there?

*A.* Yes, I did.

### Cross-examined by Mr. Richardson.

*Q.* Who gave you the letter that you speak of?

*A.* Mr. Wright.

*Q.* He gave you some letters to carry to Admiral Foley?

*A.* Yes.

*Q.* Where did he give it you?

*A.* I was at the fore-door upon the pony, and he came out to the door to me with the letter.

*Q.* To whom did you deliver it?

*A.* To the Admiral's Servant.

*Q.* At Deal?

*A.* Yes.

*Q.* What is her name?

*A.* I do not know, she took it up stairs to the Admiral directly?

*Q.* You did not see the Admiral?

*A.* I saw him that night.

*Q.* Do you mean before you left Deal?

*A.* Yes.

*Q.* This letter you delivered to some servant at the door?

*A.* Yes.

*Q.* And she carried it up stairs?

*A.* Yes.

Re-examined by Mr. Gurney.

*Q.* After she had delivered it up stairs you saw the Admiral?

*A.* Yes.

*Admiral Thomas Foley sworn.*

*Examined by Mr. Gurney.*

*Q.* On the morning of Monday the 21st of February did you receive a letter by that boy?

*A.* A letter was brought to me that that boy brought to the house, and given to me, I was in bed.

*Mr. Park.* You did not receive it from the hand of that boy?

*A.* No, it was brought to me by my maid-servant at three o'clock in the morning, I was in bed.

*Q.* Did you get up immediately?

*A.* I read the letter in bed.

*Q.* Is that the letter? (*shewing a letter to the witness.*)

*A.* This is the letter.

*Q.* Did you mark it before you parted with it?

*A.* I do not know whether I marked it or not.

*Q.* You know it again.

*A.* I inclosed it in a letter but I did not mark it.

*Q.* You inclosed it in a letter to Mr. Croker?

*A.* Yes a private letter to Mr. Croker.

*Q.* Is that the letter in which you inclosed it to Mr. Croker (*shewing a letter to the witness.*)

*A.* This is the letter.

*Q.* That letter which I first shewed you is the letter you received from your maid servant?

*A.* It is.

*Q.* I suppose you rose directly?

*A.* I rose and sent for the boy into my dressing room.

*Q.* Did you communicate the news by telegraph to the admiralty that morning.

*A.* It was very late before I began, I will tell you what I did, I questioned the boy a good deal, for I must say I did not believe the letter.

*Q.* I must not ask you what passed between you and the boy, but whether you telegraphed the admiralty?

*A.* I did not, because the weather was thick, and I further say, the message I should have sent to the admiralty would have satisfied them—

*Q.* In fact you did not telegraph the admiralty because the weather was too thick?

*A.* I did not.

*Q.* When you sent for the boy up had you the letter in your hand?

*A.* I had, it was then three o'clock and dark, the telegraph would not move.

*Q.* I take for granted you had a candle?

*A.* Of course.

*Mr. Gurney.* We will now read the letter.

*Mr. Park.* I object, with great deference to his Lordship, to that letter being read, the evidence does not bring home that to the supposed officer, who is said to be Mr. De Berenger, it does not appear from any evidence to have come out of his hand it reaches this boy by the communication of Mr. Wright, who has not been called.

*Mr. Gurney.* I will ask the witness as to the reason of Mr. Wright's not being here—he is very ill, is not he?

*A.* He is extremely ill.

*Mr. Park.* My Lord, that does not alter the law of evidence, I submit there is a chasm in that chain that precludes their reading the letter as evidence against Mr. De Berenger. I do not mean to say that might not be supplied in the absence of Mr. Wright, but that letter lying before your Lordship's Officer is not identified to be the very paper which issued forth from this supposed person. It was delivered to this youth at the door of the inn by Wright, who is ill and absent from illness, he is not present to tell your Lordship from whom he received that, and there is a chasm in the chain of evidence, nor does the Admiral say he received the letter from this boy, he received it from a maid servant.

*Lord Ellenborough (to Admiral Foley.)* When the boy came into your presence I suppose you asked him about this letter?

*A.* I did.

*Q.* Did he recognize that as the letter he had brought?

*A.* He did.

*Mr. Park.* With deference to your Lordship I should submit the letter was then open, the boy had delivered the letter shut to the maid servant, and I should have submitted, it is quite impossible that this youth could distinguish the letter, nobody doubts it is the letter, but that must be proved by legal evidence.

*Lord Ellenborough.* It is prima facie evidence. I do not speak now of the communication from De Berenger (supposing he is the person) of the letter to the boy. I do not say any thing upon that objection of yours, but that the letter which reached Admiral Foley was the letter the boy brought I think no human being can doubt.

*Mr. Park.* But still upon the original point, I submit it is not so proved as to be read in evidence.

*Lord Ellenborough.* Yes, you may resort to that if you please, the witness said he wanted an express horse to send to the Admiral at Deal, and then an express horse was got, and something was carried to the Admiral at Deal. That is the evidence as it stands.

*Mr. Serjeant Best.* So far the evidence goes my Lord, they now want to make the contents of that letter evidence, but before they can do that they must either prove that letter to be the hand-writing of Mr. De Berenger, or trace that Letter regularly from the hand of Mr. De Berenger: they have no such evidence, but all they say is, that Wright, the Landlord of the inn, took the letter out of the inn and delivered it to the boy at the door, the boy never having seen Mr. De Berenger, nor they having the smallest evidence whatever to connect the boy with him.

*Lord Ellenborough.* If there had been, the question would not have arisen.

*Mr. Serjeant Best.* I submit there is nothing to connect that letter with this person, and if it is the hand-writing of Mr. De Berenger I should think they would have no difficulty in proving that, there were other gentlemen waiting for information from France, as we hear from the witnesses, and if this letter is read Mr. De Berenger and the other Defendants may be made responsible for that letter which may have been written by one of those other persons.

*Lord Ellenborough.* I only want to get first all the facts relating to this letter. I cannot find any thing beyond that that he wanted an express horse to send to the Admiral at Deal.

*Mr. Gurney.* And that a sheet of paper was brought to him to write.

*Lord Ellenborough.* That he was preparing to write a letter and that he wanted an express horse to carry it, but as to the immediate identification of that letter you lose the intervening proof by the absence of Mr. Wright.

*Mr. Gurney.* My Lord, if there is any sort of difficulty about it, I will identify it at once by proving the hand-writing, but the Gentleman to prove that felt a delicacy in consequence of his being the Attorney for the prosecution.

*Germain Lavie, Esq. sworn.*

*Examined by Mr. Gurney.*

*Q.* You are the Attorney for the prosecution?

*A.* Yes.

*Q.* Did you see Mr. De Berenger in the custody of the messenger, in the course of the month of April?

*A.* Several times.

*Q.* In the course of those interviews did you see him write?

*A.* I did.

*Q.* Did you see him write a good deal?

*A.* Yes, a considerable deal, I saw a whole letter which he handed me across when he had written it, and it was given back and copied again, and for about an hour he was writing different things and handing backwards and forwards.

*Q.* Did you also see his papers in his writing desk?

*A.* I did.

*Q.* From the observation you made upon his writing, seeing him writing as you did at those several interviews, do you or do you not believe that to be his hand-writing?

*A.* I verily believe it to be his hand-writing from what I saw him write, but I am more impressed with its being his hand-writing, or at least the impression of its being his hand-writing is strengthened by what I saw of his writing.

*Q.* Do you believe, from what you saw him write, that that is his hand-writing.

*A.* Yes I do most solemnly, I did not see the letter till afterwards, and the moment I saw it, I concluded that to be his hand writing, and said so at the time.

*Mr. Park.* What you said at the time is no evidence, and you know that.

*Mr. Gurney.* Did your observation of it enable you to say you believed it to be his hand writing?

*A.* I have said so.

*Mr. Park.* You know as well as any man, that what you said to any body is no evidence.

*Lord Ellenborough.* It is a measure strongly indicative of his persuasion, it is an act accompanying his seeing it.

*Mr. Gurney.* Does Mr. De Berenger always write as large as that, or does he write a hand as large as that, and a smaller one also?

*A.* His usual hand is a good deal smaller than this.

*Q.* Did you find him sometimes writing larger than at other times?

*A.* Yes, there was apparently in his letters a larger hand in writing, I could positively swear that the man who wrote those I saw, wrote this, only one was larger than the other.

*Cross examined by Mr. Park.*

*Q.* You told my learned Friend just now, that you formed your mind not only from what you saw him write, but from what you saw in his writing desk?

*A.* That confirmed my mind.

*Q.* Upon your oath, if you had not seen those writings in his Desk, would you have taken upon yourself to swear that it was his hand writing?

*A.* I think I should, but that makes it much stronger in my mind.

*Q.* I ask you again and will have a positive answer to the question, if you had never seen those other writings to which you have alluded, would you upon the mere circumstance of having seen him write, have taken upon you to swear that you believed that to be his hand writing?

*A.* I could have sworn it not quite so strongly, I could have sworn to my verily believing it, but I can now swear without the least doubt that it is his.

*Q.* That is because I have examined you perhaps?

*A.* No it is not.

*Q.* You verily believe that to be his writing, do you?

*A.* Yes.

*Q.* Look at that and tell me whether you believe that to be his hand writing, (*shewing a letter to the witness*) you need not open it, I have shut it for the purpose.

*A.* Yes I do, that is more like what I saw him write than this; I believe that to be his hand writing.

*Mr. Park.* I will put a letter A upon it; will you be so good as to look at that account, (*shewing it to the witness*) and tell me whether you believe that to be his hand writing.

*A.* I can only say this is the sort of hand he writes.

*Q.* Will you swear that is his hand writing.

*A.* That appears to me to be the same sort of hand.

*Mr. Park.* I will mark this B. They are very much alike.

*A.* They are more like the sized hand he writes in common than this, this is a larger hand.

*Mr. Serjeant Best.* Do you believe these to be Mr. De Berenger's hand writing? (*shewing three papers to the witness*).

*A.* They are all like his hand writing.

*Lord Ellenborough.* I think this should be kept for your case—I never saw any thing like this in my life.

*Mr. Gurney.* I take for granted these are meant to be produced in the defence?

*Lord Ellenborough.* You must be conscious that you are doing an irregular thing in tendering them now.

*Mr. Park.* I am not conscious my Lord, of doing an irregular thing.

*Lord Ellenborough.* I mean in tendering evidence at a time when it is not open to the Defendant to do so.

*Mr. Park.* But I may try the credit of the Witness by shewing him these.

*Lord Ellenborough.* There is no doubt that every Defendant has a right to give evidence in his turn, but at present we are upon the case of the prosecution.

*Mr. Park.* Have you not shewn that Letter to various other persons in order to procure their testimony to the hand writing?

*A.* No, I have not.

*Q.* You have not attempted it?

*A.* I was always conscious that I should be able to prove the Letter, but this morning finding Mr. Wright was not come up, I asked them if they had any body at hand that could prove it, so as to avoid being called myself; but I believe I must be called at last to the examination of the papers, so that it is not so important my being called sooner or later.

*Q.* Have you attempted to get other evidence?

*A.* I have not.

*Q.* Was Mr. Stevens applied to?

*A.* Before the Grand Jury, Mr. Stevens was not only applied to, but attended.—Mr. Lees also, of the Bank of England had ascertained before I had any thing to do with the business——

*Mr. Park.* That is not my question.

*Lord Ellenborough.* Put your question distinctly.

*Mr. Park.* I ask whether Mr. Lavie had not applied to various persons to swear to De Berenger's hand writing, and finding that they would not swear to it, then he determined to swear to it himself?

*A.* No, I have not.

*Mr. Gurney.* You say you did apply to Mr. Lees of the Bank, and Mr. Stevens?

*A.* Yes.

*Q.* Mr. Lees is the Inspector at the Bank?

*A.* He is.

*The Letter was read as follows:*

Dover, one o'clock, A. M. Feb. 21st, 1814.

Sir,

I have the honour to acquaint you, that the L'Aigle from Calais, Pierre Duquin, Master, has this moment landed me near Dover, to proceed to the capital with Dispatches of the happiest nature. I have pledged my honour that no harm shall come to the crew of L'Aigle; even with a Flag of truce they immediately stood for Sea. Should they be taken, I have to entreat you immediately to liberate them; my anxiety will not allow me to say more for your gratification, than that the Allies obtained a final victory, that Bonaparte was overtaken by a party of Sachen's Cossacks, who immediately slaid him, and divided his body between them; General Platoff saved Paris from being reduced to ashes, the Allied Sovereigns are there, and the White Cockade is universal, an immediate Peace is certain.—In the utmost haste I entreat your consideration, and I have the honour to be,

Sir,<br>
Your most obedient, humble Servant,<br>
R. Du BOURG,<br>
Lt. Col. & Aid de Camp to Lord Cathcart.

To the Honourable T. Foley
Port Admiral, Deal,
&c. &c. &c. &c.

*Mr. Serjeant Best.* Your Lordship will allow me to explain. I did not ask these questions of Mr. Lavie, with a view to offer hand writing against hand writing, but to prove these Papers that I mean to offer in evidence.

*Lord Ellenborough.* They should be proved in your case; I know by mutual consent they are sometimes proved by a Witness for the Prosecution, and I did not interfere in the first instance, but when I saw it multiplying, I thought it necessary to interfere.

*Thomas Dennis Sworn.*

*Examined by Mr. Adolphus.*

*Q.* Are you the driver of a post chaise in the service of Mr. Wright, at the Ship at Dover?

*A.* Yes.

*Q.* Early in the morning of the 21st of February, do you remember taking a fare from thence?

*A.* Yes, I drove the chaise.

*Q.* With how many horses?

*A.* Four.

*Q.* Where did you drive it to?

*A.* To Canterbury.

*Q.* To what Inn?

*A.* To the Fountain.

*Q.* What sort of person was it that you drove?

*A.* I cannot say.

*Q.* Was it one person, or more than one?

*A.* Only one.

*Q.* A man or a woman?

*A.* A man.

*Q.* Was it dark?

*A.* Yes.

*Q.* Could you see how he was dressed?

*A.* No.

*Q.* Had you the Wheel horse, or the leaders?

*A.* The leaders.

*Q.* When you put the person down whom you had driven, what did he give you?

*A.* He gave me a gold Napoleon.

*Q.* Did he give you only?

*A.* He gave us one a piece.

*Q.* What became of those Napoleons?

*A.* I sold mine.

*Q.* What did you get for it?

*A.* I got a one pound note for mine.

*Q.* Do you know the name of the lad at Canterbury that took him after you?

*A.* Yes.

*Q.* What is his name?

*A.* Broad.

*Q.* Who was the other?

*A.* Thomas Daly.

*Cross Examined by Mr. Richardson.*

*Q.* Did you see Broad and Daly set off with the chaise from Canterbury?

*A.* Yes.

*Q.* It was a very dark night, was not it?

*A.* Yes.

*Q.* An hazy misty night?

*A.* Yes.

*Q.* A dark foggy night?

*A.* Yes.

*Q.* How do you remember the day this happened, from Dover you are in the habit of carrying persons in chaises and four to Canterbury frequently?

*A.* Yes.

*Q.* Day and night?

*A.* Yes.

*Q.* The carrying a gentleman in a chaise and four to Canterbury was nothing extraordinary?

*A.* No.

*Q.* How came you to remember this particular day?

*A.* I do not know.

*Q.* Upon your oath, might it not have been the 20th or the 22nd?

*A.* I cannot say indeed.

*Q.* Have you not heard other people say it was the 21st that this extraordinary affair happened?

*A.* No, I have not.

*Q.* You have not heard it talked of at all?

*A.* No.

*Q.* For aught you know it might be the 20th or the 22nd?

*A.* I cannot say.

*Re-examined by Mr. Adolphus.*

*Q.* Do you remember what day of the week it was?

*A.* No.

*Q.* Do persons often give you a Napoleon for driving them?

*A.* No, I never had one before.

*Q.* You do not remember the day of the week?

*A.* No, I do not.

*Edward Broad sworn.*

*Examined by Mr. Adolphus.*

*Q.* Are you a driver of a chaise at the Fountain at Canterbury?

*A.* Yes.

*Q.* Do you remember the last witness coming to your house with a fare early in a morning in February.

*A.* Yes.

*Q.* Do you remember what day it was?

*A.* No, I do not.

*Q.* Do you remember what day of the week it was?

*A.* No, I do not.

*Q.* Was it one gentleman you particularly remember, or more?

*A.* One gentleman.

*Q.* From whence did he come?

*A.* From the Ship at Dover.

*Q.* Did you drive the wheel horses or the leaders?

*A.* The leaders.

*Q.* He came with four horses?

*A.* Yes.

*Q.* And went away with four?

*A.* Yes.

*Q.* Where did you drive him to?

*A.* To the Rose at Sittingbourn.

*Q.* Did you see him into a chaise there?

*A.* He did not get out—the chaise went forwards.

*Q.* With four horses or two?

*A.* With four.

*Q.* Who drove him, do you remember the boys names?

*A.* Michael Finnis was one, and James Wakefield.

*Q.* What present did he make you?

*A.* I did not receive any money from him; the other boy received the money.

*Q.* What had you for your share?

*Mr. Park.* That cannot be received unless he saw it given.

*Mr. Adolphus.* Did you see the money given?

*A.* I was very busy taking the horses off.

*Q.* What had you for your share?

*A.* A Napoleon.

### Cross-examined by Mr. Park.

*Q.* Have you long lived at the Fountain at Canterbury?

*A.* Yes.

*Q.* Have you long known Thomas Dennis?

*A.* Yes, some years.

*Q.* Have you never driven a fare he brought from Dover before?

*A.* Not particularly to my knowledge.

*Q.* Your knowledge has been called to this subject, but you do not know that you ever drove one that he brought before?

*A.* I might have driven one, but he brought this I know.

*Q.* You might have driven a fare brought by him from Dover?

*A.* I might, there are a great many boys from that Inn.

*Q.* And you have driven a single gentleman before?

*A.* Yes.

*Q.* And sometimes you have driven a chaise and four?

*A.* Yes.

*Re-examined by Mr. Adolphus.*

*Q.* Did you ever receive a Napoleon before?

*Mr. Park.* He did not receive it from that person.

*Lord Ellenborough.* Did all these circumstances ever concur in any other case. Did you ever drive so early in the morning a single gentleman in a chaise and four, and receive a Napoleon from him?

*A.* No, I never did.

*Michael Finnis sworn.*

*Examined by Mr. Adolphus.*

*Q.* Are you a post-chaise driver at the Rose at Sittingbourn?

*A.* Yes.

*Q.* Do you remember the last witness bringing a gentleman in a post-chaise to your house?

*A.* Yes.

*Q.* In the month of February?

*A.* I did not take particular notice of the time.

*Q.* Was it early in the morning?

*A.* Yes.

*Q.* In a chaise and four?

*A.* Yes.

*Q.* At what o'clock in the morning might it be?

*A.* It might be somewhere about four, or between four and five I believe. I did not take particular notice, for I had no watch with me, it was dark.

*Q.* Where did you drive him to?

*A.* I drove him to the Crown at Rochester.

*Q.* That is Mr. Wright's house?

*A.* Yes.

*Q.* At what time in the morning might it be when you got to Rochester?

*A.* I cannot say, we were not much above an hour going with the gentleman—it might be an hour and ten minutes at the outside.

*Q.* Did the gentleman get out there?

*A.* Yes, he did.

*Q.* What present did he make you?

*A.* He gave us a Napoleon a piece; he gave me two, one for my fellow-servant and one for myself.

*Lord Ellenborough.* You had no opportunity of seeing his person?

*A.* I did just see him in the house when he paid me, but I did not take any particular notice of him.

*Lord Ellenborough.* He had no luggage, had he?

*A.* I do not know.

*Lord Ellenborough.* I thought he had changed chaise?

*Mr. Park.* No, he did not change chaise, only got out and in again.

*A Juryman.* Did you observe his dress?

*A.* He had a kind of a pepper and salt coat on, and a red coat under that I perceived, and a cap he had on.

*Mr. William Wright sworn.*

*Examined by Mr. Adolphus.*

*Q.* You keep the Crown Inn at Rochester?

*A.* Yes.

*Q.* Do you remember a chaise from Sittingbourn arriving at your house on the morning of the 21st of February?

*A.* Yes.

*Q.* A chaise and four?

*A.* Yes.

*Mr. Park.* I request that the questions may not be put so leading as to fix the day, for not one witness has proved it.

*Mr. Adolphus.* Have you any particular reason for remembering that day?

*A.* Yes.

*Q.* What sort of a person was it that came in the chaise?

*A.* It was a tall person rather thin than otherwise.

*Q.* Dressed how?

*A.* He was dressed in a pepper and salt great coat, with a scarlet coat under it, a Military scarlet coat; the upper coat was nearer the color of that coat I think than any thing I could state, (*pointing to the coat before produced*), the scarlet Military coat he had under that was very much trimmed with gold lace, it appeared by the candle light to be gold lace trimmed down the front; he had on also a cap, a Military cap with a broad gold lace round it—a band.

*Q.* What was the cap apparently made of?

*A.* The cap appeared to me to be made of cloth; I am not certain whether it was of cloth or fur, but it appeared to be nearly of the color of the great coat.

*Q.* Was there any thing particular about his Military coat?

*A.* On the Military coat was a star, and something suspended either from the neck or the button, I do not know which, something which he told me was some honor of a Military order of Russia.

*Q.* Was that thing at all like this? (*shewing the star to the witness.*)

*A.* Yes, it had very much the appearance of that sort of thing.

*Q.* Did the person stay any time at your house?

*A.* I should suppose I was in conversation with him about ten minutes in the parlour.

*Lord Ellenborough.* At what time in the morning was this?

*A.* The time the chaise drove into the yard I suppose was about half-past 5 o'clock; it was not earlier than that, and I suppose very little later.

*Mr. Adolphus.* What were you and he doing during these ten minutes?

*A.* I was getting some chicken for him, and cutting that chicken up and some round of beef.

*Q.* In what room were you?

*A.* In our bar parlour; I took him there, the house not being open, that being warmer than the rest of the rooms.

*Q.* What passed in that conversation you had with him?

*A.* I was first of all called up by a post-boy of my brother's at Dover, he told me he was to go forward with some letter to London, and that there was a Messenger.

*Q.* You must not state what passed with your brother's boy, but in consequence of what that boy told you what did you say to the gentleman?

*A.* I went into the yard and found the gentleman looking out at the front window of the chaise and he said he was very hungry, and could he have any thing to eat, for he had had nothing since he left Calais; I told him that he could get any thing he pleased, and should I bring him any thing by way of a sandwich, as I supposed he would not get out of the chaise, he said he would get out, and he did get out, and I took him into our bar parlour; when he got there I said "I am led to suppose you are the bearer of some very good news for this Country," he said he was, that the business was all done, that the thing was settled. I asked him if I might be allowed to ask him, what was the nature of his dispatches, and he said "he is dead!" I said "who do you mean Sir?" He said "The Tyrant Bonaparte!" or words to that effect; I believe those were the exact words. I said "is that really true Sir?" Upon that observation he said, "if you doubt my word you had better not ask me any more questions." I then made an apology for presuming to doubt his word, and requested he would be kind enough to say, as the Country was very anxious, and our town in particular, what were the dispatches; he then went on that there had been a very general battle between the French and the whole of the Allied Powers, commanded by Schwartzenberg in person; that the French had been completely defeated and Bonaparte had fled for safety. That he had been overtaken at a village, to the best of my recollection he said it was Rushaw, six leagues from Paris, by the Cossacks, to the best of my recollection that was the name of the place and the distance. That the Cossacks had there come up with him, and that they had literally torn him into pieces. That he had come from the field of battle from the Emperor Alexander himself; that he either was an Aid-de-Camp of the Emperor or of one of his principal Generals he told me, but which I am not able to say, but one I know he told me was the case, that the Allies were invited by the Parisians to Paris, and the Bourbons to the throne of France, that was pretty well all the conversation that passed. He eat very little, if he did any thing, he said he was very cold; I asked him if he would take any brandy, he said no he would not, for he had some wine in the carriage. He enquired what he had to pay, I told him what he had had had been in so uncomfortable a manner, that I should not wish to take any thing for what he had had. He did not accept of that, he threw down a Napoleon on the table and desired me to take that for what he had himself taken, and to give the servants something out of it; he meant the whole of the servants, for when he got into the chaise the ostler asked him for something, and he said he had left something with his master.

*Q.* Did he go away in the chaise that brought him, or in another chaise?

*A.* In the same chaise.

*Q.* With four horses?

*A.* Yes, with four horses.

*Q.* What were the names of the lads that drove him?

*A.* James Overy and Thomas Todd, I believe were the boys. I am not quite positive as to the names of the boys.

*Q.* Should you know the person again that you saw that morning if you were to see him?

*A.* I think I should, he was very much disguised at that time.

*Q.* Look about, and tell me whether you see him any where?

*A.* I do not immediately see any face that I should know again, that I at this moment recollect.

*Q.* Look with care round about?

*A.* That is the gentleman, (*pointing to De Berenger.*)

*Q.* Do you believe that to be the person?

*A.* Yes, I do think that is the person—really when I see the face it is the same.

*Q.* Looking again, have you any doubt of it?

*A.* I think I can swear that is the gentleman. I have no doubt of it—that certainly is the gentleman.

*Cross Examined by Mr. Richardson.*

*Q.* Had you ever seen the gentleman before?

*A.* No.

*Q.* Nor since?

*A.* No not till to-day, not to my knowledge.

*Q.* The first thing he said was that he was very hungry; and you went to get him something to eat?

*A.* Yes; and he got out of the chaise, and I got him something. We crossed the yard together.

*Q.* During all the time you were with him he was getting something to eat?

*A.* No; he was sitting in the room part of the time.

*Q.* You were busy getting him something at the time?

*A.* He was standing while I was getting it, and then he sat down; I staid to wait upon him.

*Q.* What was the whole length of the time you were with him?

*A.* I suppose ten minutes.

*Q.* The greatest part of that time he was eating, was not he?

*A.* The greatest part of the time he was talking; I do not think he ate any thing; he took a knife and fork in his hand but I do not believe he ate any thing.

*A Juryman.* Did you observe any thing particular in his dress?

*A.* He was dressed pretty much in the way I have described; he had one part of his dress I have not mentioned, which was a large white cockade hanging down very dirty, as if it had been a long time worn.

Lord *Ellenborough.* Had you any conversation with him about his communicating this intelligence in any public quarter; or did you give him any advice upon that?

*A.* No I did not. When he went away I gave him a card of the road, and requested his favors when he should come that way again; and he bowed, as if assenting.

*Q.* You have not seen him since?

*A.* No I have not.

*A Juryman.* Had he his cap on?

*A.* Yes he had it on the whole of the time I believe. I have got the Napoleon in my pocket that the gentleman gave me.

*The Witness produced it.*

*A Juryman.* What did you say was the color of the cap he had on?

*A.* I think it was very near the color if not the color of the great coat, to the best of my recollection, looking at it by candle light.

*Lord Ellenborough.* From the circumstances of his appearance, looking at that person before you, you have no doubt?

*A.* I have no doubt of it; I can swear to that gentleman, though I have never seen him since.

*James Overy sworn.*

*Examined by Mr. Adolphus.*

*Q.* Did you take up a person at your master's house at Rochester?

*A.* Yes.

*Q.* Do you recollect on what day it was?

*A.* On a Monday.

*Q.* Can you recollect the day of the month?

*A.* No I cannot.

*Q.* Where did you drive him to?

*A.* I drove him to Dartford.

*Q.* How was he dressed?

*A.* He appeared to have a great coat on.

*Q.* What house at Dartford did you drive to?

*A.* The Granby.

*Q.* What kind of a coat had he on?

*A.* A grey mixture coat it appeared to be.

*Q.* Did you see any other part of his dress?

*A.* Yes, a red coat, like an aid de camp's, it appeared to be.

*Q.* Describe the coat, was it adorned with any thing?

*A.* He had a star very full indeed.

*Q.* Did you see any thing else?

*A.* There was something about his neck hanging.

*Q.* What had he upon his head?

*A.* He had a cap with a bit of white ribband run through the cap.

*Lord Ellenborough.* How was that ribband, in the shape of a cockade?

*A.* No it was not.

*Mr. Adolphus.* What sort of a cap was it?

*A.* A cap such as officers wear, with a gold lace band round it.

*Q.* Was it day-light when you left him at Dartford?

*A.* Yes; it was about ten minutes before seven when we came to Dartford with him.

*Q.* Was it then day-light?

*A.* Yes it was day-light about two miles before we came to Dartford.

*Q.* Did you see the person sufficiently to think you should know him again?

*A.* I do not know that I should.

*Q.* What did he give you at parting?

*A.* He gave us two Napoleons, and paid me for the Dartford horses and for our horses too; he paid me one £5. note and a shilling for the Dartford horses, and the Rochester horses too, and the turnpikes.

*Q.* He gave you and the other lad a Napoleon a-piece?

*A.* Yes he did.

*Q.* Who took him up at Dartford?

*A.* Thomas Shilling and Charles Ward.

*Cross Examined by Mr. Park.*

*Q.* What was the color of his cap?

*A.* I did not take notice of it.

*Q.* There was a white ribband stuck through it?

*A.* Yes.

*Q.* You took so much notice of it you said it was like an officer's cap?

*A.* Yes.

*Q.* How do you describe an officer's cap, are there not different sorts of officers caps?

*A.* I have seen what they wear when they are not in their regimentals, those they wear in a morning, this was such a cap as they generally wear in a morning, not what they wear with their regimentals in the day-time.

*Q.* It slouched down I suppose?

*A.* Yes.

*Q.* There is a something comes down to shade the eyes?

*A.* Not on that.

*Q.* How does it slouch then?

*A.* A kind of a turn down, a little way turned down.

*Q.* What was a little way turned down?

*A.* The cap.

*Q.* What part of the cap, in the front, or where?

*A.* In the front.

*Q.* Did you observe what color it was?

*A.* No I did not.

*Q.* Whether it was a dark brown?

*A.* I did not take any notice of the color.

*William Tozer sworn.*

*Examined by Mr. Adolphus.*

*Q.* You are an innkeeper at Dartford?

*A.* Yes.

*Q.* What is your sign?

*A.* The Crown and Anchor.

*Q.* Do you remember on any particular day James Overy bringing a fare to any other house in your town?

*A.* Yes.

*Q.* What day was it?

*A.* About the 21st of February.

*Q.* What day in the week?

*A.* Monday morning.

*Q.* What sort of person was it you took notice of?

*A.* The person that I took notice of was sitting in the chaise.

*Q.* Did you speak to him?

*A.* I did.

*Q.* What passed between you?

*A.* I was informed——

*Q.* Tell us what you told him?

*A.* In the first place, I made my obedience to the gentleman in the chaise, hoping that he had brought us some good news.

*Q.* You said so?

*A.* Yes.

*Q.* What did the gentleman say?

*A.* He said he had, and that it was all over; that the Allies had actually entered Paris; that Bonaparte was dead, destroyed by the Cossacks, and literally torn in pieces, and that we might expect a speedy peace.

*Q.* Did he tell you any thing more?

*A.* No; during the conversation I saw him give James Overy two gold pieces, which afterwards proved to be French pieces, I had them in my hand.

*Q.* Do you know the name of them?

*A.* I cannot say that I do; there was ten francs or something on them.

*Q.* Did you see enough of the person with whom you conversed in the chaise to think that you should know him again?

*A.* I am positive I should.

*Q.* Look round and see whether you see him here?

*The Witness looked round.*

*A.* I cannot see him; he is not round here; I cannot say that I am positive.

*Q.* You do not see him?

*A.* No I cannot say that I do.

*Q.* Look from here to the end of the row?

*A.* No I cannot say that I am positive.

*Q.* Do you know the boys who drove the Baron away?

*A.* Yes, Shilling and ——.

*Mr. Gurney.* Before Shilling comes in, and when what I say is not heard by him, I must say that the person to be identified should hold his head so as to be seen.

*Mr. Park.* And so he did. I desired Mr. De Berenger to hold his head gently up, and he did it immediately.

*Lord Ellenborough.* The questions might go much nearer; the witnesses might be asked if that be the person: it is done always at the Old Bailey in cases of life and death, where the prisoner stands in a conspicuous situation—it is less strong in that case; but to be sure when it is proved in the way it has been, it can be of very little consequence.

*Thomas Shilling sworn.*

*Examined by Mr. Adolphus.*

*Q.* You are a chaise-driver at Dartford?

*A.* Yes.

*Q.* Do you remember on a particular day taking up a gentleman who came in a chaise and four to Dartford?

*A.* Yes.

*Q.* What day was that?

*A.* I do not rightly know the day, but I believe it was on the 21st of February.

*Q.* What day of the week?

*A.* On a Monday.

*Q.* Had you a pair of horses?

*A.* Yes.

*Q.* Upon your ride to London, did the gentleman say any thing to you?

*A.* Yes, he discoursed with me a good deal.

*Q.* Who first spoke to him in your hearing?

*A.* The first man that spoke to him in my hearing that I took any notice of, was the waiter.

*Q.* The waiter at your inn at Dartford?

*A.* Yes.

*Q.* What was the sign of your house?

*A.* The Granby at Dartford.

*Q.* What passed between him and the waiter?

*A.* The waiter asked him whether he had brought any good news; the gentleman said, yes, it was all over; Bonaparte was dead; he said he was torn in a thousand pieces; and the Cossacks fought for a share of him all the same as if they had been fighting for sharing out gold, and the Allies were in Paris; then we were ordered to go on.

*Q.* How far had you gone before this gentleman spoke to you?

*A.* To Bexley Heath, about two miles and a half.

*Q.* Had he before that said any thing to you about driving?

*A.* Not that I heard.

*Q.* When he came to Bexley Heath what did he say to you?

*A.* He told me not to hurry my horses, for his business was not so particular now, since the telegraph could not work he thought.

*Q.* Were you in sight of a telegraph then?

*A.* No.

*Q.* What sort of a morning was it?

*A.* Rather a thick morning; very frosty.

*Lord Ellenborough.* Did it appear to you to be so thick a morning that the telegraphs could not work?

*A.* It did.

*Mr. Adolphus.* What did you say to him?

*A.* I told him I thought the telegraphs could not work, for I knew almost every telegraph between Deal and London. He then said, Post-boy, don't take any notice of the news as you go along; I told him I would not unless he wished; he said I might tell any of my friends as I returned, for he dar'st to say they would be glad to hear it. He then said that he had sent a letter to the Port-Admiral at Deal, for he was ordered to do so, or he was obliged to do so, I will not be certain which.

*Lord Ellenborough.* You are sure he said so?

*A.* I am sure he said so. He said that he had to walk two miles after he came ashore before he got to the Ship at Dover. He said the Frenchmen were afraid of coming so near to Dover, for fear of being stopped, the Frenchmen that brought him; then we drove on till we came to Shooter's Hill.

*Mr. Adolphus.* Did he tell you why he had sent to the Port-Admiral at Deal?

*A.* To have the telegraphs worked, that he said was the reason.

*Q.* Did any thing further pass between you at the time?

*A.* Not any thing that I recollect.

*Q.* Had you any subsequent conversation at any other part of the stage?

*A.* Not till I got to Shooter's Hill; when I came there I alighted from my horse, and so did my fellow-servant; the gentleman then looked out of the window, and gave us part of a bottle of wine; he said we might drink that, because he was afraid the bottle should break, and some cakes with it.

*Q.* What sort of cakes?

*A.* Little round cakes; I chucked the bottle away, and handed the glass again into the chaise; he told me I might keep it, that I might have it. He then said, "Post-boy, you have had a great deal of snow here, I understand?" I said, "Yes, Sir, we have." He then said, "Here is a delightful morning, post-boy; I have not seen old England a long while before." Then he asked me, "which was the first hackney coach stand?" I told him, at the Bricklayer's Arms, was the first.

*Q.* Did he say why he asked that question?

*A.* Not a word; he said that would not do, for that was too public; he was afraid some body would cast some reflections, and he should not like that. I told him, I did not think any body would do that, that they would be so glad to hear of the news. Then he asked me, if there was not a hackney coach stand in Lambeth Road? I told him yes. Then he said, "Drive me there, post-boy, for your chaise will go faster than a hackney coach will, and so you may drive me there." I drove him to the Lambeth Road, and when I came there, there was no coach on the stand.

*Q.* Where about is the Lambeth Road?

*A.* I went from the Dog and Duck by the Asylum; this coach-stand was at the Three Stags, there was no hackney coach there. I ordered my fellow-servant to stop, and I looked round and told the gentleman there was no hackney coach there; but that there was a coach-stand at the Marsh Gate, and if he liked to get in there, I dared to say nobody would take any notice of him—I drove him up along side of a coach.

*Q.* Did he do any thing upon that?

*A.* I think he pulled up the side-blind as I came round the corner.

*Q.* Was the side-blind up?

*A.* Yes, it was up when I came there; I saw it up, but I did not see when he pulled it up.

*Lord Ellenborough.* Having been down before, it was up when you got there?

*A.* Yes, when I got there I pulled up alongside of a hackney coach.

*Mr. Adolphus.* How many hackney coaches were there?

*A.* Only one; I called the coachman, and the waterman opened the coach door, and I opened the chaise door.

*Q.* Did the gentleman go into the coach?

*A.* Yes, he did.

*Q.* How?

*A.* He stepped off my step on to that, for he stepped on the body of the coach, or on the step of the coach; I cannot say he never stepped on the ground, the coach and the chaise were too nigh together.

*Q.* Did he make you any present for your trouble?

*A.* He then held his hand down, and gave me two Napoleons; I have them here now; he did not say one was for my fellow-servant and the other for myself, but I supposed it was so (the witness produced the Napoleons.)

*Q.* Did you hear him tell the coachman where to drive to?

*A.* I did not.

*Q.* Do you know the name of the coachman or the waterman?

*A.* Yes, I do.

*Q.* What is the name of the coachman?

*A.* Crane.

*Q.* Do you know the waterman's name?

*A.* I am not rightly sure; I think they call him Bob. I know his person very well.

*Q.* How was this gentleman dressed, that you drove to town?

*A.* He was dressed with a dark fur cap—a round cap, and with white lace, of some sort, round it; whether it was gold or silver, I cannot say; he had a red coat on underneath his outer coat.

*Q.* What sort of a coat was his outer coat?

*A.* I think it was a dark coat, a kind of brown coat—but I will not swear to that.

*Q.* You saw a red coat underneath it?

*A.* Yes, I saw a red coat down as far as the waist; I did not see the skirts of it.

*Q.* Did you make any particular observation upon the red coat?

*A.* No, I think it was turned up with yellow; but I should not like to swear that.

*Q.* Had it any thing upon it?

*A.* It had a star of some sort upon it, but I was not close enough to see that, and cannot swear to what it was.

*Q.* Was that all that you observed of his dress?

*A.* No, not quite all, I think; I think upon the outer coat there was fur, a kind of white fur, the same as off a rabbit's skin.

*Q.* But that you do not recollect with certainty?

*A.* No, I should not like to swear to that.

*Q.* As you conversed so much with that gentleman, do you think you should know him again?

*A.* I should know him in a moment.

*Q.* Have you seen him since you have been in Court?

*A.* Yes, that is the gentleman (*pointing to De Berenger.*)

*Q.* Have you any doubt that is the person?

*A.* Not at all.

*Q.* Since the day you drove him, have you seen him before to-day?

*A.* I have.

*Q.* How often?

*A.* Only once.

*Q.* Where was that?

*A.* In King-street, Westminster, in a room there.

*Q.* Did you equally well know him then?

*A.* I did the moment I saw him.

*Q.* Had you ever the least doubt about him?

*A.* Never the least in the world; I knew him as soon as I saw him.

*Cross-examined by Mr. Richardson.*

*Q.* Have you not been told this morning in what part of the Court he sat?

*A.* No, I never enquired about it; I looked round when I came in and found him out in a moment; I dare say every gentleman in the Court saw me.

*Q.* Had you never seen him before this time you speak of in February?

*A.* I have seen him since, I never saw him before February, to my knowledge.

*Q.* When was it that you heard of the reward which was offered by the Stock Exchange?

*A.* I heard of it the day it was printed.

*Q.* How long after this transaction happened?

*A.* I think two or three days afterwards.

*Q.* Do you remember the Club at Dartford, called the Hat Club?

*A.* Yes, perfectly well; I was there.

*Q.* Do you remember the conversation there, whether Crane or you should get the reward?

*A.* Yes, I remember being asked, whether I thought I should get the reward, and I said I thought not.

*Q.* You produced your purse, with what you had got?

*A.* Yes, I produced my purse, and rapped it on the table in this way, but that was money I had laid out before; I had received five pounds from the gentlemen of the Stock Exchange towards my expences.

*Q.* What might be your observation, when you rapped it upon the table?

*A.* To let them know that I had it.

*Q.* Did you say any thing about the yellow boys?

*A.* Yes, those were the gold Napoleons.

*Q.* Did you not say that the gentleman applauded you, and said you were a clever fellow?

*A.* No, I did not, I would have said very wrong if I had, I am sure.

*Q.* I think they would have done you no more than justice. Did you not on that occasion say, you would swear for that side that paid you best?

*A.* No, I did not.

*Q.* On that occasion, nor any other?

*A.* No, I never did, you may depend upon it.

*Q.* Nor any thing to that effect?

*A.* No, I did not.

*Q.* Who were present at this time?

*A.* Upon my word I do not know; several members round about.

*Q.* Several neighbours?

*A.* Yes, they were members.

*Q.* Was a person of the name of Man there?

*A.* I do not know him.

*Q.* Or Wood?

*A.* I do not know such a person; there were not above a dozen of them there; but I am not there often myself.

*Q.* How many members of the club are there?

*A.* I do not know, indeed; the hat maker pays my money for me; being very much out, I am not there one time in ten.

*Q.* When you are there, you do not know who are present?

*A.* No, I do not exactly.

*Lord Ellenborough.* What is this Hat Club?

*A.* We pay a shilling a week, and have a pint of beer; I have not been there these several weeks.

*Lord Ellenborough.* You get part of your money back in a hat?

*A.* We pay twenty-four shillings, and then have a hat for it.

*Mr. Richardson.* You have described this gentleman's person before to-day?

*A.* Yes, I have.

*Q.* You have been examined upon several occasions before this?

*A.* I have been examined at the Stock Exchange, and before the Grand Jury, no where else.

*Q.* Did not you describe the person as one that had a great red nose, and a blotched face?

*A.* A red nose I said, and his face was very red that morning, for it was very frosty. I said he was pitted with the small-pox.

*Lord Ellenborough.* Red or not sure you are, of the identity of the face?

*A.* Yes, I am sure of it.

*Mr. Richardson.* It was you that told him of the stand of coaches in the Lambeth Road?

*A.* Yes.

*Q.* That is before you come to the Marsh Gate?

*A.* Yes.

*Q.* That is not far from the Asylum, is it?

*A.* No.

*Q.* You went there for the purpose of getting a coach in the first instance?

*A.* Yes.

*Q.* And then you told him he might perhaps get one at the Marsh Gate?

*A.* Yes.

*William Bartholemew was called into Court.*

*Q. (to Shilling)* Is that the waterman?

*A.* That is the waterman.

*William Bartholemew sworn.*

*Examined by Mr. Adolphus.*

*Q.* Are you a waterman attending a stand of coaches?

*A.* Yes.

*Q.* Where?

*A.* At the Marsh Gate.

*Q.* Do you know Shilling, the last witness?

*A.* Yes, by seeing him come up with post chaises from Dartford.

*Q.* He is a Dartford boy?

*A.* Yes.

*Q.* Do you remember at any time in February, his coming with a chaise with a gentleman in it?

*A.* Yes, the 21st of February.

*Q.* What day in the week was it?

*A.* On a Monday.

*Q.* With how many horses?

*A.* Four horses.

*Q.* At what time in the morning?

*A.* Between nine and half past nine in the morning.

*Q.* Was there a coach on the stand?

*A.* Yes.

*Q.* Any more than one?

*A.* No more than one.

*Q.* Who drove that coach?

*A.* One Crane.

*Q.* Did you see the gentleman get into it?

*A.* Yes, I did.

*Q.* How did he go in?

*A.* He stepped out of one into the other?

*Q.* Did you open the door and let down the step for him?

*A.* Yes.

*Q.* How was that gentleman dressed?

*A.* He had got a kind of brown cap on, and a dark drab military sort of coat.

*Q.* Was there any thing round the cap?

*A.* There was a sort of band or something round the cap.

*Q.* What had he under his military great coat?

*A.* A scarlet coat.

*Q.* Did you see any thing on the scarlet coat?

*A.* I only took notice of the lace upon it.

*Q.* Where did that gentleman order the coach to drive to?

*A.* Up to Grosvenor Square.

*Q.* To what street?

*A.* I do not recollect whether he told me any street, only Grosvenor Square.

*Q.* Do you think you should know that gentleman again?

*A.* I do not know; dress makes such an alteration.

*Q.* Look round, and see whether you can see any one.

*A.* I do not see that I can recollect him, only seeing him that half minute.

*Q.* Look at that gentleman who is stooping down to write, (*De Berenger,*) and see whether you think that is like him?

*A.* Yes, I do upon my word, but I only saw him for about half a minute.

*Cross-examined by Mr. Park.*

*Q.* You, being a waterman, take that particular notice of every body that gets into a hackney coach, that you are quite sure having seen him step from the chaise into the coach, that he is the man?

*A.* I said at first, that the dress made such an alteration that I should think I should hardly know him.

*Q.* If I were to get into your coach with this dress on, and afterwards with my ordinary dress, you would hardly know me again?

*A.* No, I should think not.

*Richard Barwick sworn.*

*Examined by Mr. Adolphus.*

*Q.* What are you?

*A.* I am clerk to Messrs. Paxtons and Company.

*Q.* Where is their house of business?

*A.* In Pall Mall.

*Q.* They are Bankers?

*A.* Yes, they are.

*Q.* Do you remember a particular circumstance in passing near the Marsh Gate any morning?

*A.* Yes, I do.

*Q.* On what day?

*A.* Monday Morning the 21st February.

*Q.* What did you observe in passing?

*A.* I observed a post chaise with four horses, it had galloped at a very great rate, the horses were exceedingly hot, and the man was getting into a hackney coach that the people there told me had come out of that chaise.

*Q.* Did you hear that person who got into the coach say anything?

*A.* No, I had no conversation with any body.

*Q.* Did you follow that coach?

*A.* I did.

*Q.* How far?

*A.* I saw it as far as the Little Theatre, in the Haymarket.

*Q.* Why did you follow that hackney coach.

*A.* Because I wanted to know what the news was.

*Lord Ellenborough.* How came you to know any thing about the news?

*A.* I was told, it was a General Officer arrived with news, and I wanted to know what it was.

*Lord Ellenborough.* You were told it was an Officer arrived with news?

*A.* Yes, I was.

*Mr. Adolphus.* Then you went to your own business, having followed this coach to the Haymarket?

*A.* Yes.

*Q.* Did he pass by any of the public offices?

*A.* Yes, he did.

*Q.* Did he stop at any of them?

*A.* No.

*Q.* He went straight to the Haymarket?

*A.* Yes, he did.

*Q.* Was that the reason why you desisted from following?

*A.* It was nine o'clock, and I must be at the office by that hour, and therefore I did not go on.

*Q.* Did you see enough of that person to know him again?

*A.* I believe, I did.

*Q.* Look at him, and see whether you know his person again?

(*The witness looked round.*)

*Lord Ellenborough.* Did you see his body?

*A.* I saw his face in the coach, he had a cap on such as the German Cavalry wear, after an evening parade, with a gold band upon it.

*Mr. Adolphus.* Have you seen that person in court?

*Lord Ellenborough.* There is no objection to his looking at the Defendant, and seeing whether he is the person.

(*The witness looked at the Defendant De Berenger.*)

*A.* I really do not know that I do see him exactly.

*Mr. Park.* This is the gentleman said to be the man.

*Lord Ellenborough.* If you do not recollect the gentleman's person, say so.

*Mr. Park.* Is the result of your looking that you do not believe this to be the man?

*A.* He is something like him.

*Q.* One man is something like another, he goes upon two legs, and has two hands, and so on.

*A.* It is like him certainly.

*William Crane sworn.*

*Examined by Mr. Adolphus.*

*Q.* Do you drive a hackney coach?

*A.* Yes.

*Q.* What number.

*A.* 890.

*Q.* On a Monday morning in February do you remember taking up a fare at the Marsh Gate?

*A.* Yes.

*Q.* What day of the month was it?

*A.* The 21st of February.

*Q.* Where did the fare come from?

*A.* From Dartford.

*Q.* Out of what?

*A.* A post chaise and four—a Dartford chaise.

*Q.* Where were you directed to drive to?

*A.* To Grosvenor Square.

*Q.* Where to there?

*A.* He did not say where in Grosvenor Square.

*Q.* Where did you set him down?

*A.* I drove him into Grosvenor Square, and then the gentleman put down the front glass and told me to drive to No. 13, Green Street.

*Q.* Did the gentleman get out there?

*A.* Yes.

*Q.* Did you hear whom he asked for?

*A.* He asked for Colonel or Captain somebody, I did not hear the name, and they said he was gone to breakfast in Cumberland Street.

*Q.* What did the gentleman say then?

*A.* The gentleman asked if he could write a note to him.

*Q.* Did he go in?

*A.* Yes, he went into the parlour.

*Q.* Were you discharged then?

*A.* Yes, the gentleman gave me four shillings before he went in, and I said, I hoped he would give me another shilling: he took out a bit of a portmanteau that he had, and a sword, and went in, and came out into the passage and gave me another shilling.

*Q.* What sort of a portmanteau was it?

*A.* A small leather one, big enough to wrap a coat up in.

*Q.* What sort of leather?

*A.* I think black leather, as well as I can recollect.

*Q.* Have you seen that person since that you drove that morning?

*A.* Yes, I saw him in King Street, Westminster.

*Q.* At the messenger's house?

*A.* At Mr. Wood's house.

*Q.* Do you see him in court?

*A.* I think this is the gentleman, here, (*pointing to De Berenger.*)

*Q.* Were you of the same opinion when you saw him at Mr. Wood's?

*A.* When I came down stairs he looked very hard at me.

*Q.* Did you know him then?

*A.* Yes, it was something of the same appearance, but he had altered himself very much by his dress.

*Cross-examined by Mr. Richardson.*

*Q.* You went to Wood's for the purpose of seeing him?

*A.* Yes, I did.

*Q.* Wood is a messenger of the Alien Office?

*A.* He lives in King Street.

*Q.* He was pointed out there as being the person in custody?

*A.* No, I walked down stairs, and met the gentleman coming up stairs.

*Q.* You thought you saw a resemblance?

*A.* Yes, I thought he was something like the same gentleman that I had carried.

*Q.* You do not pretend to be able to recollect every person you carry in your hackney coach every day?

*A.* No, but this gentleman that I took from a post chaise and four, when he got out at Green Street I saw that he had a red coat underneath his great coat.

*Q.* You did not open your coach to him, the waterman did that?

*A.* Yes, the post boy ordered me to get on the box.

*Lord Ellenborough.* When he got out you opened the door to him I suppose?

*A.* Yes, I did.

*Mr. Richardson.* Did you open the door, or the footman at the house?

*A.* I opened the door.

*Q.* And he paid you and passed into the house?

*A.* Yes, he did.

*Q.* What was the colour of his great coat?

*A.* A brown grey great coat, with a brown cape with lace to it.

*Q.* You have before described the great coat as a brown great coat, have not you?

*A.* A kind of a brown grey.

*Q.* Did not you describe it before as a kind of a brown coat?

*A.* No.

*Mr. Gurney.* I will now prove the finding the clothes in the river, and then prove the purchase of them.

*George Odell sworn.*

*Examined by Mr. Gurney.*

*Q.* Are you a waterman?

*A.* Yes.

*Q.* Do you remember in the month of February last, fishing up any bundle in the river?

*A.* In the month of March.

*Q.* Where did you fish it up?

*A.* Above the Old Swan Stairs, off against the Iron Wharfs.

*Q.* Were you dredging for any thing?

*A.* I was dredging for coals with a drag.

*Q.* What kind of a bundle did you find?

*A.* I picked up a bundle, tied up with a piece of chimney line, or window line in the cover of a calico chair bottom.

*Q.* What was in it?

*A.* I think there were two sleeves of a coat, and then a coat cut to pieces, and embroidery, and a star, and a silver coat of arms, with two figures upon it.

*Q.* How was it sunk?

*A.* With three pieces of lead, three screws, and some marks for letters.

*Q.* With some metal?

*A.* Yes, and some bits of coal.

*Q.* Did you give that which you found to Mr. Wade, the Secretary of the Stock Exchange?

*A.* Yes.

*Q.* How soon after you found it did you give it to him?

*A.* I picked it up on the Wednesday, and I carried it there on the Saturday.

*Mr. Park.* Can you give us the day of the month when you picked this up?

*A.* The 24th of March.

*Mr. Gurney.* Did you find it on the 24th of March, or give it to Mr. Wade on that day?

*A.* I picked it up on that day, about half after eleven o'clock in the day; I can bring plenty of witnesses to my picking it up.

*Q.* Are these the sort of things that you picked up? (*shewing a bundle of clothes with star, &c. to the witness.*)

*A.* These are the sort of things, but the star was not in that state it is now; the star was in half, and one of the birds was off.

*Mr. Gurney.* This, my Lord, is an order of masonry, and this I understand a Russian order of knighthood, the order of St. Ann.

*Mr. Francis Baily sworn.*

*Examined by Mr. Gurney.*

*Q.* You are of the Stock Exchange?

*A.* Yes, I am.

*Q.* Were you present with Mr. Wade, when he received the parcel from Odell?

*A.* I was,—from the last witness in the box.

*Q.* Was it delivered over to Mr. Lavie?

*A.* I believe it was, it lay upon the table some time.

*Q.* Did you examine it?

*A.* I did, very minutely.

*Q.* Are the things contained in that parcel?

*A.* I believe them to be, they appear to be the same.

*Mr. Gurney (to Mr. Lavie).* Did you receive that from Mr. Wade?

*Mr. Lavie.* I did, I took it from the Stock Exchange room.

*Q.* Mr. Wade and Mr. Baily were present?

*Mr. Lavie.* Yes, they were.

*Mr. Robert Watson Wade sworn.*

*Examined by Mr. Gurney.*

*Q.* You are the Secretary at the Stock Exchange?

*A.* I am.

*Q.* Did you, in company with Mr. Baily and other gentlemen, receive from Odell the bundle said to be found in the River?

*A.* I did.

*Q.* Was it given to Mr. Lavie?

*A.* It was.

*Q.* The star we understand was then in two pieces?

*A.* Yes.

*Q.* Was it afterwards sewn together?

*A.* It was, for the purpose of being exhibited.

*Simeon Kensington Solomon sworn.*

*Examined by Mr. Gurney.*

*Q.* I believe you are a military accoutrement maker?

*A.* Yes, I am.

*Q.* Have you a shop at Charing-Cross, and another at New-Street Covent Garden?

*A.* We have.

*Q.* On the Saturday the 19th of February do you remember any person making a purchase of any military dress at your house?

*A.* Yes, I do.

*Q.* What dress was purchased of you?

*A.* A military great coat and foraging cap.

*Q.* What is it made of?

*A.* Dark fur.

*Q.* Was any thing on it?

*A.* It had a pale gold band.

*Q.* Have you since had a cap and a coat made exactly resembling them?

*A.* I have.

*Q.* Are these the cap and the coat you have had so made? (*shewing them to the witness.*)

*A.* They are.

*Q.* Do they exactly resemble the cap and the coat you sold?

*A.* As nearly as I could possibly recollect.

*Q.* What else did the person purchase?

*A.* They purchased at our house in New Street——

*Q.* You suppose some order had been given in New-Street, did any thing come from New-Street as having been ordered there?

*A.* Yes there did.

*Q.* You were at Charing Cross?

*A.* I was.

*Q.* Did any person come to your shop at Charing-Cross and take away that which had been sent from New-Street which you furnished?

*A.* Yes, he did.

*Q.* Was there any other coat purchased besides that great coat?

*A.* There was a military regimental coat, a staff coat was brought from New-Street.

*Q.* Was that scarlet?

*A.* Yes, fitted for a staff officer the uniform of an Aid de Camp.

*Q.* With this sort of gold lace upon it?

*A.* Yes.

*Q.* Have you examined these fragments?

*A.* Yes, I have.

*Q.* Were there any ornaments besides?

*A.* There was a star and a badge.

*Q.* Look at that star and badge and tell me whether you believe them to be the same?

*A.* Yes, I do believe them to be the same.

*Q.* Why do you believe them to be the same?

*A.* The star I certainly believe to be the same, because we had the very fellow star.

*Q.* Except these two, did you ever see any star like them?

*A.* I do not know that ever I did.

*Q.* Do you believe that badge to be the same?

*A.* The badge I did not notice much.

*Q.* You sold a badge?

*A.* The badge came from our house in New-Street.

*Q.* Had you any conversation with the person?

*A.* Yes I had.

*Q.* You have examined these fragments?

*A.* I have.

*Q.* Do you believe them to be the fragments of the dress you furnished, or of such a dress?

*A.* They appear to be those materials, as far as I can judge in that state.

*Q.* And the same kind of lace?

*A.* The same description of embroidery.

*Q.* Speaking of a thing so cut to pieces, does it appear to you to consist of the remnants of the dress you furnished?

*A.* Yes, except that the scarlet is very much discoloured by being under water, it appears the same description of coat.

*Q.* Had you any conversation with the person as to the use of these things?

*A.* I had very little conversation as to the sale of the uniform, for they were already purchased before I saw him, with respect to the great coat I sold that and also the cap.

*Q.* Did he mention for what purpose they were wanted?

*A.* He observed that they were wanted for a person who was to perform the character of a foreign officer, to be sent into the country that evening.

*Q.* Did he take them away with him?

*A.* Yes he did.

*Q.* Did you offer to lend them to him?

*A.* Where he purchased the uniform——

*Q.* If that was not in your presence you will not state it—did he take them away with him?

*A.* Yes he took them away in a coach.

*Q.* Had he any portmanteau with him?

*A.* He had a small portmanteau.

*Q.* Did he beat you down in the prices?

*A.* No, he did not.

*Q.* Did he say any thing about money?

*A.* No, he made no observations, he merely paid for them.

*Q.* You were conversing with that person for some time?

*A.* For a short time.

*Q.* Have you since seen him again—have you seen any person that you believed to be the same?

*A.* I was introduced to a person——

*Q.* Where was that?

*A.* At the Parliament-street Coffee House.

*Q.* Do you believe that person you saw at the Parliament-street Coffee House to be the person who so made the purchase?

*A.* That I cannot undertake to say.

*Q.* What do you believe?

*A.* In point of appearance he resembles him, except that the person whom I served had whiskers.

*Q.* I suppose the person you saw in Parliament street had not?

*A.* He had not.

*Q.* Look at him now and tell me whether you do or do not believe him to be the person? (*The witness looked at the Defendant De Berenger.*)

*A.* This is the person I was introduced to at the Coffee-house.

*Q.* Upon the oath you have taken, what is your belief respecting him?

*A.* I really cannot undertake to swear that he is the person?

*Q.* What do you believe?

*A.* The Gentleman that represented himself to be Mr. Wilson was dressed in a different manner, he had black whiskers, and from that circumstance I could not possibly undertake to swear it was the same person.

*Q.* What is your belief?

*Mr. Park.* That belief may be founded on different facts?

*Lord Ellenborough.* To those facts you will examine, Mr. Gurney is now examining, there is no objection to the question.

*Mr. Gurney.* What is your belief?

*A.* Upon my word it is impossible for me to say.

*Q.* Do you mean to say that you have no belief upon the matter?

*A.* I mean to say I cannot undertake to swear it is the person.

*Q.* What is your belief?

*A.* I believe it resembles the person, except that the person I served had whiskers.

*Q.* Making allowance for whiskers which may be taken off in a minute, what is your belief upon the subject?

*A.* Upon my word it is impossible for me to say.

*Q.* You can certainly say what is your belief?

*Lord Ellenborough.* You are not asked as to whether you are certain, but to your belief.

*A.* If I were to say I believe it is the person I might say wrong, if I were to say I believe it is not the person I might say otherwise, it may be the person but I cannot undertake to say I believe it is.

*Mrs. Abigail Davidson sworn.*

*Examined by Mr. Gurney.*

*Q.* In the month of February last did you reside in the Asylum Buildings?

*A.* Yes.

*Q.* That is near to the Asylum?

*A.* Yes.

*Q.* Is the house within the rules of the King's Bench?

*A.* Yes it is.

*Q.* Did Mr. De Berenger lodge with you?

*A.* He did.

*Q.* Do you remember on what day he finally quitted your house?

*A.* On the 27th of February.

*Q.* What day of the week was that?

*A.* Sunday.

*Q.* Do you remember where he was the Sunday before that?

*A.* No.

*Q.* Did you see him on the morning of that Sunday?

*A.* No, on Sunday the 20th you mean, I did not.

*Q.* Did he sleep at home that night?

*A.* I cannot say.

*Q.* Did you see him that night at all?

*A.* We never attended to the door.

*Q.* Did you usually hear Mr. De Berenger in the morning?

*A.* Yes.

*Q.* Much or little did you hear him?

*A.* We heard him very frequently.

*Q.* Did you on the morning of Monday the 21st hear him as usual?

*A.* No.

*Q.* What did you use to hear of him on the mornings on which you did hear him?

*A.* We heard the bell ring for the servant.

*Q.* Once or more than once?

*A.* More than once?

*Q.* What rooms did he occupy?

*A.* The whole of the upper part of the house.

*Q.* What part did you occupy?

*A.* The parlours.

*Q.* How many rooms up stairs were there?

*A.* Four.

*Q.* And you and your husband occupied the two parlours?

*A.* Yes.

*Q.* On other mornings when you heard him besides ringing the bell did you hear any thing else respecting him?

*A.* Occasionally Mr. De Berenger would play on the violin or the trumpet.

*Q.* Did you hear him walk about?

*A.* Yes.

*Q.* Did Mr. De Berenger then wear whiskers or no whiskers?

*A.* Whiskers.

*Q.* Was there any morning on which you were at home that you did not hear his bell and his walking about?

*A.* No, I generally heard his bell.

*Q.* Did you see him come home on the Monday?

*A.* No.

*Q.* How early on that evening did you see him?

*A.* In the evening about a quarter or half past five.

*Q.* Had you heard him in the house before that time?

*A.* I heard him in the afternoon.

*Q.* You say he quitted your house on the Sunday after?

*A.* Yes.

*Q.* Do you remember any Gentleman calling there the day before he quitted with a letter?

*A.* On the Saturday night—

*Q.* He called with a letter?

*A.* Yes he did.

*Q.* Have you since seen that Gentleman again?

*A.* Yes.

*Q.* Where did you see him?

*A.* I saw him at the Temple?

*Q.* Was it at the Crown Office?

*A.* I do not know what office it was.

*Q.* Was Mr. Lavie present at the time you saw him?

*A.* Yes he was.

*Q.* Did you point him out to Mr. Lavie.

*A.* I cannot say that I should positively know the gentleman.

*Q.* Do you believe him to be the same?

*A.* Yes, I think it was.

*Q.* The same you had seen on the Saturday deliver that letter?

*A.* Yes, I think so.

*Q.* Had Mr. De Berenger two servants of the name of Smith, William Smith and his wife?

*A.* Yes.

*Q.* When he dined at home did his servants attend him?

*A.* Always.

*Q.* On the Sunday before he finally went away, Sunday the 20th, did he dine at home?

*A.* I cannot answer that.

*Q.* What was his usual dinner hour?

*A.* About four o'clock.

*Q.* Where were his servants at four o'clock on that day? At home or not?

*A.* I think they went out early on that day.

*Q.* What do you mean by early?

*A.* I mean two or half past two o'clock.

*Q.* Do you remember any thing about your key, respecting either of them, whether either of them had your key?

*A.* There was a private place where the key always hung for the accommodation of Mr. De Berenger and us.

*Q.* Where was the key put that night?

*A.* The key was always under the care of Mr. Smith.

*Q.* You did not see where he put it that night, did you?

*A.* No, I did not.

*Cross-examined by Mr. Park.*

*Q.* What Sunday was it that these servants went out to dinner at two or half past two?

*A.* On Sunday the 20th.

*Q.* You were preparing to go to chapel on that Sunday at eleven o'clock, and Mr. De Berenger went out at the time.

*A.* Mr. Davidson was going out, I did not go out.

*Q.* You were not well?

*A.* No.

*Q.* Mr. Davidson was going out.

*A.* Yes, but I did not see Mr. De Berenger.

*Q.* Did you hear your husband make an observation at the time?

*A.* Yes, I did.

*Q.* You did not yourself attend to the door?

*A.* No.

*Q.* This Gentleman had been your lodger for some years, had he not?

*A.* Nine months?

*Q.* You do not mean to represent, that he slept from his own bed on that Sunday, the 20th?

*A.* I cannot say that he did, or that he did not.

*Q.* You do not make his bed or go into his room?

*A.* No.

*Q.* Do you sleep in the parlour?

*A.* Yes, we have the two parlours.

*Q.* What is your general hour of rising in the morning?

*A.* Between seven and eight.

*Q.* Mr. De Berenger's time of trumpeting is not so early as that I suppose?

*A.* I have heard him at nine o'clock.

*Q.* He did not alarm the neighbourhood at seven o'clock?

*A.* No, I have heard him by eight or nine.

*Q.* Not so soon as that I should think in the month of February, not being very warm weather at that time?

*A.* I cannot speak to the time.

*Q.* If a person went out at eight o'clock that morning, you had no particular reason to know of it?

*A.* No.

*Q.* You had no call to look after him on the Sunday, or Monday, or Tuesday morning?

*A.* No.

*Q.* And whether he slept at home or did not, you cannot take upon yourself to say?

*A.* No.

*Re-examined by Mr. Gurney.*

*Q.* My learned Friend has asked you as to your husband observing upon Mr. De Berenger's going out on the Sunday morning: in what words did your husband make the remark as to Mr. De Berenger's going out?

*A.* He called out, our lodger is gone out with a new great coat on.

*Mr. Germain Lavie again called.*

*Examined by Mr. Gurney.*

*Q.* Who was the Gentleman that Mrs. Davidson pointed out to you?

*Mr. Serjeant Best.* I object to that, that is a leading question.

*Mr. Gurney.* I beg pardon.—Did the last witness point out any person to you at the Crown-Office, at the time of striking the Jury?

*A.* Before she came into the Crown-Office she saw Mr. Cochrane Johnstone getting out of a Hackney coach at the Crown-Office door—she then told me——

*Q.* Did she point out any person to you as having seen him before?

*A.* No, she did not then.

*Q.* Did she afterwards fix upon any person as having seen him?

*A.* No she did not, unless I can speak to what passed before.

*Q.* Did she mention having seen any person get out of a Hackney Coach?

*A.* Yes.

*Q.* Who was that person that she observed upon?

*A.* The person she pointed out to me as having seen get out of a Hackney coach was Mr. Cochrane Johnstone—she staid the whole time of the striking of the Jury, he struck the Jury himself.

*Lord Ellenborough.* Then the whole of it is, that the person who was striking the Jury, was Mr. Cochrane Johnstone?

*A.* Yes.

*Mr. Gurney. (to Mrs. Davidson).* Was that person the person that you believe brought the Letter?

*Q.* I cannot be positive to his person.

*Q.* Do you believe that to be the person?

*A.* I think it was.

Mrs. Abigail Davidson.

*Cross-examined by Mr. Serjeant Best.*

*Q.* How came you to go for the purpose of striking the Jury.

*A.* A person from Mr. Lavie came and fetched me for the purpose.

*Q.* To attend to assist in striking the Jury?

*A.* No, to see Mr. Johnstone.

*Q.* You were told Mr. Johnstone was to be there?

*A.* Yes.

*Q.* And going there you saw a person taking a part with respect to the striking of the Jury?

*A.* I saw a Gentleman get out of the coach as I was standing in the passage, I saw a Gentleman come across, that I thought was the person, but I could not be positive.

*Q.* Can you take upon yourself to swear now, that was the person?

*A.* No, I would not swear it.

*Re-examined by Mr. Gurney.*

*Q.* When you saw the person at the time he left the letter, had you any reason to know what his name was?

*A.* No, I had never seen the Gentleman before, but in conversing with Smith, Mr. De Berenger's servant———.

*Q.* Had you any conversation about him with Smith, Mr. Du Bourg's servant?

*A.* I had.

*Mr. Gurney.* I do not ask you what it was, my learned Friends may if they please.

*Launcelot Davidson sworn.*

*Examined by Mr. Gurney.*

*Q.* Are you the husband of the last Witness?

*A.* Yes.

*Q.* Mr. De Berenger we find lodged in your house?

*A.* He did.

*Q.* Do you remember on what day he quitted your house?

*A.* The 27th of February I think.

*Q.* What day of the week?

*A.* Sunday.

*Q.* Do you remember seeing him go out on the Sunday before the 20th.

*A.* Yes.

*Q.* At what hour of the day?

*A.* Before eleven.

*Q.* Have you any reason to know the time?

*A.* Yes, I had been out before, and I returned home and stood before the parlour window waiting to hear the Asylum clock strike eleven, to go to chapel.

*Q.* How was he dressed?

*A.* At that time that I saw him go out, I had seen him ten minutes before come in.

*Q.* How was he dressed when he came in before?

*A.* He had a plaid cloak on that he had worn nearly all the winter, he and I came in together, he was just before me.

*Q.* When he went out again, how was he dressed?

*A.* He had just such a coat as this on as to colour, (*the grey coat before produced.*)

*Q.* Did it appear to be new or old?

*A.* I cannot exactly say, but as he went down the yard, I said to my wife who was in the back parlour, there goes our lodger, he has a new great coat on, just before he had his plaid on when I came in.

*Q.* Did he come home again at all during that day?

*A.* Not that I saw.

*Q.* Did you see or hear him at all during that day?

*A.* No, I did not.

*Q.* Did you see or hear him the next morning?

*A.* No, I am not at home—I always go out the early part of the morning.

*Q.* At what time do you go out?

*A.* About nine.

*Q.* Before nine had you either seen or heard him?

*A.* No, I had not.

*Q.* Do you usually hear him in a morning before that time?

*A.* Yes, I generally used to hear him walking about, or ringing for his servant, or something or other.

*Q.* On that Monday morning before you went out, did you hear those things you generally did?

*A.* No, I did not, and we made the observation upon it, and also upon the servants going out at two o'clock, which was not customary.

*Q.* At what time on the Sunday did they go out?

*A.* I think about two o'clock.

*Q.* At what time did they return?

*A.* That I cannot say.

*Q.* Did they return that evening?

*A.* I dare say they did, but we never opened the door?

*Q.* Were they out or at home at four o'clock?

*A.* That I cannot say, I do not think they were at home.

*Q.* What was Mr. De Berenger's usual dinner hour?

*A.* About four o'clock.

*Q.* Did they attend him at dinner?

*A.* The man servant did.

*Q.* And the woman servant cooked his dinner?

*A.* Yes, she did.

*Q.* Did he dine at home on that Sunday?

*A.* No, he did not.

*Q.* I do not ask you what conversation took place between you and the Smiths' next day respecting the Sunday night, but did any conversation take place on that subject?

*A.* Yes, there did.

*Q.* On the Sunday afterwards he left your house?

*A.* He did.

*Q.* Did you see him go away on the Sunday after?

*A.* No.

*Cross-examined by Mr. Richardson.*

*Q.* You had nothing to do with his domestic life, with his dinner, or letting him into the house, or letting him out of it?

*A.* No.

*Q.* His servants attended to all that?

*A.* Yes.

*Q.* He might come in or go out without your observing it?

*A.* Yes, he might, but it is almost impossible I should think, because he generally gave a very loud rap at the door, and he had very few visitors.

*Q.* You yourself go out early in the morning upon your own business?

*A.* Yes, about nine o'clock.

*Q.* Do you stay out a considerable part of the day?

*A.* Yes.

*Q.* What is your business?

*A.* A broker.

*Q.* At that time you acted as a broker?

*A.* I acted as a broker's Clerk at that time.

*Q.* You are out a considerable part of the day, sometimes more, sometimes less.

*A.* Yes.

*Mr. Gurney.* Now my Lord I am going to what I have stated as the underplot, respecting M'Rae, Sandom, Lyte, and Holloway.

*Thomas Vinn sworn.*

*Examined by Mr. Bolland.*

*Q.* In consequence of a note that was left at your house, did you go to the Carolina Coffee House in February last?

*A.* I did, where I met M'Rae.

*Q.* What day in February was it?

*A.* On the 14th of February the note was dated, and I received it the 15th.

*Q.* On what day did you go to the Carolina Coffee House?

*A.* On the 15th in the morning.

*Q.* Did any body accost you there?

*A.* I met M'Rae, who was at that time in company with an elderly Gentleman, he desired me to sit down and he would be with me presently.

*Q.* Had you known M'Rae before?

*A.* I had some years.

*Q.* Did he return to you as he said he would?

*A.* He was not out of my sight, he was standing near the door, and in the course of seven or ten minutes, as far as I can recollect, he came and joined me.

*Q.* Upon his joining you what passed?

*A.* He told me he had known me a long time, and that he thought he had now an opportunity of making my fortune; that he knew from the knowledge I had of languages, particularly that of the French, I should have an opportunity of both benefiting others and myself.

*Q.* What answer did you make?

*A.* I asked him what the object was, and whether it was to travel abroad; he told me it was not to travel abroad, but it was probably to travel at home, and that almost immediately; that it was a scheme that he had in contemplation, employed by men of affluence and consequence, and that he thought no man more competent to that than myself.—On my asking him if there was any thing of moral turpitude in it, he said that there was none but that it was practised daily by men of the first consequence, it was nothing more nor less than biting the biters, or in other words, a Hoax upon the Stock Exchange. I asked him in what way I could attend to it, or in what way it was to be performed; he told me by going down to Dartford, Folkestone, or Dover, as I should receive instructions, and that, that evening, but that it was necessary to have for himself and me, two dresses appropriated to that of French Officers. I here stopped him, and asked whether he really meant me to be employed in this transaction, to which he replied, certainly, and that I should be in the first place remunerated, and ultimately have a fortune made me. I replied with indignation, that I would as soon be concerned in a highway robbery, that I thought he had known me better than to have suggested to me a plan of the kind, and expressed myself rather beyond the usual tone of my voice, hurt at it, he endeavoured to hush me by saying people would overhear us, he endeavoured to hush me by the ejaculation *ish* for that we should be overheard there.

*Lord Ellenborough.* Did he say you might probably be overheard there?

*A.* Yes, he did, and then he took me out of the Coffee-house and went up Cornhill where I left him, but recollecting this was only what was related to me, and that if ever it took place or did not, it was impossible that what I said could be any proof, I therefore considered that I had better——

*Mr. Alley.* Give us the facts if you please, and not the reasons?

*Mr. Bolland.* Do not trouble my friend with your reasons as he does not like them, but tell us what you did?

*A.* I returned and told him if he would go with me to another Coffee-house, I would introduce him to a person, who though I would not undertake the business might do it.

*Q.* What was your reason for doing that?

*A.* Only that I might have a witness.

*Mr. Alley.* I object to that reason being stated.

*Lord Ellenborough.* This is only introductory to what he is about to state. I presume no one can be more interested than I am in his narration being short?

*A.* I told him I would take him to a Coffee-house where a person was who might engage in this hoax.

*Lord Ellenborough.* I beg you will not call it by that name—such an offence as this.

*Mr. Bolland.* Did you take him to the Coffee-house?

*A.* Yes.

*Q.* What Coffee-house?

*A.* The Jamaica—there was a young man there to whom I was about to introduce him, but he turned round suddenly and I did not.

*Q.* Did any thing more pass between M'Rae and you?

*A.* No, nothing more.

*Q.* Any thing about French terms?

*A.* I recollect myself—In consequence of M'Rae returning, he asked me whether I would not give him in writing the terms *Vive le Roi—Vive les Bourbons*;—which in the expectation of his attending to this young man, (this was in the Jamaica Coffee-house) I gave him.

*Q.* Did you give him any other?

*A.* None other to my knowledge.

*Q.* Was that the letter you received from M'Rae? (*shewing a letter to the witness.*)

*A.* That is it.

*Q.* Is that M'Rae's writing?

*A.* It is.

(*The Letter was read as follows:*)

February 14, 1814.

Mr. Vinn,

Please to meet me at the Carolina Coffee-house, Birchin-lane, about eleven to-morrow, upon very particular interesting business.

Yours, very respectfully,<br>ALEXANDER M'RAE.

*Cross-examined by Mr. Alley.*

*Q.* As I have not the pleasure of knowing you, what is your business?

*A.* I am an accountant.

*Q.* Have you been acquainted for any length of time with Mr. M'Rae?

*A.* I believe five years and a half, or nearly six years.

*Q.* Have you been concerned in any business in the Stock Exchange?

*A.* No.

*Q.* You were not in the habit of buying and selling as a Broker?

*A.* No.

*Q.* It was an odd thing that Mr. M'Rae should resort to you in such a base transaction, you being in the business of an Accountant?

*A.* I have been in business and have been unfortunate, and since have been an Accountant.

*Q.* Not to lose your character I take for granted?

*A.* I hope not.

*Q.* There was no other person present to hear this conversation?

*A.* He was talking with a gentleman when I entered.

*Q.* This rests upon your own testimony?

*A.* We afterwards joined a party, but no person heard the conversation but ourselves, except that any person might hear me when I became vociferous.

*Q.* You quite met my approbation when you told me that you considered this as base as if he had asked you to go on the highway—how came you to propose a friend of yours after that?

*A.* It was merely for the purpose of having a witness to the offer to me, because if not, and this took place what I had said would have been of no effect had it been rendered completely abortive by this failing with me.

*Q.* Then am I to understand you thought it better to let this wickedness be practised in order that it might afterwards be proved?

*A.* I am sorry I am so misunderstood, I only wished it should not be promulgated to the world merely on my *ipse dixit*, but on the testimony of another.

*Q.* You did introduce him to your friend?

*A.* No, I did not, he would not be introduced. I had communicated to my friend the business in question before he came.

*Q.* How soon did you communicate this to the Stock Exchange?

*A.* I communicated it within ten minutes afterwards on that day.

*Q.* After the thing had been publicly known?

*A.* No, I went immediately on this application being made and promulgated it to Mr. Rothery, of the Atlas Printing-Office, in Houndsditch; I afterwards went to a house in Clement's lane, where I promulgated it to thirteen or fourteen different persons, and I made it public daily in all the companies I went into.

*Q.* Was that before this happened?

*A.* It was on the 15th I made public, not the name of M'Rae, but that such a thing had been offered to me, which I refused with indignity.

*Q.* Some of these gentlemen are here as witnesses to-day I suppose?

*A.* I did not think it necessary, but I am perfectly willing that they should be called, I have seen two of them in Court and probably they may be so now.

*Lord Ellenborough.* This is merely a meditated something if you think it worth while to pursue it you may.

*Mr. Alley.* He only says that it rests upon his testimony, that was all I wanted to know—you gave him two bits of French to assist him however?

*A.* After I had agreed to take him to another friend, in order to get him to that business, I certainly did mention the name of *Vive le Roi—Vive le Bourbons.*

*Q.* Would not you have thought it quite as honest and as much to your purpose to have omitted that?

*A.* You will see that that was done for the purpose I have mentioned.

*Mr. Gurney.* Was it done in order to get a conformatory witness?

*A.* It was done with that intent and that only.

*Sarah Alexander sworn.*

*Examined by Mr. Bolland.*

*Q.* You live at No. 61, Fetter-lane, do you not?

*A.* Yes, I do.

*Q.* How long have you lived there?

*A.* I have lived there ever since last September.

*Q.* Do you know Mr. M'Rae?

*A.* Yes.

*Q.* Did he lodge with you?

*A.* Not with me—he lodged on the same floor that I did.

*Q.* Is he a married or single man?

*A.* A married man; he had his wife with him.

*Q.* Do you recollect any thing passing in February last, with regard to Mr. M'Rae?

*A.* Yes, on a Saturday night.

*Q.* What Saturday night?

*A.* The 19th of February.

*Q.* Where were you at that time?

*A.* In my own room; he came into my room and brought it and gave it to his wife.

*Q.* His wife was in your room?

*A.* Yes.

*Q.* What did he bring home and give to his wife?

*A.* A small parcel; he gave it to his wife and told her it was of value and to take care of it.

*Q.* Did he say any thing else to her?

*A.* Nothing else.

*Q.* Did you see any thing more of that parcel on that night?

*A.* Not that night. On Sunday the 20th, he went out about ten o'clock, between ten and eleven.

*Q.* Did he return again and when?

*A.* He returned before twelve.

*Q.* Did he bring any thing in with him?

*A.* He brought two coats and two opera hats.

*Q.* Did he bring the two coats and two opera hats open or inclosed in any thing?

*A.* They were in a bundle.

*Q.* Did you see them?

*A.* Yes.

*Q.* What sort of coats were they?

*A.* They were very dark blue, done with braiding—Officers coats.

*Q.* What coats were they?

*A.* Like Officers coats.

*Q.* What was the braiding?

*A.* It was to ornament the coats.

*Q.* What was it done in?

*A.* In flowers.

*Q.* Of worsted or silk?

*A.* Of worsted.

*Q.* What do you mean by opera hats?

*A.* Shutting together.

*Q.* Did you remark how the coats were lined?

*A.* One was lined with white silk.

*Q.* Were the coats alike, or did one appear of more rank than the other?

*A.* One appeared of more rank than the other; one was better than the other, and so was one of the hats.

*Q.* Were the hats plain or ornamented in any way?

*A.* One was black and the other ornamented on one side.

*Q.* What with?

*A.* With a brass plate or something of that kind at the end, and a gold tassel at each corner.

*Q.* Upon his producing them did he do any thing with them?

*A.* He put them on and asked me if he looked like an Officer, and I said yes, he did.

*Q.* What did he then do?

*A.* He went out again and came home again before one and brought some white ribband with him.

*Q.* Did you see him do any thing, or hear him say any thing about that white ribband?

*A.* Yes, he wanted two cockades to be made.

*Q.* To whom did he apply to make those cockades?

*A.* To his wife—they were to be made round.

*Q.* Was any thing said to him either by you or his wife as to the purpose, to which they should be applied?

*A.* His wife asked him what they were for, and what he was going to do with them, and he said they were to deceive the flats.

*Q.* Did you see what he did with the cockades?

*A.* He put them into his pocket and took the coats in his hand, and went out saying he must be at Billingsgate to go down to Gravesend by a quarter before two.

*Q.* What did he do with the hats?

*A.* He put them into the bundle.

*Q.* He then went away, did he?

*A.* Yes.

*Q.* When did you see Mr. M'Rae again?

*A.* About the same time the next day, about half-past one, or a quarter before two, I met him in Cursitor-street.

*Q.* Did he say any thing to you?

*A.* He gave me a shilling and asked me to go to the cook's shop for his dinner.

*Q.* Did any thing else pass in Cursitor-street between you?

*A.* No, not then, I went for his dinner.

*Q.* How was he dressed then?

*A.* Just the same as he went out—in his own cloaths.

*Q.* Had he any thing with him?

*A.* A bundle.

*Q.* Was that the same bundle he took out with him apparently?

*A.* He brought home one coat and one hat.

*Q.* Did you see the contents of that bundle when he got home?

*A.* Yes, the best coat and the best hat he brought home with him.

*Q.* Did he tell you where he had been?

*A.* He said he had slept at Northfleet, but he had the appearance of not having been a bed at all.

*Q.* He appeared tired?

*A.* He appeared very tired.

*Q.* Did he bring the cockades back?

*A.* Yes, he brought the cockades back in his pocket, the ribband was taken off.

*Q.* By whom?

*A.* By his wife; and the paper they were quilled on was thrown into the fire and the ribband made use of for strings, they had not buckram, and they made up the cockades on paper.

*Q.* Was any thing done with the coat?

*A.* They took the white lining out of the coat, and carried it to the Dyers to be dyed black.

*Q.* They said they should take it to the Dyers to be dyed black?

*A.* I know they took it out of the house to the Dyers, and the coat he wore.

*Q.* Before this how long had Mr. M'Rae lodged with you?

*A.* He lodged there before I went, he went about a week before me, I went in September.

*Q.* From September to February had you lodged together in that house?

*A.* Yes.

*Q.* Had you been acquainted with him and his wife?

*A.* Never before that, but at that house we kept but one fire; coals were very dear, and we lived a good deal together there.

*Q.* Had you any means of judging Mr. M'Rae's circumstances as to poverty or wealth?

*Q.* He was poor, he never had any money except it was a shilling or an eighteen penny piece.

*Q.* After this expedition to Northfleet, how did he appear in circumstances?

*A.* Oh, better; he had a £10. note and a £1. note, and the day before he left his lodgings he had three £2. notes.

*Q.* Do you mean before he finally left his lodgings?

*A.* Yes.

*Q.* When was that?

*A.* The second of March I think it was, the second or third to the best of my knowledge.

*Q.* Do you know of his purchasing any new cloaths for himself?

*A.* Yes, on the Sunday he bought a new coat, dark green, with yellow buttons.

*Q.* What Sunday was that?

*A.* Not the 20th.

*Q.* The Sunday after his return?

*A.* Yes.

*Q.* Did he buy any other articles of dress?

*A.* A new hat.

*Q.* On what day did he buy that?

*A.* The Monday.

*Q.* Was that the Monday after his return?

*A.* The Monday after he had bought his new coat.

*Q.* Did he tell you whether it had been a successful expedition to him?

*A.* He said he was to have £.50 for what he had done.

*Q.* Had you at any time any conversation with him about the nature of his journey?

*A.* No, never. He wished when he went away that it might be kept a secret where he was gone to; he did not wish any body to know where he was going to; he seemed very much agitated, and I desired he would not tell me that I might not tell any body else, and I did not know then.

*Mr. Philip Foxall sworn.*

*Examined by Mr. Bolland.*

*Q.* You keep the Rose Inn at Dartford?

*A.* I do.

*Q.* Look at that letter, and tell me whether you received it at any time, and when, from the person whose name it bears?

*A.* I did.

*Q.* I see it purports to be from Mr. Sandom?

*A.* It was from Mr. Sandom.

*Q.* Did you know Mr. Sandom before that time?

*A.* I did, by his frequently having chaises ordered from my house?

*Q.* Did you execute that order?

*A.* Yes.

*Q.* And sent a chaise to bring the party to Dartford?

*A.* Yes; and I had horses ready, as the letter advised me.

*Q.* Had you sent chaises on a similar message before?

*A.* Yes I had, by messages, and by letter; and he also came down there in the chaise.

*Lord Ellenborough.* By a message in writing coming to you?

*A.* Yes sometimes; this came by a boy.

*Q.* You do not know his hand-writing?

*A.* No I do not.

*The Letter was read as follows:*

SIR,

Please to send me over immediately a chaise and pair to bring back to Dartford, and have four good horses ready to go on to London with all expedition.

Yours, &c.<br>
R. SANDOM,<br>
Northfleet.

Monday Morning.
*Addressed,*
*Mr. Foxall, Rose Inn, Dartford.*

*Mr. Bolland.* In consequence of that you sent a chaise to Northfleet?

*A.* I did.

*Q.* Did you see the chaise on its return from Northfleet?

*A.* Yes; the chaise drove furiously into my yard with two gentlemen and Mr. Sandom, with white cockades in their hats.

*Q.* What sort of hats were they?

*A.* They were very large cocked hats.

*Q.* Were they flat hats; what are called opera hats?

*A.* I did not see; indeed they did not take them off.

*Q.* Were they quite plain hats?

*A.* Yes, with the exception of white paper or ribband, I cannot say which.

*Q.* How were the gentlemen dressed?

*A.* In blue clothes I think; but there were such a number of persons hurrying into the yard, that I had not an opportunity of examining; the four horses were ready; I gave them another chaise, as I feared the wheels of this were not very well greased.

*Q.* Had you any conversation with Sandom, or either of the gentlemen with him?

*A.* I said to Mr. Sandom, "Will those gentlemen breakfast;" he said, "No, they have breakfasted at my house, they have been in an open boat all night, and are very much fatigued." I then asked him a question, "Who are they?" he said he did not know, but they had news of the utmost consequence, and begged I would let them have good horses.

*Q.* Did any thing else pass between you and Mr. Sandom?

*A.* No, further than my asking where to; and they said to Westminster. I told the boys I supposed they were going to the Admiralty.

*Cross-examined by Mr. Serjeant Pell.*

*Q.* What time was it you received the note?

*A.* I think the note must have been received about seven o'clock.

*Q.* In the morning?

*A.* Yes; the boy was unacquainted with the town, and he went to the house opposite with the note, and a man pointed to me as I was standing at the door.

*Q.* At what time did the chaise come with Mr. Sandom and those gentlemen?

*A.* I think it could not exceed an hour; I was quite surprised at the chaise coming back in so short a time.

*Q.* What is Mr. Sandom, do you know him?

*A.* I only know him from his occasionally having horses to take him to Northfleet; I understood he lived there.

*Q.* How long had he lived there?

*A.* That I really cannot say; I think he had been in the habits of occasionally having horses from me for nine months before that time.

*Foxall Baldry sworn.*

*Examined by Mr. Bolland.*

*Q.* You are a post-boy at the Rose at Dartford?

*A.* I ride occasionally.

*Q.* Did you ride on the morning of the 21st?

*A.* I did.

*Q.* Do you recollect a chaise coming from Northfleet to your house?

*A.* Yes I do.

*Q.* Who was in that chaise do you recollect?

*A.* I have seen one of the gentlemen since; I did not know Mr. Sandom at the time personally.

*Q.* Was Mr. Sandom one of those persons?

*A.* Yes he was.

*Q.* Do you know the other two of those persons?

*A.* I do not.

*Q.* Did you drive either of the pair of horses that took those gentlemen to town?

*A.* I drove the leaders.

*Q.* Did they give you any orders as to which way they were to go?

*A.* Just as we were coming to Shooter's Hill, Mr. Sandom got out of the chaise with one of those other gentlemen, walked some little distance, and when he came back I was altering my harness; and he beckoned me, and said, My lads we do not want you to distress your horses up this hill, but when you get up you may get on a little: He asked what the gates were, and said, I shall give you twelve shillings a-piece for driving; but as to saying to what part I did not know at the time; my fellow-servant at the wheel ordered me to go over London Bridge, down Lombard Street, along Cheapside, over Blackfriar's Bridge, down the New Cut, and when I was in sight of the Marsh gate I was ordered to stop.

*Q.* Did you take that course?

*A.* I did.

*Q.* How was Mr. Sandom drest?

*A.* Why I really cannot say, but I think he had a brown great coat on.

*Q.* How were the other two persons dressed?

*A.* They were in blue great coats I think.

*Q.* Do you recollect what sort of hats they had?

*A.* They had round hats when they left me.

*Q.* What sort of hats had they when they got into the chaise?

*A.* They had military hats on.

*Q.* Was there any ornament in the hats?

*A.* A paper or ribband, I cannot tell which.

*Q.* Had the horses any ornaments upon them?

*A.* Yes, laurels.

*Q.* Do you know by whose orders they were put on?

*A.* No, I do not.

*Q.* You were near the Marsh gate you say?

*A.* Yes, I could see the Marsh-gate when I pulled up.

*Q.* Did the parties get out there?

*A.* Yes.

*Q.* How were they dressed then?

*A.* They had taken off their military hats and put round ones on, and they walked away.

*Q.* At what hour in the morning was it when you got to the Marsh gate?

*A.* I should think about eleven o'clock; I cannot say for half an hour.

*Q.* Did Mr. Sandom give you any thing?

*A.* Not at that time.

*Q.* Did he pay for the chaise?

*A.* He did not, not there.

*Q.* Has he since given you any thing?

*A.* He asked us what house we stopped at, I told him the Bull at Kent Street end, and he came to us there, and gave my fellow-servant a one pound note, and the remainder in silver for him and me together.

*Q.* Did he pay for the chaise?

*A.* He did not pay for the chaise.

*Q.* Did either of the other two return with him?

*A.* They did not.

*Mr. Francis Baily called again.*

*Examined by Mr. Bolland.*

*Q.* In consequence of enquiries that had been made, did Mr. Holloway attend the Committee of the Stock Exchange?

*A.* He did.

*Q.* Did Mr. Lyte attend also?

*A.* Afterwards he did with Mr. Holloway; first Mr. Holloway came, and denied having any knowledge of the transaction.

*Q.* Did you see him again at any other time?

*A.* Yes, very near the time of the bill being found; I cannot tell whether before or after that, he came with Mr. Lyte and confessed that he was the person who had planned that plot, or participated in it.

*Q.* State what he said as nearly as you can recollect?

*A.* He said that he had done it with a view to obtain money by a rise in the public funds; and Mr. Lyte stated, that he was one of the parties who had been employed by Mr. M'Rae, at Mr. Holloway's suggestion; at Holloway's or M'Rae's.

*Q.* Did either of them say who were the actors in the plot?

*A.* Mr. Lyte said that he and Sandom and M'Rae rode in the post chaise from Northfleet to Dartford, and afterwards from Dartford to London.

*Lord Ellenborough.* In whose presence did Lyte state this?

*A.* Mr. Wakefield was present, Mr. Lavie was present, and a Mr. Chaumette.

*Q.* Was Holloway present then?

*A.* Yes he was; they both came together.

*Q.* What Lyte stated was in the presence of Holloway?

*A.* Exactly so. Holloway stated that he did it with a view of obtaining money, by the rise in the funds.

*Q.* Did he state any thing more?

*A.* He stated that he was not aware of the serious turn it would take; that he did not contemplate it in that point of view at first; but finding that it had taken so serious a turn, he had come forward and confessed it, in the hope that the Stock Exchange would not pursue it to extremities, and carry on the action against him, or the prosecution: He was asked whether he had any connection with Lord Cochrane, Cochrane Johnstone, or Mr. Butt, which he denied.

*Cross-examined by Mr. Serjeant Pell.*

*Q.* Do you know what it was that immediately led to Mr. Holloway's making this communication to the Stock Exchange?

*A.* No I do not; nothing more than the publicity of the measures which they were taking to follow up the parties, I believe.

*Q.* Did you not learn at the time from Mr. Holloway during this conversation, and from Mr. Lyte, that M'Rae had offered to come forward for a very considerable sum of money and state his knowledge of the transaction?

*A.* That had been stated before publicly I believe in Mr. Cochrane Johnstone's letter.

*Q.* I ask as to the conversation at the time, do you recollect whether or not at the time of this interview between Holloway, Lyte, and the gentlemen of the Stock Exchange, any thing was said about M'Rae's having offered to be a witness for a large sum of money?

*A.* There was certainly something said, but whether it was mentioned first by the gentlemen of the Stock Exchange, or by Mr. Holloway, I cannot recollect.

*Q.* Did not Mr. Holloway state, that in order to prevent the gentlemen of the Stock Exchange paying a large sum of money for the communication that would be paid in fact for nothing, he would come forward and state the part of the transaction in which he was concerned?

*A.* I believe he did.

*Q.* It was understood by the gentlemen of the Stock Exchange, was it not, that that communication of M'Rae's was supposed to extend to my Lord Cochrane's part in the transaction?

*Mr. Gurney.* What was understood cannot be asked.

*Mr. Serjeant Pell.* I ask as to what was said at the time, was it not said that M'Rae's communication was to affect Lord Cochrane's share in the transaction?

*A.* I do not recollect that that was stated.

*Q.* I think you stated that Mr. Holloway or Mr. Lyte distinctly asserted, that this business of theirs had nothing to do with that in which Lord Cochrane was concerned?

*A.* He did.

*Q.* Do you know what was the sum that it was stated M'Rae was to be a witness for, was not it so large a sum as £10,000?

*A.* That sum had been stated in a letter which passed?

*Q.* Was it not stated in the conversation?

*A.* I believe it was; but the subject of the communication of M'Rae was so little attended to by the Committee, that it never entered their heads that any such sum should be paid.

*Q.* Was there any letter, or any writing of Mr. Holloway's produced at the time?

*A.* I really cannot fix my memory.

*Q.* Have you any recollection of any letter of his having been produced at the time?

*A.* Certainly none that I can recollect.

*Q.* Do you not know that Mr. Holloway had written a letter to the Committee of the Stock Exchange upon this business?

*A.* I really do not know it; it may possibly have been.

*Cross-examined by Mr. Park.*

*Q.* This person Holloway was asked whether he had any connection with Lord Cochrane, Mr. Cochrane Johnstone, and Mr. Butt, and he denied it?

*A.* He did.

*Q.* Did he not, in the same conversation, deny that he had any connection, not only with those persons, but De Berenger also?

*A.* Certainly.

*Q.* That you dropped?

*A.* Yes, I did not mean to drop it.

*Cross-examined by Mr. Alley.*

*Q.* At the time this conversation passed between you and Holloway, M'Rae was not there?

*A.* He was not.

*Q.* It was all in his absence?

*A.* It was in his absence, it was in Mr. Lavie's office.

*Lord Ellenborough.* The evidence of course can operate only against Holloway and Lyte, who were there.

*Mr. Joseph Fearn sworn.*

*Examined by Mr. Gurney.*

*Q.* You are a stock broker?

*A.* I am.

*Q.* How long have you known Mr. Butt?

*A.* Several years.

*Q.* Were you introduced by him to Mr. Cochrane Johnstone and to Lord Cochrane.

*A.* Yes.

*Q.* In the month of February last, were you employed either by Mr. Butt or Lord Cochrane, or Mr. Cochrane Johnstone, to make any purchases for them in the funds?

*A.* Yes, I was.

*Q.* At that time where was your office of business?

*A.* No. 10, Cornhill.

*Q.* Was it No. 10 or No. 86, about the 12th of February?

*A.* I believe it was No. 86.

*Q.* Had Mr. Butt an office?

*A.* He had somewhere about that time an office in Sweetings Alley.

*Q.* From the 12th of February to the 19th of February, did you see Mr. Butt daily?

*A.* I think I did.

*Q.* At your office or at his?

*A.* Both.

*Q.* Did you generally see him alone, or in company with either of the other persons?

*A.* Frequently all three together.

*Q.* You mean Mr. Cochrane Johnstone, Lord Cochrane, and Mr. Butt?

*A.* Yes.

*Q.* When you did business for Lord Cochrane, did you in all instances take orders from him or from any person for him?

*A.* Sometimes from him, and sometimes from Mr. Butt.

*Q.* After you had acted for him upon the orders of Mr. Butt, did he recognize those orders?

*A.* Always.

*Q.* From the 12th till the 19th, did you make various purchases and sales for them?

*A.* I did.

*Q.* On the evening of the 19th, what balance had he in his hand; Lord Cochrane's transactions I believe were only in omnium?

*A.* No.

*Q.* The amount was £139,000, was it not?

*A.* Yes.

*Q.* That is to say, that he had that balance of omnium?

*A.* Yes.

*Q.* What balance of omnium had Mr. Cochrane Johnstone on that day?

*A.* £120,000.

*Q.* One hundred and twenty, or one hundred and thirty thousand?

*A.* I have not drawn out the balance here.

*Q.* What was Mr. Cochrane Johnstone's consol account on that day?

*A.* £100,000.

*Q.* How much had Mr. Butt of omnium at the same time?

*A.* I think about £160,000.

*Q.* Is not the omnium £130,000.

*A.* I should think more than that; I believe it was £154,000.

*Q.* How much his consols?

*A.* £168,000.

*Q.* On the morning of the 21st of February, did you sell them all?

*A.* I did.

*Q.* Omnium and consols and all?

*A.* Yes.

*Q.* On the morning of Monday the 21st, did you remove to any other office than that you had before occupied?

*A.* Yes, I did.

*Q.* Where was that office?

*A.* No. 5, in Shorter's Court.

*Q.* Is that close to the side door of the Stock Exchange?

*A.* Yes, it is.

*Q.* How many rooms were there?

*A.* Three.

*Q.* Had you one?

*A.* I had one and a small closet; Mr. Butt had another up stairs with Mr. Johnstone and my Lord Cochrane, and the ground floor was occupied by Mr. Lance.

*Q.* Was he a clerk of yours, or employed by them?

*A.* He was employed by them.

*Q.* Had you taken that office, or had it been taken for you?

*A.* Mr. Johnstone had taken his with one room or two rooms, I am not sure which.

*Q.* Had the office been taken for you, or had you yourself gone and taken it?

*A.* They had taken those two rooms, I believe, without intending to take any more; but as I was not pleasantly situated, and was rather too far from business, I wished to have an office there, if they could procure it; several of my friends went to look at it, and finding it convenient, I requested them to take the whole of it, if they could, in order that I might be accommodated.

*Lord Ellenborough.* Whom do you mean by friends, Mr. Cochrane Johnstone?

*A.* No, other persons for whom I did business.

*Mr. Gurney.* When was this done?

*A.* In the course of the week preceding.

*Lord Ellenborough.* When you say Mr. Cochrane Johnstone took a room for you, do you mean at this place?

*Q.* They had taken those two rooms, I believe, for themselves, without reference to my having any thing to do there.

*Mr. Gurney.* Did they afterwards take a third?

*A.* They afterwards took the whole that is in my possession.

*Q.* You have all of them in your possession now?

*A.* I have.

*Q.* On the morning of Monday the 21st of February, how soon did you see either of those gentlemen?

*A.* They were in the habit of being at the office as early as I myself attended.

*Q.* At your office in Cornhill?

*A.* Yes.

*Q.* How early did you see them at your office that morning?

*A.* I believe at about ten, or a little past.

*Q.* Whom did you then see.

*A.* I think, Mr. Butt and Mr. Johnstone.

*Q.* Are you positive upon that subject?

*A.* I am sure they were both there in the course of the morning.

*Q.* Are you positive whether any body else was with them?

*A.* No, I think nobody else.

*Q.* Business begins in the Stock Exchange I believe at ten o'clock.

*A.* Yes.

*Q.* At what price had consols for time left off on Saturday?

*A.* I can hardly say.

*Q.* Did they open on Monday morning pretty much as they had left off on Saturday evening?

*A.* I think they did.

*Q.* How soon after you had been in the Stock Exchange, did any good news come?

*A.* I think it was near eleven.

*Q.* What news had arrived?

*A.* I cannot take upon me to say; I only knew in general, with perhaps every body in the house in business, that there was some news, but we rarely enquire into particulars of news, it is enough that facts are produced.

*Q.* You were doing a good deal of business at that moment, and must have heard something of it; did you hear any thing about a messenger arriving at Dover?

*A.* I have heard so much since that, I cannot take upon myself to swear what I heard, whether that a messenger had arrived at Dover, or that Bonaparte was killed, but one of the two certainly.

*Q.* Did you hear that Bonaparte was killed?

*A.* Yes.

*A Juryman.* Were those gentlemen with you at the time the news arrived?

*A.* They were—not my Lord Cochrane.

*Mr. Gurney.* Had the good news an immediate effect upon the funds?

*A.* Yes, it had.

*Q.* After the funds had begun to rise, did you sell?

*A.* I began to sell before the rise took place.

*Q.* What was the first price you sold at?

*A.* Omnium at twenty-nine and a quarter.

*Q.* That was the first price you sold at?

*A.* Yes.

*Q.* Do you mean to say that omnium opened that morning at twenty-nine and a quarter?

*A.* I rather think it did.

*Q.* However, the first price you sold at was twenty-nine and a quarter?

*A.* Yes.

*Q.* What was your next price?

*A.* £29-3/8, 29-1/2, and 30-1/2.

*Q.* At what did you sell the consols?

*A.* Beginning at 70-5/8ths, 71-1/4, 71-7/8ths, 72, and 72-1/4.

*Q.* In what manner did you receive instructions for these various sales; they were sold in different parcels?

*A.* Yes, I came frequently to my office from the Stock Exchange to Mr. Butt and Mr. Cochrane Johnstone.

*Q.* And you reported to them and received orders?

*A.* Yes.

*Q.* Did you receive notes likewise?

*A.* I was in the constant habit of doing so.

*Q.* Did you do so that morning?

*A.* I am not quite certain; but I am in the constant habit of receiving notes from them.

*Q.* Do you remember hearing in the course of the morning, of a post chaise coming through the city?

*A.* I did.

*Q.* Did that occasion a still further rise in the funds?

*A.* I do not know.

*Q.* Before business left off, the funds fell again?

*A.* They did.

*Lord Ellenborough.* About what o'clock did the funds fall?

*A.* I believe about two.

*Mr. Gurney.* It was discovered at that time that the good news was not true?

*A.* It certainly was not believed.

*Q.* Have you an account of the different purchases from the 12th to the 21st, taken from your books?

*A.* I have.

*The Witness delivered in the Accounts.*

*Mr. Serjeant Best.* From what are those taken?

*A.* From my books.

*Mr. Gurney.* Have you carried those accounts down to the 5th of March?

*A.* I have.

*Q.* Has Mr. Baily, also had access to your books, to take the different balances?

*A.* He has.

*Mr. Gurney.* The reading of this would not be very intelligible, a sight of it perhaps would be the best thing.

*Lord Ellenborough.* We must have the sum total or the results.

*Mr. Gurney.* I will give your Lordship the result after the examination of several stock brokers; Mr. Baily has abstracted the whole.

*Mr. Serjeant Best.* I shall carry back the accounts considerably earlier; that should be understood. If I put in accounts of an earlier date, it must not be considered that I am giving evidence in so doing.

*Mr. Gurney.* I take it the same, as if my learned friend cross examined Mr. Fearn upon that subject.

*Cross-examined by Mr. Serjeant Best.*

*Q.* You have spoken of these gentlemen engaging in stock transactions, you have been carried back no further than February the 8th, they had all three of them bought to an enormous amount long before that time—had they not?

*A.* Certainly.

*Q.* And as to sales, had they not sold very large sums, long antecedent to the month of February?

*A.* Oh yes.

*Q.* Can you state as to my Lord Cochrane, for instance, had he not sold hundreds of thousands before that time?

*A.* Yes.

*Q.* I would ask you, did he not from time to time, down to that time, continue to be selling large sums?

*A.* Yes.

*Q.* With respect to Mr. Cochrane Johnstone—on the 10th or 11th of February, had he not a balance of £100,000.

*Mr. Gurney.* To save my learned friend time, my account shews every day's purchases, and every day's sales from that time.

*Mr. Serjeant Best.* Be so good as to look at that printed paper, and tell me whether that is not a correct statement of Mr. Cochrane Johnstone's account with you.

*A.* I cannot tell from this book.

*Mr. Gurney.* I believe the accounts will agree to a farthing, from the time they each begin.

*Mr. Serjeant Best.* Then the larger sales will appear upon this paper without troubling his Lordship to take them down upon his notes; there were very large sales for all of them several days precedent to the 21st.

*A.* Yes, there were.

*Q.* I believe they began these speculations as early as the month of November, did they not?

*A.* Yes.

*Q.* Mr. Butt managed principally—very much for these gentlemen—for Lord Cochrane particularly?

*A.* Yes, he did.

*Q.* Lord Cochrane, you have told us, was not there on the morning of the 21st?

*A.* No, he was not.

*Q.* For a great many days, I believe I may say months, had you not been directed to sell their stock whenever it should so rise, that you could get one per cent?

*A.* Yes.

*Q.* You have told us that on the morning of the 21st, you began to sell before the news came?

*A.* Yes.

*A Juryman.* He said before the rise took place.

*Mr. Serjeant Best.* You found when you came there in the morning, that the stocks had got to such a pitch as that you could sell consistently with the orders they had given you?

*A.* It was so.

*Lord Ellenborough.* At what hour was that?

*A.* Ten o'clock.

*Mr. Serjeant Best.* Did you not sell out very large sums before either of them came near the place that morning?

*A.* I think I had began to sell before they came, but I cannot say positively.

*Q.* Had you not sold to a considerable amount, if you can tax your memory with it, or refresh your memory by looking at any book?

*A.* I think I had.

*Q.* Can you tell us to what amount you had sold before any of them came?—I do not ask to a few shillings, we deal in thousands here.

*A.* I cannot positively say—I had done much before I saw either of them, for I was in the habit of doing twenty or thirty and reporting to them.

*Q.* Do you mean thousands?

*A.* Yes.

*Q.* You think you had sold considerably before you saw them?

*A.* I think I had.

*Lord Ellenborough.* Cannot you fix the time of your sale?

*Mr. Gurney.* I shall prove the prices every half hour.

*Mr. Serjeant Best.* I am not at all conversant in those things, never having speculated in stock at all, but I am told it is the practice sometimes to sell stock which the persons have not to transfer?

*A.* I have heard of such things.

*Q.* Consequently, if I had been at the Stock Exchange that morning, and had found the Omnium up at 34, which I believe it was that morning——

*Mr. Bolland.* No, thirty two.

*Mr. Serjeant Best.* If I had been at the Stock Exchange that morning, and had found the Omnium up at 32, and had known that the good news must soon turn out to be all invention, I might have sold if I had liked, a million of stock, according to the practice of the Stock Exchange, though I did not happen to have a sixpence.

*A.* It certainly might have been done.

*Q.* Is it not the practice for a man who wishes to gamble in the funds, to sell stock which he has not, when he thinks they will fall?

*A.* I know it is done.

*Q.* A man who thinks the stocks may fall, may sell stock he has not, to any person who thinks they may rise?

*A.* It certainly is done.


*Q.* Did either my Lord Cochrane, Mr. Cochrane Johnstone or Mr. Butt, make any such sales on that day to your knowledge, you having stated you were their Broker—do you know of their having sold on that day any stock which they had not purchased before?

*Lord Ellenborough.* Are you not putting this gentleman in a situation of peril?

*Mr. Serjeant Best.* If he admits it.

*Lord Ellenborough.* Why should you place him in such a situation to deny or affirm? This does not affect the charge.

*Mr. Serjeant Best.* I ask whether it was done by those persons?

*Lord Ellenborough.* But that would be done through a broker.

*Mr. Taddy.* If your Lordship will allow me to suggest on behalf of the witness, that in an action for the penalties, the question would be whether he knew they were possessed of the stock, or not, and this would go to make out his knowledge.

*Mr. Serjeant Best.* Do you know whether either of those persons on that day sold any stock or omnium, which they had not purchased before?

*Lord Ellenborough.* That question must be limited to any thing in which you have not had participation in the way of sale, otherwise you may criminate yourself—having given you that caution, you may do as you please.

*A.* They did not.

*Lord Ellenborough.* That is not imputed to them.

*Mr. Serjeant Best.* The use I mean to make of it I have no objection to state now.

*Lord Ellenborough.* No, you need not, I leave it entirely to your judgment.

*Mr. Serjeant Best.* I think you told us before, those gentlemen told you, whenever the stock rose to one per cent, above what they had bought at, to sell.

*A.* Yes, they did.

*Q.* With respect to the taking of this office, when did you first see it?

*A.* In the course of the week anterior to the 21st of February.

*Q.* Mr. Butt had before an office in Sweeting's Alley.

*A.* Yes.

*Q.* He found that an inconvenient one and he took these rooms in Shorter's Court, he and Mr. Johnstone?

*A.* Yes.

*Q.* Those were taken for Mr. Butt, were they not?

*A.* I believe so.

*Q.* I believe you went to the rooms as to the rooms of Mr. Butt?

*A.* I did.

*Q.* I believe you thought upon seeing Mr. Butt's room, that the situation was a very convenient one for yourself?

*A.* Yes.

*Q.* And therefore you suggested, did you not, that you should like a room in the same house?

*A.* I think I did.

*Q.* In consequence of this suggestion did not Mr. Butt give up to you the room he had taken for himself, and take another in the same house for himself?

*A.* Yes, he did.

*Q.* And the room being taken in this manner, you put up your name "Fearn, Stock Broker."

*A.* On the Monday.

*Q.* Did you do that at your own idea or was it suggested to you by any body?

*A.* It was the same transparent blind I had at my former office, which I removed and put in the window.

*Q.* Your name in gold letters?

*A.* In black letters.

*Q.* You took your furniture?

*A.* The rooms were furnished.

*Q.* I believe after thus finding your Customers liked the situation, you desired Mr. Johnstone to purchase the lease of the house for you.

*A.* Yes, I did.

*Q.* Was that before or after the 21st?

*A.* I think after.

*Lord Ellenborough.* Then that does not apply.

*Mr. Serjeant Best.* You had taken it before the 21st and got into possession on the 21st.

*A.* Yes.

*Q.* One of your reasons for taking it was that some of your customers were particularly pleased with it.

*A.* Yes.

*Q.* That was on the Thursday in the week before.

*A.* I believe it might be.

*Q.* You have told us you did not see Lord Cochrane on that morning, how many days previously to that had you seen him?

*A.* I think I saw him on the Saturday.

*Q.* You are not quite certain of that?

*A.* No, I am not.

*Q.* Does it appear whether he bought any thing on that day.

*Mr. Gurney.* It appears from the account that he bought 20,000 and sold 17,000.

*Mr. Serjeant Best.* You have told us that all those three persons, Mr. Cochrane Johnstone, Lord Cochrane, and Mr. Butt, were very large speculators; did they always speculate the same way, or on the contrary, when one bought did not the other very often sell?

*A.* It has been the case.

*Q.* Has not that happened often, several times?

*A.* Yes it has, several times.

Re-examined by Mr. Gurney.

*Q.* On that day they all sold?

*A.* Yes they did.

*Q.* They all acted together on that day.

*A.* Yes they did.

*Q.* Where did Lord Cochrane reside on the 21st of February?

*A.* I do not know.

*Q.* How soon after did you know his residence in Green-Street?

*A.* Not at all until the printed paper of the Stock Exchange came out.

*Q.* Did you know that Lord Cochrane resided at the time in Green-Street?

*A.* Only by report.

*Q.* Not from Lord Cochrane?

*A.* No.

*A Juryman.* You say they did not sell any stock but what they had before purchased, do you mean such as they had bought and paid for, or only such as they had contracted for the purchase of, was it actually bought and transferred to them?

*Mr. Taddy.* That is the very thing I have taken the liberty of suggesting to your Lordship.

*Lord Ellenborough.* He has before said they had not sold any of which they had not become the proprietors before, so that he is predicating of them that they had purchased this, for they could not otherwise become proprietors.

*A Juryman.* Is it not a purchase for time altogether, are they not all time bargains both the omnium and the stock?

*A.* This is one of those questions I cannot answer.

*Lord Ellenborough.* Gentlemen, he objects to answering the questions as it may criminate him, but the offence charged may have an effect upon the funds, in which not only these individuals are concerned, but every person who has transactions in Stock, the persons belonging to the Court of Chancery, who have to purchase or sell, may be influenced by an improper elevation or depression of the funds, that does not affect the question as to the crime charged upon this record, you will consider Mr. Gurney whether you will persist in the questions, because this man demurs to the answering the questions, being a party in the transaction.

*Mr. Gurney.* You do decline answering that question?

*A.* Yes I do.

*Mr. Robert Hichens sworn.*

*Examined by Mr. Gurney.*

*Q.* I believe you are a Stock-Broker?

*A.* Yes I am.

*Q.* Have you for some years past known Mr. Cochrane Johnstone?

*A.* Yes.

*Q.* I believe you have not done business for him till the present year?

*A.* No.

*Q.* From the 8th of February to the 19th did you make various purchases for him.

*A.* Yes I did.

*Q.* At the leaving off of the business on Saturday what was the balance.

*A.* £250,000.

*Q.* That was all omnium.

*A.* Yes it was.

*Q.* Have you taken from your books a statement of the business you did?

*A.* I have memorandums that will enable me to answer any questions.

*Q.* Has Mr. Baily from your books taken an account of purchases and sales?

*A.* I furnished Mr. Baily with a copy of it.

*Mr. Gurney.* Then through Mr. Baily I will give all the particulars of it.

*Lord Ellenborough.* Whether purchased with money or no they take upon themselves the disposition of that fund, shewing that they had an interest in the rise and fall of the funds, and that they sold on the Monday and gained a profit.

*Mr. Gurney.* Yes my Lord. On Monday morning the 21st how soon did you see Mr. Cochrane Johnstone?

*A.* I think between ten and eleven I cannot say exactly.

*Q.* Where did you see him?

*A.* I think I met him as I was coming out of the Stock Exchange.

*Q.* How near ten or eleven?

*A.* I think it must have been about a quarter before eleven but I cannot say positively.

*Q.* Did you receive any directions from him as to what you were to do with respect to the omnium?

*A.* I received an order from him on the Saturday, to sell £50,000 at one per cent. profit, and that I had sold before I saw him.

*Q.* At what had you sold it?

*A.* At 29.

*Q.* Did he give you any further instructions what to do with the remainder?

*A.* He then ordered me to sell a certain quantity at an eighth per cent more.

*Q.* In short did you sell the whole of it that day by his directions?

*A.* I did.

*Q.* At what prices?

*A.* At 29, 29-1/8, 29-1/2, 30-3/4, and 30-7/8.

*Lord Ellenborough.* At those different prices did you dispose of the whole which Mr. Cochrane Johnstone held on that 21st.

*A.* Yes.

*Q.* At one or other of those prices.

*A.* Yes.

*Cross-examined by Mr. Topping.*

*Q.* Can you tell me what was Mr. Cochrane Johnstone's balance on the 15th?

*A.* I think £465,000.

*Q.* On the 16th how much was that reduced?

*A.* On the 16th I sold £200,000.

*Q.* Reducing the balance of course to £265,000.?

*A.* Yes.

*Q.* Upon the 17th what did you sell?

*A.* On the 17th I bought £50,000. and sold £115,000. reducing the balance to £200,000.; on that Saturday I bought £50,000.

*Q.* And you had his directions upon that Saturday to sell at one per Cent.?

*A.* To sell £50,000. at one per Cent. profit.

*Q.* And you had done that before you saw Mr. Cochrane Johnstone at all?

*A.* Yes, I had.

*Mr. William Smallbone, sworn.*

*Examined by Mr. Gurney.*

*Q.* You are a Stock-broker, I believe?

*A.* Yes.

*Q.* Did you shortly before the 21st of February make any purchases for Mr. Cochrane Johnstone?

*A.* Yes.

*Q.* You had made two purchases only, I believe, the 12th and the 14th?

*A.* Yes, only two purchases of £20,000. each.

*Q.* When did you sell them out?

*A.* On the 21st of February.

*Q.* At what did you sell them out.

*A.* 28-1/8, 29-1/4, and 29-1/2.

*Q.* By whose order did you sell them out?

*A.* I sold Mr. Johnstone's by his order; I sold Mr. Butt's by his order.

*Q.* Was that order from Mr. Cochrane Johnstone received on the Monday, or before the Monday?

*A.* In part it was received on the Monday, but a part on the Saturday.

*Q.* You had also, I believe, made purchases in Omnium for Mr. Butt?

*A.* I had.

*Q.* To the amount of £40,000 I believe?

*A.* Yes.

*Q.* Was that £40,000 left as a balance on Saturday the 19th?

*A.* Yes.

*Q.* And all sold out on the Monday?

*A.* Yes, all sold on the 21st.

*Q.* Have you given Mr. Baily a statement from your books of that?

*A.* Yes.

*Q.* And of the prices at which it was sold?

*A.* Yes.

*Lord Ellenborough.* Now what is the result of all these accounts?

*Mr. Gurney.* I am going to call one person more, and then I will give your Lordship the totals.

*Q.* You had bought for Mr. Cochrane Johnstone, £40,000, and on that 21st you sold it all?

*A.* Yes.

*Q.* You had bought for Mr. Butt £40,000, and on the Monday you sold it all?

*A.* I sold it all on Monday.

*Lord Ellenborough.* If he sells all the sum is immaterial, if you prove that he sold all of the several amounts, it furnishes a constructive motive for what has passed.

*Cross-examined by Mr. Scarlett.*

*Q.* When was it you had purchased the £40,000 for Mr. Cochrane Johnstone?

*A.* On the 12th and the 14th.

*Q.* Did Mr. Johnstone send you the order to purchase it?

*A.* Yes.

*Q.* Was it upon his own account?

*A.* No, it was upon his own account, the order was from him.

*Q.* But not upon his own account?

*A.* No, it was not.

*Q.* Was the whole £40,000 purchased at two different times?

*A.* Yes, it was.

*Q.* You stated to my learned Friend, that he gave you an order to sell a part of it on Saturday?

*A.* Yes, he gave me an order on Saturday.

*Q.* What was it?

*A.* To sell at a quarter profit if I had an opportunity.

*Q.* I take for granted that opportunity did not occur on the Saturday?

*A.* No, it did not.

*Q.* Otherwise you would have sold it on the Saturday?

*A.* Certainly.

*Q.* On the Monday you say he gave you an order as to the other £200,000?

*A.* Yes.

*Q.* Had you sold the first £20,000 before you saw him on the Monday?

*A.* Yes, I had.

*Q.* At what time in the morning had you sold it?

*A.* I think about half past ten.

*Q.* When did you first see Mr. Johnstone?

*A.* I saw him soon after I had sold out, between ten and eleven.

*Q.* His order had been confined to £20,000 on the Saturday?

*A.* Not exactly to £20,000; if I saw an opportunity of selling any at a quarter profit I was to sell.

*Q.* When you saw him on the Monday, did he then order you to sell the remainder?

*A.* Yes.

*Q.* Did you sell it immediately.

*A.* As soon as an opportunity offered to sell it at a profit.

*Q.* Was that early in the day?

*A.* Yes, about eleven I believe.

*Q.* When was it that you first heard any rumour of good news in the morning?

*A.* Soon after the market opened, between ten and eleven.

*Q.* You say you had purchased £40,000 for Mr. Butt?

*A.* Yes.

*Q.* When was that?

*A.* The 12th, 14th, and 18th of February.

*Q.* Different sums on those days?

*A.* Yes.

*Q.* Had you any order from Mr. Butt as to the sales?

*A.* To sell whenever I saw an opportunity of selling at a quarter profit, or three eighths as the circumstances might allow.

*Q.* How long have you known Mr. Butt?

*A.* About six months.

*Q.* Had you had any transactions with him before in that way?

*A.* Yes.

*Q.* He had occasionally employed you?

*A.* Yes, he had.

*Q.* Who introduced you to Mr. Johnstone?

*A.* Mr. Johnstone was in Mr. Butt's office when I first saw him there in Sweeting's Alley.

*Q.* It was through Mr. Butt you became acquainted with Mr. Johnstone?

*A.* Yes, it was.

*Q.* If any person had known that this news was false, and had been disposed to be a bear, he might have made his fortune by selling that day, might not he?

*A.* Certainly.

*Q.* By selling for account?

*A.* Certainly.

*Q.* You had no directions from either of those Gentlemen to sell more than they had bought that day?

*A.* No I had not.

*Cross-examined by Mr. Richardson.*

*Q.* You stated to my learned Friend that you had bought large quantities of Omnium on account of this Gentleman, had any of it been paid for.

*A.* Shall I answer that question my Lord?

*Lord Ellenborough.* If the Witness looks at me I must tell him he need not answer any question that implicates him in a crime.

*Mr. Richardson.* You decline answering that question?

*A.* Yes, I do.

*Q.* You will decline answering any other questions that you think implicate yourself.—Were any of those purchases real purchases for stock transferred, or on account?

*A.* It was for Omnium—that cannot be transferred.

*Q.* You spoke of Consols?

*A.* No this was Omnium.

*Q.* Was it all bought or paid for, or on account?

*A.* I decline answering that question.

*Q.* With respect to the Consols had any of them been paid for or transferred?

*A.* I had no Consol account.

*Mr. Richardson.* I will state to your Lordship the object I have in that; I submit it is incumbent upon the prosecutors to prove in support of the allegations of their indictment, which charge a conspiracy for the purpose of enabling Mr. Cochrane Johnstone and the other gentlemen, to sell divers large sums of Government Securities, and so on, that they had an interest in those Government Securities.

*Lord Ellenborough.* That applies only to the two first counts.

*Mr. Gurney.* If I leave my case imperfect, my learned friends will take advantage of it.

*Lord Ellenborough.* It does not apply to the third count, certainly there is a particularity which is quite unnecessary in the others; it states that by certain devices and contrivances they endeavoured to raise the price of the funds, to the prejudice of His Majesty's subjects, to an undue elevation, and so on, there is enough to let in the general evidence.

*Mr. Gurney.* And there is enough in the first count, independently of the sales.

*Mr. Richardson.* The first count states this to be to enable these gentlemen to sell Omnium, and Three per Cent. Consols, at larger prices than they would otherwise have sold for; I submit to your Lordship, that in support of that it is for the prosecutors to shew that they had such to sell?

*Lord Ellenborough.* That will be an observation at the close if they leave their proof imperfect; perhaps I accede to you, but that would only apply to one count, they have six more counts, I do not say that they are all safe counts, but you will see what they propose taking their verdict upon.

*Mr. Malcolm Richardson sworn.*

*Examined by Mr. Gurney.*

*Q.* I believe you are a bookseller and also act as a stock broker.

*A.* I am.

*Q.* You are not a Member of the Stock Exchange.

*A.* No, I am not.

*Q.* In the afternoon of Saturday the 19th of February, did Mr. Butt, make any application to you on the subject of stock.

*A.* On the morning of that day.

*Q.* What did he apply to you to do?

*A.* He applied to me to purchase a quantity of Omnium.

*Q.* How much did he mention?

*A.* He mentioned on the first instance as much as £150,000.

*Q.* What answer did you give to that?

*A.* I hesitated to execute such a commission as that to that extent.

*Q.* How much did you purchase for him?

*A.* £20,000.

*Q.* On that Saturday?

*A.* Yes, in the morning I speak of.

*Q.* What did you do with that £20,000?

*A.* I received instructions to sell it again, if I could get a quarter per cent profit.

*Q.* Did you get a profit and sell it again?

*A.* In a short time I did get three-eighths per cent profit, and consequently sold it again without waiting for instructions.

*Q.* Did you then by his instructions make any further purchase for him?

*A.* I did in the latter part of that day purchase first £20,000 and then £10,000.

*Q.* On the morning of Monday the 21st did you sell out that £30,000?

*A.* I did.

*Q.* In pursuance of instructions received on the Saturday or on the Monday?

*A.* On the Saturday, at the time I saw him.

*Q.* At what profit did you sell?

*A.* At three-fourths per cent profit.

*Q.* What was the price?

*A.* 28-1/4.

*Q.* Have you given the account of this to Mr. Baily?

*A.* Yes I have.

*Cross-examined by Mr. Brougham.*

*Q.* You were partner with Mr. Fearn, Senior, Mr. Butts, broker, were not you?

*A.* Yes, formerly I was.

*Q.* Did you not apply to Mr. Butt, stating that you had a wife and family, and wishing him to give you some employment.

*A.* Mr. Butt had been known to me ten or twelve years, and known to Mr. Fearn, Senior, only as being one of my customers in the book line.

*Q.* Did you not apply to Mr. Butt yourself to ask him to serve you.

*A.* Not upon this occasion at all.

*Q.* Will you hear the question first, and then answer it. Did you never before this apply to Mr. Butt to give you some of his business?

*A.* Yes I did.

*Q.* And he did give you some of his business upon this day?

*A.* He did.

*Cross-examined by Mr. Richardson.*

*Q.* Was any of the Omnium bought for Mr. Butt, paid for?

*A.* I would rather decline answering that.

*Mr. Francis Baily called again.*

*Examined by Mr. Gurney.*

*Q.* These gentlemen have informed us that they have furnished you with the exact statements of all the purchases and sales; have you drawn out from their statements the purchases and sales, and the daily balances of each?

*A.* I have. It may be necessary to state, Mr. Richardson has not furnished me with a written account, but I have taken it down now from his own mouth.

*Q.* Have you from that made out a general statement of the several accounts containing the daily purchases, the daily sales, and the daily balances?

*A.* I have.

*Q.* For Mr. Cochrane Johnstone, Lord Cochrane, and Mr. Butt?

*A.* Yes.

*The account was delivered in and read, as follows;—*

| 1814 Feb | General Statement of A. Cochrane Johnstone's Omnium Account, from 8th to 21st Feb. 1814 |||||||||||| A. Cochrane Johnstone's Consol Account from 12th to 21st Feb. 1814 ||| Lord Cochrane's Omnium Account 14th to 21st Feb. 1814 |||
|---|---|---|---|---|---|---|---|---|---|---|---|---|---|---|---|---|---|---|
| | through Fearn ||| through Hichens ||| through Smallbone ||| TOTALS ||| through Fearn ||| through Fearn |||
| | Daily Purchases | Daily Sales | Daily Balances | Daily Purchases | Daily Sales | Daily Balances | Daily Purchases | Daily Sales | Daily Balances | Daily Purchases | Daily Sales | Daily Balances | Daily Purchases | Daily Sales | Daily Balances | Daily Purchases | Daily Sales | Daily Balances |
| 8 | 10,000 | | 10,000 | | | | | | | 10,000 | | 10,000 | | | | | | |
| 9 | 47,000 | 10,000 | 47,000 | 20,000 | | 20,000 | | | | 67,000 | 10,000 | 67,000 | | | | | | |
| 10 | 78,000 | 105,000 | 20,000 | 150,000 | | 170,000 | | | | 228,000 | 105,000 | 190,000 | | | | | | |
| 11 | 115,000 | 35,000 | 100,000 | 95,000 | | 265,000 | | | | 210,000 | 35,000 | 365,000 | | | | | | |
| 12 | | | 100,000 | | | 265,000 | 20,000 | | 20,000 | 20,000 | | 385,000 | | | | | | |
| 14 | 96,500 | 100,000 | 96,500 | 200,000 | | 465,000 | 20,000 | | 40,000 | 316,500 | 100,000 | 601,500 | 100,000 | | 100,000 | 100,000 | | 100,000 |
| 15 | 13,500 | | 110,000 | | | 465,000 | | | 40,000 | 13,500 | | 615,000 | | | 100,000 | | | 100,000 |
| 16 | 18,500 | 10,000 | 118,500 | | 200,000 | 265,000 | | | 40,000 | 18,500 | 210,000 | 423,500 | | | 100,000 | 50,000 | | 150,000 |
| 17 | 11,000 | 19,500 | 110,000 | 50,000 | 115,000 | 200,000 | | | 40,000 | 61,000 | 134,500 | 350,000 | | | 100,000 | | 50,000 | 100,000 |
| 18 | 38,000 | | 148,000 | 50,000 | | 250,000 | | | 40,000 | 88,000 | | 438,000 | | | 100,000 | 36,000 | | 136,000 |
| 19 | | 18,000 | 130,000 | | | 250,000 | | | 40,000 | | 18,000 | 420,000 | | | 100,000 | 20,000 | 17,000 | 139,000 |
| 21 | | 120,000 | 10,000 | | 250,000 | | | 40,000 | | | 410,000 | 10,000 | | | | | 139,000 | |

| Feb | General Statement of R. G. Butt's Omnium Account, from 8th to 21st Feb. 1814 |||||||||||| R. G. Butt's Consol Account from 12th to 21st Feb. 1814 |||
|---|---|---|---|---|---|---|---|---|---|---|---|---|---|---|---|
| | through Fearn ||| through Richardson ||| through Smallbone ||| TOTALS ||| through Fearn |||
| | Daily Purchases | Daily Sales | Daily Balances | Daily Purchases | Daily Sales | Daily Balances | Daily Purchases | Daily Sales | Daily Balances | Daily Purchases | Daily Sales | Daily Balances | Daily Purchases | Daily Sales | Daily Balances |
| 8 | 10,000 | | 10,000 | | | | | | | 10,000 | | 10,000 | | | |
| 9 | 50,000 | 10,000 | 50,000 | | | | | | | 50,000 | 10,000 | 50,000 | | | |
| 10 | 78,000 | 110,000 | 18,000 | | | | | | | 78,000 | 110,000 | 18,000 | | | |
| 11 | 115,000 | 33,000 | 100,000 | | | | | | | 115,000 | 33,000 | 100,000 | 46,000 | 20,000 | 26,000 |
| 12 | | | 100,000 | | | | 20,000 | | 20,000 | | | 120,000 | | 87,000 | 113,000 |
| 14 | 96,500 | 100,000 | 96,500 | | | | 10,000 | | 30,000 | 106,500 | 100,000 | 126,500 | | | 113,000 |
| 15 | 13,500 | | 110,000 | | | | | | 30,000 | 13,500 | | 140,000 | | 55,000 | 168,000 |
| 16 | 18,500 | 10,000 | 118,500 | | | | | | 30,000 | 18,500 | 10,000 | 148,500 | 40,000 | | 208,000 |
| 17 | 11,000 | 19,500 | 110,000 | | | | | | 30,000 | 11,000 | 19,500 | 140,000 | | | 208,000 |
| 18 | 38,000 | | 148,000 | | | | 10,000 | | 40,000 | 48,000 | | 188,000 | | | 208,000 |
| 19 | | 18,000 | 130,000 | 50,000 | 20,000 | 30,000 | | | 40,000 | 50,000 | 38,000 | 200,000 | | 30,000 | 178,000 |
| 21 | | 154,000 | 24,000 Sold too much. | | 30,000 | | | 40,000 | | | | 24,000 Sold too much. | | 168,000 | 10,000 |

*Q.* What appears at last to be the gross balance held by each of them on the 19th February; what is Mr. Cochrane Johnstone's balance of Omnium from all those different accounts, on the 19th February?

*A.* £420,000.

*Q.* Now state Mr. Cochrane Johnstone's Consol Account.

*A.* £100,000.

*Q.* What was the balance of Lord Cochrane's Omnium account?

*A.* £139,000.

*Q.* Now state Mr. Butt's.

*A.* £200,000.

*Q.* And it appears, I see, that there were £24,000 sold too much on the Monday.

*A.* Exactly so; there was that quantity sold more than he had purchased.

*Q.* What was Mr. Butt's Consol Account?

*A.* £178,000, and he sold only £168,000.

*Lord Ellenborough.* Then there was £24,000 too much of his Omnium, and £10,000 too little of his Consols sold?

*Mr. Gurney.* Exactly so. Now what was the gross amount of their account of balances on that day?

*A.* £759,000 Omnium, and £278,000 Consols.

*Q.* As we are not so well acquainted with Omnium as you are, if that were reduced to Consols what would they have amounted to?

*A.* It may be necessary to state, that every thousand pounds Omnium consists of £1100 Reduced and £670 Consols, therefore the whole amount of that would be £1,611,430 three per cents.

*Q.* Now upon that amount, what would the fraction of a single eighth per cent. be?

*A.* £2014:5:9.

*Lord Ellenborough.* The whole of this fund was cleared on the 21st, except £10,000 Consols, and it was oversold by £24,000 Omnium?

*A.* Exactly so.

*Mr. Gurney.* Have you calculated from the accounts, the profits made by those sales of the 21st?

*A.* I have.

*Q.* To what does it amount?

*A.* Exactly £10,450.

*Q.* That is the total of the three. Can you give me the proportion of each?

*A.* For Lord Cochrane £2470, Mr. Cochrane Johnstone £4931:5, Mr. Butt £3048:15.

*Q.* From the state of the market on the morning of the 21st if no news had arrived such as raised the funds on that day, could any persons have sold this large quantity of Omnium and Consols without very much depressing the market?

*A.* I should think not certainly.

*Q.* Do you remember at what price Omnium left off on Saturday the 19th?

*A.* I have referred back to the books; I cannot state from my own memory.

*Q.* Have you the books here?

*A.* No; they are the books of the Stock Exchange.

*Q.* Mr. Wetenall's accounts?

*A.* Yes.

*Q.* How soon after the business at the Stock Exchange began on the morning of the 21st did the news arrive there?

*A.* I should think in about half an hour after, but I really am not quite certain to that point.

*Lord Ellenborough.* The business begins at ten, I believe?

*A.* Yes.

*Mr. Gurney.* As soon as the news came, had it a sensible effect on the funds?

*A.* Yes; a gradual effect, according as the report was believed.

*Q.* Do you remember after some time whether there was any check or decline?

*A.* Yes; there was about the middle of the day.

*Q.* I mean the first decline.

*A.* Yes; afterwards they recovered.

*Q.* To what was that recovery owing?

*A.* It was generally attributed to the news that came through the city.

*Q.* You mean the chaise coming through the city?

*A.* Yes; it was generally believed it was a confirmation of the former report.

*Q.* Did that second rise which took place upon the chaise going through the city, extend still higher than it had been on the report of the arrival of the messenger?

*A.* I think it did.

*Cross-examined by Mr. Park.*

*Q.* You are not under the same restraint as the other persons are, can you tell us whether these were real transactions, or only fictitious ones which daily take place at the Stock Exchange?

*A.* The accounts which were given in, I think were given in for time, but I have only taken out the figures.

*Lord Ellenborough.* I should imagine the witness would say that from the magnitude of the accounts he would think they were for time?

*A.* Certainly.

*Mr. Park.* I want to know, for I have never had Omnium in my life, whether you are not competent to say from your knowledge of these accounts, that these are all what they call time bargains?

*A.* There is nothing stated upon the face of these accounts as to what days the purchases are made for; possibly they may be for time.

*Q.* I ask you whether from your knowledge of these accounts and the investigations you have made, they are not time bargains?

*Lord Ellenborough.* He has no personal knowledge of them, he can know nothing but from the magnitude of the sum, he may suppose they must have been time bargains.

*A.* Certainly; there is nothing upon the face of the accounts to lead to any such conclusion.

*Mr. James Wetenall, sworn.*

*Examined by Mr. Gurney.*

*Q.* I believe you are employed by the House to take the prices of the day at the Stock Exchange?

*A.* I am.

*Q.* At what price did Omnium leave off on Saturday the 19th of February?

*(The Witness referred to a paper.)*

*Mr. Serjeant Best.* Where do you get those accounts from?

*A.* I collect them from the Stock Exchange.

*Mr. Gurney.* Do you go about all day long taking the prices?

*A.* I collect them at different times in the course of the day.

*Q.* You go about taking an account from all the persons who are there?

*A.* I take them from different persons who are in the market.

*Mr. Serjeant Best.* This is a printed paper?

*A.* Yes.

*Mr. Gurney.* It is printed under your directions, I believe?

*A.* Yes.

*Q.* Is your original paper destroyed?

*A.* It is.

*Q.* Is this paper a copy from that of yours?

*A.* Yes.

*Mr. Serjeant Best.* Did you ever compare this with the paper on which you took down the prices?

*A.* Yes.

*Q.* Where do you get the contents of your written paper?

*A.* From the gentlemen in the Stock Exchange.

*Mr. Serjeant Best.* I submit that this paper cannot be evidence. The Witness states that he collects from the gentlemen in the Stock Exchange, the prices at which they buy and sell, from time to time, in the course of the day; he says he compares this printed paper with the original written paper; I am not objecting to that, but I submit, the written paper itself could not be evidence.

*Lord Ellenborough.* It is all hearsay, but it is the only evidence we can have; it is the only evidence we have of the price of sales of any description. I do not receive it as the precise thing, but as what is in the ordinary transactions of mankind received as proper information, and I suppose there is hardly a gentleman living who would not act on this paper.

*Mr. Gurney.* At what price did Omnium leave off on Saturday the 19th of February?

*A.* 26-3/4.

*Lord Ellenborough.* Do you furnish the Bank with these papers?

*A.* Yes.

*Mr. Gurney.* Was that 26-3/4 the money price or the time price?

*A.* The money price.

*Q.* The time price, I believe, is about one per cent. higher?

*A.* In general.

*Q.* At what price did Omnium commence on the Monday following?

*A.* 26-1/2.

*Q.* That is the money price?

*A.* The money price.

*Q.* Therefore the time price was 27-1/2?

*A.* I did not take the time price.

*Q.* After this news arrived what did it get up to?

*A.* As high as 30-1/4.

*Q.* At what time was that?

*A.* That is impossible for me to say.

*Q.* How soon did it get up to 30-1/4?

*A.* I cannot say; it did rise to that by degrees.

*Q.* Did it stand at that, or rise or fall?

*A.* It fell by degrees to 30, and from that to 28.

*Lord Ellenborough.* So that the rumour had a continuing effect to the close of the day?

*A.* Yes.

*Mr. Gurney.* Did it fall back so low by one and a half as it began in the morning?

*A.* No.

### Cross-examined by Mr. Serjeant Pell.

*Q.* Do you remember at what time in the course of the day the report came to the Stock Exchange, of a chaise coming through the city?

*A.* I cannot say at what time it was.

*Q.* Then perhaps you cannot tell whether or not the Stocks rose again upon any report of that kind arriving there?

*A.* According to my recollection the Stocks rose a second time; they rose at first, then they fell, and then they rose again.

*Q.* But you cannot tell at what time that was, or to what cause it was attributable?

*A.* It was attributable to a chaise arriving.

*Q.* You remember that?

*A.* Yes.

*Q.* See whether you cannot remember how long it was after the opening of the business of the day that they so rose; might it be three hours afterwards?

*A.* It was in less than three hours, I think.

*Q.* It was less than three hours that they rose the second time you mean?

*A.* Yes; the second time.

*Q.* Have you a distinct recollection of this. Though you cannot remember the precise point of time at which it took place, have you distinct recollection that they rose at first, then fell, and then rose again.

*A.* Yes; I have a perfect recollection of that, but I cannot tell the time.

*Cross-examined by Mr. Park.*

*Q.* How often in the course of the day do you take that account?

*A.* Not at any particular stated times.

*Q.* You have nothing to do with buying or selling stock, I presume.

*A.* Not on my own account.

*Q.* But you are a Stock Broker?

*A.* I am.

*Q.* Then when you are not otherwise employed you fill up that paper from time to time?

*A.* No; if I perceive there are any particular fluctuations, I then make it my business to collect the prices.

*Q.* Do you mean to represent that the Stocks had not risen from what they ended at on Saturday before any news came to the Stock Exchange; had not they risen considerably that morning?

*A.* I think not, because if I recollect, there were reports in the morning that news had arrived.

*Q.* We have heard from some gentlemen that they sold stock as soon as the Stock Exchange opened; now I ask whether stock had not been sold at a rise before the news arrived?

*A.* Yes.

*Mr. Gurney.* But you say before the market opened there were some reports of a Messenger having arrived?

*A.* Yes.

*Mr. Charles Addis, sworn.*

*Examined by Mr. Gurney.*

*Q.* Have you a house in Shorter's-court?

*A.* No, I have not; I am concerned for a gentleman who has some property there.

*Q.* You have the letting of a house for a gentleman there?

*A.* I have.

*Q.* Was any application made to you in the week prior to the 21st of February for any part of that house?

*A.* Yes, on the 15th or 16th, I think Mr. Cochrane Johnstone applied to me for an Office in a house, the letting of which was under my management.

*Q.* What number in Shorter's-court did he finally fix upon?

*A.* It is number 5, the house almost immediately adjoining the Stock Exchange.

*Q.* Did he on that day take any part of the house of you?

*A.* He took one room for an office in that house on that day.

*Q.* The house in which Mr. Fearn is now?

*A.* Yes.

*Q.* How soon did he take any more?

*A.* He called on the following day and engaged another office.

*Q.* That was the 16th then?

*A.* I believe it was the 16th, I will not be positive, and he called on the following day the 17th, being the third time.

*Q.* Did he, when he called on the 17th, write that letter in your office (*handing it to the Witness.*)

*A.* This is a letter he left in my absence in the office, on which day I cannot say, but this was a letter that he left for me.

*Q.* That was on the third day after he had engaged the three offices?

*A.* Yes.

*Q.* He had then engaged all three?

*A.* Yes.

*Q.* Are they three rooms in the same house?

*A.* Three rooms in the same house.

*Q. (To Mr. Fearn)* Is that letter Mr. Cochrane Johnstone's hand writing? *(handing it to the Witness.)*

*A.* I believe it is.

*It was delivered in, and read as follows:—*

"Sir,—I called again upon you to know if you have Powers to sell the house, part of which I have taken, as I find there are several persons in the house at present, which is rather awkward, and makes it too public.

"If you have powers to sell I will immediately treat with you; have the goodness therefore to leave the terms with your clerk, or send them to me at No. 18, Great Cumberland-street. I will however call again this day before I return to the West end of the town.

I am, Sir,<br>Your obedient Servant,<br>(Signed) A. COCHRANE JOHNSTONE."

*(Addressed)* Mr. Addis.

*Cross-examined by Mr. Serjeant Best.*

*Q.* I believe he took the first room for Mr. Butt expressly?

*A.* Yes; and gave me a reference to him at Mr. Fearn's, who then lived in Cornhill.

*Q.* And the next time he came he said he wanted it for Mr. Fearn?

*A.* No; he said then he wanted it for Mr. Butt.

*Q.* And the third time he said he wanted it for Mr. Fearn?

*A.* Yes.

*Q.* Mr. Fearn has now the whole.

*A.* Yes.

*Mr. James Pilliner, sworn.*

*Examined by Mr. Gurney.*

*Q.* Are you a Stock Broker?

*A.* Yes.

*Q.* Prior to the 21st of February had you made any purchases for the Defendant Holloway, in Stock or Omnium?

*A.* I had, in both.

*Q.* How much of either was he possessed of before business began on Monday the 21st of February?

*A.* £20,000 Omnium and £20,000 Consols.

*Q.* Did you sell that out on that Monday?

*A.* I sold £20,000 Omnium and £14,000 Consols.

*Mr. Serjeant Pell.* Does your Lordship think, in consequence of what you have suggested already, that the Witness is bound to answer to the nature of the stock?

*Lord Ellenborough.* I am not apprized whether it is a real sum or not at present.

*Mr. Serjeant Pell.* The reason I now interpose is, that if this should turn out to be a transaction which was not real, the Witness would not be bound to answer any question respecting it, because it may tend to criminate himself, and involve him in penalties. The mere circumstance of his having sold stock at all that day, supposing it not real stock, would warrant him in declining to answer these questions.

*Lord Ellenborough.* Whether he sold any thing is a link in the chain, or else you might exclude all the transactions of the day, because they might ultimately connect with the vicious sale.

*Mr. Serjeant Pell.* Suppose it should turn out to be a time bargain, these questions would be material to convict this person of an offence, the amount sold would be very material; therefore if he is not bound to answer the last question———

*Lord Ellenborough.* I do not prohibit him; I am only to tell him that if these are bargains which are against law, he is bound to know the law, and if it would involve him in any penalty he need not answer the question.

*Mr. Serjeant Pell.* All I would request then is, that your Lordship would now suggest to the Witness that he need not answer any question that will tend to criminate himself.

*Lord Ellenborough.* If it will convict you in penalties, you are not bound to answer any question.

*Mr. Serjeant Pell.* I was only taking the liberty to suggest that that admonition may be given in the early part of the examination.

*Lord Ellenborough.* I cannot tell a witness he is not bound to answer a question, until I see that it has some bearing and probable tendency to accuse him;

otherwise I must rummage all the statute books for penalties to put the witnesses on their guard—I must not only carry all the penal laws in my head, but mention them to every witness who comes before me upon any subject.

*Mr. Gurney.* Did you see Mr. Holloway on the morning of the 21st?

*A.* Yes I did.

*Q.* Did he give you any directions?

*A.* I beg to decline answering that question.

*Mr. Gurney.* I submit to your Lordship he is not at liberty to decline answering that question.

*Lord Ellenborough.* You may answer that question. Did he give you any directions?

*A.* He did.

*Mr. Gurney.* What to do?

*A.* I must beg to decline answering that question.

*Lord Ellenborough.* You need not answer to what you did; but you must state what he proposed to you to do, unless you did it afterwards, and the having done it would involve you in a penalty.

*Mr. Gurney.* What did he give you directions to do?

*A.* To sell stock.

*Q.* Was it to sell all he had, or part of what he had?

*A.* To sell all.

*Q.* At what time on Monday was it?

*A.* About the middle of the day.

*Cross-examined by Mr. Serjeant Pell.*

*Q.* What is Mr. Holloway?

*A.* A wine merchant.

*Q.* Where does he live?

*A.* In Martin's-lane, Cannon-street.

*Q.* Have you known him any time?

*A.* I have known him upwards of twenty years.

*Q.* How long have you acted for him as his broker?

*A.* Perhaps two years.

*Mr. James Steers sworn.*

*Examined by Mr. Gurney.*

*Q.* Are you Stock Broker to the Accountant General of the Court of Chancery?

*A.* I am.

*Q.* Did you as broker to the Accountant General, make purchases on Monday the 21st February?

*A.* I did.

*Q.* At what prices?

*A.* I made purchases to the amount of £15,957:10:8, at 71-5/8 per cent.

*Q.* Consols I suppose?

*A.* Yes, I have got them down in various sums.

*Q.* Was that the high price of the day, or the price at which stock opened in the morning?

*A.* I got to my office I think about eleven o'clock, or a little before, I took the orders from the Accountant General's office.

*Q.* At what time did you begin making your purchases?

*A.* I think from eleven to a quarter after eleven.

*Q.* Had the news then considerably raised the Stocks?

*A.* It had.

*Lord Ellenborough.* Is that all you did that day?

*A.* That is all I did that day.

*Mr. Gurney.* Did you do business for any body besides the Accountant General on that day?

*A.* I cannot speak to any thing but what I did for the Accountant General.

*Lord Ellenborough.* Though you cannot speak to any thing else in precise sums, do you recollect that you did buy for any body else on that day besides the Accountant General?

*Q.* I can speak to an entry on my books on that day, but I cannot say whether I did the business myself. I do not recollect doing any thing else myself besides that bargain.

*A Juryman.* At what price could you have bought that lot of Consols on Saturday?

*A.* I can state the purchases I made on Saturday to the Court; I purchased on Saturday the 19th for the Accountant General £6894:11:4 at 70 per Cent.

*Mr. Gurney.* I have called for Lord Cochrane's Affidavit, it is admitted by my learned friends that notice has been given to produce it, and it is not produced.

*Mr. John Wright sworn.*

*Examined by Mr. Adolphus.*

*Q.* Where do you live?

*A.* At No. 5, Panton-square.

*Q.* Do you know where Lord Cochrane lives?

*A.* At No. 13, Green-street, Grosvenor-square.

*Q.* Had you occasion to see Lord Cochrane in February or March last?

*A.* Almost every day in February and in March last.

*Q.* In the course of that time did he deliver in a paper to you?

*A.* Yes he did.

*Q.* What was it?

*A.* He delivered several papers to me.

*Q.* What was done with that? (*shewing a paper to the witness.*)

*A.* Lord Cochrane brought me that affidavit for the purpose of getting it inserted in the newspapers.

*Q.* Did you do so?

*A.* I did, I got it printed in slips, and distributed a copy of it to each of the newspapers.

*Q.* Have you a copy of it?

*A.* I have not.

*Q.* Have you one of the slips?

*A.* No, I have not.

*Q.* Did you receive any other copies of affidavits purporting to be affidavits of persons of the name of Smith?

*A.* No, I had no concern whatever with Smith.

*Q.* Smith and his wife?

*A.* Certainly not, I know nothing of the printing of them.

*Q.* Was the Morning Chronicle one of the papers in which you put Lord Cochrane's affidavit?

*A.* Yes, it was.

*Mr. Park.* It must not be said to be Lord Cochrane's affidavit, till that is proved.

*Lord Ellenborough.* He printed something purporting to be Lord Cochrane's affidavit. I have taken it that Lord Cochrane delivered several papers, one purporting to be an affidavit which this witness inserted in the newspapers.

*Mr. Park.* But when once the expression is used by my learned friend, persons do not get rid of it again.

*Lord Ellenborough.* If he published it as an affidavit, it is quoad him an affidavit.

*Mr. Park.* To be sure, my Lord.

*Cross-examined by Mr. Serjeant Best.*

*Q.* You have said that he brought this paper to you, giving you directions to have it printed?

*A.* He wished it to be inserted in the newspapers.

*Q.* Tell us all that he said to you at the time; did he not at the time when he was giving you directions to print it, say, that if De Berenger was the man, he had given the Stock Exchange the clue to it?

*A.* After reading the affidavit, his Lordship said "I once saw Captain De Berenger at dinner."

*Lord Ellenborough.* Was this at the time?

*A.* Yes; he said "I once saw Captain De Berenger at Mr. Basil Cochrane's—I have no reason to think that Captain De Berenger is capable of so base a transaction, but if he is, I have given the gentlemen of the Stock Exchange the best clue to find him out."

*Lord Ellenborough.* Did he say what sort of clue he had given?

*A.* The clue as to De Berenger.

*Mr. Gurney.* By his affidavit?

*A.* Yes, that by that he had given them the best clue.

### Re-examined by Mr. Adolphus.

*Q.* When was it this affidavit was given to you?

*A.* I cannot state the day.

*Q.* Was it so late as March?

*A.* No, it must be about the 27th or 28th of February I think, but the newspaper will prove the date; it might be the first or second of March, I cannot speak to that.

*Q.* Was it not after the 11th of March?

*A.* I cannot state indeed.

*Q.* It was given to you the day before it appeared in the Morning Chronicle?

*A.* It was the day before, about three o'clock.

*Mr. Gurney.* Look at that (*shewing a pamphlet to the witness*) have you received one of those pamphlets either from Mr. Cochrane Johnstone, Lord Cochrane, or Mr. Butt?

*A.* Lord Cochrane gave me one of those at my own request, hearing it was published.

*Q.* Look at that which purports to be an affidavit of Lord Cochrane.

*Mr. Serjeant Best.* Is that the identical book Lord Cochrane gave you?

*A.* No.

*Mr. Gurney.* Read the affidavit and tell me whether you know that to be verbally and precisely the same?

*Mr. Serjeant Best.* I submit to your Lordship that will not do.

*Mr. Gurney.* Where is your copy of the pamphlet?

*A.* It is at home.

*Mr. Gurney.* Will your Lordship allow him to go home and fetch it.

*Lord Ellenborough.* Certainly.

*Mr. Malcolm Richardson called again.*

*Examined by Mr. Gurney.*

*Q.* You are a bookseller?

*A.* Yes.

*Q.* Were you employed by Mr. Butt to publish that pamphlet?

*A.* Not absolutely employed by him to publish it, but I sold it for him at his request, he wrote to me to know whether I would sell it for him.

*Lord Ellenborough.* This should be a publication by Lord Cochrane, to make the affidavit evidence against him.

*Mr. Gurney.* Certainly, my Lord, and if my learned friends wish it, I will wait till the witness comes back.

*Mr. Serjeant Best.* I have no wish to lay any impediment in the way, therefore if your Lordship thinks there is no impropriety in my permitting it to be read now, I will do it?

*Lord Ellenborough.* I leave it to your judgment, whether your resistance does you more good than the admission.

*Mr. Serjeant Best.* I will not resist it certainly. If I had the original I would deliver it up in a moment, but the fact is, we have not the original.

*The Affidavit was read as follows:*

"Having obtained leave of absence to come to town, in consequence of scandalous paragraphs in the public papers, and in consequence of having learnt that hand-bills had been affixed in the streets, in which (I have since seen) it is asserted that a person came to my house, at No. 13, Green-street, on the 21st day of February, in open day, and in the dress in which he had committed a fraud; I feel it due to myself to make the following deposition that the public may know the truth relative to the only person seen by me in military uniform, at my house, on that day.

COCHRANE."

March 11, 1814.
13, Green-street.

"I, Sir Thomas Cochrane, commonly called Lord Cochrane, having been appointed by the Lords Commissioners of the Admiralty, to active service (at the request, I believe, of Sir Alexander Cochrane) when I had no expectation of being called on, I obtained leave of absence to settle my private affairs previous to quitting this country, and chiefly with a view to lodge a specification to a patent relative to a discovery for increasing the intensity of light. That in pursuance of my daily practice of superintending work that was executing for me, and knowing that my uncle, Mr. Cochrane Johnstone, went to the city every morning in a coach.

"I do swear, on the morning of the 21st of February (which day was impressed on my mind by circumstances which afterwards occurred) I breakfasted with him at his residence in Cumberland-street, about half past eight o'clock, and I was put down by him (and Mr. Butt was in the coach) on Snow-hill, about ten o'clock; that I had been about three quarters of an hour at Mr. King's manufactory, at No. 1, Cock-lane, when I received a few lines on a small bit of paper, requesting me to come immediately to my house; the name affixed, from being written close to the bottom, I could not read. The servant told me it was from an army officer, and concluding that he might be an officer from Spain, and that some accident had befallen to my brother; I hastened back, and I found Captain Berenger, who, in great seeming uneasiness, made many apologies for the freedom he had used, which nothing but the distressed state of his mind, arising from difficulties, could have induced him to do. All his prospects, he said, had failed, and his last hope had vanished, of obtaining an appointment in America. He was unpleasantly circumstanced, on account of a sum which he could not pay, and if he could, that others would fall upon him for full £8000. He had no hope of benefiting his creditors in his present situation, or of assisting himself. That if I would take him with me he would immediately go on board and exercise the sharp-shooters, (which plan Sir Alexander Cochrane, I knew, had approved of.) That he had left his lodgings and prepared himself in the best way his means allowed. He had brought the sword with him which had been his fathers, and to that, and to Sir Alexander, he would trust for obtaining an honourable appointment. I felt very uneasy at the distress he was in, and knowing him to be a man of great talent and science, I told him I would do every thing in my power to relieve him; but as to his going immediately to the Tonnant, with any comfort to himself, it was quite impossible, my cabin was without furniture, I had not even a servant on board. He said he would willingly mess any where. I told him that the wardroom was already crowded, and besides I could not with propriety take him, he being a foreigner, without leave from the Admiralty. He seemed greatly hurt at this, and recalled to my recollection certificates which he had formerly shewn me, from persons in official situations. Lord Yarmouth, General Jenkinson, and Mr. Reeves, I think, were amongst the number. I recommended him to use his endeavour to get them, or any other friends, to exert their influence, for I had none, adding that when the Tonnant went to Portsmouth, I should be happy to receive him; and I knew from Sir Alexander Cochrane, that he would be pleased if he accomplished that object. Captain Berenger said, that not anticipating any objection on my part from the conversation he had formerly had with me, he had come away with intention to go on board and make himself useful in his military capacity;— he could not go to Lord Yarmouth, or to any other of his friends, in this dress, (alluding to that which he had on) or return to his lodgings where it would excite suspicion (as he was at that time in the rules of the King's Bench) but that if I refused to let him join the ship now, he would do so at Portsmouth. Under present circumstances, however, he must use a great liberty, and request the favour of me to lend him a hat to wear instead of his military cap. I gave him one which was in a back room with some things that had not been packed up, and having tried it on, his uniform appeared under his great coat; I therefore offered him a black coat that was laying on a chair, and which I did not intend to take with me. He put up his uniform in a towel, and shortly afterwards went away in great apparent uneasiness of mind; and having asked my leave, he took the coach I came in, and which I had forgotten to discharge in the haste I was in. I do further depose, that the above conversation is the substance of all that passed with Captain Berenger, which, from the circumstances attending it, was strongly impressed upon my mind, that no other person in uniform was seen by me, at my house, on Monday the 21st of February, though possibly other officers may have called (as many have done since my appointment;) of this, however, I cannot speak of my own knowledge, having been almost constantly from home, arranging my private affairs. I have understood that many persons have called under the above circumstances, and have written notes in the parlour, and others have waited there in expectation of seeing me, and then gone away, but I most positively swear that I never saw any person at my house resembling the description, and in the dress stated in the printed advertisement of the members of the Stock Exchange. I further aver that I had no concern, directly or indirectly, in the late imposition, and that the above is all that I know relative to any person who came to my house in uniform on the 21st day of February, before alluded to. Captain Berenger wore a grey great coat, a green uniform and a military cap. From the manner in which my character has been attempted to be defamed, it is indispensibly necessary to state that my connexion in any way with the funds, arose from an impression that in the present favourable aspect of affairs, it was only necessary to hold stock in order to become a gainer without prejudice to anybody; that I did so openly, considering it in no degree improper, far less dishonorable; that I had no secret information of any kind, and that had my expectation of the success of affairs been disappointed, I should have been the only sufferer. Further, I do most solemnly swear that the whole of the Omnium on account, which I possessed on the 21st day of February, 1814, amounted to £139,000 which I bought by Mr. Fearn (I think) on the 12th ultimo at a premium of 28-1/4, that I did not hold on that day any other sum on account in any other stock directly or indirectly, and that I had given orders when it was bought to dispose of it on a rise of one per cent, and it actually was sold on an average at 29-1/2 premium, though on the day of the fraud it might have been disposed of at 33-1/2. I further swear, that the above is the only stock which I sold of any kind on the 21st day of February, except £2000 in money which I had occasion for, the profit of which was about £10. Further, I do solemnly depose, that I had no connexion of dealing with any one, save the above mentioned, and that I did not at any time, directly or indirectly, by myself or by any other, take or procure any office or apartment for any broker or other person for the transaction of stock affairs."

"COCHRANE."

*Mr. James Le Marchant sworn.*

*Examined by Mr. Bolland.*

*Q.* Are you acquainted with Captain De Berenger?

*A.* I was so.

*Q.* When did your acquaintance with him commence?

*A.* About 18 months ago.

*Q.* How long did it continue?

*A.* It continued until the 16th of February to the best of my knowledge.

*Q.* Between those periods was Captain De Berenger in the habit of calling upon you frequently?

*A.* He was, from the 10th to the 16th of February.

*Q.* At what period of the day?

*A.* At different periods.

*Q.* Did he pass his evenings with you?

*A.* Occasionally.

*Q.* In conversations with him, did you ever collect from him, whether he had any connexion with Lord Cochrane or Mr. Cochrane Johnstone?

*A.* I did—with both.

*Q.* State to the Court what he has told you.

*A.* He stated that he was about to go to America under the command of Lord Cochrane; on his mentioning this, I put the question to him, how he possibly could do it under the embarrassments that he laid under, upon which he answered, all was settled on that score.

*Q.* Do you recollect upon what day this conversation passed?

*A.* I should think nearly about the 14th, to the best of my recollection, he said, that for the services he had rendered Lord Cochrane and Mr. Cochrane Johnstone, whereby his Lordship could realize a large sum or large sums of money by means of the funds or stocks, one of the words, that his Lordship was his friend, and had told him a few days before, that he had kept unknown to him till that period, a private purse for him De Berenger.

*Q.* Did he state to you whether there was any particular intimacy between him and Lord Cochrane, or Mr. Cochrane Johnstone?

*A.* He frequently mentioned particular intimacy of dining, breakfasting and supping with his Lordship. He said, in which purse he had placed or deposited a certain per centage out of the profits which his Lordship had made by his stock suggestions.

*Q.* Did you afterwards hear of the events of the 21st of February?

*A.* I did so.

*Q.* Did you upon that make known to any parties, and to whom, your suspicions of Captain De Berenger having been active in them?

*A.* I did so.

*Q.* To whom were those communications made?

*A.* To Captain Taylor of His Majesty's 22nd regiment of foot, and Lieutenant Wright in the Honorable East India Company's Service.

*Q.* Did you collect in any conversations you had with Captain De Berenger, that Lord Cochrane and Mr. Cochrane Johnstone consulted him in any transactions of Stock?

*Mr. Park.* That is a pretty good leading question.

*Mr. Bolland.* Did he state to you any thing respecting their consulting him as to stock transactions?

*A.* Most undoubtedly, or I should not have drawn the conclusions I did.

*Q.* For what was he to have a per centage?

*A.* For the ideas he had given to Lord Cochrane, enabling him to make a profit in the stocks.

*Q.* Did he extend that to Mr. Cochrane Johnstone, or Lord Cochrane?

*A.* To both.

*Mr. Serjeant Best.* I am aware that your Lordship will not consider this as evidence against Lord Cochrane, or Mr. Cochrane Johnstone.

*Lord Ellenborough.* No; it is admissible evidence, the effect of it is another thing.

*Cross-examined by Mr. Serjeant Best.*

*Q.* You have been corresponding with my Lord Cochrane.

*A.* I have so.

*Q.* You are now a prisoner in the King's Bench, I believe?

*A.* No; I am not.

*Q.* You have told my Lord Cochrane?——

*Mr. Bolland.* Have you ever had any communication with Lord Cochrane but in writing?

*A.* None individually.

*Mr. Bolland.* Then I object to any questions except as to letters.

*Mr. Serjeant Best.* You are a gentleman whose appointment Government have stopped?

*A.* It is not stopped.

*Q.* Suspended?

*A.* It is not suspended.

*Q.* You mean to state that upon your oath?

*A.* I state that I hold the situation of Secretary and Register to the Court of Antigua and Montserrat.

*Q.* You have not been prevented from going out?

*A.* In consequence of being compelled to give my evidence either at this court or some other court.

*Q.* And not on any other account?

*A.* Not that I know of.

*Q.* You know of no other reasons why Government have prevented your going out, but that you may be kept here as a Witness?

*A.* Yes.

*Q.* You mean to state that broadly?

*A.* Precisely.

*Q.* Is that your hand writing? (*shewing a letter to the Witness*)

*A.* It is.

*Q.* Just look at these; are these your hand writing? (*shewing other letters to the Witness.*)

*A.* That is not.

*Q.* That is Lord Cochrane's hand writing, is it not, you have got one in your pocket that is a copy of one that Lord Cochrane wrote to you in answer to one of your letters?

*A.* I will look at it. (*the Witness read the letter over.*) This is precisely the same as one I have in my pocket.

*Q.* You have got that letter about you?

*A.* I have.

*Q.* Have you not proposed to my Lord Cochrane to lend you money, and have you not told his Lordship that if he would not——

Mr. *Bolland.* My Lord, he says he has had no communication but in writing.

*A.* I have had no communication with Lord Cochrane but in writing.

Mr. *Serjeant Best.* Would you have given this evidence if you could have obtained a loan of money from Lord Cochrane?

*A.* Most undoubtedly; I must have been compelled to do it upon oath if brought forwards in a court of justice.

*Q.* I will not have a reasoning answer, but a direct answer, and that answer I will have taken down. Would you have given this evidence here if you could have obtained a loan of money from Lord Cochrane?

*A.* If my Lord Cochrane had not called me forwards, of course I should not have given an evidence, but he has compelled me.

*Q.* That will not do, I will put the question again; I want an answer, yes, or no, to this; would you have given this evidence if you could have obtained a loan of money from Lord Cochrane?

*A.* I hardly consider that question as fair; if his Lordship says it is I will answer it.

*Lord Ellenborough.* I rather think the terms of the question embrace some communications; he says he has had no communications about a loan in any way but in writing, and I think you cannot in that way travel indirectly to the contents of a letter; if the letter says any thing about a loan of money, you may give it in evidence.

*Mr. Serjeant Best.* Will your Lordship allow me to put it in this way. I have no right to ask the contents of any letter but with humble deference to your Lordship; I have a right to ask this man what passed in his own mind, for it does not yet appear that he put it upon paper; if the question had been what have you written to Lord Cochrane? that would have been objectionable, but surely I have a right to ask him what is passing in his own mind upon the subject, to know the motives from which this gentleman, of whom I shall speak by and by, comes to speak.

*Lord Ellenborough.* Do you give your evidence from resentment in consequence of having some loan refused to you?

*A.* None individually—none whatever.

*Mr. Bolland.* My Lord, I must object to my learned friend Mr. Serjeant Best getting the effect of a correspondence which was in writing.

*Lord Ellenborough.* He does not refer to it, but one cannot but be conscious after what has passed, that all that has ever passed about a loan has been in writing, therefore it would be the most ingenuous course to put it in.

*Serjeant Best.* I certainly mean to read this man's letters.

*Lord Ellenborough.* I asked him in the strongest manner possible, do you now give your evidence in resentment for having a loan, or any other benefit withheld from you? You may press that if you please.

*Mr. Serjeant Best.* I will put it in the way your Lordship suggests. Do you not now give your evidence in consequence of your being angry with Lord Cochrane for refusing to lend you money?

*A.* No. So help me God.

*Q.* Now take care. Do you know a gentlemen of the name of Palfreyman?

*A.* I have met him twice, I think, within this fortnight past.

*Q.* You have no resentment against Lord Cochrane whatever I understand you?

*A.* None whatever.

*Q.* You have never so expressed yourself to Mr. Palfreyman?

*A.* I am persuaded I never have.

*Q.* You never have told Mr. Palfreyman then that you would be his ruin?

*A.* Never.

*Q.* Nothing like that?

*A.* Never.

*Q.* That you would assist the Stock Exchange?

*A.* Never.

*Q.* Nothing of the sort?

*A.* I have already answered you.

*Q.* That will not do. Where did you come from now?

*A.* I came from the Gloucester Coffee House.

*Q.* I should have thought you had been in a coffee house, it is after dinner time I suppose. You are sure you never said any thing of the kind?

*A.* I have repeated it three or four times.

*Q.* You know this gentleman very well, Mr. Palfreyman?

*A.* A very slight acquaintance.

*Q.* Now I ask you another thing—Did you ever disclose this conversation with Mr. De Berenger till after Lord Cochrane refused you a loan?

*Lord Ellenborough.* If any application you made for a loan was in writing, you are not bound to answer that question.

*Mr. Serjeant Best.* My question was as to the time of the disclosure to the Stock Exchange, I will certainly read his letters; this does not touch me, but my learned friends of Counsel for De Berenger had not seen these letters. My question is, whether you ever disclosed the matter you have stated to day against De Berenger till after you were refused a loan by Lord Cochrane?

*Lord Ellenborough.* But if the proposition for loan was in writing, the letter must explain itself.

*Mr. Scarlett.* If we are not allowed to examine this witness as to his motives and his conduct as to these letters, I do not see how these letters could ever be made evidence.

*Lord Ellenborough.* You cannot examine him as to his motives, without producing the letters, that would be extracting the most unfair testimony in the world; I know nothing about the man, I never saw his face before to-day; but he, as a witness, has a right to the common protection of the law of the land, and not to have garbled questions put to him.

*Mr. Scarlett.* We do mean to read the letters.

*Lord Ellenborough.* And then you may call him back to ask him any questions upon them; but I would not have him answer without the letters being read.

*Mr. Brougham.* My learned friend merely referred to the letters as a date, not to the substance of the letters.

*Lord Ellenborough.* But he has said that he never had any communication with Lord Cochrane, but by letter, therefore the request for a loan, if any one was made, must have been by writing, and if he is to be questioned about that request in writing, he ought to have the terms of that request in writing read before the jury, so as to give a pointed answer to it.

*Mr. Brougham.* With great submission, my learned friend, did not ask as to the contents of the correspondence, but in point of date and time merely; he put this question, Was your information given to the Stock Exchange previously or subsequently to that correspondence, whatever the contents of that correspondence were?

*Lord Ellenborough.* I never heard that question put till this moment. Previous to some supposed correspondence, without stating the nature of that correspondence, was the information given by you to the Stock Exchange?

*A.* No, it was given by Lord Cochrane in his publication of the correspondence in the Morning Chronicle.

*Lord Ellenborough.* We cannot get on without the letters.

*Mr. Serjeant Best.* I have no objection to the letters being read now.

*Lord Ellenborough.* That would disturb the order of the proceedings.

*Cross examined by Mr. Richardson.*

*Q.* The conversation with Mr. De Berenger was about the 14th of February?

*A.* Yes it was.

*Q.* Have you not reason to know that about that time he had expectations of getting some employment in America?

*A.* He mentioned it to me himself.

*Q.* To serve under Sir Alexander Cochrane who had a command?

*A.* To serve under Lord Cochrane as I understood.

*Q.* He expressed his anxious desire and wish to be so employed?

*A.* Particularly so.

*Q.* He expressed a hope that he might make himself useful to the cause, by drilling the sharp shooters, and other things of that sort?

*A.* That was what he represented.

*Q.* Did you not know that he had had experience as a volunteer officer in a particular department?

*A.* I had a very high opinion of him as being acquainted with that science.

*Q.* He had been a Captain for a considerable number of years in the Duke of Cumberland's Corps of Sharp Shooters?

*A.* Adjutant I understand.

*Q.* You considered him as a man of science and skill in that department?

*A.* I did.

*Q.* Do you not know that he was making preparations at that time in order to go to America if he should be successful in procuring the appointment he was soliciting?

*A.* Not making preparations, those I know nothing of.

*Q.* That it was his anxious wish and desire to go you heard from him?

*A.* Yes.

Re-examined by Mr. Bolland.

*Q.* Did the Stock Exchange apply to you, or did you go to them to give information.

*A.* The Stock Exchange applied to me and sent me a subpœna.

*Q.* Was the application made to you after Lord Cochrane's publication, or before?

*A.* After Lord Cochrane's publication. The information that I gave to the two gentlemen, Captain Taylor and Lieutenant Wright was prior to Lord Cochrane's affidavit, or its ever being mentioned in my hearing that Mr. De Berenger was implicated in this business.

*The Honorable Alexander Murray sworn.*

*Examined by Mr. Bolland.*

*Q.* You are in His Majesty's service as an officer?

*A.* Not at present.

*Q.* I believe you have the misfortune at present to be in the King's Bench.

*A.* I am.

*Q.* In the rules?

*A.* In the inside.

*Q.* Are you acquainted with Captain De Berenger, and how long have you been so.

*A.* About a year and a half I have been.

*Q.* Who introduced you to Captain De Berenger?

*A.* Mr. Tahourdin, who was my solicitor, and likewise the solicitor of Mr. De Berenger.

*Q.* In consequence of that introduction did a considerable intimacy take place between you and the captain?

*A.* There did.

*Q.* Were you frequently together?

*A.* Very frequently; when I first went over to the rules of the Bench, I lodged with Mr. De Berenger in the same house for about one month, till I took a house of my own.

*Q.* Had you at any time any conversation with Captain De Berenger previous to the 21st of February with respect to Lord Cochrane and Mr. Cochrane Johnstone?

*A.* Towards the end of January I think, or perhaps the beginning of February.

*Q.* What was the substance of these conversations?

*A.* It happened one Sunday between one and two o'clock, Mr. Harrison called upon me, and we were conversing about a pamphlet he was writing.

*Q.* That Mr. Harrison was writing?

*A.* Yes; it was relative to the trial between Mr. Basil Cochrane and Mr. Harrison.

*Q.* That impressed the day upon your recollection?

*A.* Yes.

*Q.* Did Captain De Berenger come in that day?

*A.* Yes; he came in during the conversation and joined in it.

*Q.* Did any thing pass from Captain De Berenger on that day respecting Mr. Cochrane Johnstone and Lord Cochrane?

*A.* I at that time knew he was employed by Mr. Cochrane Johnstone.

*Q.* From whom did you understand that?

*A.* From Mr. De Berenger himself, that he was employed by Mr. Cochrane Johnstone in planning out a small piece of ground behind his house in Alsop's Buildings.

*Q.* What passed at that time about Mr. Cochrane Johnstone?

*A.* He mentioned that there was a transaction going on.

*Q.* Does the circumstance of the pamphlet bring back to your recollection what Sunday it was?

*A.* I cannot state the day of the month, but it was towards the end of January or the beginning of February.

*Q.* State what Mr. De Berenger then said?

*A.* He said that they had a plan in view——

*A.* Who had?

*A.* That De Berenger had, with Mr. Cochrane Johnstone and Lord Cochrane, that provided it succeeded, it would put many thousand pounds in the pocket of Mr. Cochrane Johnstone and Lord Cochrane.

*Q.* Upon hearing this, did either you or Mr. Harrison ask Captain De Berenger what the plan was?

*A.* I did, and he declined answering it; I said, "is it the plan with regard to Ranelagh which it was proposed to build in Alsop's Buildings, on Mr. Cochrane Johnstone's land," and he said "no, it is not, it is a far better plan."

*Q.* Did you collect from Mr. De Berenger's conversation with you, whether there was any particular intimacy between him and Mr. Cochrane Johnstone and Lord Cochrane?

*A.* I knew there was a very particular intimacy between him and Mr. Cochrane Johnstone, but I did not understand it was with Lord Cochrane at all; I understood he was a more recent acquaintance.

*Q.* From what did you collect that; what did Mr. De Berenger say to you that induced you to believe he was intimate with Mr. Cochrane Johnstone?

*A.* He was constantly with him; he was there almost every day.

*Q.* You say that his acquaintance with Lord Cochrane was recent?

*A.* I do.

*Q.* When you understood him to be acquainted with Lord Cochrane, did he state any thing with regard to his visits to Lord Cochrane?

*A.* He did not.

*Cross-examined by Mr. Park.*

*Q.* You have known Mr. De Berenger a great while?

*A.* Yes, I have.

*Q.* He is a man of very considerable science and attainment I am told?

*A.* Very much so.

*Q.* I believe you happen to know that he was at that time, or had been about that time engaged in some plan of Mr. Johnstone's about building a place called Vittoria, in consequence of the great victories?

*A.* It was to be called Ranelagh I understood, I never heard of the name Vittoria.

*Q.* He had been engaged for a considerable time before in drawing a plan?

*A.* He had, which I had seen.

*Q.* And that led him, as you understood, to be very much with Mr. Cochrane Johnstone?

*A.* It did.

*Q.* Alsop's Buildings is somewhere near Mr. Cochrane Johnstone's house?

*A.* Mr. Cochrane Johnstone has a house there, and this is the ground immediately behind it, about an acre, which is in garden ground, and which was to be converted to that use.

*Q.* Something upon the plan of the old Ranelagh?

*A.* Something upon an improved plan of Mr. De Berenger's.

*Q.* You have seen the plan you say, which Mr. De Berenger drew for Mr. Cochrane Johnstone?

*A.* Yes.

*Q.* How long ago is that?

*A.* I cannot exactly say how long ago it was.

*Q.* Was it before this conversation a good while?

*A.* Before this conversation; when I was in the habit of calling upon him.

*Q.* About the close of the last year probably?

*A.* About that time, I cannot exactly say.

*Q.* Was it not a very beautiful plan that he had drawn for this Ranelagh?

*A.* It was.

*Q.* It required, from the nature of it, a considerable deal of time and labour?

*A.* It did certainly.

*Q.* Do you know whether Mr. De Berenger was very much employed in plans of that kind for the Royal Family and others?

*A.* He was.

*Lord Ellenborough.* If you see any tendency to the advantage of your client, I will not interrupt you, but at present this seems to have no bearing.

*Mr. Park.* I assure your Lordship, and I know I shall have credit for believing what I state, I would not at this hour of the night pursue it if it was not important, but I feel it necessary when it is stated that there has been a wonderful intimacy, from which, conspiracy is sought to be inferred.

*Lord Ellenborough.* I will not ask you to go into your reasons, if you only say you think it material.

*Mr. Park.* As far as you have seen Mr. De Berenger, for the length of time you have described, do you not believe him to be a man of honor and integrity?

*A.* I certainly do from every thing I have seen; I saw nothing but the most perfect gentleman during the time I lodged under the same roof.

*William Carling sworn.*

*Examined by Mr. Adolphus.*

*Q.* Whose servant are you?

*A.* The Honorable Basil Cochrane's.

*Q.* Are you in his service still?

*A.* Yes.

*Q.* Did Mr. Cochrane Johnstone and my Lord Cochrane visit at your master's house?

*A.* Yes.

*Q.* Have you ever seen them there in company with Captain De Berenger?

*A.* Yes; Baron De Berenger is the name I have given in.

*Q.* The gentleman who sits there now?

*A.* Yes.

*Q.* Did he come there once, or oftener, within your memory?

*A.* Twice.

*Q.* Who brought him?

*A.* I do not know that any body brought him in particular, he came to dine there as a visitor.

*Q.* With whom?

*A.* Not with any body in particular; invited by the Honorable Basil Cochrane.

*Q.* Was that upon days when Mr. Cochrane Johnstone and Lord Cochrane were there?

*A.* Mr. Cochrane Johnstone and Lord Cochrane dined there once; Lord Cochrane did not the second time?

*Q.* As far as you could observe, did Lord Cochrane and Mr. Cochrane Johnstone appear to be acquainted with the Baron De Berenger, or to be then first introduced to him?

*A.* They appeared to be acquainted with him.

*Cross-examined by Mr. Topping.*

*Q.* Can you tell us what time this was?

*A.* In January the first time, and the next in February, but I cannot say what day.

*Q.* You live with Mr. Basil Cochrane?

*A.* Yes.

*Q.* He is related to Lord Cochrane?

*A.* Yes, he is uncle to Lord Cochrane.

*Q.* And Mr. Basil Cochrane having a dinner party, Baron De Berenger was one of the party, and Lord Cochrane another?

*A.* Yes.

*Q.* And Mr. Cochrane Johnstone another?

*A.* Yes.

*Q.* Did the dinner party consist of any other?

*A.* Yes, the first time, Admiral Cochrane (Sir Alexander), his lady, and some more ladies and gentlemen.

*Q.* Was that the day Lord Cochrane dined there?

*A.* Yes, it was.

*Q.* Then upon another occasion, Mr. Basil Cochrane having a diner party, Mr. Cochrane Johnstone formed one of the party, and Baron De Berenger another?

*A.* Yes.

*Q.* Was there an indiscriminate mixture of ladies and gentlemen again then?

*A.* Yes.

*Q.* And Lord Cochrane was not there?

*A.* He was not.

*Q.* You have been asked whether Baron De Berenger and Lord Cochrane and Mr. Cochrane Johnstone appeared to be acquainted—did Baron De Berenger appear to be acquainted with Admiral Cochrane?

*A.* I cannot say.

*Q.* You were merely a servant attending at table?

*A.* Yes.

### Cross-examined by Mr. Richardson.

*Q.* From the conversation that passed, did you understand whether Baron De Berenger was going to America to serve under Admiral Cochrane.

*A.* I did not.

### Mr. Barnard Broochooft sworn.

### Examined by Mr. Bolland.

*Q.* You are Deputy Marshal of the King's Bench?

*A.* I am clerk to the Marshal of the King's Bench.

*Q.* Do you know Baron De Berenger?

*A.* Yes.

*Q.* Was he, during the latter end of the last year, and the beginning of the present, a prisoner in the King's Bench?

*A.* Yes.

*Q.* How long had he been confined there?

*A.* I think from the latter end of the year 1812.

*Q.* Till what time?

*A.* I am not prepared to state the day but till within about six weeks.

*Q.* Have you the book of rules here?

*A.* I have not.

*Q.* Did you miss him at any time?

*A.* Yes some months.

*Mr. Park.* I waive the objection to your asking your questions, so far as I am concerned for Mr. De Berenger.

*Mr. Bolland.* Who were the securities for Mr. De Berenger?

*A.* Mr. Cochrane, a bookseller, in Fleet-street, and Mr. Tahourdin, the attorney.

*Q.* You made search for him and could not find him?

*A.* Yes.

*Cross-examined by Mr. Serjeant Best.*

*Q.* That Cochrane was not at all connected with the Dundonald family?

*A.* I asked the question, and I understood not.

*Cross-examined by Mr. Park.*

*Q.* Mr. Cochrane is partner in the house of Mr. White, of Fleet-street?

*A.* Yes.

*Q.* I believe you saw Mr. De Berenger on the morning of the 21st very early, did not you?

*A.* No.

*Q.* Recollect yourself, because I understand you did see him that morning?

*A.* I cannot recollect having seen Mr. De Berenger for a very great length of time, and I think long previous to that?

*Q.* I have reason to put the question, or I should not to you, not doubting the veracity of your answer; recollect whether you did not see him near the King's Bench Prison, very early on that morning?

*A.* I have nothing by which I can charge my recollection.

*Q.* The security was given a considerable time ago for the rules?

*A.* A very considerable time ago, nearly two years ago I should think.

*Q.* It was not for a very large sum?

*A.* Under £400. I think.

*Q.* You will excuse my asking, but the security is generally nearly commensurate with the debt?

*A.* They generally do take it for the amount as nearly as possible, calculating the costs.

*Q.* More than the debt then?

*A.* Yes.

*Mr. Bolland.* Was Mr. Ralph Sandom a prisoner in the King's Bench Prison?

*A.* Twice he has been a prisoner.

*Q.* Was he on the 21st of February?

*A.* I have not the books, and cannot state that.

*Mr. Joseph Wood sworn.*

*Examined by Mr. Gurney.*

*Q.* Are you a Messenger of the Alien Office?

*A.* I am.

*Q.* Did you on the 3d or 4th of April leave London in order to apprehend De Berenger?

*A.* I did on the 4th.

*Q.* Had you a warrant of the Secretary of State?

*A.* I had.

*Q.* How long had you had it in your possession?

*A.* Ever since the 17th of March.

*Q.* Where did you find him?

*A.* At Leith.

*Q.* On what day?

*A.* On the 8th of April.

*Q.* Did you find him in possession of any writing desk?

*A.* Of this one. (*producing a portable desk*).

*Q.* Did that writing desk contain papers and bank notes?

*A.* Yes.

*Q.* Before you parted with any of those papers or bank notes did you mark them?

*A.* Yes I did.

*Q.* When did you mark them?

*A.* I marked them before the Grand Jury the day of the bill being found.

*Q.* Have they been in your possession from the day you marked them?

*A.* They have from the hour I took Mr. De Berenger.

*Q.* Were there any pieces of coin in the writing desk also?

*A.* There were guineas and half guineas, and in the pocket book there were two Napoleons. (*the witness opened the desk.*)

*Q.* The bank notes are in parcels I believe?

*A.* Yes they are.

*Q.* Give me the packet with the 67.

*They were handed in.*

*Mr. Gurney.* I believe it will be more clear if I do not open them now till I have proved them?

*A.* Here are two packets, and a pocket book containing a fifty pound note and four five pound notes, the Napoleons are in the pocket book.

*Q.* There is a memorandum book also and a paper of memorandums?

*A.* There are.

*The Witness delivered them in.*

*Q.* There is a road book besides?

*A.* Yes there is.

*Mr. Park.* There are some papers of which I have heard no proof; there is a paper, in which it is stated there is some pencil mark, I have heard no proof of any pencil mark, or any writing; it is not evidence because it is in his pocket-book because one has many things in a pocket-book which are not in one's hand-writing.

*Mr. Gurney.* This is the writing.

*Mr. Park.* I shall not look at it; I do not know his hand-writing.

*Mr. Gurney.* Mr. Jones, I will trouble you to read the first article in that memorandum-book.

*Mr. Park.* That cannot be done.

*Mr. Gurney.* It is found in his letter-case.

*Mr. Park.* I object till his hand-writing is proved; the finding a manuscript in my possession, is not sufficient to warrant its being read as evidence against me; your Lordship might confide some paper to me, and it would be very hard to read that against me.

*Lord Ellenborough.* It is *prima facie* evidence I think, subject to any observations you make upon it.

*Mr. Park.* It is found in that thing, not in his pocket.

*Lord Ellenborough.* (*to Wood*) Was it under his lock?

*A.* It was in his possession when I took him.

*Mr. Park.* Am I to be answerable for all manner of things sent to me by my friends?

*Lord Ellenborough.* I think a paper found under the lock and key of the party, is *prima facie*, readable against him; it is subject to observations. If you do not go further, the reading this as found in his possession, is doing little.

*Mr. Gurney. (to Mr. Lavie)* Do you believe that to be Mr. De Berenger's writing?

*A.* I have no doubt about it.

*Mr. Park.* Is it in pencil or ink?

*A.* In ink.

*Mr. Serjeant Best.* That cannot be evidence against the Cochranes.

*Lord Ellenborough.* No, if it was transmitted by him in writing to the others, it would be evidence against them; but it purports to be only a memorandum of his own.

*Mr. Gurney.* Certainly not, my Lord.

*The Extract was read as follows:*

"To C. I. by March 1st 1814, £350—£4 to 5000—assign one share of patent and £1000 worth shares of Jn. De Beaufain at Messrs. H. to their care.—Believe from my informant £18,000 instead of £4800—suspicious that Mr. B. does not account correctly to him as well as me. Determined not to be duped. No restrictions as to secresy—requesting early answer."

*Mr. Gurney.* That is all I wish to read.

*Mr. Park.* I never heard a word of this.

*Mr. Gurney.* Very likely not.

*Cross-examined by Mr. Richardson.*

*Q.* Did you carry this box of papers before the Grand Jury?

*A.* Yes I did, the writing desk.

*Q.* By whose orders was that done?

*A.* By orders of the Secretary of State, of Mr. Beckett; I was subpœnaed to bring it before the Grand Jury, and I carried the subpœna to take directions from Mr. Beckett the Under Secretary of State.

*Q.* You received Mr. Beckett's orders to do it?

*A.* With the subpœna I told Mr. Beckett I had received an order to take it before the Grand Jury, and I did so.

*Mr. Park.* There are no subpœnas for the Grand Jury.

*Mr. Gurney.* There are indeed, Crown Office subpœnas.

*Mr. Richardson.* By whose order were the seals put on at Edinburgh taken off?

*A.* By order of Mr. Beckett.

*Q.* That was before you went before the Grand Jury?

*A.* Yes.

*Q.* Has the box remained in your possession ever since you took it at Edinburgh?

*A.* Yes, ever since when I went a journey to Holland; in my absence Mr. Tahourdin wished to see it, and Mr. Musgrave opened it for him.

*Q.* Except the time you took a journey to Holland it has been in your possession?

*A.* Yes.

*Q.* Had the seals been opened before that time, before you went to Holland?

*A.* They had.

*Q.* In whose possession was it during the time of your absence?

*A.* Mr. Musgrave's, and he delivered it up to me again.

*Q.* Who is Mr. Musgrave?

*A.* One of the clerks in the Office.

*Q.* How long were you absent?

*A.* A week or ten days.

*Q.* Has it been in your possession ever since your return?

*A.* Yes, it has.

*Q.* Were you present all the time it was before the Grand Jury?

*A.* I was; I left it on the Grand Jury table when I went out, but I locked it, and I had the key.

*Q.* With all its contents locked up in it?

*A.* Yes.

*Q.* Were you present when Mr. Wakefield of the Stock Exchange, and Mr. Lavie called, I think on the very day that Mr. De Berenger arrived in London?

*A.* I was.

*Q.* Was that at your house?

*A.* No it was not.

*Q.* Where was it?

*A.* At the Parliament Street Coffee House.

*Q.* That was the place you carried him to first?

*A.* No, first to the Secretary of State's Office, and afterwards to the Parliament Street Coffee House.

*Q.* The day of your arrival those Gentlemen came there?

*A.* They were there.

*Q.* Mr. Wakefield and some other Gentleman?

*A.* Mr. Wakefield and another Gentleman.

*Q.* Who was the other Gentleman?

*A.* I do not exactly recollect.

*Q.* Was it not stated to him by those Gentlemen that they did not wish to press him if he would furnish information against Lord Cochrane, Mr. Cochrane Johnstone, and Mr. Butt?

*A.* I do not recollect hearing those names mentioned.

*Q.* Against the other Gentlemen?

*A.* No, I do not recollect hearing that.

*Q.* Did they not state that what they wanted was information from him to fix the guilt upon others?

*A.* Not to my recollection.

*Q.* Or any thing to that effect?

*A.* I do not recollect any thing of the kind, I did not exactly listen to the conversation.

*Q.* He was in your custody, and you in the room all the time?

*A.* Not exactly; I was there the greatest part of the time.

*Q.* Be so kind as to recollect yourself, it was only in the month of April last that this happened, many circumstances have called this to your recollection since; what was the conversation that passed; what did they state to him as to his furnishing information?

*A.* There were some gentlemen wanted to speak to Mr. De Berenger; Mr. Wakefield went very close to Mr. De Berenger, and I declare to you upon my oath I do not recollect any particular words.

*Q.* The substance is all I want?

*A.* I really do not recollect the substance.

*Q.* Was any thing said as to his furnishing information: recollect, that you are to tell the whole truth upon your oath, as far as you recollect it; what was said upon that subject, as far as you can recollect?

*A.* Mr. Wakefield did say something to him, but I really do not recollect.

*Q.* Was it to that effect?

*A.* Mr. Wakefield put some questions to Mr. De Berenger respecting this business, the Stock Exchange business; but the exact conversation, which I did not listen to, I cannot say.

*Q.* Respecting the other persons supposed to be concerned, was not that the effect of it?

*A.* Something to that effect I think, but I did not listen to the conversation.

*Lord Ellenborough.* What is the effect? only something about other persons, that is no effect.

*Mr. Richardson.* What was the effect of it?

*A.* Mr. Wakefield put some questions respecting the Stock Exchange, I did not attend exactly to what it was.

*Lord Ellenborough.* You had better call Mr. Wakefield, who put the questions, than he who did not hear what passed.

*Mr. Park.* We cannot call Mr. Wakefield; he is one of the Prosecutors, he is one of the Stock Exchange.

*Lord Ellenborough.* I know nothing about Mr. Wakefield; as long as the question is sperate I am willing to hear it put, but it has been put ten times and the same answer returned.

*Mr. Richardson.* Did you hear names mentioned?

*A.* I did not.

*Q.* Did you hear them tell him, that their wish was that he should furnish information, to bring home the guilt to others?

*A.* I remember the word information, and that is all I recollect.

*Q.* That they wanted information?

*A.* That is all I recollect.

*Q.* Before this conversation took place, did not Mr. De Berenger say that he wished to be attended by Counsel, if they wished to converse with him?

*A.* Mr. De Berenger did answer something, but I cannot state what it was; I did not attend to the conversation.

*Q.* Before these Gentlemen were introduced by you to him, did he not say that he was exhausted by his journey, and unwilling to see them, unless he could have some person present?

*A.* He did; he said he was very unwell, and exhausted by his journey.

*Q.* And desired not to see them, unless some person was present with them?

*A.* Yes, I think he did say something of that kind, that he was very faint with his journey.

*Q.* But nevertheless you introduced them to him that evening?

*A.* They were in the room with him, they came into the room with him; that was at the time that Mr. Wakefield was in the room, I believe.

*Mr. Park.* That he was very unwell, and would not answer unless some person was with him?

*Lord Ellenborough.* Did he say that he was unwilling to answer, without having some friend present?

*A.* I do not recollect that; but he said he was very unwell, and exhausted with the journey.

*Mr. Park.* Nevertheless a long conversation did take place, did it?

*A.* I believe Mr. Wakefield was there about ten minutes or a quarter of an hour, not more than that.

*Re-examined by Mr. Gurney.*

*Q.* Did you put your marks upon these things before you went to Holland?

*A.* Yes, I did.

*Mr. Joseph Fearn called again;*

*Examined by Mr. Gurney.*

*Q.* Be so good as to look at that check dated the 10th of February 1814 [*shewing it to the Witness*] did you give that check to Mr. Butt?

*A.* I did on the day of its date, the 10th of February.

*Mr. Joseph Brumfield sworn;*

*Examined by Mr. Gurney.*

*Q.* Are you the clerk that paid the check on the 10th of February?

*A.* I am not.

*Q.* Is Mr. Evans here?

*A.* I believe not; I have not seen him.

*Mr. William Smallbone called again;*

*Examined by Mr. Gurney.*

*Q.* On the 19th of February 1814, did you draw that check [*shewing it to the Witness*]?

*A.* Yes.

*Q.* For whom?

*A.* For Lord Cochrane.

*Q.* Did you give it to Lord Cochrane?

*A.* I did.

*Q.* For Lord Cochrane?

*A.* Yes.

*Q.* To pay for gains upon the stock account?

*A.* Not gains exactly, but upon the stock account.

*Q.* To whom personally did you give it?

*A.* To Lord Cochrane.

### Cross examined by Mr. Serjeant Best.

*Q.* Was Mr. Butt in the office at the time?

*A.* Yes, I think he was.

*Q.* Do you recollect whether you gave it into the hands of Lord Cochrane or Mr. Butt?

*A.* I think into the hand of Lord Cochrane; I feel satisfied in my mind that I gave it to Lord Cochrane and not to Mr. Butt.

*Q.* If you gave it to Lord Cochrane, did you see Lord Cochrane hand it over to Mr. Butt?

*A.* No, I cannot say that I did.

*Q.* Have you no recollection one way or the other?

*A.* No.

*Q.* Nor is your recollection very distinct whether you gave it to one or the other?

*A.* I have no reason to think I gave it to Mr. Butt.

*Q.* Mr. Butt frequently acted for Lord Cochrane?

*A.* Not with me.

*Lord Ellenborough.* Do you believe you gave it to Lord Cochrane?

*A.* I do, but I am not certain whether I laid it before him upon the table, or gave it into his hand.

*Lord Ellenborough.* You presented it to him, and gave it into his reach, so that he might take it?

*A.* Yes.

*A Juryman.* You charged him with it in account?

*A.* Yes, I did.

[*The check on Messrs. Jones, Loyd & Company, dated the 10th of February 1814, for the sum of £.470. 19s. 4d. was read.*]

*Edward Wharmby sworn;*

*Examined by Mr. Gurney.*

*Q.* Are you clerk to Jones, Loyd & Company?

*A.* Yes.

*Q.* Look at that check [*handing it to the Witness*] did you pay that check?

*A.* Yes, I did.

*Q.* On what day?

*A.* On the 19th of February.

*Q.* In what Bank notes did you pay it?

*A.* In one of £.200.

*Mr. Serjeant Best.* From what are you speaking.

*A.* I have a copy of the notes.

*Q.* Is the book here?

*A.* No.

*Mr. Gurney.* You were directed to bring the books with you,—you must go and fetch them.

*Benjamin Lance sworn;*

*Examined by Mr. Gurney.*

*Q.* On the 26th of February did you give that check to Mr. Butt?

*A.* Yes, I did. [*The check was handed in.*]

*Mr. Gurney.* Perhaps, my Lord, I had better wait till the witness brings the books; I am extremely sorry for the loss of time?

*Lord Ellenborough.* It will be more clear.

*Mr. Gurney.* I have a little more evidence to give under this head, if your Lordship will allow me to give that now, the letter which I opened, offering Mr. M'Rae's discovery.

*Mr. Joseph Fearn called again;*

*Examined by Mr. Gurney.*

*Q.* Look at that letter, [*shewing a letter to the witness,*] do you believe that to be Mr. Cochrane Johnstone's hand-writing?

*A.* I do.

*Q.* Do you believe that also to be Mr. Cochrane Johnstone's hand-writing?

*A.* Yes, I believe that also to be the same that is dated the 18th of April.

[*The letters were delivered in, and read as follow:*]

"To the Chairman of the Committee,
"Stock Exchange, No. 18, Great Cumberland-street, 12th April 1814.

"Sir,

"I have this moment received a letter, of which the enclosed is a copy, and lose no time in transmitting it to you for the information of the gentlemen composing the Stock Exchange Committee; from the bearer of the letter, I am given to understand, that Mr. M'Rae, is willing to disclose the names of the Principals concerned in the late hoax, on being paid the sum of £.10,000. to be deposited in some banker's hands, in the names of two persons, to be nominated by himself, and to be paid to him on the conviction of the offenders.

I am happy to say, that there seems now a reasonable prospect of discovering the authors of the late hoax, and I cannot evince my anxious wish to promote such discovery, more than by assuring you that I am ready to contribute liberally towards the above sum of 10,000*l.* and I rest assured, that you will eagerly avail yourselves of this opportunity, to effect the proposed discovery (an object you profess to have so much at heart) by concurring with me in such contribution.

I have the honour to be, Sir,
Your obedient humble servant,
(Signed) *A. Cochrane Johnstone.*"

[*The inclosure was read as follows:*]

"April 12th.

"Sir,

"I authorize the bearer of this note, to state to you that I am prepared to lay before the Public, the names of the persons who planned and carried into effect the late hoax, practised at the Stock Exchange the 21st of February, provided you accede to the terms which my friend will lay before you.

> I am, Sir,
> Your obedient Servant,
> *A. M'Rae.*"

To the honourable,
Cochrane Johnstone.

> "No. 18, Great Cumberland-street,
> 18th April 1814.

"Sir,

"I have to request, that you will be so good as to inform me what are the intentions of the Stock Exchange, on the subject of the letter which I addressed to you relative to the proposal of Mr. M'Rae.

Lord Cochrane, Mr. Butt, and myself, are willing to subscribe 1,000*l.* each, in aid of the 10,000*l.* required by Mr. M'Rae; the bearer waits your answer, which, to prevent any mistake, I hope you will find time to commit to writing.

> I am, Sir,
> Your obedient servant,
> *A. Cochrane Johnstone.*"

To Mr. Charles Laurence,
Chairman of the Committee
of the Stock Exchange.

[*Mr. Gurney to Mr. Fearn.*]

*Q.* Look at the address of that letter [*shewing a letter to the witness*] is that address Mr. Cochrane Johnstone's hand-writing?

*A.* I believe it to be so.

[*The letter was read as follows.*]

"To the Committee of the Stock Exchange.

> No. 18, Great Cumberland-street,
> 14 March 1814.

As the report of the Stock Exchange Committee conveys an idea to the public, that they estimated delinquency by the enormous profits which accrued to Lord Cochrane, Mr. Butt, and myself, on the sale of Stock upon the 21st day of February, and as the public prints have estimated the gains, some at 100,000*l.* others at 75,000*l.* and none under 30,000*l.* I pledge myself to prove that the whole profits are as follow; viz.

| Lord Cochrane | £.1,700. |
|---|---|
| Mr. Butt | 1,300. |
| Mr. Cochrane Johnstone | 3,500. |

If the Committee had acted impartially, they would have published a statement of all the purchases and sales effected by every broker on that day, with the names of the parties, that the Public might have drawn their conclusions. To obviate this omission on the part of the Committee, I am preparing for the press a correct statement of all sums bought for the parties before-mentioned, together with the names of those from whom the Stock was procured, and to whom sold; whereby it will be seen, who were the purchasers at an early hour on the 21st day of February.

*A. Cochrane Johnstone.*

Charles Laurence, Esq.
Chairman of the Committee of the Stock Exchange.

*Mr. Gurney.* I apply that to the memorandum I before read, by which it appears that he states his own gains and Mr. Butt's to be £.4,800. subtracting Lord Cochrane's; the whole is £.6,500.

*Edward Wharmby called again;*

*Examined by Mr. Gurney.*

*Q.* On what day in February did you pay that check? [*shewing it to the witness.*]

*A.* The 19th of February.

*Mr. Serjeant Best.* Is that entry in the book your own hand-writing?

*A.* It is.

*Mr. Gurney.* In what Bank notes did you pay it?

*A.* In one of two hundred pounds, No. 634.

*Q.* What other notes?

*A.* Two, of one hundred pounds each.

*Q.* What are the numbers?

*A.* 18,468 is one of them, and the other 16,601.

*Q.* Was there a £.50.?

*A.* Yes, No. 7,375.

*Mr. Gurney.* It is not necessary to mention the other, because I do not trace it.

*Cross-examined by Mr. Serjeant Best.*

*Q.* You do not know to whom you paid that?

*A.* No, I do not.

*Lord Ellenborough.* You paid it to the bearer of that check for £.470, in discharge of that check?

*A.* Yes, I did.

*Mr. Thomas Parker sworn;*

*Examined by Mr. Gurney.*

*Q.* You are a coal-merchant?

*A.* Yes.

*Q.* Does Lord Cochrane deal with you?

*A.* He did.

*Q.* Did you receive from him in payment a bank note of fifty pounds.

*A.* To the best of my recollection I did.

*Q.* On what day?

*A.* I do not exactly know the day; but some time in the beginning of March I think, or probably in the end of February.

*A Bank Clerk produced the £.50. note No. 7,375.*

*Q.* Did Lord Cochrane make that payment to you in that bank note?

*A.* Yes, I believe he did.

*Mr. Serjeant Best.* Is that your own memorandum?

*A.* Yes; I write on the back of the notes, and that is my hand-writing.

*Benjamin Lance called again;*

*Examined by Mr. Gurney.*

*Q.* On the 24th of February, did you go to the Bank to exchange any bank notes for smaller notes?

*A.* I did.

*Q.* By whose desire did you go?

*A.* Mr. Butt's.

*Q.* Are those the two notes you received from him to exchange? [*shewing the witness the two notes for £.100. each, produced by the bank clerk.*]

*A.* They are.

*Lord Ellenborough.* Have you seen those £.100. notes, which you carried to the Bank to exchange for smaller notes?

*A.* I have this moment.

*Mr. Gurney.* What did you receive in exchange for them?

*A.* I received two hundred notes for one pound each.

*Q.* What did you do with those notes?

*A.* I gave them to Mr. Butt.

### Cross-examined by Mr. Scarlett.

*Q.* Have you any connexion with Mr. Smallbone.

*A.* Yes, I am with Mr. Smallbone.

*Q.* Do you remember at any time, on the 15th of February, Mr. Butt lending Lord Cochrane two hundred pounds, in order to make up a sum that he had to pay?

*A.* Yes.

*Q.* On the 15th of February?

*A.* Yes, it might be on the 15th of February.

*Q.* Do you remember going with that check [*shewing it to the witness*] which was afterwards given by Mr. Smallbone, to get the money?

*A.* Yes, that check for £.470. 19*s.* 4*d.*

*Q.* That bears date the 19th of February?

*A.* Yes.

*Q.* You were the person who took that to the banker's, to get the money for it?

*A.* Exactly so.

*Q.* You say you know Mr. Butt did lend Lord Cochrane two hundred pounds?

*A.* So I understood; I did not see him lend it.

*Mr. Gurney.* He does not know that it was lent?

*Mr. Scarlett.* How do you know that it was lent?

*A.* Only by Mr. Butt saying so.

*Lord Ellenborough.* At what time?

*A.* The 15th of February.

*Lord Ellenborough.* This check is dated the 19th?

*Mr. Scarlett.* You received in payment for that check, two notes of £.100. each?

*A.* Yes, I did.

*Q.* What did you do with those two notes of 100*l.* each?

*A.* I gave them to Lord Cochrane.

*Q.* That was on the 19th of February?

*A.* Yes, it was.

*Q.* Were you present when Lord Cochrane paid those notes back to Mr. Butt?

*A.* I was not.

*Q.* Though you were not present when those notes were given by him to Mr. Butt, do you know that those notes were in Mr. Butt's hands afterwards?

*A.* I know of receiving them from him.

*Q.* Though you paid them to Lord Cochrane upon the 19th, did you not afterwards receive them from Mr. Butt?

*A.* I received the two £.100. notes I have now looked at from Mr. Butt.

*Q.* It was by Mr. Butt's desire you changed them for small notes at the Bank?

*A.* Yes.

*Q.* That you say was the 24th of February?

*A.* Yes.

*Q.* For Mr. Butt?

*A.* Yes.

*Q.* Was Lord Cochrane in the city at that time?

*A.* Not that I know of.

*Q.* Do you know on the 15th of February of any loan made by Mr. Smallbone to Lord Cochrane?

*A.* Yes, I do.

*Mr. Gurney.* Do you know that of your own knowledge, or how do you know that?

*A.* I know that of my own knowledge.

*Mr. Scarlett.* I believe you know that my Lord had a certain sum to make up to pay what he owed at that time?

*A.* He had.

*Q.* How much was that amount?

*A.* I am not prepared to tell you the exact amount.

*Q.* Was it between six and seven hundred pounds?

*A.* More than that.

*Q.* Do not you know that he was without the money in the City, to make it up at that time?

*A.* He was.

*Q.* How much did he borrow of Mr. Smallbone?

*A.* I cannot say exactly.

*Q.* Was it £.450.?

*A.* £.450. I think, was advanced by me as clerk to Mr. Smallbone.

*Lord Ellenborough..* In all £.450.

*A.* In all £.450.

*Q.* £.250. in these bank notes?

*A.* No, £.450. besides these bank notes.

*Lord Ellenborough.* The £.450. is to be added to these bank notes?

*Mr. Scarlett.* The witness was not present when Mr. Butt lent the £.200. I was about to shew, that besides the £.450. that Mr. Smallbone lent, Lord Cochrane wanted £.200. more, and that he went out to get it.

*Lord Ellenborough.* Did you see the £.200. lent to Lord Cochrane?

*A.* No.

*Q.* How do you know it was lent?

*A.* Because I was told so by Lord Cochrane.

*Lord Ellenborough.* Then it comes to nothing?

*Mr. Scarlett.* He knows the fact that he wanted the £.200. You advanced £.450. yourself?

*A.* Yes, I did.

*Lord Ellenborough.* In gold or bank notes?

*A.* In bank notes.

*Q.* In what description of bank notes?

*A.* The money was lent in fact by Mr. Smallbone, and he made up the difference; it is not usual to pay in bank notes, and we made it up in checks; his Lordship had left his money at the west end of the town.

*Mr. Scarlett.* You advanced his Lordship £.450.?

*A.* Yes.

*Q.* Was that all that he wanted, or did he want more?

*A.* No, he wanted £.200. more.

*Lord Ellenborough.* This advance must all be in paper?

*Mr. Scarlett.* Yes, my Lord, it is not material to my purpose to shew how Mr. Butt made this advance to him.

*Lord Ellenborough.* If it was a loan and you rely upon it as such, you must shew in what it was?

*A.* The £.450. was in a check.

*Lord Ellenborough.* Then that check must be shewn.

*Mr. Scarlett.* Mr. Butt was not present, was he?

*A.* Not that I know of.

*Q.* At what time Lord Cochrane gave these two £.100. notes to Mr. Butt you do not know, do you?

*A.* No.

*Q.* But it was not by Lord Cochrane's desire you took them to the Bank.

*A.* No; by Mr. Butt's.

*Mr. John Bilson sworn;*

*Examined by Mr. Gurney.*

*Q.* Look at these two £.100. notes; on the 24th of February; were those two notes of £.100. each brought to the Bank to be exchanged for one pound notes?

*A.* They were entered for payment in the Bank on that day.

*Q.* Have you there the book in which your own entries are made, or those which are made by Mr. Northover?

*A.* I have the book in which is my own hand-writing.

*Q.* What notes did you pay this in?

*A.* One pound notes.

*Q.* You make the entries, and the other clerk gives over the notes?

*A.* Yes.

*Q.* Have you all the numbers there?

*A.* Yes, I have.

*Mr. Gurney.* I am sorry to trouble your Lordship with having these numbers read; they do not happen to be in sequence. Will you go over those numbers?

*A.* 27th August, No. 1,048.

*Lord Ellenborough.* You had better see what you apply your proof to, otherwise he must go through the list.

*Mr. Gurney.* I am told these clerks have examined all these notes. You have looked over all these notes found in Mr. De Berenger's trunk, have you not?

*A.* I have not looked over them to-day; we looked over them before the Grand Jury.

*Q.* Look over that parcel, and tell me whether you paid all that parcel [*handing a parcel of bank notes to the witness.*]

[*The Witness and Mr. Thomas Northover examined the notes.*]

*A.* Yes; those were paid.

*Q.* There are forty-nine in number?

*A.* Yes.

*Lord Ellenborough.* Were all those forty-nine part of the two hundred pounds that were given in exchange for the two £.100. notes?

*A.* They were.

*A Juryman.* What were the numbers of the two £.100. notes?

*A.* No. 16,601 and No. 18,468.

*Mr. Hilary Miller sworn;*

*Examined by Mr. Gurney.*

*Q.* You are a clerk in the Bank?

*A.* Yes.

*Q.* Have you forty-seven one pound notes that have come into the bank?

*A.* I have fifty-seven [*the witness produces them.*]

*Mr. Gurney.* (*to Bilson and Northover*) Look and see whether those fifty-seven are also part of the same payment?

*Miller.* I believe that part of those notes were received at another period.

*Mr. Northover.* They do not appear to arise from this transaction.

*Mr. Gurney.* I will state to your Lordship the effect of this; perhaps it is hardly worth pursuing; they came into the bank from various quarters, and Mr. De Berenger's name is upon them, but not in his hand-writing.

*Mr. Bilson.* Here are some of them in this account.

*Lord Ellenborough.* They do not appear to be evidence.

*Mr. Gurney.* Then I will not pursue that.

*Thomas Christmas sworn;*

*Examined by Mr. Gurney.*

*Q.* Were you clerk to Mr. Fearn, in February last?

*A.* I was.

*Q.* Do you recollect being sent on the 24th of February to change a note for two hundred pounds?

*A.* Yes.

*Q.* By whom were you sent?

*A.* By Mr. Fearn.

*Q.* Where did you go to change that note?

*A.* To Messrs. Bond & Pattesall.

*Q.* Look at that bank note (No. 634), is that the bank note which you changed?

*A.* Yes.

*Q.* What did you receive in exchange for it?

*A.* Two notes of £.100. each.

*Q.* Did you take those two notes of £.100. each to the bank?

*A.* Yes.

*Q.* For what did you change them there?

*A.* Two hundred notes of one pound each.

*Q.* What did you do with those two hundred notes of one pound each?

*A.* I gave them to Mr. Fearn.

*Q.* In whose presence?

*A.* Two or three gentlemen in his office.

*Q.* Who were those gentlemen?

*A.* I do not recollect.

*Q.* Were Mr. Butt or Mr. Cochrane Johnstone there then?

*A.* No, they were neither of them there then.

*Q.* Did you see what Mr. Fearn did with those notes?

*A.* No, I did not.

*Q.* Did you put your name upon the two £.100. notes before you gave them into the bank?

*A.* I put Mr. Fearn's name upon them.

[*Mr. Miller produced two £.100. notes.*]

*Q.* Are those the two?

*A.* Yes they are.

*Q.* What are their numbers?

*A.* 19,482 and 19,592.

*Mr. Joseph Fearn called again;*

*Examined by Mr. Gurney.*

*Q.* On the 24th of February did you receive from Christmas two hundred notes of one pound each?

*A.* Yes.

*Q.* To whom did you give those notes?

*A.* To Mr. Butt.

*Q.* Did you see what Mr. Butt did with them?

*A.* He gave them to Mr. Cochrane Johnstone.

*Mr. John Bilson and Mr. Thomas Northover called again.*

*Mr. Gurney.* Did you on the 24th of February pay a £.100. Bank note No. 19,482?

*Mr. Bilson.* We paid to Fearn on that day two hundred one pound notes for two notes of £.100. each.

*Q.* Are those the two notes for which you paid them, [*shewing them to the Witness*]?

*A.* Those are the two notes.

*A Juryman.* What are the numbers?

*A.* 19,482, the 4th of February 1814, and 19,592 of the same date.

*Mr. Gurney.* I am now going to put into the hands of the witnesses sixty-seven notes found in Mr. De Berenger's writing desk, for him to see whether they are not part of those he paid for those two £.100. notes?

[*The Witnesses compared them.*]

*Mr. Bilson.* These are part of the notes we paid to Fearn on the 24th of February.

*Lord Ellenborough.* The whole sixty-seven?

*A.* Yes.

*Mr. Joseph Fearn;*

*Cross-examined by Mr. Brougham.*

*Q.* When Christmas brought back these two hundred one pound notes from the bank, you say they were given to Mr. Butt?

*A.* Yes.

*Q.* And you say Mr. Butt afterwards gave them to Mr. Cochrane Johnstone?

*A.* Yes.

*Q.* Did you see him give them?

*A.* Yes.

*Q.* Did you see Mr. Butt give him the other two hundred one pound notes he got from Lance?

*A.* No.

*Q.* You were not present then?

*A.* No, I was not.

Mr. *Adolphus.* We wish Mr. Wood now to produce out of the desk a watch, which he found in the possession of Mr. De Berenger.

[*The Witness produced two watches.*]

*Q.* Were they both in the box when you found it?

*A.* They were.

*Mr. Bishop Bramley sworn;*

*Examined by Mr. Adolphus.*

*Q.* What are you?

*A.* A watchmaker and silversmith.

*Q.* Do you live at Hull?

*A.* Yes.

*Q.* Look at those watches that lie there; did you sell those watches?

*A.* No, neither of those.

*Q.* Did you sell a watch to the gentleman who sits there?

*A.* Yes.

*Q.* For how much money?

*A.* Twenty-nine guineas and a half, £30. 19*s.* 6*d.*

*Q.* When was that?

*A.* The 4th of March.

*Q.* What name did he pass by?

*A.* We did not hear any name.

*Q.* How did he pay you?

*A.* In one pound Bank of England notes.

*Q.* Did you write any name upon them?

*A.* I put my own initials upon them.

*Q.* So that you will know them again if they are produced?

*A.* Yes.

[*Mr. Miller produced some bank notes.*]

*Mr. Adolphus (to Bramley.)* Look at those, and see whether those are part of what you received?

*A.* All these notes we took of the gentleman we sold the watch to, on the 4th of March.

*Q.* And that is the gentleman who sits there? (*pointing to De Berenger.*)

*A.* Yes.

*Lord Ellenborough.* What mark have you put upon them to know them again?

*A.* My own initials and the dates; it is written at the top end of the note.

*Q.* How are you enabled to say that those seven notes are what you received from the person who bought that watch?

*A.* We took no other Bank of England notes on that day.

*Q.* You marked them at the time you received them?

*A.* Yes, I received twenty in the forenoon, and the other eleven in the afternoon, and I marked them and paid them away the same afternoon.

*Cross-examined by Mr. Park.*

*Q.* I understand you to say neither of those watches found in the possession of Mr. De Berenger is the watch you sold?

*A.* Neither of them.

*Q.* You wrote upon all the notes?

*A.* Yes.

*Q.* Those are the only seven you have seen since?

*A.* Yes.

Mr. *Gurney.* You paid them all away?

*A.* We did.

*John Bilson and Thomas Northover called again.*

Mr. *Gurney.* Have the goodness to look over your book, and see whether those seven were part of the two hundred that were paid to Fearn?

[*The Witnesses examined them.*]

Mr. *Bilson.* Those seven notes were part of the property paid to Fearn on the 24th of February.

*Benjamin Lance called again;*

*Examined by Mr. Gurney.*

*Q.* On the 25th of February, did you give Mr. Butt a check on Prescott & Company, for £.98. 2*s.* 6*d.*?

*A.* On the 26th of February I did.

*Q.* Is that the check? [*shewing it to the witness.*]

*A.* That is the check.

*John Isherwood sworn;*

*Examined by Mr. Gurney.*

*Q.* Are you clerk to Prescott & Company?

*A.* I am.

*Q.* Look at that check, did you pay that?

*A.* I did.

*Q.* On what day?

*A.* The date of it the 26th of February, I think.

Mr. *Park.* That is an entry in your own hand-writing.

*A.* It is.

Mr. *Gurney.* Did you pay a 50*l.* note?

*A.* Yes.

*Q.* What number?

*A.* No. 13,396.

*Q.* Did you pay also a forty pound note?

*A.* Yes, No. 6,268.

*Q.* Look at that, is that the £.40. note?

*A.* Yes, that is the note.

*Mr. Gurney.* Mr. Miller, will you produce the £.50. note? [*Mr. Miller produced it, and it was shewn to the Witness.*]

*A.* This is the note.

*Mr. John Seeks sworn;*

*Examined by Mr. Gurney.*

*Q.* Look at that cancelled bank note for £.50. did you receive that bank note in payment from any person?

*A.* I gave change for it.

*Q.* On what day?

*A.* I cannot exactly recollect.

*Q.* About when; have you any minute on the back of it?

*A.* Here are some letters here that I know it by.

*Q.* To whom did you give change for it?

*A.* Mr. De Berenger's servant, Smith.

*Q.* The day you cannot exactly fix?

*A.* I cannot.

*Mr. Serjeant Best.* I submit to your Lordship, that is no evidence, until they call Smith.

*Mr. Gurney.* On referring to Mr. De Berenger's memorandum book, I find "W. S. £.50." which I consider as connecting itself with this.

*Mr. Park.* That book is not proved.

*Mr. Gurney.* It is proved by being found in the trunk.

*Mr. Park.* I object to that book being read; that is not the book which was before proved; as to that, Mr. Lavie gave some evidence of the hand-writing before the entry was read.

*Mr. Germain Lavie called again;*

*Examined by Mr. Gurney.*

*Q.* Do you believe that to be the hand-writing of Mr. De Berenger?

*A.* Yes I do, most certainly.

*Cross-examined by Mr. Park.*

*Q.* I observe this is pencil writing you have been speaking to; did you ever see any writing of this person in pencil before?

*A.* No, never.

*Q.* There is no difference in a man's writing with a pencil and with a pen?

*A.* I conceive that to be written by Mr. De Berenger.

*Q.* It is exactly like the character of that letter which has been given in evidence upon your testimony?

*A.* Yes, it is the same sort of writing.

*Mr. Serjeant Best.* I submit to your Lordship, still I am not removed from my objection. There is first a check of £.98. 2*s.* 6*d.*; then an attempt is made to trace £.50. of that into the hands of Mr. De Berenger; the way in which that is attempted is, that a person says he gave change for that note of £.50.;— beyond that, they have produced a pencil memorandum, proved to be in the writing of Mr. De Berenger, at least there is some evidence of that; that pencil memorandum is merely this, not that a particular bank note; not that the note which came into the hand of the witness, and for which he gave change, but that a bank note of £.50. was paid to W. S. It does not appear that it was that bank note, and this, I submit, is no evidence in a criminal case.

*Mr. Gurney.* I submit to your Lordship it is evidence, *valeat quantum*, it does not prove that Smith received that bank note from De Berenger, but that it came from De Berenger's servant; I shall give no other evidence to bring it home to De Berenger, and I submit that it is admissible evidence, as that which is proved to come so near as the child, the wife, or the servant.

*Lord Ellenborough.* I think it is not evidence; it does not get the length of William Smith; but even if it were to be taken to refer to William Smith, it does not connect it with this bank note, or any other means of payment. I cannot translate "W. S." into "William Smith my servant," and "£.50." into "this £.50. bank note." You do not call William Smith.

*Mr. Gurney.* No, certainly not, my Lord,—I shall leave that to my learned friends.

*Mr. Benjamin Bray sworn;*

*Examined by Mr. Gurney.*

*Q.* Where do you live?

*A.* At Sunderland.

*Q.* Will you look at this £.40. note, [*shewing the witness the note just produced,*] did you receive that £.40. note from any one?

*A.* From the waiter of the Bridge Inn at Sunderland.

*Q.* Did you see Mr. De Berenger about the time of the receipt of it?

*A.* I had seen him often prior to that.

*Q.* At Sunderland?

*A.* Yes.

*Q.* A waiter brought it to you?

*A.* Yes, with Major Burne's compliments.

*Q.* He brought you some message with it?

*A.* Yes, I gave him six £.5. notes for it, and ten £.1. notes.

*Q.* Bank of England notes?

*A.* No, of the Durham Bank.

*Q.* Did any thing pass between you and Mr. De Berenger afterwards, on the subject of that note?

*A.* The waiter returned in a few minutes afterwards.

*Q.* Did any thing pass afterwards between you and Mr. De Berenger, on the subject of that note?

*A.* Yes, he came shortly afterwards to take his leave of me.

*Lord Ellenborough.* Where did he come to?

*A.* To my house.

*Q.* What shop do you keep?

*A.* I am a druggist and agent to the Durham bank.

*Mr. Gurney.* How long had Mr. De Berenger been at Sunderland?

*A.* I had known him there from the 7th to the 21st of March. I apologized for not being able to send more Bank of England paper in exchange for the Durham bank notes; the waiter having been to request that I would send him Bank of England paper, I gave him a message to Mr. De Berenger.

*Q.* You made him an apology for not having sent him more bank paper in exchange?

*A.* Yes.

*Q.* In exchange for the note you had at first received; for that note?

*A.* Yes.

*Q.* What did Mr. De Berenger say, on your making the apology?

*A.* I apologized for not having sent him more Bank of England paper, and he acknowledged having received the whole of the notes I had sent him from the waiter.

*Q.* By what name did Mr. De Berenger go there.

*A.* Major Burne; he gave me his name.

*Q.* Is that the gentleman you have been speaking of? *(pointing to De Berenger.)*

*A.* Yes.

Cross-examined by *Mr. Richardson.*

*Q.* How do you know that £.40 note to be the note you received?

*A.* By a copy that I made at the time.

*Q.* Have you got that copy with you?

*A.* This is a copy of my waste book—the waste book is at Sunderland.

*Q.* You identify it by means of the copy which you have made from your waste-book, which book you have left at Sunderland.

*A.* Yes; and also from my initials on the back of the note.

*Q.* Made at the time?

*A.* A day or two afterwards.

*Lord Ellenborough.* Before you parted with it?

*A.* Yes.

*Mr. Richardson.* You are the agent of the Durham Bank?

*A.* Yes.

*Q.* You have a great many notes passing through your hands?

*A.* Yes.

*Lord Ellenborough.* Are you sure that when you made that memorandum, you had perfectly in your recollection from whom you took that note?

*A.* Yes, perfectly.

*Mr. Richardson.* You did not keep this distinct from your other notes?

*A.* No.

*Q.* You mixed it with your other notes?

*A.* Yes.

*Q.* You marked it several days afterwards?

*A.* I marked it between the 31st of March and the 4th of April, when I remitted it.

*Q.* You put your name upon every bank note that passes through your hands?

*A.* No, I do not.

*Q.* Why did you put your name upon this?

*A.* I cannot give a satisfactory answer why.

*Q.* Do you generally put your initials on notes that pass through your hands, or not?

*A.* No, I do not.

*Q.* How came you to do so in this particular case?

*A.* I have before answered that I cannot give a satisfactory reason.

*Q.* At Sunderland, which is a place of great business, do not a large number of bank notes pass through your hands?

*A.* Yes, there do of course.

*Lord Ellenborough.* Did the transaction of your sending Durham notes, and his objecting to not having more bank notes, fix the circumstance of the £.40. note more strongly in your memory?

*A.* I have not had another £.40. note since that.

*Q.* Nor had you at the time?

*A.* No, I had not.

*Q.* Nor since?

*A.* No.

Mr. *Gurney.* The only remaining head of evidence that I have to trouble your lordship with, is with respect to a check for £.56. 5s. paid by Mr. Fearn to Mr. Butt, and the produce of that.

*Mr. Pattesall sworn;*

*Examined by Mr. Gurney.*

*Q.* Are you a partner in the house of Bond & Company?

*A.* I am.

*Q.* Look at that check of Mr. Fearn's, did you pay that?

*A.* I did not.

*Q.* Who did pay it?

*A.* Mr. Evans, a clerk of ours.

*Q.* Is Mr. Evans here?

*A.* Upon my word I cannot tell.

Mr. *Gurney.* He has been expressly desired to be in attendance.

*Lord Ellenborough.* Then call him upon his subpœna if he does not appear.

Mr. *Gurney.* Just look and see whether the entry is Evans's hand-writing.

*A.* It is Evans's hand-writing.

*Thomas Evans was called on his subpœna, and did not appear.*

*Lord Ellenborough.* This entry then will be of no use to you.

Mr. *Gurney.* No, my Lord; it was mentioned that there were two Napoleons in the letter case: Mr. Wood has those two Napoleons to produce.

[*Mr. Wood produced two Napoleons.*]

Mr. *Gurney.* This, my Lord, is the evidence on the part of the prosecution.

---

Mr. *Serjeant Best.* I wish to apprize your Lordship that I think it will be necessary for the defendants to call witnesses.

*Lord Ellenborough.* I should wish to hear your opening, and to get into the defendants case, if I can; there are several gentlemen attending as witnesses, who, I find cannot, without the greatest public inconvenience, attend tomorrow.

*Mr. Park..* The difficulty we feel, I am sure your Lordship will feel as strongly as we do the fatigue, owing to the length of our attendance here; but we will proceed if your Lordship desires it.

*Lord Ellenborough.* I would wish to get into the case, so as to have the examination of several witnesses, upon whom the public business of certain offices depend, gone through, if possible.

*Mr. Park.* I have undergone very great fatigue, which I am able to bear; but I would submit to your Lordship the hardship upon parties who are charged with so very serious an offence as this, if their case is heard at this late hour; and then a fresh day is given to my learned friend to reply.

*Lord Ellenborough.* It will not be a fresh day when you will be here by nine o'clock, and the sun will be up almost before we can adjourn; I will sit through it if you require it, rather than that.

---

*Mr. Alley.* On the part of M'Rae, I shall not trouble your Lordship with any witnesses or observations.

---

MR. SERJEANT BEST.

May it please your Lordship,

Gentlemen of the Jury,

I assure you I am extremely sorry on my own account, and still more sorry on your account, that it will be necessary for me, if I am able to do it, to take up a considerable portion more of your time, in the discussion of this most important question; a question, certainly, of great importance to the public; a question, of great importance to the three individuals whose interests are committed to my charge; for, gentlemen, upon the issue of this question, with reference to them, depends whether they are to hold the situation in society which they have hitherto held, or whether they are to be completely degraded and ruined.

Gentlemen, allusions in the course of the day have been made to that which passes at the Old Bailey; no sentence that can be passed there, can be felt more by the persons on whom it is passed, than a verdict of Guilty will be felt by these three persons.

Gentlemen, from the attention I have observed every one of you giving to the evidence, and from the accuracy of the notes that have been taken by the noble and learned Judge, I have, at this late hour, this consolation left to me, that whatever I may omit, you will supply; whatever I shall not be able to impress upon you, in the manner it ought to be impressed upon you, will be brought to your consideration by his Lordship, and that that explanation which I shall feel myself unable to give, he will be in a situation to give; and with this hope, I proceed to call your attention to the case of these gentlemen:—My Lord Cochrane, Mr. Cochrane Johnstone, and Mr. Butt; the interests of the other defendants being committed to much abler hands.

Gentlemen, there are very few of the introductory observations that were made to you by my learned friend, which I am in a condition, or feel any disposition to dispute. I by no means dispute, that what is charged in this indictment is not an offence of very considerable magnitude; if I was satisfied that it was not an offence which the law of the country reaches, I protest to you, that I would not take any objection upon that score; because I am quite convinced that acquittal, upon such a ground as that, would be an acquittal that would not answer the purpose of the respectable gentlemen that I represent before you.

Gentlemen, I have observed some of my learned friends asking questions, which seemed calculated to obtain answers on which some legal objection might be founded. I hope you will recollect, that I have never asked any such questions; on the contrary, I have avoided looking at the indictment, lest I should see any thing that should force an objection upon me, and prevent this case from being decided upon its merits.

Gentlemen, I certainly do admit, that it is a crime, and a crime of a great magnitude, for any person, by means of the circulation of false news, to attempt to raise the price of the public funds; in consequence of which, individuals who are fair purchasers of such funds, are compelled to pay more than the stock they purchase is fairly worth. I hope, whoever were the authors of this, which has been called, and improperly called, a hoax, will suffer for their offence; but when we are reminded, that certain persons have suffered by it, I must say, that the fair purchasers who have suffered, are but few in comparison to those who are objects of no compassion, namely, the gamblers who attended at the Stock Exchange upon this occasion.

Gentlemen, I admit also, that which has been stated by my learned friends, that it is not necessary, for the purpose of bringing home the crime of conspiracy to any individual who may be charged with it, that you should call a person who was present at any of the consultations—shew the casting of the different parts of those who were to act in the drama, and point out distinctly who those were who were to perform, and how afterwards they have performed these parts. I admit that all this is not necessary to be proved: conspiracy, like every other offence, may be brought home by circumstantial proof. Indeed, circumstantial proof is, in many cases, more satisfactory than that which is direct and positive, because it is free from the suspicion of falsehood. But I deny, upon this occasion, that there are any circumstances that bring home the crime of conspiracy to any of the three persons whom I represent. All that is proved may be true, and yet the defendants may be innocent. The circumstantial evidence that alone can warrant conviction, is the proof of such facts as could not have happened had the accused been innocent.

Gentlemen, whether Mr. De Berenger be the Colonel Du Bourg who pretended to bring the news from France, or not, it is not for me to discuss; I shall leave that question to my learned friend Mr. Park, who is counsel for Mr. De Berenger, and who, I hope, will be able to satisfy you that Mr. De Berenger is not that Colonel Du Bourg; if he is not that Colonel Du Bourg, then there is no evidence against either of the parties I represent. But admitting, for the purpose of my presenting the case to you which I am called upon to support, that De Berenger is that Du Bourg, still it is another question, whether either of these defendants were connected with De Berenger; and I do, notwithstanding what has been stated to you by my learned friend, that he was perfectly certain that he should bring home the guilt charged by this indictment to all the defendants, submit most confidently, that there is no evidence against either of my clients.

Gentlemen, it is extremely difficult, amidst such a mass of evidence as has been laid before you, to bring one's attention, or to call your attention immediately to the evidence that applied to any particular person. I will take the three cases in the order in which they stand upon this indictment; and the first of those three for whom I am concerned, is my Lord Cochrane.

Now, gentlemen, let us examine the evidence that is offered to you, to prove that he is connected with this conspiracy. It consists in this, that my Lord Cochrane did, on the 21st of February, sell £.139,000 Omnium; and further, that Mr. De Berenger was, on the morning of the 21st of February, at the house of Lord Cochrane. Gentlemen, as far as I can collect, from the attention I have been able to give to the evidence, I have stated the utmost effect of the evidence against my Lord Cochrane; for, gentlemen, though it was suggested by my learned friend, Mr. Gurney, that he should trace some of the notes which were found in the desk of Mr. De Berenger into the hands of my Lord Cochrane, I beg to state, that there is not one single note traced into the hands of my Lord Cochrane. I admit that there are notes found in the chest of De Berenger, traced into the hands of the other two defendants; but I believe I shall be able, by and by, satisfactorily to shew you how these notes came from the hands of one of the defendants into the hands of De Berenger, and to prove that they came into the hands of De Berenger, under circumstances altogether unconnected with that which is the subject of your enquiry; but I am, for the present, only considering the case of Lord Cochrane; and I would beg the favour of his Lordship now to refer to his notes, and I am persuaded his Lordship will go along with me in the observations I am making, that there is no evidence whatever to bring home any one of the notes to my Lord Cochrane.

Gentlemen, the only part of the evidence which has the least tendency to connect my Lord Cochrane, by means of the notes, with Mr. De Berenger, is the evidence that was given by a person of the name of Lance; there is not one other witness that attempts to state, that a single note traced from the hands of Lord Cochrane, ever was found in the hands of Mr. De Berenger; now, if you will have the goodness to attend to Lance's evidence, you will find that there were for a time put into the hands of Lord Cochrane two £.100 notes, which were afterwards found at the Bank, and in exchange for which two hundred one pound notes were given to the person changing them, and that a considerable quantity of those £.1 notes have certainly been proved to be found in the chest of Mr. De Berenger; but permit me to state, that though those two £.100 notes, by which one hundred £.1 notes were afterwards produced, are for a short space of time shewn to be in the hands of Lord Cochrane, that the same witness tells you, that those £.100 notes were got back from my Lord Cochrane again, before they were exchanged at the Bank; for he tells you, that he carried those two £.100 notes to the Bank *for Mr. Butt.* Gentlemen, my learned friend, who cross-examined Mr. Lance, certainly could not get from him that he was present at the time when my Lord Cochrane paid those two notes into the hands of Mr. Butt; but it is perfectly clear, from that which he subsequently stated, that at some period before they found their way into the Bank, and before they can furnish any means of proof against the parties, they must have been returned to Butt's; these notes might have been in the hands of any one of you, gentlemen; but the question is, on whose account the two hundred £.1 notes were received from the Bank, for it is these small notes which can alone connect the party with Mr. De Berenger. Now, I say, Mr. Lance, in a part of his evidence, stated, that though he was not present at the time Lord Cochrane returned the two £.100 notes to Butt, yet that he afterwards received those notes, not from the hands of Lord Cochrane, but from the hands of Mr. Butt; for Mr. Butt he went to the Bank; for Mr. Butt he got the two hundred £.1 notes, and those two hundred £.1 notes he delivered back into the hands of Mr. Butt. Gentlemen, I am sure therefore, that if I have made myself understood upon this part of the case, I have completely released Lord Cochrane from the effect of this evidence, for though the two large notes were once in his hands, these notes were never in the hands of De Berenger. The notes found on him were the small notes given in exchange for them at the Bank, and these were given to Mr. Butt, and not Lord Cochrane. It is perfectly clear, therefore, that though these had been in the hands of Lord Cochrane, from the money transactions taking place between them every day, it was Mr. Butt that was the possessor of those notes, at the time the £.1 notes were obtained for them; I am satisfied, therefore, you will see that this evidence does not connect Mr. De Berenger with Lord Cochrane. I am quite confident, therefore, that I am right, when I state to you, that my learned friend's attempt to draw an unfavourable inference from the circumstance of De Berenger being in possession of notes which once belonged to Lord Cochrane, is completely answered; and then I state again, that the only points which remain for your consideration, with respect to Lord Cochrane, are, first; the large sale of stock on the 21st of February; and, next, De Berenger being at his house on that day; with respect to the last circumstance, that is proved only by Lord Cochrane's affidavit, and I think I shall shew that Lord Cochrane, in that affidavit, completely explains that circumstance.

Gentlemen, with respect to the large sale on the 21st of February, I do not think the Committee of the Stock Exchange have conducted themselves quite fairly in a criminal case; because, in a criminal case, it is not fit to take up a piece of evidence just exactly at that point where it will suit the purpose of those who offer it, keeping back other evidence which they know is extremely important, which they must know is calculated to do away the effect of that which they offer. Now, gentlemen, for the purpose of implicating Lord Cochrane, the Stock Exchange have instructed my learned friend, Mr. Gurney, to state, and Mr. Gurney did, in pursuance of his instructions, state most expressly, that Lord Cochrane began his Stock Exchange speculations about one week before the 21st of February; and, till I cross-examined Mr. Fearn, you must necessarily have understood, as well from the statement of counsel, as from the evidence that has been offered, that Lord Cochrane, about six or seven days only antecedent to the 21st of February, had purchased the whole of the £.139,000 that was sold out on that day; that his lordship had never speculated in the funds before, and, therefore, that all his purchases must have been made in order that he might have so much stock to sell at this particular time. But, gentlemen, it turns out that Lord Cochrane had been deeply speculating in the Stock Exchange for several months before, and so the inference, that he purchased this stock with a view to the event that happened on the 21st of February, is rebutted; that Lord Cochrane did not first begin to buy this £.139,000 merely for the purpose of selling on the 21st of February, is most clearly proved by the testimony of Fearn and of Hichens, who say, that so early as the month of November preceding Lord Cochrane had bought very largely, and had sold very largely; and that he continued to buy and to sell, down to the very period of the last sale taking place; it is impossible, therefore, when the evidence is laid before you, that you can collect, merely from the circumstance of his selling so large a sum as £.139,000 on the 21st of February, that he was guilty of a conspiracy to occasion a rise in the funds on that day. The witness did not come prepared to state to you, what had been the extent of the sales made by Lord Cochrane on antecedent days; but when he states that he sold largely, (I think I may venture to say, that he sold nearly as much on previous days as on this occasion); you will find therefore nothing to distinguish the conduct of Lord Cochrane on the 21st of February, from that which had been his conduct on many days precedent.

Gentlemen, I trust therefore, that in a criminal case, you will think that the inference of criminality which is supposed to arise merely from the circumstance of the sale of this large quantity of stock, is rebutted by the fact I have now brought under your consideration; but you will have the goodness also to bear in mind another circumstance. I did expect, when I heard the case opened with so much confidence against Lord Cochrane, that you would hear of some particular directions being given to sell on that day; but, gentlemen, how does that fact turn out; no particular directions are given to sell on that day, but Lord Cochrane's general directions, from the first moment when he became a speculator in stock, were, that whenever any event should happen by which the stocks should be raised, one per cent. the broker was not to wait for particular directions, but to sell; and this large sale of £.139,000, from whence the inference is drawn, that Lord Cochrane necessarily knew of the conspiracy which had taken place, was made under these general directions. It is also to be observed, that Lord Cochrane was never present in the city a single hour during the 21st; there is no evidence given that he was there; on the contrary, all the witnesses that have been examined, have told you they did not see him there; all the stock was therefore sold on that day, without any interference on his part; and as it appears beyond all question, a very considerable part of the stock of all these gentlemen was sold before any of them came into the city, and without any particular directions on the subject of the sale of it.

Gentlemen, the sale of the stock which Lord Cochrane possessed, considering the circumstances under which he became possessed of it, and the circumstances under which it was sold, furnishes, I submit to you, no proof that he was privy to what they have called the hoax. I beg pardon of the noble and learned judge, for using this term, after the observation that his lordship has made upon it. I did not use it for the purpose of treating with levity the crime contained in the indictment; but it has been so frequently applied to this crime, both before and since the prosecution was instituted, that it is difficult in the hurry of speech to avoid using it.

Gentlemen, another circumstance has transpired, which I think furnishes a strong observation in favour of all my clients; namely, the practice of selling both stock and omnium, which the seller is not at the time of such sale in possession of. If Lord Cochrane had been privy to the fraud, would he have contented himself with merely selling the stock that he had previously purchased. Would you not have found him selling to every buyer that offered (and on the 21st of February there was no scarcity of buyers at the advanced prices) stock and scrip in any quantity; if he had been privy to the fraud, he must have known that the bubble would soon burst, that the funds would fall back to their former prices, and that by every sale that he so made, he must be a great gainer; yet he is not found selling the value of a shilling in this manner; nothing is sold but what had been previously bought, and that sold under general directions given to the broker previous to the day of sale, and previous to the time when the conspiracy could have been conceived. If his lordship had been one of the conspirators, he must have been found to have made many more thousands of pounds by the speculations of this day, than he either is or can be proved to have made hundreds. Avarice, always insatiable, which had in this case impelled the defendant to hazard every thing that was dear and valuable to him in life, stops short in the hot pursuit of its object, at the very moment when the most abundant means of gratification are brought within its reach. Does not then the inference of innocence, arising from what he did not sell, although he might have sold much, outweigh the inference of guilt, arising from what he actually did sell; what he did on this day, it is not only possible but probable that he might have done, and yet be innocent of the conspiracy with which he is charged; what he did not do, he could not have omitted to do, if he had been guilty.

My learned friend, Mr. Gurney, has told you, that the circumstance of his selling out as he did, proves his privity to the conspiracy. Men who were unconscious of the risk, says my learned friend, did not sell on the first rise in the market, but held their stock in the expectation of gaining still higher prices; but the defendant, knowing that the falsehood of the news would soon be discovered, and that its effect on the funds must be of very short duration, sells his whole stock on the opening of the market. I should have felt the force of this argument, had you found Lord Cochrane on the Stock Exchange, pressing his brokers to complete their sales; but when you find that his lordship was not present, and gave no directions for immediate sales, but that his stock was sold under orders given before the fraud could have been thought of, I trust that you will find it not worthy of much attention. If, however, you are to decide on the guilt or innocence of Lord Cochrane from the transactions of the 21st of February, you will look at the whole of his conduct, and when pressed to find that the circumstance of his selling is proof of his guilt, you will say, that the circumstance of his not selling more than he did, is a still stronger proof of his innocence. My learned friend will have an opportunity in his reply, of accounting why his lordship and his supposed co-conspirators did not sell more; and I think he will find it a task that will transcend even his powers, to account for it in a manner compatible with their guilt.

Gentlemen, the only remaining point relative to Lord Cochrane is this; that on the morning of the 21st of February Mr. De Berenger went to the house of his lordship. Gentlemen, it is material for your consideration how the Stock Exchange got the knowledge of that fact. Gentlemen, but for my Lord Cochrane, the Stock Exchange never would have known of the existence of any such person as De Berenger; but for my Lord Cochrane, it is impossible that the Stock Exchange could have instituted this prosecution, because it was by Lord Cochrane's affidavit only that the name of De Berenger was given to them. I am aware my learned friend stated to you, that the Stock Exchange had some reason to suspect that a Mr. De Berenger had been engaged in it before this affidavit was published; but, Gentlemen, my learned friend has offered no proof of the grounds of such suspicion; the only proof that he has offered upon the subject, is the proof which my Lord Cochrane's affidavit furnished him with. Now, Gentlemen, I have a right to say, that the mere circumstance of Lord Cochrane's introducing the name of Mr. De Berenger for the first time, in that affidavit, is of itself sufficient to repel the inference arising from the circumstance of De Berenger's going to his house. But, gentlemen, I am sure you will bear in mind the very important evidence that was given by Mr. Wright upon that subject. My learned friend may repeat again the observation with which he introduced this prosecution, that those who are wicked are not always wise, and that it so happens frequently, that men do acts without considering the consequences of those acts, and that it is in consequence of this want of consideration that criminality is often brought home to delinquents; but it appears from Mr. Wright's testimony, that Lord Cochrane was fully aware of the consequence of the affidavit that he was about to publish. Mr. Wright, the printer, who was called for the purpose of shewing that this affidavit had been printed by Lord Cochrane, tells you, that when he received the instructions from Lord Cochrane to print the affidavit, Lord Cochrane said this, *I have no reason to think De Berenger was the man, but if he was, I have given the Stock Exchange a clue to him*; so that you see, at the very moment that his lordship published that affidavit, he was perfectly aware of the consequence of what he was about; and he must know, that if the Stock Exchange could not find out who this man was who came to his house, it would be impossible for them to reach his lordship. He must know that they were likely to remain for ever ignorant who that person was. He comes forward and tells them who that person was, recollecting at the time he makes the disclosure, that if that person be guilty, he would by the act he was about to do deliver him over to their justice. What must those persons think of Lord Cochrane? who after this can consider him as implicated in the guilt of this conspiracy? the guilty men knowingly and advisedly point out to their prosecutors, the only course by which they can be hunted down; such guilty men must be men of too weak understandings to be answerable for their conduct either to God or their country. In the declaration that Lord Cochrane made to Mr. Wright, he did that justice to Mr. De Berenger which his knowledge of that gentleman compelled him to do; he said he did not think him guilty; but if he was guilty, he was about to give him up to the punishment that he justly merited. Gentlemen, there is more of simplicity, more of fair dealing in this behaviour, than was ever found connected with so much guilt as is imputed by the indictment that you are trying, to this defendant.

Gentlemen, let us look at the affidavit itself; my learned friend indulged himself with making upon it a great number of very harsh observations. It is easy to raise suspicions; but suspicion and conviction are different things. Recollect, that before you can convict Lord Cochrane, you must be convinced that this affidavit is altogether false. Gentlemen, it might possibly be said, that that noble Lord, not reflecting on the consequences of such an offence as that imputed to him by this indictment, might be engaged in it; but you must impute to Lord Cochrane a much more serious offence, one for which want of consideration will be no excuse, after that affidavit has been laid before you, or it is impossible for you to say that he can be convicted of this conspiracy; for it will not be forgotten by you, that at the close of that affidavit, my Lord Cochrane does, in the most solemn manner protest, that he is altogether innocent of the offence which is imputed to him by the Stock Exchange Committee. Gentlemen, I cannot put that better to you than in the words of the affidavit itself; after stating every thing that had taken place with respect to De Berenger coming to his house, his Lordship says, "Further, I do solemnly depose, that I had no connexion or dealing with any one, save the above mentioned, and that I did not directly or indirectly, by myself, or by any other, take or procure any office or apartment for any broker or other person for the transaction of Stock affairs."

Gentlemen, it is said that this affidavit has only been sworn before a magistrate; a lawyer, like my learned friend, knows that upon an affidavit so sworn a party cannot be indicted for perjury; but my learned friend will have a great difficulty in convincing you, that Lord Cochrane, whose education has been different from that of my learned friend, knew that he was not liable to that punishment. I am persuaded that he conceived himself as completely amenable to the guilt of perjury, as if that oath had been taken in a court of justice. But is the temporal danger that awaits an act of this sort, the only thing that could prevent a person of the character and situation in life of this noble person, from making such an affidavit. What reason has my learned friend given you to-day? What reason can you collect from the former life of this noble person, (for he has been before you, and has lived in the view of the public), that can induce you to believe that he is so completely lost to all sense of that which is right and wrong, to all sense of what is due to himself, as to go before a magistrate to make an affidavit, in which he must know he was deposing to that, which at the time he was making the deposition was absolutely false? Gentlemen, I ask you what evidence you have upon which you are to find this noble person, not only guilty of a foul conspiracy, but also of the still higher crime of wilful and corrupt perjury? Gentlemen, I am quite satisfied, you will not feel that there is any evidence in this cause, which can weigh down the testimony which my learned friend has thought proper to put in. I say the oath of Lord Cochrane makes the evidence offered on the other side kick the beam; that there is nothing to put in competition with the affidavit which my learned friend has himself given in evidence.

But, gentlemen, let us look at the narrative given in the affidavit, and see whether there is any thing improbable in it. Lord Cochrane states, that he had gone out on the morning of the 21st, with his uncle, not to go into the city, but to go to a man of the name of King, who was engaged in making for him a lamp, for which he was about to obtain a patent; is that true, or is it false? It is true, according to all the evidence in the cause; there is no doubt that Lord Cochrane did set out with Mr. Cochrane Johnstone, for the purpose of going towards the city. Did he go into the city? No one witness has shewn that he did. On the contrary, I think it may be taken as admitted, that he never was in the city on that day. Here then this part of the affidavit is most unquestionably confirmed. He states, that having proceeded to the house of this man, who was assisting him in preparing this lamp, he received a note in which he was desired to come home; then he states, he was informed that the person who brought the note was in the dress of an officer; and Lord Cochrane goes on to state, that imagining it was some officer who had just come from Spain, (and probably you may know, gentlemen, that Lord Cochrane, who is himself serving in the navy, has a very gallant brother at this time serving in the army in Spain, and with respect to whom, I believe I shall shew you in evidence, that he was exceedingly ill, and was considered to be in very great danger), he immediately connected that officer with his brother in Spain, and he proceeded in a hackney coach to his house, hoping for some account of his brother in Spain.

Gentlemen, it appears that the officer turned out to be Mr. De Berenger. Lord Cochrane then gives you an account of what Mr. De Berenger represented to be his object in coming to his lordship's house; he says that

Mr. De Berenger had previously made applications to him to take him out to America, for the purpose of exercising his men in small arms, and that Mr. De Berenger renewed his application that morning to him to take him in the Tonnant, the ship to the command of which his Lordship was then appointed, and in which he was about to sail to America. Gentlemen, is this true? we have the evidence of Mr. Murray, a gentleman called on the part of the prosecution; we have the evidence of another person, of whom I cannot speak in the same terms as I do of Mr. Murray, for I shall by and by shew you that he is entitled to no credit, who certainly, as far as he speaks in favour of Lord Cochrane, is entitled to consideration; but where he speaks against Lord Cochrane, as I shall shew you, he is entitled to no consideration, for that he has vowed he will bring on the ruin of Lord Cochrane, in consequence of the refusal of a loan of money. We have it in evidence, that Mr. De Berenger did expect to go to America, under the protection of Admiral Cochrane and Lord Cochrane; the narration in the affidavit is thus confirmed by this evidence; the affidavit then goes on to state, that Mr. De Berenger told Lord Cochrane, that he had left the King's Bench, and come to Lord Cochrane for the purpose of going to America. That he, Lord Cochrane, stated to De Berenger, that it was impossible for his lordship to take him, that his ward room was full; and further, that De Berenger being a foreigner, his Lordship could not take him without the consent of His Majesty's Government; that he might go on board ship at Portsmouth; but in the meantime he must get the permission of His Majesty's Government, upon which his lordship says, De Berenger said he would go to the noble Lord, whom I have the honour to see in court, to get that permission; his affidavit then states, that De Berenger said to his lordship, I must take a great liberty with you, for it is impossible I can go to the first Lord of the Admiralty in the dress in which I now am; upon which he, Lord Cochrane, not suspecting that Mr. De Berenger had been making an improper use of the dress he had on, or his views in wishing to change it, furnished him with a coat and hat.

Here my learned friend, Mr. Gurney, makes an observation which I am sure he will be exceedingly sorry for having made; because he would not intentionally, in a criminal case, prejudice the case of the defendant by any argument that is not borne out by the facts of the case; he says, Did Lord Cochrane think it a right thing for his lordship to do, to furnish De Berenger with the means of escaping from his creditors? Gentlemen, there was no such thing thought of at the time, as the escaping from the King's Bench prison; the cloaths were to enable De Berenger to go to the Admiralty, and to Lord Yarmouth; and it was for the purpose of appearing before Lord Yarmouth and Lord Melville, that this change of dress was asked for, and not for the purpose of escaping out of the kingdom, and avoiding his creditors; whether Lord Cochrane was wise or not in acceding to this request, it is not for us to decide to-day; but I am sure you will feel it was straining the English law too much, to say of a good-tempered English sailor, that he is guilty of a conspiracy, because he yields to a request, to which a person more hacknied in the tricks practised on them, would not have acceded. If my learned friend could have shewn you, that all that the affidavit states, respecting De Berenger's going to America, was the invention of Lord Cochrane since the 21st of February, that nothing of the sort had ever been thought of before, such proof would have falsified the affidavit. But so far from offering any such evidence, all the evidence adduced confirms the statement in the affidavit; and yet my learned friend still ventures to ask you to disbelieve what Lord Cochrane has sworn, although his oath is unopposed by any testimony, and supported by all the testimony given in the cause.

Gentlemen, it is not my business to argue before you, that Mr. De Berenger went that morning to Lord Cochrane, expecting to obtain leave to go to America; it is enough for me that I satisfy you, that he pretended that that was the object of his visit; but why did he go there at all? Why my learned friend, Mr. Gurney, has given you the reason for his going to some person's house before he went to his own. He has told you, that it would have been highly imprudent, if he was Colonel De Bourg, for him to go to his own lodgings; the Stock Exchange would have had no difficulty in finding him out by means of the post-boys, had he driven home. He determined therefore to make a pretence for stopping at some other person's house; and what had passed between him and Lord Cochrane, afforded him a pretence for going to his lordship's.

Gentlemen, bear in mind this; you are to decide this cause upon evidence; you have no positive evidence of any thing that passed in the house of Lord Cochrane, except that evidence which my learned friend, Mr. Gurney, has given you from Lord Cochrane himself; you have had evidence upon the oath of my Lord Cochrane, that whatever concealed objects this gentleman had, the avowed object in going there, was that which he has stated; and in which, I say again, he is completely confirmed by all the evidence that has been offered in this cause. Gentlemen, if it was not for this purpose—if this was not the pretence on which Mr. De Berenger went there, he was much more intimate with Mr. Cochrane Johnstone than he was with Lord Cochrane; why did not he go there; Mr. Cochrane Johnstone lived only in the next street; if he went to the one house or to the other, because of a connection between him and these parties in a conspiracy, why happens it that he did not go to the house of the party with whom he was most intimate.

Gentlemen, there is another circumstance you will not fail to observe; it appears from this affidavit, and will appear from the testimony of witnesses whom I shall call, that Lord Cochrane was sent for to his house by Mr. De Berenger; now, in my humble judgment, that is an extremely strong circumstance to shew, that whoever was connected in this scheme, Mr. De Berenger could not have considered Lord Cochrane as privy to it. If Lord Cochrane was engaged in this conspiracy, what object could De Berenger have for sending for him back from the city, about half past ten in the morning; why, if he and De Berenger had been parties to this conspiracy to raise the price of stocks, Mr. De Berenger could not want to see Lord Cochrane; why therefore was his Lordship to be sent for out of the city, at the very time when his presence in the city was essential to the consummation of the fraud. This therefore shews to you, I think most clearly and satisfactorily, that De Berenger had sent for him on the pretence that Lord Cochrane states in his affidavit, and that Lord Cochrane was not informed of what was passing in the city, nor was in any wise privy to it.

Gentlemen, I have stated to you, that it appears to me that every part of the affidavit of Lord Cochrane is confirmed by the evidence which has been given by Mr. Murray, and by all the other evidence offered in the cause; that from all of it you may collect, that De Berenger did go there under the pretence stated, and that he did not go there as a place at which he was to terminate a journey which he had undertaken in concert with Lord Cochrane and others, for the purpose of raising the price of the funds. But knowing the evidence I have, I will not leave it upon this evidence, for this is a case too important to the honour and character of Lord Cochrane, for me to leave any thing undone which I think may possibly tend to produce that verdict, which I am sure every one of you will by and by feel rejoiced to give; I shall therefore adduce before you other evidence confirmatory of such parts of Lord Cochrane's affidavit as are capable of confirmation. Gentlemen, it has been said that this affidavit is false in this; that it states, that Mr. De Berenger when he came to Lord Cochrane's had on a green coat, whereas it is proved by several witnesses that he had on a red one; but let me suppose that their account as to the colour of the coat is true, and that Lord Cochrane's account is incorrect; would such a mistake, for it is impossible that it can be any thing but a mistake, weaken the credit due to Lord Cochrane. Men do not commit crimes, unless impelled to the commission of such by some strong motive; what object could Lord Cochrane possibly have for stating that this gentleman came in one coloured coat rather than another? Gentlemen, I think I can account for the mistake; my Lord Cochrane made this affidavit a great many days, I think some weeks, after the transaction had taken place; Mr. De Berenger belonged to a corps of riflemen in this country, commanded by Lord Yarmouth, and the proper dress of Mr. De Berenger, as a member of that corps, was a green uniform; my Lord Cochrane had often seen Mr. De Berenger in this green uniform. His lordship, when he made his affidavit, recollected the circumstance of Mr. De Berenger's being dressed in a military uniform, but there being nothing to fix on his lordship's mind the colour of the uniform, the sort of dress in which he had been accustomed to see Mr. De Berenger presented itself to his lordship's mind, as the dress De Berenger wore when his lordship saw him last. Gentlemen, I have now made all the observations that have occurred to me on this affidavit; I cannot, however, take my leave of it, without again intreating you to consider the circumstances under which it was made; remember Mr. Wright's evidence, and say if any thing can more strongly evince Lord Cochrane's consciousness of his innocence, than the publication of this affidavit. Gentlemen, you have been told, and truly told that Lord Cochrane is a public character. From the high station in which he was born, and the still higher place in the eyes of his countrymen to which his public services have raised him, his lordship may, without indulging any blameable vanity, one day expect to fill one of the proudest situations in the country.

Is a man so circumstanced likely to commit so sordid a crime as that with which he is charged? No prospect of gain could hold out any temptation to Lord Cochrane to put in hazard what he now possesses.

The public character which you have been reminded he possesses, would of itself repel such a charge as that which is made against him, though it were supported by much stronger evidence than has been offered in support of this indictment.

Gentlemen, I come now to the case of Mr. Cochrane Johnstone; and with respect to him, I find that the charge is attempted to be made out against him upon these grounds; first of all, that he was a very great speculator in the funds. Gentlemen, I charge again upon the Stock Exchange the same unfair mode of proceeding, with respect to Mr. Cochrane Johnstone, which they pursued in the case of Lord Cochrane: with respect to Mr. Cochrane Johnstone, they take up the case, I think, on the 8th, but my learned friend applied his observations principally to the 12th of February. Now, gentlemen, so far from that being a fair statement of the transaction, it appears most clearly, that Mr. Cochrane Johnstone had been speculating in the funds, and speculating as desperately from the month of November, as he was in this month of February. But another thing is pressed against Mr. Cochrane Johnstone, the largeness of his balance on the 21st of February, which is stated to be £.420,000; now, gentlemen, I am astonished that the Stock Exchange should instruct my learned friend to say any thing to you upon that subject, producing the account which they have produced; if Mr. Cochrane Johnstone had never had so large a balance before, there would have been something in the argument; but cast your eye up that page, and you will find that Mr. Cochrane Johnstone, who is supposed to have been desirous of getting a quantity of stock into his possession, to sell on the 21st of February, had on the 14th £.615,000; so that this gentleman, who is supposed by the prosecutor's case, to have meditated a fraud by the sale of stock on the 21st, is found reducing his balance immediately before that day from £.615,000 to £.420,000; to contrive and carry into execution such a trick as that which has been practised, must have taken many days. It certainly must have been in contemplation as early as the 14th, how then can the prosecutors account for Mr. Johnstone's conduct in selling between the 14th and 21st, if Mr. Cochrane was one of the persons who had been contriving to put into his possession all the stock that he could purchase, for the purpose of selling it on the 21st; this is so entirely inconsistent with what must have been the view of a man engaged in a transaction of this sort, that a view of this paper is sufficient to show that there could not have been such an intention; look at this paper, and you will see what he was in the habit of selling; look at his daily sales, and you will find that he began selling; on the 9th that he sold £.10,000, on the 10th £.105,000, on the 11th £.35,000, on the 14th £.100,000, on the 16th £.10,000, on the 17th £.19,500, and on the 19th, this gentleman, who is supposed to have meditated such a fraud as this on the Monday following, sells out £.18,000. Let any man in his senses, any man not carried away with the feelings which agitate the Stock Exchange, in consequence of their having been outwitted; for these sharps, who are called flats by one of the witnesses, did not like to be taken in by other sharps. Let any dispassionate man look at this paper, and say whether Mr. Johnstone could have contemplated the rise in the funds that took place on the 21st.

Gentlemen, it is said that he made a very large profit; that will not prove much, because he was making this sort of profit on several occasions before. What was the general habit of his business, as to the Stock Exchange? Why, that he was content with a very small profit, constantly telling his brokers, that whenever they could get a profit they were to sell, and he was acting in the very same way, until the day on which this transaction took place.

Gentlemen, I have also to observe particularly, that though he did go into the city on the Monday morning, he was in the habit of going every morning; he did not get there any earlier on that day than on any previous day, and so far from his being concerned in the sale of this stock, a very considerable quantity (Hichens speaks to £.50,000) had been sold before he or any one of these gentlemen came there; how is it possible therefore to say, from the circumstance of his being possessed of this stock, and selling it, that he was implicated in this transaction; on the contrary, I ask you, looking at the whole of this evidence, ask yourselves this plain question, whether he was not selling on the 21st upon the same principles as he had been selling to an immense amount on the preceding days on which sales had been had?

Gentlemen, with respect to profit, I believe that will appear somewhat different from what it has been stated, if you cast up the amount of profits. We are sought to be charged with a fraud. Why? because these three gentlemen all together made a sum of £.10,000, which, however, these gentlemen of the Stock Exchange have put their hands upon, and nobody is likely to get at, as they state it; I believe the whole did not amount to more than £.6,000, but the prosecutors state it at £.10,000, that is to be divided among the three, another person taking a share too; but if profits have any thing to do with it, you will find the sales made by Mr. Cochrane Johnstone alone on the 17th, produced a profit of above £.8,000; how, therefore, can you presume, merely from the circumstance of the profits made on the 21st, that he was connected with this conspiracy? Gentlemen, he was near the Stock Exchange, and if in the secret, he certainly would have availed himself of the practice to which I have alluded, namely, selling at a favourable moment, stock he was not in the possession of; all the brokers have been examined, and not one of them has been able to tell you of one single shilling stock sold by these gentlemen, or either of them, of which they were not actually in the possession. It is impossible, if he is so rapacious a man as to engage in a speculation to ruin his fortune and his character, to account for his not taking advantage of such a state of things.

Gentlemen, next to the profit made by Mr. Cochrane Johnstone, is his having been engaged to take a house for Mr. Fearn; and here I was led to expect that my learned friend would falsify the statement made upon oath by Mr. Cochrane Johnstone; he was to prove, that what he had sworn to, or offered to swear to, of his not having taken the house was untrue; it is enough for me to say, that that is not proved; it is an unfounded statement of my learned friend, proceeding from misinstructions which have been given to him by his clients; but on the subject of taking this house, my learned friend must have felt the distress of his case when he pressed it upon you.—Why, gentlemen, what are you desired to find? not that these parties were generally engaged in stock-jobbing transactions; not that these parties had conceived an intention of dealing for a continuance in the stocks; but that they had planned a scheme by which, at one stroke, they were to cheat all persons who came to engage with them in the Stock Exchange; the fraud was to be over in a single day; they wanted no office for that; that could be wanted only for the purpose of carrying on that scheme of stock-jobbing, which these persons began in November, and have actually continued long subsequent to the 21st of February; but does it not appear that my learned friend is wrong in his instructions. According to the papers we have seen (most improperly circulated) a house was taken for Mr. Fearn, without his knowing any thing about it; and Mr. Fearn found himself seated in the office, without knowing how he came there.—Does that turn out to be the fact? No; it turns out that Mr. Butt had an office before, which he did not like; Mr. Cochrane Johnstone took another office for Mr. Butt; Mr. Fearn came to look at Mr. Butt's office, liked it, and it was kept for him. In consequence of this, this office, which you are told was taken by Mr. Cochrane Johnstone for Mr. Fearn, without his knowledge, was taken by Mr. Fearn for himself, because he found the house to be a convenient one; and it was suggested to him by his friends, that such a house would be extremely convenient to them. Upon this, Mr. Butt agreed to give up one of the rooms he had, and allowed Mr. Fearn to take possession of that room. Gentlemen, there is another thing which proves that the taking of this house had nothing to do with this particular day; you find, that Mr. Fearn not only continued to possess these rooms, sticking up his name there, but that he liked them so well, he has since taken the whole house, and now continues to occupy it.

Gentlemen, what is the next head of evidence pressed against Mr. Cochrane Johnstone? It is, that Mr. Cochrane Johnstone called, and left a letter on Saturday the 26th, at the lodgings of Mr. De Berenger. Gentlemen, in the first place, I have to observe, that it was but very loosely and unsatisfactorily proved, that Mr. Cochrane Johnstone was at the house of Mr. De Berenger on that day; but I will admit it, for that is the best way, perhaps. I never have denied, that Mr. De Berenger was acquainted with Mr. Cochrane Johnstone; I never denied that they were in the habit of dining together, and if they were, where was the harm of his leaving a note at the house of Mr. De Berenger.

Gentlemen, I did expect, as there has been so much activity (an activity by the bye that has gone beyond the proper line) in seizing the papers of this gentleman, that we should have seen the letter that Mr. Johnstone left at De Berenger's; but no such letter is produced, and although the prosecutors have got possession of every paper belonging to De Berenger, not a scrap of paper has been produced in the handwriting of my clients; all that is proved is, that Mr. Cochrane Johnstone called upon De Berenger, as one acquaintance would call upon another. Gentlemen, God forbid, that because he does so, it should be conceived that he is a party with Mr. De Berenger in this scheme, if he has been concerned in it.

Gentlemen, the next attempt is this, and a miserable one it is; all possible means have been had recourse to, for making it out; for not only has Mr. Basil Cochrane's servant been subpœnaed by the Stock Exchange, to prove who are the persons dining at his house, but the females of this family have been subpœnaed to this place, and kept here for the purpose of proving the same facts which might have been admitted at any hour of the day, and not only subpœnaed, but that subpœna sent by a person whose presence was the most insulting of any one who could have been selected in this town, and who could have been selected for no other purpose than that of offering insult to the members of this family.

Gentlemen, the next circumstance in this case is, that some money was found in the chest of Mr. De Berenger, which certainly had passed through the hands of Mr. Cochrane Johnstone. Gentlemen, I think you have a clue already given you, by which you can account how De Berenger became possessed of Mr. Johnstone's money. But I shall offer other evidence on this part of the case; I will shew most satisfactorily how that money came into De Berenger's hands. You have had it proved already, that Mr. De Berenger is an extremely ingenious artist; you have had it proved, that he was engaged by Mr. Cochrane Johnstone, for the purpose of planning a new Ranelagh, to be called Vittoria, near Alsop's Buildings. Now, I will prove to you, by a witness I will call, that part of this money was paid by Mr. Cochrane Johnstone to De Berenger, for the plans he had drawn for Mr. Johnstone of the projected garden; and the remainder was lent to Mr. De Berenger on his note of hand, by Mr. Johnstone. Fifty pounds was advanced in September last, when the plans of the garden were begun; and £.200 more was paid in the month of February, the 25th or 26th of February. Mr. De Berenger, at the time he was paid for his plans, stated that his distresses were such, that though what he had received was all he had a right to ask of Mr. Cochrane Johnstone, in satisfaction of that which was due to him for what he had done at Vittoria Gardens, yet he hoped Mr. Cochrane Johnstone would advance him £.200 more, by way of loan. Mr. Cochrane Johnstone was exceedingly desirous of relieving the distresses of Mr. De Berenger; but he would not do it, unless he found he would be effectually relieved by the proposed loan. I will prove to you, therefore, that he took same days to consider of it; and on being satisfied on that point, he did lend De Berenger another £.200; and this money was paid in that manner to Mr. De Berenger and Mr. De Berenger has given his note for it, payable in six months.

Gentlemen, my learned friend told you, that bank-notes were good things to trace crimes; certainly they are. The finding of the notes puts me to give some account of them. I will do that by the evidence I have stated; and I have a foundation laid for the proof that I shall offer, by the evidence produced already in the cause. I have seen the plans; you shall see them; and after you have seen them, if you are called upon by the evidence produced in this cause to convict De Berenger, which I hope you will not be, you will lament that you are bound to convict a man whom you will find to be possessed of so much ingenuity and taste. You will find that the sum paid is but a small remuneration for the attention he had paid, and the skill he had bestowed, in the service of Mr. Cochrane Johnstone; but whether he was well or ill paid is not the question; the payment of the money, I admit, renders some explanation necessary, and I will give it to you.

Gentlemen, I come now to the case of Mr. Butt; and with respect to him the case is very much like that of Mr. Cochrane Johnstone, therefore I shall have occasion to trouble you with but few observations. He is found to have had a large balance on the 21st of February, but he had as large a one before; he sold on this day, but he had sold a much before. He made only £.1,300 on that day; he had made much more on other days; there is not an atom of evidence connecting him with Mr. De Berenger; but the taking of the office applies to him as well as to Mr. Cochrane Johnstone, and also the circumstance of some notes being traced into his hands. Here, gentlemen, I have a difficulty with respect to Mr. Butt, which I cannot explain by evidence so well as I can the transactions of Mr. Cochrane Johnstone; but I am persuaded you will feel that I can, by observation, as completely relieve him from the effect of those notes being in the hands of Mr. De Berenger, as I have Mr. Cochrane Johnstone. I will shew you, by the testimony I shall call, that this debt discharged to Mr. De Berenger, or the sum advanced by way of loan, was principally paid in one pound notes; if so, that will account for the whole of these one pound notes; and as to its going through the hands of Mr. Butt instead of Mr. Cochrane Johnstone, is it any thing wonderful, when you find him acting as a sort of agent for Mr. Cochrane Johnstone, that they should have passed through his hands? But it will appear, that all the notes found in the trunk of Mr. De Berenger got into that trunk, either through the loan or payment of Mr. Cochrane Johnstone. One of the witnesses called for the prosecution has proved the payment by Mr. Cochrane Johnstone of the sum of £.200; but whether that relieves him from the whole or not, are you to say a man is guilty of a conspiracy on such a ground as this? I cannot call these persons for each other; being joined in the indictment, I am deprived of that opportunity. I do not find fault with the prosecutors so doing; but you must be content, under these circumstances, with the best explanation I can offer to you, with respect to that which appears against this gentleman. I shall offer you the best evidence the nature of the case admits; and I cannot do more. If direct evidence cannot be offered, you will not expect it, as my learned friend says on the part of the prosecution, I say on the part of the defendants, and much more strongly. If you see my clients offer you the best evidence the nature of the case admits of, with that I am sure you will be content.

Gentlemen, with respect to Mr. Butt, there is not a tittle of evidence bringing him into connection with Mr. De Berenger; no man has proved that ever they were seen in the same room; no person has ever brought them into connection together; and it is merely because Mr. Butt is a great purchaser of stock, and some of Mr. Butt's money is found passing through the hands of Mr. Cochrane Johnstone into the hands of Mr. De Berenger, that you are desired to find them all connected together in this conspiracy.

Gentlemen, I have divided these three persons cases; but there is an observation common to all the cases, which I feel it my duty to make to you.

My learned friend said, he could not put them in the same room together; but I think if these persons were conspirators, he would have found no difficulty in bringing them nearer together than he has done. I think he might have shewn, that about the Stock Exchange, or at some place or other, they were at some time or other all acting together; we have eight or nine different persons, Mr. de Berenger, Mr. Cochrane Johnstone, Mr. Butt, Lord Cochrane, Mr. Sandom, Mr. Holloway, Mr. Lyte, Mr. M'Rae, all charged as co-conspirators; did any man ever see all these persons together; between a great number of them there is not the least proof of connection; you are desired to find a conspiracy proceeding upon this supposition, that all these parties were acting in concert; and yet between two of the parties, there is no more connection proved to have existed, than there is between you and me, or you and any one of these parties.

Gentlemen, this observation I should have a right to make on any case of a conspiracy. I should have a right to say, it is too dangerous to say these persons were engaged together in a conspiracy; but, Gentlemen, permit me to call your attention to a particular fact proved in this case which negatives the connection of my clients in this conspiracy;—you have two persons who are stated to have made a confession of their guilt; one of these gentlemen appears to have felt the impropriety of his conduct, and in a moment when he had recollected himself, and recollected the offence of which he had been guilty, had gone with a mind disposed to make the fullest compensation that he could to those whom he had injured, and to state all that he knew of the transaction; he goes and he states, that having heard that a Mr. M'Rae was willing to give up the persons who were parties to this conspiracy, on the payment of a large sum; he considers it improper, that the Stock Exchange should be plundered of this large sum, by the extortion of Mr. M'Rae; and therefore, to prevent their paying this large sum to Mr. M'Rae, he (Holloway) goes to the Stock Exchange, and tells them all that Mr. M'Rae could tell them; and what does he say; it would have been enough if he had not said that Mr. Cochrane Johnstone, Lord Cochrane, Mr. Butt and himself, were connected; but he says, in the most distinct terms, that he knew nothing of Lord Cochrane, Mr. Johnstone, or Mr. Butt. The way in which the case is put to you, is, that all these parties were acting altogether; if so, one of the actors must know who were the other persons that were engaged; and Mr. Holloway, who was an actor, declares that he knew nothing of either Mr. Cochrane Johnstone, Mr. Butt, or Lord Cochrane; but Lyte, who was present when Holloway made this declaration, does not contradict; he acknowledges his own guilt, and asks for mercy, but he does not attempt to inculpate my clients. I ask, are you against evidence; against the evidence offered by the prosecutors, for this evidence forms a part of the prosecutors case, to say that these persons were connected with the conspiracy.

Gentlemen, if Mr. Holloway could, at the time he was disposed to make confession of his own guilt, have gone the length of saying, I can prove that Lord Cochrane is a conspirator, I can prove that Mr. Cochrane Johnstone is a conspirator, he would not have been here to-day to answer for his crime; he would not only have been paid, but most amply rewarded, if he could have given any testimony by which the conviction of my clients could have been obtained.

Gentlemen, there is another circumstance I must take leave to press upon you. It seems to me that a conspiracy of this sort could never be carried into effect without some broker being concerned in it. If my clients had been concerned, they would certainly have consulted some of the brokers who have been examined. It is impossible that they could have kept the secret from these brokers; and yet I think it is perfectly clear that they knew nothing of it. It is not pretended by the prosecutors that they had, and from the fairness with which they have given their evidence, it is but just to acquit them of any participation in it.

Gentlemen, I beg to be understood in what I am now about to say, as not intending to impute any thing wrong to Government or to the Stock Exchange; though I think I may venture to say, that what has been done as to the breaking open the trunk, and the searching for these papers, cannot be justified by law; for I know of no law that justifies the Government of the country, or any magistrate whatever, in breaking open trunks and taking away papers on suspicion of a misdemeanor; yet I am not disposed to impute blame to public officers, when impelled by proper and adequate motives, they go a little beyond the strict letter of the law; but where such powers have been exerted to detect guilt, if guilt had existed, it could not have escaped detection. There has been a degree of activity exercised to bring home the guilt to these persons, which I never saw on any former occasions; liberties have been taken which I never saw in a case of misdemeanor before. All De Berenger's papers have been ransacked and taken from him, at a moment when he could have no idea that they would be taken, and therefore could not have destroyed or secreted any, and yet not a single paper is found (but the bank notes), not a single letter; the parties to the conspiracy are never brought together in connection, and it does not appear that there has been any communication by letter. Here seems to be a conspiracy without any possible means of conspiring. I do not see how men are to conspire without communicating with each other, and I am not aware of any other modes of communication than conversation or writing; yet you are desired to find several persons guilty of a conspiracy, without any communication having been proved to have been had between them, and without any writing of any sort having been found.

Gentlemen, there is one other circumstance to which I would wish to allude; not that it concerns my clients, for I am persuaded his lordship will tell you the evidence given by that extraordinary man, Le Marchant, does not bear upon either of my clients, because though where several engage in a conspiracy, you may offer evidence that will affect any one of them, yet the declarations of one cannot affect another; now Mr. Le Marchant was never in the company of Lord Cochrane, he never heard one word that Lord Cochrane said; all that he speaks of are conversations with Mr. De Berenger, which may be evidence against Mr. De Berenger, but in point of law or common sense are no evidence against Lord Cochrane; but I will dispose of this man for the sake of the country, that he may never be sent out of the country in any office. I will shew you that he is a man utterly unworthy of credit, for I will prove to you by his own letters that he comes forward to-day, because Lord Cochrane has refused to lend him money; gentlemen, I have a letter of his, in which he desires to have an interview with Lord Cochrane; he has admitted his own hand-writing to the letters, which I will by and by put in. Lord Cochrane very properly gives no answer to the first letter desiring an interview; on the 7th of April 1814, the first being on the 6th April; on the very next day, Lord Cochrane not answering him, he writes an impertinent letter to Lord Cochrane, which you shall hear read; but I produce it for the purpose of introducing the letter which he admits Lord Cochrane wrote to him, and his answer, from which I argue Lord Cochrane's innocence, and this man's infamy. If Lord Cochrane had felt himself a guilty man, he would not have denied this man when he suggested that he could be of use to him in this cause, but you will find from Lord Cochrane's letter, he says, "I should have hoped, that circumstanced as I am, and attacked by scoundrels of all descriptions, that a gentleman of your understanding might have discovered some better reason than that of silent contempt."

*Mr. Gurney.* My learned friend has not yet proved that letter.

*Mr. Serjeant Best.* I proved that he had the original in his hand; this is the letter of the guilty Lord Cochrane to the innocent Mr. Le Marchant, in answer to the two applications for an interview. "Sir, I should have hoped, circumstanced as I am, and attacked by scoundrels of all descriptions, that a gentleman of your understanding might have discovered some better reason than that of silent contempt;" that is, what he complains of to Lord Cochrane in his second letter, "to account for the delay of a few hours in answering a note; the more particularly as your note of the 6th led me to conclude, that the information offered to me, was meant as a mark of civility and attention, and was not on a subject in which you felt any personal interest." A more prudent letter than that, I defy any man in Lord Cochrane's situation to write. A guilty man catches at any twig, but Lord Cochrane does not answer this gentleman at first, and when pressed by a second letter, he tells him the reason; it is unsafe you and I should meet, I cannot trust you, I am surrounded by scoundrels who are attempting to charge upon me a crime of which I know I am innocent.

Gentlemen, having stated to you in what light this letter shews Lord Cochrane, I beg to read you the last letter of this man, who has offered his evidence to-day; and I will then ask you, whether upon the testimony of such a man as this, you will convict one of the most suspicious characters that ever was produced in a court of justice; whether you would in any cause, of ever so trifling importance, give the least consideration to it. "I ask your lordship's pardon of my letter of yesterday, and which was written under the supposition of being treated with silent contempt;" so that this gentlemen put the true construction upon it, certainly. "To convince you of the high respect I have for your lordship, I have the honour to enclose to you a statement of what I know relative to the 21st February, and I also now declare solemnly, that no power or consideration shall ever induce me to come forward as an evidence against you, and that all I know on the subject shall be buried for ever in oblivion. Thus much I hope will convince you I am more your friend than an enemy, as my testimony, corroborated by the two officers, would be of great import, not (believe me) that I myself doubt in anywise your lordship's affidavit; but De Berenger's conversation with me, would, to your enemies be positive proof. As for my part, I now consider all that man told me to be diabolically false;" and yet he has to-day come forward to tell you the truth, and the whole truth; he has told you what De Berenger said, and has not stated the qualification, that he did not believe one word of it. "If my conduct meets your approbation, can I ask for a reciprocal favour, as a temporary loan, on security being given; I am just appointed to a situation of about £.1,200 a year, but, for the moment, am in the greatest distress, with a large family; you can without risk, and have the means to relieve us, and, I believe, the will of doing good. Necessity has driven me to ask your lordship this favour; whether granted or not, be assured of my keeping my oath now pledged, of secrecy." He has kept that oath, I dare say, as well as he has kept this; he went and gave information, and comes forward to-day to give evidence; you remember how he fenced with the evidence. I ask you, whether you believe, after I have read this, one word of what he has said. I ask you, whether this is not taking advantage of the situation of this noble lord. I am sorry to see that a man can act so scandalous a part, who has the honour of being appointed to a situation of £.1,200 a year; but I am quite satisfied the moment the Government know this, that suspension which does exist, will be continued, and that this man will never be sent to the office to which he was destined. I am quite satisfied, that when this letter is read, you will feel, that even as it respects Mr. De Berenger, for it is applicable only to him, his evidence can have no influence in any court of justice whatever, for that it comes from a man who, in the clearest and most unequivocal manner, declares himself most infamous, and most unworthy of credit.

Gentlemen, I am conscious that fatigued as I felt myself, when I rose to address you, after having been thirteen or fourteen hours in court, I have very imperfectly discharged the duty which I owed my clients; but, gentlemen, I hope they will not suffer, from not having their case presented to you as it ought to have been. Gentlemen, I do not press upon you the considerations which, in criminal cases, are often pressed, and with propriety pressed, upon juries. I do not ask you to take this case in a merciful point of view; I do not press upon you the common observation, to temper your justice with mercy. I ask you to look at this case fairly and impartially; if the guilt of these gentlemen be made out, so that you, upon your oaths, must declare them guilty, say so, dreadful as will be the consequence to all these parties; but unless their guilt is made out, if there be nothing but suspicion, you will not, upon your oaths, say that suspicion is conviction.

Gentlemen, you will recollect the situations of life in which all these men are; they have all up to this moment been the best possible characters, two of them are persons of very high and distinguished situations in life, members of a very noble family; and with respect to one of them, he has reflected back on a long and noble line of ancestors, more glory than he has received from them; and it would be the most painful moment of my life, if I should to-night find that that wreath of laurel which a life of danger and honour has planted round his brows, should in a moment be blasted by your verdict.

MR. PARK.

May it please your Lordship;

Gentlemen of the Jury,

If my learned friend, at the close of his address to you, thought it necessary to make an apology for the fatigue which he had endured in the course of this day, and during his address to you; it becomes much more necessary for me to make such an apology, when it is now sixteen hours and a half since I left my own dwelling. Gentlemen, notwithstanding that, I have a very serious and important duty to discharge to the person who now sits by me, and I have no difficulty in calling upon you, in the most serious manner, fatigued and exhausted as you may be, for your attention; you must not permit, I take the liberty of saying, as you regard the oath you have taken, you must not permit that fatigue to disable you from attention to the statement and the evidence that are to be laid before you.

Gentlemen, the case has become an extremely serious and a most important one; for the gentlemen for whom my learned friend the Serjeant has addressed you, I have nothing to say; they have been well and ably defended;

but I am to address you on behalf of a gentleman totally unknown to me till this day, when I saw him in Court. He is represented to me as a gentleman of very high descent, and though he has been unfortunate in his pecuniary circumstances, he has been proved, before you to-day, to be man of very considerable attainments, and of high and literary character; it is therefore your duty, and I know it is a duty you will honestly and faithfully discharge, not to allow what my learned friend cautioned you well against, but immediately fell into the very same course himself; not to allow any thing like prejudice to bias any of your minds.

Gentlemen, I am no flatterer of persons who sit in your place; and I have no difficulty in telling you twelve gentlemen, that, though I have no doubt you are honorable men, you cannot have lived in this city, in which you are all merchants, for the last two months of your lives, without having every hour of the day, and at every meal at which you sat down, had your ears assailed by accounts of this transaction, and there is no one, however honourable he may be, who can prevent his mind being biassed by circumstances stated in common conversation. Gentlemen, I only know this matter publicly; but I declare one could hardly go into any company, where the discourse has not been turned upon this very circumstance we are now discussing; how difficult is it then for you to recollect, that you are not to decide upon any thing you heard before you came into that box, but upon the evidence produced before you. But, did my learned friend himself follow that course which he prescribed to you? Did he embark no prejudice into this matter? My learned friend will give me leave to say, that I own it is quite new to me, that in discussing criminal matters, the counsel for the prosecution are to argue it and labour it as they would a cause between party and party:—I dare say I have been extremely faulty in that respect, but having been engaged in criminal prosecutions, chiefly in the service of His Majesty, I never thought myself at liberty so to treat criminal prosecutions. I have generally acted on the opposite scheme, and mean, till corrected, so to continue to act; but at all events, I am surprised that my learned friend, with whose good nature in private life we are all acquainted, should have introduced before you, that which I say my learned friend's great experience in courts of justice told him, before he pronounced it, he had no right to read in evidence before you. I do not speak lightly of this; you will remember we had an affidavit, supposed to have been made by William Smith, read verbatim from some pamphlet my learned friend had in his hand; he knew perfectly well that it could not be given in evidence; if William Smith was called as a witness, undoubtedly my learned friend might ask him, whether he had not sworn the contrary at another time; but it will be for my learned friend to explain to you, under what rule it was, that he was at liberty to read such a document as a part of his speech, which, by the rules of law, could not be received in evidence in this place.

Gentlemen, there was another circumstance which my learned friend has introduced to prejudice this case; and unless I have deceived myself, or my ears have deceived me, I have heard no such evidence given in the cause, as my learned friend stated; a stronger statement to prejudice could hardly be made in a case of this sort; but I heard no such question put to Wood, the messenger, and I listened with all the attention I could to his examination.— My learned friend stated, that Mr. De Berenger had been extremely anxious to get back into his hands the identical notes; that no other notes would serve him; that he must have those notes, and those only delivered back. Was this stated without any reason by my learned friend? Certainly not; it would have been, if the fact had corresponded with the statement, an extremely strong argument on the part of my learned friend against this gentleman for whom I am counsel. But my learned friend, and his learned coadjutors, never put to any witness, at any one period of this cause, the question, whether Mr. De Berenger made any such application to their knowledge? and all this is a gratuitous statement of my learned friend, but a statement that went to prejudice, or was intended to prejudice, your minds upon the subject, and it undoubtedly was very important.

Gentlemen, this may have been said in places unknown to me; it may have been said in newspapers for aught I know to the contrary; but, thank God, I never read newspapers with that attention some gentlemen do, for I think it is a great waste of time. If men are in public situation, they must read them; but I have heard no statement in evidence of that circumstance, which my learned friend Mr. Gurney so much relied upon, and so much reasoned upon in his statement to you.

Gentlemen, it was also said, that there had been publications in this case; I do not know by whom those publications have taken place. There was some evidence given by Mr. Richardson, of a publication by Mr. Butt; that I suppose my learned friend has seen; I have not; but I do not go along with my learned friend in this; I do not agree, that these are the necessary consequences of a free press; I have always been of opinion, and always shall, because it is firmly rooted in my mind, that all previous publications on one side or the other, tending to inflame the minds of the Jury, who are to try questions between the King and his subjects, or between party and party, on whatever side they may be published, are most highly and extremely improper. I think it is a disgrace, that the press of this country has engendered such an avidity in the public mind to have these things detailed to them; that they indulge it to a degree subversive of all justice. Hardly a case has happened within our own observation of late years, that the whole of the case has not been detailed before it came to trial, so that it is impossible but that the minds of the jurymen (and men cannot divine whether they shall be jurymen or not) should receive a bias upon this subject; but it is very hard that all the obloquy which such publications merit, should be thrown upon the defendants. Did that self-constituted Committee of the Stock Exchange, of which I shall speak much more plainly by and by, and tell you what I think of that committee; did that self-constituted Committee of the Stock Exchange, who have brought forward this as a charge against the defendants, make no publication; did they not placard on the doors of their Stock Exchange, the names of these gentlemen, members of the legislature, and persons standing so high in the country? Why did they set so infamous an example? I admit to follow it was bad; but to set it, I insist, was much worse.

Gentlemen, whatever blame may have attached upon some of the defendants, if they have made these publications, my client, Mr. De Berenger, is not implicated in any such transactions. Those who have published have only followed the example set them by the prosecutors on this occasion.

Gentlemen, there are certain rules of evidence on subjects of this nature, with which I am sure you are in a great degree acquainted, but upon which you will hear more from his Lordship by and by. It is quite clear that no declarations of one party, though he may be indicted with the others, can be evidence against the other defendants, unless they be present at that declaration. My learned friend, the Serjeant, has so fully gone through the general nature of the case, that it would be impertinent in me to do it; but I shall observe such things as occur to me, on the different species of proof on the part of the prosecution, and I think I shall most decidedly convince you, that even as the case stands, if it was not to be met by the evidence by which it will be met, it would be impossible for you to convict any of these parties, for whom my learned friend and myself are counsel.

Gentlemen, I will presently come to the evidence by which Mr. De Berenger is supposed to be traced from Dover to London; but the great point upon which my learned friend relied, as affecting him after he came to London, was the contradictory statement, as it is supposed, of Lord Cochrane in his affidavit. Gentlemen, first, upon the subject of what are called voluntary affidavits. It is extremely absurd in magistrates ever to take them; no man who knows the law, if he knew he was taking a mere voluntary affidavit, would swear the person before him; but as far as the magistrates are concerned, it is impossible from the nature of the thing, that they should know whether they are voluntary affidavits or not, for there is a great part of the business of magistrates which does not depend upon the hearing of parties, and unless they were to read every affidavit through, which would be to impose a great burthen upon them, they must sometimes swear a party to a voluntary affidavit.

But, Gentlemen, let us look to Lord Cochrane's situation in this matter. I will suppose that Lord Cochrane knew he was not liable to the pains and penalties of perjury by law; but is Lord Cochrane so reduced in the scale of society by any thing that has yet appeared before you, that you will say he has not only joined in committing the fraud in this conspiracy charged, but that he is a person wholly unworthy of credit, and who, though he may not be subjected to the penalties of perjury, is lost to all sense of duty, so that he would, because he could not be prosecuted at law for the perjury, put his name to a direct and absolute falsehood. I believe no man would say of Lord Cochrane, that he had so utterly thrown off all regard to religion, to the sanction of an oath, properly so called, and to the responsibility he stands under in conscience, as that he would go before a magistrate and make an affidavit, because he could not be prosecuted. I think the supposition is so shocking and so degradatory to him as a man, an officer and a christian, that you will not come to that conclusion. That Lord Cochrane is a brave man, that he has served his country well, no man will deny. Does Mr. Baily then, do the three other brokers, who demurred to the question put to them as to time bargains; do all this mass of people, constituting the Stock Exchange, now standing within the sound of my voice, mean to say, that because Lord Cochrane has acted so improperly (for I so consider it) as to enter into a time-bargain, therefore he is not to be believed upon his oath? If so, Gentlemen, the Stock Exchange and its doors must be shut up for ever; and the great men who stalk about as the self-constituted Committee of the Stock Exchange, must not have any thing to do in future, because time-bargains are their daily bread; they are at that species of traffic daily, conducting themselves in a manner, whether they like it or not, I say, is most highly disgraceful.

Gentlemen, is Lord Cochrane to be believed or not? have you any ground for saying, that this noble Lord has been guilty, not of perjury in the common sense of the word, but of perjury of a much higher kind, in my view, for which he must be accountable, for which he knows he must be accountable, if he has sworn that which he knows to be false, and which he cannot have done without being one of the most worthless men in the world. Gentlemen, what has he said? and I beg your particular attention to it, because the evidence of the brokers will not tally with the statement at all; he has sworn that he breakfasted with his uncle, Mr. Cochrane Johnstone, in Cumberland place, which is at a considerable distance (whatever my learned friend may suppose about it) from Green-street Grosvenor-square; it is on the other side, I believe, of the Oxford Road, and near the top of it. It is proved that he breakfasted with him, for Crain's evidence is, that when he set down Mr. De Berenger at the door, the answer was, that he was gone to Cumberland Place. What does Lord Cochrane state; that he went with his uncle in a hackney coach, which took him into the city at the hour of ten in the morning. I beg his lordship's particular attention to that part of the affidavit. Now, Gentlemen, when is it that these time-bargains are supposed to have been made, in consequence of news which it is alleged Mr. De Berenger brought. It is sworn that they were made before eleven o'clock in the day. Why, Gentlemen, we are forgetting distances. If Lord Cochrane was set down at Snow-hill at ten in the morning, if he afterwards came back, as he did, to Green-street Grosvenor-square, being sent for by his servant or Mr. De Berenger, he could not be back before half-past ten or nearly eleven, and I defy all mankind to state how he could after that have communicated to the Stock Exchange, the news this gentleman was supposed to be dispersing abroad, so as to affect the price of stocks. The whole of the transaction took place before eleven in the day, and he was not sent for from Snow-hill till after ten. Why, if this gentleman had been a conspirator with Lord Cochrane, when he heard that Lord Cochrane was gone to Snow-hill, he would have gone on to Snow-hill, then they would have been near the purlieus of that place where all this infamy is daily transacting; instead of that Lord Cochrane comes back. It is too ridiculous and absurd, says my learned friend, to suppose that Lord Cochrane should be coming back to see an officer. I hope, gentlemen, that will not appear to you to be absurd under the circumstances he has sworn to. I can hardly conceive a motive stronger on the mind of a brave man and a good officer for going back, than that stated by him. He was not acquainted with Mr. De Berenger's hand-writing, though Mr. Cochrane Johnstone was. Having a brother in Spain, he expected that he should receive accounts of him from a brother officer; is that an unnatural sensation? I trust it will never be so in the bosom of any one to whom I am addressing myself; it is one of the most natural that can be stated, and under that impression he goes back, and holds the conversation which has been stated.

Gentlemen, it is stated to you by my learned friend, the Serjeant, and he has better means of proving these things than I have, that the grounds upon which this matter rests, as far as Lord Cochrane is concerned, will be fully explained. The gentleman for whom I appear was, at that time, under duress on account of debt; and Mr. Tahourdin, now his attorney, was his security for that debt. He was a distressed man, and was desirous of going out to Sir Alexander Cochrane, who had had conversation with this gentleman, whose bravery and whose character nobody will dispute; and it will be proved to you Sir Alexander Cochrane had made application to the noble lord near his lordship, to enable him to go out to America; but he could not go, because His Majesty's ministers thought (and I dare say most wisely) that it was not fit to give him the rank which he claimed, being a foreigner by birth, though he had been long serving in this country with the approbation of His Majesty's Government. He was a member of the corp of sharp shooters, of which Lord Yarmouth or the Duke of Cumberland was the colonel. He was the adjutant of that regiment, and he had that military garb and dress which might have been sworn to by Lord Cochrane in the way my learned friend supposes, or in consequence of the facts which I have to state. I do not know why I am placed here at all, if I am to take for granted facts because witnesses have sworn them; therefore I say, Lord Cochrane might either mistake, upon the grounds upon which the learned Serjeant has stated it; or the fact might be, as my learned friend has stated, that he was not the man. I know that some of the witnesses have sworn that he was the man whom the hackney coachman took to Lord Cochrane's, but whether he had this uniform on which is stated, I have no means of proving from his declaration; but I have Lord Cochrane's affidavit as to his wearing that which was his proper uniform.

Then, gentlemen, upon my Lord Cochrane's affidavit it stands, and I say that at present there is not evidence enough to meet it. We have not often had the experience of that which has been done to-day; I believe not above twice in my professional life have I seen a prosecutor put in an answer in Chancery of the person who was defendant, and then negative that answer; but I say, there is not that negation of Lord Cochrane's story which can set it aside. You are bound to take all that Lord Cochrane swears upon the subject; and he has sworn to you that Mr. De Berenger did not communicate to him any single fact respecting the stocks, but that all his communication was with respect to his then distresses. Now, gentlemen, where is the inconsistency of that which appears upon the evidence before the Court, and that which will be produced. If this gentleman was desirous of going out with Lord Cochrane in the Tonnant, and if he had done that which I am not commending, though I shall presently shew it is not so culpable as it at first appears. He had no right, I acknowledge, to break the rules of the King's Bench, having the benefit of those rules, but where is the great wickedness of it? He gave bail to the marshal to answer the risk; but if he had come out of that place, dressed as you hear, by my Lord Cochrane, he had done so with a view of going immediately off to Portsmouth; and when my Lord Cochrane could not take him, though there was no inconsistency in his coming in that uniform, which was to be useful to him if he got out to America, there was a great deal of difficulty, at twelve or one in the day, in his returning in that garb or dress into the rules of the King's Bench prison, for he had not only to walk from the place whence those rules began to the house of Davidson, but first of all to where the rules began; and therefore, though it might be imprudent in Lord Cochrane, I shall prove that he did lend clothes to Mr. De Berenger, for that he returned in the black clothes to his lodgings, and that he had in a bundle those clothes which he had taken out on his back. There appears to me nothing so absurd in the story as to induce you to say, that Lord Cochrane has written to the public that which was wholly and absolutely false within his own knowledge, in order to deceive the public.

Gentlemen, when this person found that he could neither go with Lord Cochrane, nor in any other capacity, to Sir Alexander Cochrane, who was then out of the kingdom, you will ask me, why did he then escape from the Rules? Gentlemen, I will tell you:—The fact is, though he was only in duress for £.350; and although this gentleman who sits near him, who is his attorney, and will be called as a witness in the cause, was the principal creditor, who had been his surety for the Rules, he escaped from the Rules, under the apprehension that he should have detainers against him for four thousand pounds more. He asked this gentleman permission to go out of the Rules. I am not prepared to defend the act; but he was the only person who was beneficially interested in his remaining in the Rules; for he and Mr. Cochrane, in Fleet-street, having given this bail, the marshal of the King's Bench could, of course, come upon them for the amount of that sum; and I will prove to you, that he had the leave of this gentleman to go, and that this gentleman took the debt upon himself. He went to Sunderland, and afterwards to Leith; and he went there to avoid that which he was apprehensive of, namely, detention by his other creditors, to this very large amount.

Gentlemen, when we talk of prejudice upon this subject, this very thing has been attempted to-day to be put upon his lordship; and you, as a matter of prejudice against Mr. De Berenger, namely, that Mr. Tahourdin, who was attorney for Mr. Cochrane Johnstone, and Mr. Cochrane (a relation as it was supposed of this family, or there was no sense in it) were his bail. But, gentlemen, Mr. Broochooft has negatived the fact; he states that he did not even know Mr. Cochrane Johnstone. Mr. Tahourdin was a creditor of Mr. De Berenger to the amount of four thousand pounds, but he had so good an opinion of him that he consented to his liberating himself; and as to the other security, Mr. Cochrane the bookseller, he is no more a relation of the family of Dundonald, than I who do not know the persons of any of them; but he is a friend of Mr. Tahourdin, whose sister is married to Mr. White, Mr. Cochrane's partner; that is the history of the transaction on which it is supposed that Mr. Cochrane Johnstone has been putting in bail, because Mr. Tahourdin was his attorney; but it will appear that bail was put in two years ago, and that Mr. Tahourdin did not become acquainted with Mr. Cochrane Johnstone till long after that time.

Gentlemen, there have been other prejudices attempted here; they are prejudices that I think could never have entered into the mind of any liberal man; they must have entered first into the minds of the Stock Exchange Committee, for no gentleman could think of such a thing; that which I refer to is, that which my learned friend the Serjeant has commented upon, the proof of Mr. De Berenger being a friend of Mr. Cochrane Johnstone, from the circumstance of his dining with the family. Gentlemen, is every one who dines there to be considered as a conspirator? they are not a committee sitting over their bottle and hatching this infamy; but it appears that he dined twice at the house of Mr. Basil Cochrane (who is not implicated in this), not alone, but with Sir Alexander Cochrane, and a great number of ladies and gentlemen; and at another time Mr. De Berenger and Mr. Cochrane Johnstone also dined at Mr. Basil Cochrane's.

Gentlemen, I am told, and I believe, after what I have heard in this cause, for I have heard it from Mr. Murray, that Mr. De Berenger is a man of great abilities; his Society and his company were much courted till his misfortunes put him out of the general run of society; was there ever such a thing attempted till this moment, as that you were from such circumstance to prove a conspiracy as against these persons? On what ground can it be said that his connexion with Mr. Cochrane Johnstone is a matter of complaint against him? I have proved what it was; I have proved, out of the mouth of Mr. Murray, and shall prove again if necessary, that the meeting of these gentlemen there was not a meeting of business; was there any thing in the conversation when Mr. De Berenger came in, in the presence of Mr. Harrison, that gives the least suspicion of a connexion with Mr. Cochrane Johnstone? it appears only, that he being an ingenious man, engaged himself in this Ranelagh that was building, from which it was expected (probably it will terminate in nothing) by Mr. Cochrane Johnstone, that he would derive great benefit; this gentleman, being consulted on the plan first proposed, recommended another from which he conceived Mr. Cochrane Johnstone would make a great deal more money; there is nothing in the connexion more than that. Are you from that circumstance to infer that this gentleman was guilty of any conspiracy? as to any negociation on this subject, you hear nothing nor see nothing. You do not find him at any one period of time with Mr. Cochrane Johnstone. You hear of his dining twice in company with him at the house of Mr. Basil Cochrane; you do not hear of him at all there, except about this Ranelagh; but you are desired from that to infer criminality.

But gentlemen, this is a most important transaction; my learned friend has told you he will more satisfactorily explain it by the evidence upon the subject; there is no doubt of the gentleman who sits before me being in distress of circumstances, but at the same time a most ingenious man; and having done various works of art for Mr. Cochrane Johnston, the latter thought himself indebted to him about two hundred pounds, and paid him the money. Gentlemen, all I can say upon this is, that there is no conspiracy amongst us here, for I do assure you, that until I came into this place, and saw my learned friends, except my learned friend Mr. Topping, with whom I had spoken on the subject, I did not know that the others were concerned for the defendants upon this occasion; but I hear my learned friend state that which I trust he has the means of proving, but which my unfortunate client has not, not only because many of his papers have been immediately taken from him by the messenger, in the manner described, but because he is himself a close prisoner in Newgate, under a warrant of the Alien Office, and therefore has not the same means and opportunity of conferring with his Counsel; for I have never placed myself in that situation, and do not mean hastily to go there, for it is not a very agreeable service, and I would take no man's retainer, if I thought that I must do so; there has not therefore been that communication which we should have had, if our client had been a free man. But I shall prove by some witnesses of my own, that which will give a considerable colour to my case, and shall pray in aid all the evidence given by any other witnesses on this side of the question.

Gentlemen, before I leave this part of the case, I would wish also to remind you that we have had another piece of evidence given against my unfortunate client, by a man of the name of Le Marchant. I will venture to say, and I hope you have observed, that a much more extraordinary witness never did present himself in that box. It does not become me (and I am the last man to do it) to arraign any one act of His Majesty's ministers, but I believe that the exhibition made this day in the presence of some of His Majesty's ministers, will have been sufficient to set aside any intention of sending him out under an appointment, if it ever prevailed in their minds; for I do say, I think he would disgrace any country from which he was sent on any public business whatever; I think he would not be long in any situation, before he disgraced himself as a man, and brought disgrace upon those who employed him. But gentlemen, I do not know whether you observed another thing, which is, that he shot out of court as if he had had a sword stuck into him, and appeared no more; I never saw any thing so marked as his conduct was upon that occasion.

My learned friend has called your attention to his letter, which I never saw till he read it; my client was protesting against his testimony; but I cannot call him as a witness against this man's evidence, which Mr. Richardson endeavoured by his cross-examination to alter, because it was our duty to endeavour to get some alteration of that evidence, not knowing how he had conducted himself. I do earnestly beg of you to recall to your attention, the answers he gave to my learned friend, the Serjeant; did he not positively say upon that examination, that he was only kept by His Majesty's ministers in this country to give evidence, and that he had not given his evidence at all from a feeling of resentment, because Lord Cochrane had not complied with his request in giving him money. Gentlemen, when this correspondence comes to be read by his lordship's officer, is it possible you can believe one word of that; he in this letter, which is the last my learned friend stated, and the only one on which I will comment, stated that he believed every thing that De Berenger had told him respecting Lord Cochrane, was false. If it was all false, as it respected Lord Cochrane, it was all false as it respected himself, for this man had no time-bargains as the other gentlemen had, he was to derive no immediate benefit, except as you believe that man. I beg your particular attention to that, that he is the only person who swears to his having a per centage in this matter. I think I am correct in that statement, that Le Marchant is the only person who says De Berenger told him that he was to have a per centage upon the stock. Now gentlemen, this conversation having been on the 14th of February, seven days before this transaction, he makes the observation in this letter, that he verily believes that every thing De Berenger told him respecting Lord Cochrane was false.

If it was all false, it must be false with respect to De Berenger himself, and according to his own statement he must have invented this story, merely to implicate Lord Cochrane in the transaction; it is absurd gentlemen not to speak to you as men of understandings. Do you believe that this letter has any other sense, than give me so much money, or I will do so and so? After threatening him, he says, "As for my part, I now consider all that man told me to be diabolically false," and then without even a new paragraph in his letter, "If my conduct meets your approbation;" what conduct meets his approbation, that he would say in all places and at all times that this man's statement was diabolically false, as far as respected Lord Cochrane; "Can I ask a reciprocal favour, as a temporary loan, on security being given;" then he goes on to say, "I am just appointed to a situation of about £.1,200 a-year; but for the moment am in the greatest distress, with a large family; you can without risk, and have the means to relieve us, and I believe the will of doing good." And then, because Lord Cochrane most wisely refuses to comply with this request, we have this man set up in the box, to tell you this supposed story of De Berenger, which De Berenger has no means of contradicting; but which I say is so incredible, and so contradicted by the letter under his own hand, that I think jurymen, if it stood upon his testimony alone, or even supported by one or two witnesses to other things, would do most unrighteously if they convicted upon such testimony as that fellow has given, for I never saw a man so disgrace himself as he done.

Now gentlemen, with respect to the proof of Mr. De Berenger's hand writing, as to those things which were found in his box. I put Mr. Lavie's evidence out of the question; at first his lordship put it, that it was slight evidence; but that it was evidence subject to my observations, the thing being found upon him; gentlemen, supposing there was no evidence of his hand-writing, I can only say he must be well clothed in innocence who can escape, if a man is to be convicted, merely because a paper is found upon him; if a man writes to me a paper containing matter of a criminal nature, and I happen not to destroy it, I must immediately be convicted. I do not mean that his Lordship has said so; but if I am to be convicted because a paper is found upon me, then a man may be in danger from every letter he receives from a correspondent; I am sorry to say that I receive a great many letters which I do not answer; but does my possession of the letters give ground for inferring an approval of all contained in those letters. If you were to convict this gentleman on account of any memorandums found in his possession, because they are found there, I do think a great injustice indeed would be worked.

But, gentlemen, Mr. Lavie has proved his hand-writing. I shall call witnesses to contradict Mr. Lavie; but do not misunderstand me, I believe Mr. Lavie to be a very honourable person, and one who would not tell you a falsehood; but I say he has not the means of knowledge. I can only say, gentleman, that a man must be much more attentive to hands-writing than most of the persons of my profession, in which I include Mr. Lavie, if he can swear to a hand-writing, because he has seen that hand-writing once. I have seen my learned friends near me write many times, but I could not swear to their hands-writing; if I saw a very bad hand indeed, I should say it was Mr. Serjeant Best's; but let me caution you; you are trying these defendants for a conspiracy; you are trying them for a crime of the greatest and most enormous magnitude; you are trying them for an offence that will shut these gentlemen, if you find them guilty, out of the pale of all honourable and decent society; and therefore, though this subject is one, which, from the singularity of it, may create a smile, it is a matter which you will not smile upon when you come to pronounce your verdict; because upon your verdict must the happiness of these gentlemen depend. Will you, upon the evidence of Mr. Lavie, honourable as may believe him to be, and just as you may believe him to be, say that he has those means of knowledge which he professes to have.

Gentlemen, I am placed in a very awkward situation as to that paper, which my client assures me he never saw, and I mean to call witnesses to prove, that he is not the writer of it; I do not think it necessary, but I will do it, for it shall not rest upon me that I have not done my duty. But I am placed in an awkward situation as to the hand-writing; I do not complain of it, but the witnesses into whose hands I must put that paper, have never seen it. Mr. Lavie has seen it; he has had an opportunity of conning it over; but I think he might have done better than to have given his own testimony of this Mr. de Berenger's writing. Mr. de Berenger is not an obscure man in the city of London; he has lived in this country twenty-five years; he tells me there was no man acquainted with his hand-writing, who could be called to prove this to be his hand-writing; and that no witness to speak to that could be found; but Mr. Lavie went to him improperly; for the Stock Exchange had no more right to break in upon Mr. de Berenger, at the Parliament-street coffee-house, than any one of you. I say it was an impertinent intrusion; this gentleman was brought up on a warrant not respecting this affair, but on a warrant from the Secretary of State, whilst he was fatigued and tired, as he stated to the messenger; still most disgracefully the messenger allowed Mr. Lavie and the Stock Exchange Committee to pump him upon this matter. How the handwriting is attempted to be proved, it does not become me to say further; but I put papers into the hand of Mr. Lavie, the hand-writing of which, if they be of the hand-writing of Mr. De Berenger, I will venture to say that the paper lying before his Lordship is not; because I have eyes as well as Mr. Lavie has; and I think I can speak to any hand-writing as well as he can. I say it is not the same hand-writing as these, if my eyes do not deceive me; and I shall put it into the hands of persons who have known Mr. De. Berenger long, and they shall say whether it be his hand-writing or not. Gentlemen, if it be not his hand-writing, which I must assume, I say the whole of that Dover case falls to the ground; because the main sheet-anchor of the whole of the Dover case is that paper. Why do I say so? Because all the witnesses who have come from the Ship Inn at Dover, Marsh, Gerely, Edis, (Wright is not here, being ill;) these men one and all, speak to the person called Du Bourg, as being the person who sent this letter, as aid-de-camp to Lord Cathcart; they all say it was this man, as they believe, that wrote that letter, and sent it off to Admiral Foley. I say, gentleman, that story, as applied to Mr. De Berenger, falls to the ground, if that letter was not the hand-writing of Mr. De Berenger; inasmuch as the letter is now supposed to be traced into the hands of Admiral Foley, from the Ship Inn at Dover, by the conveyance of the little boy. If Mr. De Berenger was not the writer of it, then Mr. De Berenger was not the man who was at that inn.

Gentlemen, it was said by Mr. Gurney in his opening, that he should call the landlord and landlady of the house at which Mr. De Berenger lodged, to prove that he did not sleep at home that night; but they have proved no such thing. I expected, from my learned friend's statement of it, and I am sure he expected it, or he would not have so stated it, that they would have proved that. The man says, he does not know who comes in and who goes out, being the clerk of a stockbroker, and being a good deal out; he says, Mr. De Berenger comes in without their interference; he has his own servants; and all he reasons from is the fact, that he did not hear him blow his French horn at eight or nine o'clock on the Monday morning, which I shall prove to you he could not do, for that Mr. De Berenger went out to Lord Cochrane's at eight o'clock. These people do not swear, that he did not sleep at home; all they say is, that they do not know whether he was at home or not.

Now, Gentlemen, upon the subject upon which I am about to address you, I do not think it absolutely necessary to go into it; and I should not at this hour in the morning call evidence, but in a matter so highly penal as this is, and where I am placed in so delicate a situation, and in which, thank God, I can very seldom be placed, I do not think it right to act on my own judgment, where my client assures me that he was not the man, and is an innocent person; and that he is determined (because he knows perfectly well that what he says is the truth) to have his witnesses called; he shall have those witnesses called, for I chuse to have no responsibility cast upon me that does not belong to my situation. Gentlemen, I shall prove to you most completely that which will dispose of the case, if it is believed. I trust I have already shewn, that it is a case depending upon such frail testimony, as it stands, that it is not worthy of any degree of credit. But I am instructed, that I shall be able to call five or six witnesses, who all saw this gentleman in London, at an hour which was impossible, consistently with the case for the prosecution, and who have no interest, and had better means of knowledge than those who have been called before you.

Gentlemen, I do not mean to say those witnesses who have been called before you have been perjured; but I mean to say, they had not the same means of knowledge with my witnesses; and that, except one of them, or two at the utmost, they had not the day light to assist them in observations they made upon this traveller. Be so good as to recollect the circumstances under which he was supposed to have come to Dover; he is found knocking at the door of the Ship Inn, about one in the morning; the man belonging to the opposite house, having been carousing there at a most astonishingly late hour for a reputable tradesman, in the town of Dover, the hatter, the cooper, and the landlord, being sitting together, hear a knocking at the door; and they find a man in the passage of the house. Whom do they find there? a man dressed in the manner you have heard described; but the person who sees him, and holds the candle in the passage, has a very short conversation with him; the whole time he saw him did not exceed five minutes, and in that time he went up to call the landlord; he put the pen, ink and paper, into his room, and then he left him; he did not see him without his cap, and yet he swears he is the man; and he is not singular in that, for there are many others swear to the same.

Gentlemen, it is a prejudice my client has to encounter, that we have been engaged in this case seventeen hours; and that my learned friend, Mr. Gurney, who opened the case, was in the full possession of his powers, and that he has in a measure forestalled your minds by the evidence he has given, and that the evidence given by me has to eradicate the impressions which his statements and his evidence have made. Gentlemen, I put questions to one of the witnesses which his lordship thought were not of any weight, and *per se* they were not strong; but when we are proving identity every little circumstance goes to the question, aye or no; we had some witnesses swearing to a slouch cap, one which comes over the eyes, and another swearing that it was like the coat, *grey*; another that it was a dark brown. If the *fac simile* is correct, there are discordances in the evidence which raise a suspicion in my mind, a suspicion not that the witnesses are perjuring themselves, but that they had not sufficient means of knowledge upon the subject; and that you are called upon to convict this gentleman of a base and infamous crime, from which, except from the evidence of Le Marchant, he was to derive no benefit unless the £.400 was a *bonus*, and that upon the evidence of witnesses, who, however respectable, had very little means of observation; for it was not day light hardly even when they left Dartford; and the morning we hear was a foggy morning, and therefore, except Shilling's evidence, we have not evidence that this is the man in *day light*; we have no evidence of any persons who saw him in daylight, and identify him as being the person who came from Dover to London; Shilling's evidence I admit, is, as to his seeing him in day light, and his evidence is extremely strong undoubtedly.

Gentlemen, I am quite aware, though I have not practised a great deal in criminal courts, that the evidence of an *alibi*, as we call it, that is evidence to prove that the person was not upon the spot, is always evidence of a very suspicious nature; it is always to be watched therefore; but I am sure that I shall have his lordship's sanction for this; that if the witnesses to be called have all the means of knowledge upon the subject, if the generality of them have no interest at all in the matter of discussion, and if they prove the *alibi* satisfactorily, there is no evidence more complete than that of *alibi*, and that *alibi* will produce advantage in favour of the person who sets it up, according to the nature of that case which is made against him; and if it be merely circumstantial evidence, although that is in some cases much stronger than positive testimony, yet if the evidence against that person is chiefly mere evidence of identity of person, I say that the proof of the *alibi* will receive stronger confirmation, if those witnesses who undertake to identify have not had sufficient means of knowledge upon the subject.

Hear then, Gentlemen, how I shall prove this case. This person, by the consent of his bail, Mr. Tahourdin, as I have told you, was continually soliciting for the situation he was desirous of obtaining, for the purpose of going out to America under Sir Alexander Cochrane; he was therefore continually violating the rules; and in order to do that with safety, he used to go down a passage and take water, instead of crossing Westminster Bridge; because he thought that on Westminster Bridge he should be more likely to be met by the officers, and so more likely to get to the ears of the marshal, so as to lose the benefit of the rules; he was well known to the usual watermen plying there; and I have two watermen here, who will prove to you that on that Sunday morning, which was the first Sunday after the frost broke up, so as to open the river Thames, which had been shut a considerable time, that on the first Sunday after, namely, the 20th of February, this gentleman crossed at that ferry to go over to the Westminster side. Gentlemen, I shall prove to you, that in the course of that day he was at Chelsea; he had been known at Chelsea, having lived there for a considerable time before he was in the rules of the Bench. I will prove that he had called at a house which I will not name, because we shall have that from the witnesses from whence the stage coaches go; that the ostler at that house perfectly well knew him, and that he knew his servant; that he told him the coach had gone off at an early hour in the evening, and there was no coach to go for some time; he will tell you, that he knew this gentleman, and is positively sure that he was there. I shall prove that he went to another house in the course of that evening; and I have two or three of the members of that family who saw and conversed with him between eight and nine in the evening of the Sunday, so that by the course of time, it was absolutely impossible that he could have been at Dover by one in the morning, if he had been at this gentleman's house at eight in the evening. I shall prove that after that he went home to his lodgings. I shall prove that he slept in his lodgings; that his bed was in the morning made by his maid servant; that he constantly slept at home, and that he did that night. I have his servants here who will prove these facts. I allow that he went out that morning, and went out in regimentals, which they will describe to you, and went to Lord Cochrane's upon the errand I have described to you.

Now, Gentlemen, in addition to that, there will be the evidence to be given by my learned friend, Mr. Serjeant Best, which I have a right, as far as it applies to Mr. De Berenger, to pray in aid for him. Does it not immediately go to shew, that it is impossible, but that these persons who have been examined for the prosecution, must have been mistaken? I do not ask you to presume that these persons have knowingly said what is not true; but this made a great noise, and persons were sent to see Mr. De Berenger, and from some similarity of person believed him to be the man. I do not indeed believe the account given by one of the witnesses, Mr. St. John; he told a story the most singular, that he being the collector of an Irish charitable society, with no other means of livelihood, found himself at Dover searching for news, by desire of the editor of a newspaper, and he was afterwards on coming up, sent to Newgate to see Mr. De Berenger, who was exposed to the view of every person who chose to look at him. Mr. De Berenger was fixed upon as the man, and you are asked to presume that he fled, because he knew he was the man. Gentlemen, you will take all these circumstances into your consideration, and they will account for the mistake in the testimony of the witnesses for the prosecution; but St. John tells you, that he found himself by *accident* at Westminster. I do not call that an accident at all, for it appears that he walked down to Westminster to see his person; he went and took a good view of his person, when he was standing upon the floor of the court of King's Bench, pleading to his indictment, for being in custody he must be brought into court to plead to it; this fellow says, he was not in court, but he put his head within the curtain, where he could see this gentleman, he heard the officer read to him, and he says that he answered something; I do not care whether he heard what passed, he saw sufficient to know that he was the person in custody. I cannot, under these circumstances, believe this fellow when he tells you, that he went by *accident* down to Westminster, for it appears evidently that he went by *design*. I say there is a readiness and a desire on the part of the Stock Exchange, to follow this up, I think, with an improper spirit.

Gentlemen, we have had this case dressed up to-day; and it has been attempted to induce you to believe, that the transactions of the Stock Exchange were all laudable. Gentlemen, I say they are infamous; but my learned friend would persuade you, that all the infamy rests upon those who deceived these poor creatures. It is very true, as his lordship says, the circulation of a false report is not innocent, for that may operate against you or me going fairly to buy stock; but I think there has been an excess of zeal on this business; some of these witnesses were carried to Mr. Wood's, at Westminster, and they all fixed upon Mr. De Berenger, not corruptly, but in consequence of being carried there, and his being pointed out as the man by Mr. Lavie and some of his clerks; they come readily enough and fix upon him; the deaf man not so easily, but at last he did it too; and it struck me, the question I put to that deaf man was extremely relevant. I cannot tell by a witness's face whether he is merely an actor or not, and especially when my instructions tell me he is mistaken; I wished therefore to know, whether he was not looking round the court to give it the air of probability, and whether he had been standing behind, so as to see the others point out Mr. De Berenger, whom they all knew, because most of them had seen him since that time; some of them had not I admit; he is a soldierly-looking man, and a man likely from the description to be fixed upon. My learned friend seemed to think that one of the witnesses had not a fair opportunity of seeing his person, in consequence of his holding down his head; the fact was, he was taking notes (for he has taken a very full note); but without meaning to do anything improper, I said, hold up your head, and he did so immediately; his recognizance was to appear here to-day, not fearing to have all enquiry made respecting him and as it appeared to me; he did not on any one occasion attempt to conceal his person from their observation, I do say, gentlemen, that the means of knowledge of these witnesses are so slight, that if I call witnesses to prove, not by vague surmise, never having seen him before, that he was in their society and company that evening so late, as to render it impossible that he should have been at Dover that night. But supposing that the evidence of *alibi* should not be satisfactory, it then comes back to the other observations made in the prior part of the defence.

Gentlemen, this is the general nature of the defence I have to make to you. You will, I have no doubt, endeavour to free yourselves from all prejudice infused into your minds; and will come to your conclusion with a desire to do justice. And I trust that you will, in the result of this long hearing, be enabled to pronounce, that this defendant, for whom I am counsel (not meaning by that to exclude any of the rest, but he is the only one committed to my care) is not guilty of the charge imputed to him.

MR. SERJEANT PELL.

May it please your Lordship,

Gentlemen of the Jury,

My two learned friends, who have preceded me, Mr. Serjeant Best and Mr. Park, have both stated to you the peculiar difficulties under which they laboured, in consequence of the great fatigue which they had both undergone. I am sure you will agree with me, that that topic, so pressed by them, will come with still greater force from me; for, as the night advances, the fatigue becomes greater, and the mind more exhausted. Gentlemen, it is under the full persuasion that you and his Lordship are also much oppressed with fatigue, that I can venture to promise you my address will not be very long. But I trust, that considering the point which it will be necessary for me to expatiate upon, you will be ultimately of opinion, that my address, although not long, is still effectual for the interest of my clients.

Gentlemen, I stand in a most peculiar situation, because, upon the notes of the noble Lord, it is distinctly proved, that two of the persons for whom I am counsel, Mr. Holloway and Mr. Lyte, have admitted themselves to be guilty of that, which no man can for one moment hesitate to say is extremely wrong. Gentlemen, I think it is also sufficiently proved, that Sandom, the third person for whom I am counsel, was in the chaise which was driven from Northfleet to Dartford, and from Dartford to London; and on my part, I should consider it a most inefficient attempt, if I were to attempt, for one moment, to persuade you that Mr. Holloway and Mr. Lyte, together with Mr. Sandom, have not been most criminally implicated in this part of the transaction; but, gentlemen, although I admit this in the outset, and very sincerely lament, that men who have hitherto maintained a very respectable situation in life, should have been tempted to involve themselves in so disgraceful an affair; yet I think, unless I am mistaken in my notion of law, as applying to that record on which you are to give your judgment, it will be found that they are entitled to your acquittal.

Gentlemen, I feel myself under a difficulty, also, in another respect. I must differ from all my learned friends who have preceded me in this trial, I mean, my learned friend Mr. Gurney, of counsel for the prosecution; my learned friend Mr. Serjeant Best, as counsel for Mr. Cochrane Johnstone, Mr. Butt, and Lord Cochrane; and Mr. Park, as counsel for Mr. De Berenger. I am not here to find fault with the committee of the Stock Exchange for prosecuting this inquiry; whether that committee is composed of honourable men or not, is to me a matter of perfect indifference. If they have been actuated by a sincere desire of bringing to justice persons who have been guilty of criminal conduct, I, for one, am not disposed to complain of them. Gentlemen, I cannot agree with my learned friend Mr. Gurney, or my learned friend Mr. Serjeant Best, in what, in different parts of their address, they stated to you as being the leading features of this prosecution; for my learned friend Mr. Gurney, in the outset of his address to you, stated, that what he called the Northfleet plot was only a part of the Dover conspiracy—was subsidiary to it. I think his expression was, that they both formed different parts of one entire plot, and that those who were guilty of one must be taken to be guilty of both; although Mr. Holloway, in his confession, had acquitted Lord Cochrane and Mr. Cochrane Johnstone, of having any part or share in the Northfleet conspiracy. Now, gentlemen, I will state to you in the outset, that I mean to consider the case in a different point of view. I have not the slightest doubt on earth, that what was done by Sandom, Lyte, and M'Rae, when they left Northfleet on the morning of the 21st of February, was altogether unconnected, and was utterly unknown to, that person, whoever he was, who came from Dover, and that he had no sort of connection with it. Gentlemen, if I am right in establishing this point; if you shall ultimately be satisfied that Mr. Holloway, Mr. Sandom, and Mr. Lyte, who I admit were concerned in that part of the business, were altogether unconnected with the person who came from Dover, and who has been stated to-day to be involved with Lord Cochrane and Mr. Cochrane Johnstone, I apprehend that the three defendants for whom I appear cannot be found guilty. That my learned friend Mr. Gurney considers the case in this point of view is beyond all question, for he opened it to you as part of this case, that what he called the Northfleet conspiracy, was a part of the Dover plot, and was in furtherance of it; and he not only has so stated it in his address, but, as I read the record, it is so stated upon the record; for, in the very first count of the indictment you are now impanelled to try, it is set forth, that Sandom, M'Rae and Lyte took the chaise from Northfleet, and so passed on to London, in furtherance of that plot which was originated at Dover. Gentlemen, I submit to you, therefore, on behalf of these gentlemen for whom I appear, that their guilt or innocence with respect to this particular trial will depend upon this circumstance;—did they form, or did they not form, parts and members of that single plot in which it is supposed the three or four other gentlemen were concerned?

Gentlemen, I certainly have not the good fortune to appear for men of the high rank of those on whose behalf my learned friends Mr. Serjeant Best and

Mr. Park have addressed you. I can introduce no such eloquent topics as those which my learned friend Mr. Serjeant Best has touched upon. I cannot illustrate the character or the situations of life of the gentlemen for whom I appear, with the terms in which Mr. Park has spoken of his client De Berenger. I know of no claims to honour from any ancestry to which they can justly entitle themselves; they are men in a respectable, but in a humble line of life, compared with the other defendants upon the record; but I know, that it is not upon that account that you will be less disposed to give a ready and a willing ear to any topics that may be urged in favour of their legal innocence.

Gentlemen, as I followed the evidence, there was but one point of coincidence, in which these persons who came from Dartford to London, could be at all connected with the person who came from Dover, and it was in the very slight circumstance of the chaises driving to the same place; and my learned friend, Mr. Gurney, in furtherance of that which he submitted to you as against Holloway, Sandom and Lyte, as an ingredient, and a necessary ingredient, in their conviction, stated to you in the opening, that he should prove they went to the same place. I could not but be struck with that circumstance, because I knew it was one from which a connexion might fairly be felt; I was therefore anxious to watch the evidence which applied to that part of the case, and so far from finding that the person who came from Dover, under the name of Du Bourg, went to the Marsh Gate by design, I find that he went there altogether by accident; for by the evidence of Shilling, the person who drove him, if I do not mistake it altogether, he first proposed to drive him to the Bricklayers Arms in the Kent Road, and when he got there he found there was no hackney-coach, and then to use the very expression of the witness, "I told him there was a stand at the Marsh Gate, and if he liked to go there nobody would observe him;" so that it is quite obvious, that the supposed Colonel Du Bourg went to the Marsh Gate, in consequence of having been driven by the suggestion of Shilling. I admit that Sandom, Lyte and M'Rae went there by their own direction; but it is equally clear that Du Bourg went there in consequence of there being no hackney-coach at the Bricklayers Arms, and in consequence also of Shilling advising him to go there for the purpose of obtaining one. The only circumstance therefore in the cause, which shews a coincidence of plot between the one at Northfleet and the one at Dover, is this circumstance respecting the carriages driving to the Marsh Gate; and it will appear upon his Lordship's notes, as with reference to Du Bourg, the going of Du Bourg to the Marsh Gate at Lambeth was purely accidental.

Gentlemen, my learned friend, Mr. Gurney, was so aware of the necessity of proving a connexion between these parties, that he stated another circumstance; and I think, in the course of his address, those were the only two which he adduced, for the purpose of shewing that there was any fair probability that could lead the Court to believe that the person assuming the name of Du Bourg, and Holloway, Sandom, M'Rae and Lyte, had concurred in any part of this most scandalous transaction. My learned friend stated, that he should shew an intimacy between Mr. Sandom and De Berenger, when both of them were prisoners within the Fleet prison, and that they became acquainted there.

*Mr. Gurney.* My learned friend has misunderstood me, I said they were prisoners at the same time; that was the extent of my statement.

*Mr. Serjeant Pell.* I am very much obliged to my learned friend; I am by no means disposed to mis-state him; I find he did not state it quite so strongly as I had supposed, but the inference he meant to raise in your minds, was, unquestionably, that both being prisoners at the same time within the walls of the same gaol, it was fair to conclude, considering the other parts of the case, that an intimacy had existed between them. Now let us see how that part of my learned friend's statement is made out.—Mr. De Berenger was unfortunately a prisoner within the Rules of the King's Bench Prison in the month of February last; he had been so for some time. I think it does not exactly appear, with respect to Mr. Sandom, according to the evidence of Mr. Broochooft, the officer, who was called for that purpose, when or for how long Mr. Sandom first went there, or how long he continued there, but far from Sandom's being a prisoner in that gaol during the time when Mr. De Berenger was confined there, my Lord will find upon his notes, as given by a person of the name of Foxall, that Sandom had lived at Northfleet for nine months before he sent for the chaise on the 21st of February. You observe therefore, gentlemen, that there is not the slightest reason to believe, as far as the evidence extends, that either Mr. Sandom, Mr. Holloway, or Mr. Lyte, had any knowledge or acquaintance with the other defendants.

But, Gentlemen, I will mention another circumstance, which puts that out of all doubt:—I allude to the confession of Mr. Holloway, a confession made in the presence of Mr. Lyte, and with his concurrence. He admitted that he had used means for the purpose of inducing a persuasion that a revolution had taken place in France, which unquestionably at that time was not true. How stands the circumstance? There was a person of the name of M'Rae, who was spoken to by Vinn, the first witness called by Mr. Gurney to this part of the transaction. Vinn told a most extraordinary story, and I will venture to say, that with respect to Mr. Vinn, if the case of all the defendants had stood upon the testimony of such a man as that, no human being, who had been accustomed to watch the manners and the terms which witnesses use in courts of justice, could have believed him for a moment. His story was this.—That on the 15th of February, M'Rae met him at the Carolina coffee house, and he proposed to him to frame a conspiracy for the purpose of raising the funds; and Vinn asked him if there was any moral turpitude in the transaction. No human being could doubt for a moment, that such a transaction would be deep in moral turpitude. He says, that he told him he would as soon engage in a highway robbery, as in such a transaction; and then immediately he told him, that though he would not himself, he could find somebody else who would engage in that dirty office. Can any human being believe such a story as this? What passed between him and M'Rae upon that occasion, I am unacquainted with; but I know enough of your sober judgment, to be sure of this, that no conversation which Vinn states to have taken place between M'Rae and him, when Holloway, Sandom and Lyte, were not present, will be by you permitted to affect their interests.

Now, gentlemen, the next stage in this transaction, in which Mr. M'Rae appears, is, I think, a very singular one; he appears in a letter, I think, from Mr. Cochrane Johnstone, to be the person proposed, who, for £10,000 would make known the whole of this affair. It is a very singular part of this most curious story. This letter is sent to the Stock Exchange; M'Rae proposes, that he shall be the person who is to detect the whole of this scandalous transaction, and he proposes to himself the great reward of £10,000. Only observe, what Mr. Bailey has stated to you took place on Holloway's being acquainted with this circumstance. Holloway, knowing that M'Rae had been concerned in this, which I shall term a second plot;—knowing that M'Rae could not communicate any thing, at least as far as Holloway had reason to believe, that could at all affect that which was the greater object of the Committee of the Stock Exchange, namely, the conviction of Lord Cochrane, Mr. Cochrane Johnstone, Mr. Butt, and Mr. De Berenger, for that is the end and aim of the present prosecution; and as to the clients for whom I appear, Mr. Holloway, Mr. Lyte, and Mr. Sandom, I firmly believe, if the Stock Exchange had not been of opinion they would have derived some benefit from the conviction of my clients, they would no more have been put forward on the present occasion, than I or any of my learned friends should have been. No, gentlemen, the other defendants are the game the prosecutors are attempting to catch, and it is only for the purpose, in some shape or other, of confusing and confounding two separate and distinct parts, with a hope that in some degree the transaction of Holloway, Sandom, Lyte and M'Rae, in reference to the journey from Northfleet, on the 21st of February, may be connected in your minds with the other defendants, that they are introduced upon the present record.

Gentlemen, do me the favour to recollect what Mr. Baily has stated to-day. It was this;—Mr. Holloway, finding there had been some proposition on the part of M'Rae, to make known all that he was acquainted with in the transaction, and that M'Rae had demanded the sum of £.10,000, before he would be induced to relate that which he knew, Mr. Holloway applied to the

Committee of the Stock Exchange, and stated this to them, in the presence of Mr. Lyte;—"I admit that we were concerned in that affair when the chaise went from Northfleet to Dartford; I admit we were concerned with those persons when they came through London (and it would be vain and most impertinent if I were to take up your time to deny it), but I deny that we knew any thing of the other parts of the business; we are altogether ignorant of it." Now, gentlemen, is Mr. Holloway to be believed in any part of that which he said? I take it my learned friend will contend, that he is to be believed in all that made against himself, and all that made against Lyte, who was present; but is he not to be believed in the other part of his story? Will my learned friend contend, that he can take the one part, and reject the other? I am satisfied he will not. If you take the whole, then it appears, that Holloway and Lyte admitted that Sandom was privy to their plan, but that they were altogether unconnected and unacquainted with the business which took place at Dover, and had no more to do with Mr. Cochrane Johnstone, Mr. Butt, Lord Cochrane, or Mr. De Berenger, than any of you whom I have the honour of addressing.

Gentlemen, I should have supposed, in a prosecution of this kind, that if there had been any connection between the two plots, it would have been traced in some way or other; you observe the minute points which have been made in every other part of the prosecution. There has been labour unexampled; witnesses brought from the most distant parts of the kingdom; no expence spared; every thing done that could be done to make good the charge against four of the defendants upon the record. Is it not a most extraordinary thing, if Holloway, Lyte and Sandom, were at all connected with Lord Cochrane, Mr. Cochrane Johnstone, or the two other gentlemen, that no trace can be found, no clue can be discovered, that can connect the one with the other. Under circumstances so singular as these, there being not only no evidence of any connexion, but there being an express contradiction on the part of Holloway and Lyte, and the only connecting circumstance being explained away, I mean as to both the chaises driving to the Marsh Gate, I think you will be of opinion with me, that the two plots are altogether distinct from each other, and that my clients, although morally guilty, must be acquitted upon the present charge.

Gentlemen, I cannot but feel, that a kind of prejudice against my clients may have arisen in your minds; I am not only surprised at it, but I should have been surprised if it had not found its way there. Here is a plot conducted in the most artful and most scandalous manner;—persons of the highest authority imposed upon, dresses bought, and the whole drama got up with the greatest skill. God forbid, that I should for one moment insinuate that it was accomplished by any of the other defendants upon the record. I am bound to believe, from the character of all these gentlemen, that they are not guilty; but however this may be, still we get back to that which forms the main feature of my defence for these three gentlemen. Are they, or are they not privy to this scheme? Gentlemen, I was observing to you, that some prejudice must necessarily arise in your minds; it is my case that there were two separate plots; they are, as far as the evidence extends, two different transactions on the same day; a prejudice, however, must arise in your minds, because when you find both these transactions point to producing the same effect, you would naturally be disposed to believe, that all the persons who were concerned in both, were equally acquainted with both. You well remember the strong disposition there was at that time, for every person, those at least who were disposed to do unjust and unfair things, to invent such reports as should enable them to sell their stock at an unreal price; and I submit to you, that supposing Holloway, Sandom and Lyte, had intended to do so, there is nothing very singular in their doing it on the day when the other transaction took place. I am fortified in the opinion, that the one plot is not connected with the other, because I find another part of the evidence which disconnects them altogether, and it is this;—from the evidence of the broker who was called to prove the sale of stock, or the directions to sell stock, on the 21st of February, (a person of the name of Pilliner) it turns out that Holloway did not give him any directions to sell his stock till the middle of the day. Now the middle of the day was the time when the chaise drove through the City of London. If Holloway had been connected with those who were engaged in the first plan, I think you will be of opinion, that he would have taken advantage of the most beneficial state of the market, and sold his stock as early as when he found that conspiracy had produced its intended effect upon the funds, so that, in addition to other circumstances, this also shews that Holloway had no connexion with the other transaction.

Gentlemen, I cannot but be struck at the singularity of Mr. M'Rae's withdrawing from the field of battle. M'Rae certainly has performed a very singular part upon this occasion; he proposed to sell himself for £.10,000; he would have had the Stock Exchange to believe, that he had been let into the secrets of my Lord Cochrane, Mr. Cochrane Johnstone, Mr. Butt, and Mr. De Berenger;—the first object he had in view, was to persuade the Stock Exchange that he knew the whole of their concern in the transaction. A pleasant sort of a gentleman, to ask the sum of £.10,000, to induce him to tell all that he knew, when no human being can doubt that all M'Rae knew was, that which has been proved by the witnesses, as to Sandom, Lyte and Holloway, namely; that M'Rae was in a chaise which passed through the City of London, coming from Northfleet. This man, who has the audacity to propose the receiving £.10,000, turns out to be a miserable lodger in Fetter-lane, who after he had carried into execution the whole of his part of the conspiracy was rewarded—but how? was he rewarded as he would have been by such wealthy persons as the gentlemen whose names stand upon this record? If they had engaged M'Rae in this scandalous affair, do you believe they would have left him on the Monday morning, with nothing but a £.10 note in his pocket? It appears, by the woman with whom he lodged, that he was before in a state of abject poverty, and that afterwards he was seen with a £.10 note, and that he bought a new hat and a new coat—and this is the man who proposes to receive £.10,000 from the Stock Exchange to tell all he knew. Gentlemen, I think I am not very much deceived myself, if I say, that you will be of opinion, that a man who was in the situation of M'Rae, was not very likely to have known of transactions which would have involved the four first defendants upon the record, in such a serious prosecution as that under which they now labour; and it is not the least singular part of his conduct, that he makes no defence to-day.

Now, gentlemen, you observe the manner in which (subject to my Lord's correction) I put the defence of the three defendants for whom I appear. I have stated to you, that Holloway and Lyte have admitted themselves guilty of most immoral conduct, for I never can believe that such transactions as these, let them be conducted by whom they may, are not immoral in the highest degree. Holloway, at all events, has since done all he can to make amends; he has confessed his guilt; he has come forward with Lyte, knowing and feeling that they had done wrong, with a view to protect the Stock Exchange against giving that monstrous sum for an imperfect discovery. Had Holloway or Lyte been concerned with any of the other defendants on the record, I submit there is the strongest reason to believe, that when he confessed his own guilt, he would not have been backward in speaking of theirs. He was not aware of the effect I am giving to his defence when he made it; and if he has done no more than that which he has stated, I submit to you, under his Lordship's correction, that you cannot find him guilty; and I submit to you, upon the reasoning with which I commenced my address to you, that whatever Sandom, Holloway and Lyte did, is not at all connected with what Du Bourg, or the person so calling himself, did; that what they did is not connected with what the other three defendants on the record are supposed to have done; that there is not only no connexion proved between the two, but as far as the evidence extends that connexion is negatived; and then I submit to you, if you are of that opinion, these persons must be acquitted; because, as I apprehend, two distinct conspiracies included in one count, both being different offences, cannot be permitted to be proved in a court of justice. Crimes must be kept separate; persons must know what the charge is, on which they are called upon to defend themselves, and miserable would be the situation of persons charged with the commission of crimes, if one crime was connected with another totally distinct and separate from it, and both were brought under one and the same charge, to unite in the same defence.

Gentlemen, I have stated to you, that the gentlemen for whom I appear are in a very humble situation in life. Mr. Holloway is a wine merchant, Mr. Lyte was formerly an officer in a militia regiment, Mr. Sandom is a private gentleman of small fortune;—they are none of them, by their situation in life, apparently likely to be connected with any of the other defendants upon the record. What is there that should lead you to believe they are so? Mr. Holloway and Mr. Lyte stand under a sufficient load of guilt already; they have admitted themselves guilty of what they did on that day. Will you, therefore, because they admitted themselves guilty of one part of the day's infamy, put upon them the infamy of the whole? Will you do this, because the two plots happen to take place on the same day? Can you not, in your recollection, find, in former times, the same sort of coincidence? Do we not know that such things have happened; that plots of a similar description, carried on by different parties, but having the same end, have taken place on the same day? Have there not been much more curious coincidences than chaises driving to the same point of destination, and the persons in the carriages leaving them there? Have juries ever been satisfied that such coincidences should lead to proving a connection with plots in other respects dissimilar?

Gentlemen, it is upon these grounds, therefore, I submit to you, these three defendants are not guilty of the offence charged upon this record. I shall trouble you with no witnesses;—there is nothing for me to repel. If I am right in my notion of the law;—if I am right in the persuasion that you can see nothing in the evidence connecting the two plots together;—and if my opinion of the law is sanctioned by my Lord, when he shall address himself to you, there is nothing I have to answer for. It is out of my power to prove, by any evidence, that these three persons were not connected with any of the other defendants upon the record; such a negative as that I can never establish, and therefore I can have no proofs.

Gentlemen, such is the situation in which the three gentlemen for whom I appear stand. I have expressed my sentiments upon the subject as shortly as I could. It is undoubtedly a great misfortune to my learned friends, as well as myself, that we should have been called upon to make our defences, when both you and we are so much exhausted.

There is but one other circumstance for me to mention, it is but a slight one;—the person who came up from Dover appears to have paid all his post-chaise drivers in foreign coin; there is no pretence for saying that any thing was paid by my clients but in Bank of England notes; there is nothing in that respect, therefore, connecting these two parties together; and if they are not connected together, I trust you will find Mr. Holloway, Mr. Sandom, and Mr. Lyte, not guilty of this charge.

*Lord Ellenborough.* Gentlemen of the Jury; It appears to me this would be the most convenient time for dividing the cause, as the evidence will occupy considerable time, probably. I cannot expect your attendance before ten o'clock.

*It being now three o'clock on Thursday morning, the Court adjourned to ten o'clock.*

# Court of King's Bench, Guildhall.

*Thursday, 9 June 1814.*

The Court met, pursuant to Adjournment.

**EVIDENCE FOR THE DEFENDANTS.**

*Mr. Brougham:*—We will first read the letters which were proved yesterday?

*Lord Ellenborough:*—These are read to contradict Le Marchant?

*Mr. Brougham:*—Yes, they are, my Lord; he proved the handwriting himself.

[*The following Letters were read:*]

"Glo'ster Hotel, Piccadilly,
6th April 1814.

"My Lord,

"Although I have not the honour of your acquaintance, I beg leave to address you, to solicit an interview with your lordship, for the purpose of explaining a conversation I had with Mr. De Berenger, a few days prior to the hoax of the 21st February last, and which must be interesting to you. If your lordship will condescend to appoint an hour, I will not fail attending punctually at your house, or elsewhere.

I have the honour to be,
my Lord,
your Lordship's most obedient
humble servant,
J$^s$ Le Marchant."

Rt. Hon. Lord Cochrane,
&c. &c. &c.

"Glo'ster Hotel, Piccadilly, London,
7th April 1814.

"My Lord,

"I had the honor yesterday to address your lordship, for the sole purpose of giving you that information you are not aware of; and knowing my letter was delivered (your lordship being at home when it was presented at the door), I beg to say, that I am now justified, from your silent contempt and defiance thereof, *to make my information public*; and which I should not have done before consulting you on that head, my sole wish being to state facts, and not to be considered acting underhand. As I feel exonerated from the last charge, and being in a certain degree called on to give my evidence relative to 21st

February last; and as the rank I hold in society will *give weight* to my *testimony*, *with the witnesses* I shall bring forward on the occasion, I feel justified in the steps I am about to take, nor can your Lordship blame me in so doing, understanding the business in question will be brought before Parliament on a future day. I am sorry to have intruded myself on your Lordship's notice, by addressing you yesterday; but, to be correct, I thought it my duty to inform you by this, what have been and are my intentions.

I have the honour to be,<br>
my Lord,<br>
your Lordship's most obedient<br>
humble servant,<br>
*J. Le Marchant.*"

Rt. Hon. Lord Cochrane, M.P.
&c. &c. &c.
No. 13. Green-street, Grosvenor-square.

"13, Green-street, April 8th, 1814.

"Sir,

"I should have hoped, circumstanced as I am, and attacked by scoundrels of all descriptions, that a gentleman of your understanding might have discovered some better reason than that of "silent contempt," to account for the delay of a few hours in answering a note; the more particularly as your note of the 6th led me to conclude, that the information offered to me was meant as a mark of civility and attention, and was not on a subject in which you felt any personal interest.

I am, Sir,<br>
your obedient servant,<br>
*Cochrane.*"

Colonel Le Marchant,
Glocester Hotel.

"Glo'ster Hotel, Piccadilly,<br>
"8th April 1814.

"My Lord,

"I ask your Lordship's pardon for my letter of yesterday, and which was written under the supposition of being treated with silent contempt. To convince you of the high respect I have for your Lordship, I have the honor to enclose to you a statement of what I know relative to the 21st February; and I also now declare solemnly, that no power or consideration shall ever induce me to come forwards as an evidence against you, and that all I know on the subject shall be buried for ever in oblivion. Thus much I hope will convince you I am more your friend than an enemy; as my testimony, corroborated by the two officers, would be of great import, not (believe me) that I myself doubt in any wise your Lordship's affidavit, but De Berenger's conversation with me would to your enemies be positive proof; as for my part, I now consider *all that man told me to be diabolically false*. If my conduct meets your approbation, can I ask for a reciprocal favour, as a temporary *loan*, on *security* being given.—I am just appointed to a situation of about £.1,200 a year, but for the moment am in the greatest distress, with a large family; you *can* without risk, and have the *means* to relieve us, and I believe, the *will* of doing good. Necessity has driven me to ask your Lordship this favour. Whether granted or not, be assured of my keeping my oath now pledged, of secrecy; and that I am with the greatest respect,

My Lord,<br>
your Lordship's most obedient<br>
humble servant,<br>
*J<sup>s</sup> Le Marchant.*"

Right Hon. Lord Cochrane,
&c. &c. &c.

*J<sup>s</sup> Le Marchant's* Statement and Conversation with *R. de Berenger.*

"I became intimately acquainted with De Berenger about eighteen months ago, and have continued so till a few days prior to the hoax of 21st February last. He was in the habit of calling on me at the Glo'ster Coffee House, Piccadilly; and did so frequently, between the 10th and 16th of last February. He generally called late in the evening, saying he had dined with Lord Cochrane: Once he called about noon, stating he had breakfasted with his Lordship, had been with him on particular business, and was to return to dinner: he mentioned being very intimate with Lord Cochrane and the Hon. C. Johnstone; that they were kind friends to him, with whom he frequently dined. In his apartments, in the rules of the King's Bench, he shewed me the devices he was drawing for Lord Cochrane's lamp invention. The last time he called upon me, it was very late; he appeared elated somewhat by drinking, having (as he said) dined with his Lordship; and in consequence of there being company, he could not then shew Lord Cochrane a copy of a memorial he had written to the Duke of York, praying to be given field officer's rank, and to be appointed to be sent out under Lord Cochrane, for the purpose of instructing the marines in rifle exercise; that his Lordship was very anxious to have him on board of his ship; that he objected going, unless with field-officer's rank, hoping to procure a majority; and that Lord Cochrane had said he would try and get him a lieutenant-colonelcy. De Berenger shewed me his memorial to the Duke, the head of which not being in propriâ formâ, I corrected; it was very long, and related to the losses his family had sustained as American loyalists; also on the cause of his first coming over to England. On my asking him, if the Duke of York was to appoint him, how he could extricate himself out of his difficulties and leave the Bench, he answered, '*All was settled on that score; that in consequence of the services he had rendered Lord Cochrane and Mr. C. Johnstone, in devising, whereby they had and could realize large sums by means of the funds or stocks, Lord Cochrane was his friend, and had told him a day or two ago, that for those services his Lordship had, unknown to him (De Berenger) kept a private purse for him, placing therein a certain per-centage on the profits Lord Cochrane had gained through his stock suggestions; and that now this purse had accumulated to an amount adequate almost to liberate him from the Bench.*' When he said this, he appeared overjoyed, and said it in such a manner as to make me credit him. He remained with me this said evening, drinking hollands and water, till near two o'clock in the morning. On his leaving me, I thought of the conversation, especially that part which related to the funds, and conceived, from the numerous stock-jobbing reports, whereby the funds raised or were depressed, that he must have been deeply concerned in it. A few days after the 21st of February, it was whispered that Lord Cochrane was concerned in the hoax. Immediately, De Berenger's former conversation with me forcibly occurred to my mind, and I then mentioned to two friends, with whom I was in company, (*and this prior to Lord Cochrane's affidavit, or De Berenger's name being mentioned*), that I would lay my existence De Berenger was the sham Colonel De Bourg, and I stated my reasons for supposing so. Recollecting myself afterwards, I made them, as officers, pledge their oath and word of honour, that what I had said on the subject they would never repeat, or even hint at; and I am most fully persuaded they have not. The same day, but prior to the conversation above mentioned, the hoax being the topick in the coffee-room, I said, I thought I knew more than any one relative thereto, except the parties concerned, but I never mentioned any name whatever; yet some days after, I received two anonymous twopenny-post letters, recommending my giving up my information, either to Ministers or the Members of the Stock Exchange Committee; that I might depend on their secrecy, and an ample reward, in proportion to my report: of course these letters were left unnoticed. As soon as I suspected De Berenger to be Colonel De Bourg, I called twice on him, but could not get admittance; I also gave one of the officers above alluded to, a letter of introduction to De Berenger, for him to gain information on the rifle manœuvres: he called; was not admitted; left the letter; and, as well as myself, has heard nothing since of De Berenger.

"To the whole of this I can solemnly make oath; and I am sure I can bring the two officers in question to swear to what I said to them, and *the time when*, although I have never since spoken to them on that subject.

*Jˢ Le Marchant."*

*The Right Honourable Lord Viscount Melville sworn.*

*Examined by Mr. Scarlett.*

*Q.* Your lordship is acquainted, I believe, with Admiral Sir Alexander Cochrane?

*A.* I am.

*Q.* I believe that Sir Alexander Cochrane has been lately appointed upon a distant service?

*A.* He has.

*Q.* Does your lordship recollect any application made to you by Sir Alexander Cochrane, on behalf of Mr. De Berenger?

*A.* I recollect Sir Alexander Cochrane, several times, more than once I am certain, applying to me, that Mr. De Berenger might be allowed to accompany him in his command, to remain with him on the North American station, to which he was appointed.

*Q.* Does your lordship recollect about what time those applications were made?

*A.* I do not recollect as to the precise time, but it was a short time before Sir Alexander Cochrane sailed upon his command.

*Q.* Does your lordship recollect about what time Sir Alexander Cochrane sailed?

*A.* I think I should say about five or six months ago; but I am not at all positive.

*Q.* Does your lordship recollect the particular service that Sir Alexander Cochrane recommended the gentleman for?

*A.* Sir Alexander Cochrane was desirous that this gentleman should accompany him, for the purpose of instructing, either a corps to be raised in that part of the world, or the royal marines, in the rifle exercise; and afterwards, when Sir Alexander Cochrane wished that an officer of engineers should accompany him, and when I stated my knowledge, from other circumstances connected with His Majesty's service, that it would be difficult to give him that assistance, from the small number of engineer officers that could be procured, Sir Alexander Cochrane mentioned, that as an engineer officer, he would be quite satisfied with Mr. De Berenger.

*Q.* Does your lordship recollect, whether any particular rank was necessary or usual to accompany such an appointment, or whether it was solicited by Sir Alexander Cochrane?

*A.* I think there was, but I am not positive; I recollect perfectly explaining to Sir Alexander Cochrane, that as far as related to His Majesty's naval service, I could not agree to the appointment; and I recommended to Sir Alexander Cochrane to apply to the Secretary of State, or the Commander in Chief, stating, that if they agreed to it, I should have no objection to Baron De Berenger's accompanying Sir Alexander Cochrane.

*Q.* Was Lord Cochrane appointed to a vessel to join Sir Alexander Cochrane afterwards?

*A.* He was.

*Q.* The Tonnant?

*A.* Yes; I think he was appointed before Sir Alexander Cochrane sailed; but of that I am not positive.

*Q.* Before Sir Alexander sailed to join him upon that station?

*A.* Yes; I am not quite positive about that, but it was very nearly about that time.

*Mr. Park.* I had my Lord Melville as a witness in my brief, not knowing that my friend would call him; I should have called his lordship to these facts, if my friend had not.

*Lord Ellenborough.* Your lordship has no personal knowledge of Mr. De Berenger?

*A.* No.

*Colonel Torrens sworn.*

*Examined by Mr. Brougham.*

*Q.* You are secretary to the Commander in Chief?

*A.* I am.

*Q.* Do you remember any application being made in the department with which you are connected, in behalf of Captain De Berenger?

*A.* I do.

*Q.* About what time was that?

*A.* It was in the latter end of December, or the beginning of January.

*Q.* Do you recollect by whom the application was made?

*A.* Sir Alexander Cochrane.

*Q.* What was the purport of it?

*A.* Sir Alexander came to me twice, I think, if not three times, to urge the appointment of Mr. De Berenger to go to America, for the purpose of applying his talents as a light infantry officer, to the service on which Sir Alexander Cochrane was about to embark.

*Q.* Were any difficulties started to this application?

*A.* Great difficulties.

*Q.* What objection was made to it?

*A.* I represented——

*Lord Ellenborough.* I do not know to what point this applies?

*Mr. Brougham.* Merely that it confirms the statement made by Lord Cochrane, and shows a connexion between the different parties, consistent with that statement.

*Lord Ellenborough.* It shows that he was acquainted with Sir Alexander Cochrane, and that he recommended him to the appointment; we are not trying the propriety or impropriety of the orders of Government?

*Mr. Brougham..* No, my lord; but Lord Cochrane's statement refers to the difficulty itself.

*Lord Ellenborough.* But what the difficulties were is not at all material; it would be going into that with which we have nothing to do?

*Mr. Gurney.* I do not object to it.

*Mr. Brougham.* I will not enter into it, my lord. In consequence of those difficulties which were felt, the appointment did not take place?

*A.* It did not.

*Q.* But the appointment, in consequence of this application, came under the consideration of the Commander in Chief's office?

*A.* Certainly.

*Q.* Were those difficulties, without asking what they were, particularly personal to Captain De Berenger?

*Lord Ellenborough.* No; that we cannot ask.

*Mr. Park.* It goes to character?

*Lord Ellenborough.* Then put the question to character at once; you must not go indirectly into it, if Colonel Torrens knows his character at all.

*Mr. Park.* You do not know, personally, his character?

*A.* I do not, personally.

*Q.* Are you acquainted with the hand-writing of Mr. De Berenger?

*A.* Not in the least.

*Q.* You have never seen him write?

*A.* I never did.

*Q.* Have you received letters, purporting to be from him upon subjects of business, and have you answered and acted upon those letters?

*A.* I do not recollect, since I have been military secretary ever to have received any.

*Q.* He had been, I believe, in the rifle corps of the Saint James's.

*A.* I believe he had.

*Lord Ellenborough.* Do you know him, personally?

*A.* I know nothing of him, personally.

*Henry Goulburn, Esq. M. P. sworn.*

*Examined by Mr. Serjeant Best.*

*Q.* You are under secretary of state for the colonial department?

*A.* I am.

*Q.* Can you tell us, whether any and what application was made to your department for Mr. De Berenger going abroad with Lord Cochrane?

*Lord Ellenborough.* The terms of the application I think we cannot hear; I do not think Government secrets (when I say secrets, I mean the detail of them) ought to be stated; we cannot go further than the fact, that an application was made.

*Mr. Serjeant Best.* That is all we want, my lord; was any application made to the colonial department?

*A.* Yes; there was.

*Q.* By whom?

*A.* By Sir Alexander Cochrane.

*Lord Ellenborough.* All this must have been in writing, I should think?

*A.* Yes, it was.

*Lord Ellenborough.* You have laid this basis, that there had been some application, and that it had been in contemplation, that he should go out as connected with the service.

*Mr. Park.* That is all we wish, we want to show a connexion with the Cochranes, without this illicit connexion.

*Lord Ellenborough.* No doubt there had been an intimacy and connexion; whether for good or ill is the question?

*Mr. Serjeant Best.* And this confirms in terms the statement contained in the affidavit of Lord Cochrane.

*William Robert Wale King sworn.*

*Examined by Mr. Scarlett.*

*Q.* What are you by business?

*A.* A tin-plate worker.

*Q.* Were you employed, in the course of last summer and this last winter, by Lord Cochrane, respecting the making him any lamps?

*A.* Yes, I was.

*Q.* What was the business on which you were employed?

*A.* In the manufacture of signal lanthorns and lamps.

*Q.* For the use of the navy?

*A.* Yes.

*Q.* Was it a new sort of lamp?

*A.* Yes; for which Lord Cochrane has since obtained a patent.

*Lord Ellenborough.* A patent cannot be proved in that way.

*Mr. Scarlett.* My friend, Mr. Gurney, has intimated to me that he will not object to it. Was his Lordship in the habit of coming to your manufactory, while you were so employed?

*A.* Nearly every day.

*Q.* Do you recollect his lordship being there on the 21st of February last?

*A.* Yes.

*Q.* Where is your manufactory?

*A.* No. 1, Cock-lane, Snow-hill.

*Q.* Do you recollect about what time in the morning he came?

*A.* Between ten and eleven it was that he was with me.

*Q.* Was there any particular time when he was accustomed to come?

*A.* That was about the time he usually came.

*Q.* Do you remember the circumstance of any note being brought to him by the servant, whilst he was there?

*A.* Yes, I do perfectly well.

*Q.* Were you present when the note was delivered to him?

*A.* I was.

*Q.* What did his lordship do on receiving that note?

*A.* He immediately opened it, and retired into the passage of the manufactory; he came into the workshop again, and shortly after went away.

*Q.* What time of the day was this?

*A.* Between ten and eleven.

*Q.* What time had his lordship been at your manufactory before the servant came?

*A.* It might be a quarter of an hour, but I cannot speak precisely to that.

*Mr. Park.* How far is Cock-lane from Grosvenor-square?

*A.* I should suppose a mile and a half.

*Q.* I should think it was two miles, did you ever walk it?

*A.* No; I do not know that I have.

*Lord Ellenborough.* That is not of much consequence, I should think.

*Mr. Gurney.* Any distance my friends please.

*Mr. Park.* It is of consequence when it comes to eleven o'clock, the stock was all sold by that time.

*Lord Ellenborough.* Did you see him read the note which he received?

*A.* I saw him read the note in the passage of the manufactory.

*Lord Ellenborough.* He made no observation upon reading it?

*A.* No; not that I heard.

*A Juryman.* Did it occupy any time?

*A.* No.

*Lord Ellenborough.* His Lordship did not make any observation upon reading it?

*A.* No; I think only that he said, Very well, Thomas.

*Mr. Bowering sworn.*

*Examined by Mr. Brougham.*

*Q.* What are you?

*A.* A clerk in the Adjutant General's office.

*Q.* Do you know whether Lord Cochrane's brother, Major Cochrane, was with the army in the south of France, at the beginning of this year?

*A.* He is so returned in the returns from the 15th hussars.

*Q.* About that time, do you also know, whether or not he was upon the sick list?

*A.* He is returned "sick present" on the 25th of January.

*Lord Ellenborough.* That return did not reach you on the 25th of January?

*A.* No.

*Lord Ellenborough.* When did it reach you?

*A.* I do not know; it was received in the regular course, but I cannot state the day.

*Mr. Brougham.* Over what space of time did that return extend?

*A.* From the 24th of December to the 24th of January.

*Thomas Dewman sworn.*

*Examined by Mr. Scarlett.*

*Q.* Are you a servant of my Lord Cochrane's?

*A.* Yes.

*Q.* Have you been an old servant in the family?

*A.* I have been so for about seventeen years.

*Q.* Do you remember carrying his lordship a note any morning in February, to Mr. King's lamp manufactory?

*A.* Yes, I do, perfectly well.

*Q.* Do you remember a gentleman coming to Lord Cochrane's house in a hackney coach?

*A.* Yes.

*Q.* Did you know the gentleman?

*A.* I had never seen him in my life before that time, nor yet since.

*Q.* Did the gentleman send you with a note to my lord?

*A.* Yes, he did; he first asked me where he was gone to, and I told him, he was gone to Cumberland-street to breakfast, because his lordship told me so.

*Q.* That was to his uncle's?

*A.* It was.

*Q.* Did you go to Cumberland-street after him?

*A.* I did.

*Q.* Not finding him at Cumberland-street, where did you go to seek him?

*A.* I came back to our house in Green-street, with the note; I informed the gentleman who had written the note, that he was not there; and the gentleman said, Pray do you know where he is gone to, or where his lordship could be found? I told him, I thought I could find him, but I thought I might be too late; for when his lordship went out, he said to me, Thomas, after you have got your breakfast, follow me, with that globe glass, to Mr. King's; I had been there.

*Q.* You had been to Mr. King's before?

*A.* Yes; on Saturday I went with some things, and this globe glass I should have taken on Saturday, but I forgot it.

*Q.* His lordship having told you to follow him with this globe glass to Mr. King's, you supposed he might be there?

*A.* Yes.

*Q.* Was that the reason for taking the note to him there?

*A.* Yes; I told the gentleman that I most likely should find him at Mr. King's, as I was going to follow him there with this glass; whether this gentleman had come or not, I should have gone there with this glass.

*Q.* You took the note with you?

*A.* He took the note from me, and said, I will add two or three more lines to it.

*Q.* Did you take the note to his lordship at Mr. King's?

*A.* I did.

*Q.* Did you see him there?

*A.* I did; I enquired of Mr. King's men—

*Q.* I did not ask you whether you enquired of Mr. King's men, but, whether you saw him there?

*A.* I did.

*Q.* Did his lordship read the note in your presence?

*A.* He did.

*Q.* Did you leave him there, at Mr. King's?

*A.* I left him at Mr. King's.

*Q.* Had his lordship another man-servant at that time?

*A.* Not in Green-street; no one but me.

*Q.* Where was his other servant?

*A.* His other servant was at his lordship's country seat, near Southampton, and had been there two or three months before that.

*Q.* Had he discharged any servant?

*A.* Mr. Davis he had given warning to, a month after his lordship was appointed to the Tonnant?

*Q.* When did Davis quit him?

*A.* Davis left him about two days, or three days it might be, before he went into Green-street; his time was up then, but he was in Green-street.

*Lord Ellenborough.* For what purpose is this?

*Mr. Scarlett.* Only to shew that we cannot find this person.

*A.* Davis was not in his lordship's service at that time, but he happened to be in the kitchen when the gentleman came.

*Q.* What is become of Davis?

*A.* He is gone with Admiral Fleming, to the West Indies.

*Mr. Park.* Do you recollect what time of the day this gentleman came to your master's?

*A.* As near ten as possible; I think a little past ten.

*Q.* It was so late as that, when he arrived there?

*A.* Yes.

*Q.* You were hired to go into the country, in the room of my lord's steward, who was going to sea with him?

*A.* Yes.

*Lord Ellenborough.* I thought you had been in the family seventeen years?

*Mr. Park.* You had been with Lord Dundonald?

*A.* Yes; I was engaged with Lord Cochrane ever since last February.

*Q.* You were in Lord Cochrane's peculiar service only from February?

*A.* No.

*Q.* You said something about having been seventeen years in the service?

*A.* In the family.

*Q.* Chiefly with Lord Dundonald, the father?

*A.* Yes, and with two of his sons.

*Q.* You did not return home from King's immediately?

*A.* I did not arrive in Green-street till near two, having a father living in Castle-street.

*Q.* You do not know whether Lord Cochrane saw this person at his house when he came back, or how long they were together?

*A.* No, I do not.

*Mr. Serjeant Pell.* You have lived with Lord Cochrane several years?

*A.* No, in the family; only since Christmas with his lordship.

*Q.* Do you know the person of Mr. Holloway?

*A.* No, I do not, not even when I see him.

*Q.* Do you know a person of the name of Lyte?

*A.* No.

Lord *Ellenborough.* What did Lord Cochrane say or do when you gave him this note?

*A.* He said, "Then I must return."

*Q.* That was all that he said?

*A.* Yes; I saw him come out of Mr. King's.

*Q.* You know the different members of the family?

*A.* Yes.

*Q.* Do you know the major?

*A.* Yes, I attended on the major when he first went into the army.

*Q.* I mean Major Cochrane?

*A.* The brother of Lord Cochrane,—the younger brother.

*Q.* The brother who is in Spain or France?

*A.* Yes, he was there lately.

*Q.* All that Lord Cochrane said was, "Well, Thomas, I will return?"

*A.* Yes, that was all that he said.

[*Mr. Poole, of the Patent Office, was called, but did not answer.*]

Mr. *Gurney.* I will admit the patent to be of any date you please.

Mr. *Brougham.* It is a patent for the invention of a lamp; the date is 20th of February.

Mr. *Gurney.* I will take my learned friend's word for that.

Mr. *Brougham.* That is the case on the part of my Lord Cochrane.

Mr. *Scarlett.* The next witness is to the case of Mr. Cochrane Johnstone.

Mr. *Park.* I shall use him also.

*Mr. Gabriel Tahourdin sworn.*

*Examined by Mr. Scarlett.*

*Q.* How long have you known Mr. De Berenger?

*A.* About five or six years.

*Q.* Were you the person that introduced him to Mr. Cochrane Johnstone?

*A.* I was.

*Q.* How long ago?

*A.* In May 1813.

*Q.* You were well acquainted with Mr. Cochrane Johnstone.

*A.* I had not been well acquainted with him at that time.

*Q.* Do you know, whether Mr. Cochrane Johnstone, at that time, was in possession of a garden or some premises at Paddington?

*A.* Yes, in Alsop's Buildings.

*Q.* Which he was desirous of improving?

*A.* He was.

*Q.* What was the occasion of your introducing Mr. De Berenger to him?

*A.* It was mere chance.

*Q.* Did you, or anybody else, to your own knowledge, recommend Mr. De Berenger as a person who could assist him in planning that place?

*A.* I had previously introduced him: I will just state the circumstance that led to my introduction.

*Q.* I do not know that the circumstance is in the least material. You say the introduction was at first accidental; was there, in consequence of that accident, any connection with them, as to Mr. De Berenger assisting him in this plan?

*A.* Yes.

*Q.* The place was intended to be called Vittoria?

*A.* Yes.

*Q.* Did Mr. De Berenger employ himself in preparing a plan, as an artist?

*A.* He did, which plan is here (*producing it*).

Lord *Ellenborough.* The exhibition of the plan cannot be important, I should think.

Mr. *Scarlett.* It may become material, because Mr. Cochrane Johnstone had paid him for the plan.

*Lord Ellenborough.* Whether there were colonades, and so on, or not, I should think cannot be material.

*Mr. Park.* The production of the plan is necessary only, to shew that it is worth the money which was paid.

*Lord Ellenborough.* I only wish to avoid useless particularity; I do not wish to curtail you of the least particle of proper proof.

*Mr. Scarlett.* Do you know, whether, in the month of September in the last year, Mr. De Berenger had made considerable progress in that plan?

*A.* He had; he had nearly completed it.

*Q.* He had not quite completed it?

*A.* No.

*Q.* Do you know whether, shortly before Mr. Cochrane Johnstone went to Scotland in September, he made him any payment on account of that?

*A.* He did, through my medium.

*Q.* Besides the plan, had De Berenger prepared a prospectus, with a full and minute description of the objects of the design?

*A.* He had.

*Q.* Had he got that printed?

*A.* He had; he made him one payment of £.100.

*Q.* Do you know that Mr. Johnstone had got a number of his prospectus, to take with him to Scotland?

*A.* He had.

*Q.* In the month of September, last year?

*A.* Yes, early in October; the first or second of October, I think.

*Q.* Do you know of any payment made by Mr. Johnstone since that time, upon account of that plan?

*A.* Yes; it was not made by me.

*Q.* Were you present when it was made?

*A.* No.

*Q.* I understood you to say, you knew that the payment was made?

*A.* By letters.

*Q.* Were the letters sent to you?

*A.* Yes.

*Q.* They passed through your hands?

*A.* Yes, they did.

*Lord Ellenborough.* The moment it gets into a letter, that moment the parol statement ends.

*Mr. Scarlett.* Certainly, my Lord. Do you know whether any application was made by Mr. De Berenger after the plan was completed, for payment?

*Mr. Gurney.* Were you present?

*Mr. Scarlett.* Or did you convey any draft?

*A.* Yes, I conveyed a letter, and I spoke several times.

*Q.* To Mr. Johnstone.

*A.* Yes, upon the subject of the paying him for the plans.

*Q.* Without at present alluding to any letter, do you know what was the price that De Berenger asked for the remainder of the plans?

*A.* No price, I believe, was ever stipulated; no price was ever fixed till February last. Mr. Johnstone and myself had repeated conversations on the subject of the price of the plans, and as to the remaining sum that he should pay him.

*Q.* You made repeated applications to Mr. Johnstone to pay him?

*A.* I did, always in a delicate way, not saying, that Mr. Berenger required so much; but he requested I would take a mode of giving a hint to Mr. Johnstone, as to the payment; a hint he was always ready to take.

*Q.* Have you any means of knowing what was the money Mr. Johnstone did pay him?

*A.* Yes, I think I have.

*Q.* When was the payment?

*A.* In February.

*Lord Ellenborough.* At what time in February.

*A.* Mr. Johnstone sent me a letter on the 22d of February, enclosing a letter to him from Mr. De Berenger.

*Mr. Scarlett.* He sent to you, on the 22d of February, a letter he had received from Mr. De Berenger?

*A.* He did.

*Q.* Did you keep the letter?

*A.* I did, here it is (*producing it*).

*Lord Ellenborough.* De Berenger's letter was enclosed in one of Mr. Cochrane Johnstone's?

*A.* Yes.

*Q.* Were the letters by the post? had they any post-mark upon them?

*A.* No; this letter was delivered.

*Q.* The delivery and date were cotemporary with the transaction, namely, about the 22d of February?

*A.* Yes, it was on the 22d of February I received it.

[*The letters were read, and are as follow.*]

"18, Great Cumberland-street,
"22d February 1814.

"My dear Sir,

"I have received the enclosed letter from the Baron; and as I mean to pay him this week for his plans, pray let me know if you have advanced him any money on my account, in addition to the £.50, which I paid him on account last year. You will perceive that he wishes a loan of £.200, in addition to this sum, and that he offers me as security, Colonel Kennedy's assignment. I have told him, that if this sum can be of real service to him, I will advance it to him, I will take his note for the amount; and if he is ever able to repay me, good and well; if not, I shall have had the satisfaction of serving him.

"As I shall receive the middle of next month a considerable sum of money, you will oblige me very much, if you will have the goodness to let me know, what it would cost me to purchase an annuity for the mother of my three natural children. I wish to settle £.200 a year upon her, and £.100 a year upon each of them; her age is 23, past; my eldest boy will be five years next May, the second boy four years next October, and the third one year next April; they are all healthy. I have in my will made a provision for them, but I wish to alter this mode of settlement for them, from motives of delicacy to my daughter, Miss Cochrane Johnstone, as I would not wish to insert their names along with hers.

"I will send you as soon as possible the statement about Lady Mary Lindsey Crawford, to enable you to give the answer to the bill in chancery.

"Pray settle my account with Dawson and Wrattislaw, as I wish to clear off all demands upon me as soon as possible. Whatever sum you say they ought to receive, I will pay them. I hope you are expediting the Wendover papers.

Believe me to be,<br>my dear Sir,<br>yours respectfully,<br>*A. Cochrane Johnstone.*"

Addressed to
Gabriel Tahourdin, Esq.
King's Bench Walk,
Temple.

"London, February 22d 1814.

"My dear Sir,

"I beg to assure you, that I would not have complained to you of the disappointment and inconvenience which Colonel Kennedy's unreasonable delay of completing the purchase of the share in the oil patent created, had it not reached your ears from other quarters. I cannot agree with you, that his "want of cash" is a sufficient excuse; because in that case, he ought to have stated that instead of artificial reasons. Had he completed his contract at the price agreed on, namely, £.1,500, I should be liberated from this place, and be able to equip myself for the American expedition (which I do not relinquish) without encroaching on any friend.

"You have often kindly pressed me to let you know what would satisfy me for the two plans, MS. &c. connected with them. I really have never made a charge of this kind, and am at a loss how to calculate, much less to make a demand; but those who can perceive the labour, time, difficulties and contrivance, which the awkwardness of the ground created, may better be able to say, if £.250 for every thing, is unreasonable. At all events, it is not a charge, but I leave it to you; and in case you deem it extravagant, am ready to submit the whole to the valuation of any competent person. What regards the drawing, planning and superintending, Donovan, and the brass-cutter, in completing the two pieces of furniture, I am determined not to accept any thing for; these you must (forgive a strong word) do me the favour of accepting.

"Should Colonel K. not come to town, I shall feel greatly obliged by your assisting me with the above sum, in the course of a week. Pray favour me by calling on Mr. G. Tahourdin, in order to see the conditions of the assignment, which lays there, executed by me. He will also show you the Colonel's extraordinary letters, and all my answers; at least I imagine that he has, if not all, most of them.

"Could I in the course of seven or eight days (in addition to the £.250) procure about £.200, either from the Colonel or from you, on account of Colonel K's. £.1,500, for which you might hold the assignment as a security, I should be enabled to proceed immediately to the Tonnant; for I still think Lord Cochrane might obtain leave for my going *on board*, at all events; I yet have hopes, though his lordship seemed in doubt; perhaps you will obligingly urge his endeavours. I fear a much greater difficulty, for I have heard it hinted, that some creditors, fearful of my going to America (which I have too openly talked of), contemplate to lodge detainers against me. Among these however, Mr. Tahourdin is *not*; for I thought it my duty to tell him, and he handsomely consented to my endeavours against America, as the only means to recover from my many losses.

"My plan is to go on board, if possible, with a view to begin to drill the marines in rifle-shooting and exercise, and *any* of the crew in sword, pistol and pike use; if my creditors pursue me there, I could draw for the balance of £.900, to silence some of them (I mean after taking from £.1,500, £.200, to refund to you, in case you now oblige me with an advance, and £.400, to protect my securities for the rules); and if this cannot be completed with the Colonel time enough, and for which reason I flatter myself that you will assist me with your friendly interference, I see but one mode, that of going abroad the moment I find my creditors hostile; for although I may find £.350 to £.400, to pay the rules, I cannot find means in haste to satisfy the rest, although I have offered to assign considerable properties. In the latter case, might I not from abroad proceed to America, there to join the Admiral, as a volunteer, and at my own risk.

"Forgive my anxious and tedious suggestions, which your own feeling heart, and friendly interest in my future successes, have in some degree courted, and grant me your pardon for not attending to your good humoured hint about long letters. Even should you refuse my request, in regard to the £.200, I shall be thankful for your reply; but if it should convey your consent, the sum shall immediately be employed towards the honest but hazardous service of your country, although it hesitates by proper rank, and otherwise to encourage my loyal, and I trust zealous endeavours. Forgive the sound but frank style of this letter, owing to disappointments which would be intolerable, if the recollection of your kindness did not curb and relieve him, who must ever gratefully subscribe himself with unalterable esteem,

dear Sir,<br>
your faithful and obliged,<br>
humble servant,<br>
*C. R. De Berenger.*"

To the
Hon. Cochrane Johnstone,
&c. &c. &c.

P.S. Apropos.—You have paid me £.50. on account;—may I trouble you to tender my most respectful assurances to Miss J.; that I hope most sincerely to hear that her indisposition discontinues. Should you no longer want the books, perhaps the bearer may bring them. Will lowness of spirits be received as an apology for this slovenly letter and crippled sheet?

*Lord Ellenborough.* This does not appear to have come by the twopenny post?

*Mr. Park.* No my Lord; but there is an indorsement upon it.

*Lord Ellenborough.* De Berenger was in the King's Bench; he had not servants to send with it?

*Mr. Park.* Yes, my Lord; it is sworn to by the Davidsons, that he had a man and a woman servant.

*Lord Ellenborough.* Probably he sent one of them, as you propose to call them, perhaps they may prove that.

*Mr. Scarlett.* There is a reference in that letter to an assignment of some property that De Berenger had?

*A.* Yes.

*Q.* Was such an assignment prepared at your office?

*A.* It was; it was an assignment from Mr. De Berenger to Colonel Kennedy.

*Q.* What was the subject of the assignment?

*A.* It was an assignment of a share of a patent.

*Mr. Gurney.* We are getting so very wide of evidence, that I must object, which I am very loth to do.

*Mr. Scarlett.* There was something referred to, that might be a security to Mr. Johnstone.

*Lord Ellenborough.* That refers to something which is the real thing; that is all you can prove by this witness.

*A.* Yes, it does, my Lord.

*Mr. Scarlett.* Mr. Johnstone having written you that letter which has been read, to ask your opinion about De Berenger, did you state to him what was your opinion, as to his power of extricating himself?

*A.* I had some conversation with Mr. Johnstone, as I had had several times.

*Q.* In consequence of the letter which has just been read?

*A.* Yes; I replied to the letter shortly, and I had conversation with him in consequence.

*Lord Ellenborough.* Do you know whether Mr. Johnstone made any answer to the letter?

*A.* To the Baron? I really do not.

*Mr. Scarlett.* Is that your answer to Mr. Johnstone? (*shewing a letter to the witness.*)

*A.* Yes, it is.

*Mr. Scarlett.* If your Lordship will allow that to be read.

*Lord Ellenborough.* When did you write that?

*A.* I wrote that the 23d of February, the day after I received the letter.

*Q.* It is addressed to Mr. Cochrane Johnstone.

*A.* It was sent to Mr. Cochrane Johnstone.

*Q.* How came your answer to be in your hands?

*Mr. Scarlett.* It was handed over by us just now; it was given me by Mr. Cochrane Johnstone's attorney.

[*The letter was read, as follows:*]

"My dear Sir,

"In reply to your favour of yesterday, I beg to inform you, that the only sum I have paid the Baron on your account, since you advanced him the £.50, is a trifle of about £.7 or £.8, which he paid for the printing of the prospectus's of Vittoria. You are very kind in assisting him so much; I have done it till my purse is empty; but had it been otherwise, I would still have assisted him to the extent of my means, notwithstanding the little foolish difference between us.

"I will attend to your wishes respecting the annuities, I will settle with Dawson and Wrattislaw as speedily as possible.

"The Wendover business is proceeding; but I am awkwardly circumstanced, not having all the documents before me; in Lady M. L. Crawford's business I should wish to attend with you on the spot. Pray excuse haste

I am, dear sir,<br>
your's faithfully<br>
*Gab<sup>l</sup> Tahourdin.*"

Temple,
23d Feb. 1814.

*Lord Ellenborough.* Where is the cover of this letter: the cover should be produced, for letters of this sort may be written after their date, and one wishes to have some external thing that cannot deceive; there is no post-mark to any of these letters.

*Mr. Scarlett.* Did you write that letter on the day of which it bears date?

*A.* Yes, I did; it was not sent by the post, I believe; I cannot charge my memory, whether it was or not?

*Q.* I see there is a lady alluded to, Lady Mary Crawford Lindsey; was she a tenant to Mr. Cochrane Johnstone?

*A.* No, she was not a tenant; she had purchased a house of his.

*Q.* There was a business to settle with her?

*A.* Yes.

*Q.* Do you know the fact, that in consequence of this correspondence which has been read, Mr. Johnstone did pay Mr. De Berenger any sum of money?

*A.* Only from the parties having acknowledged, the one the having paid it, and the other the having received it.

*Q.* You were not present when the money was paid?

*A.* No, I was not.

*Q.* Was there any receipt taken for the money?

*A.* Yes, there was.

*Q.* Did you take the receipt?

*A.* No, I did not.

*Lord Ellenborough.* Did you see it at the time of the receipt?

*A.* There were two receipts at the time.

*Q.* Do you know of its existence, by seeing it at the time when it purports to bear date?

*A.* A little afterwards; a few days afterwards.

*Q.* When did you first see it?

*A.* A few days afterwards; I really believe the £.50 receipt I handed myself to Mr. Johnstone, but I cannot charge my memory with it.

*Lord Ellenborough.* You saw it in the month of February, or when?

*A.* The £.50 receipt, which was in September or October, I believe I handed over to Mr. Johnstone myself; the other I did not.

*Mr. Scarlett.* When did you first see the other receipt; was it in February?

*A.* I think within two or three days after it was given.

*Lord Ellenborough.* Have you both the receipts there?

*Mr. Scarlett.* We have, my Lord.

*Lord Ellenborough.* Then hand them in, if he proves that he saw them about the date?

*A.* This receipt of the 20th of September 1813, I handed myself over to Mr. Johnstone.

[*It was read, as follows.*]

"London, Sept$^r$ 20, 1813.

"Received of the Hon$^{ble}$ Cochrane Johnstone, the sum of fifty pounds (by the hands of Gab$^l$ Tahourdin, Esq.) on account of large plans, &c.

"*C. Random De Berenger.*"

———
£.50 — —
———

*Mr. Scarlett.* You have another receipt in your hands, that bears date the 26th of February?

*A.* Yes.

*Q.* That money did not pass through your hands?

*A.* No.

*Q.* When did you first see that receipt?

*A.* In three or four days afterwards, when Mr. Johnstone called upon me; Mr. De Berenger and I were not at that time upon favourable terms; that will account for my not having delivered it over to him.

[*It was read, as follows.*]

"London, February the 26th, 1814.

"Received of the Hon^{ble} A. Cochrane Johnstone, the sum of two hundred pounds, being the balance of some drawings, plans and prospecti, delivered.

"*C. R. De Berenger.*"

£.200 —— ——

*Mr. Scarlett.* I observe, that in that correspondence there is mention made, besides the payment of £.250 of a loan of £.200?

*A.* Yes.

*Q.* Were you present at the passing of any money?

*A.* No, I was not.

*Q.* When did you first see that paper? (*handing one to the witness.*)

*A.* I saw it at the same time with the last receipt for £.200.

*Q.* What is it?

*A.* A note of hand for £.200.

*Q.* You saw that two or three days after it bears date?

*A.* Yes, I did.

[*It was read as follows.*]

£.200 —— ——

"London, February the 26th, 1814.

"Six Months after date, I promise to pay to the Hon^{ble} A. Cochrane Johnstone, the sum of two hundred pounds.

"*C. R. De Berenger.*"

Payable at Gab^l Tahourdin, Esq.
N° 8, King's Bench Walk, Temple.


*Mr. Scarlett.* With respect to those letters you received from Mr. Johnstone, do they contain your indorsement upon the back of them?

*A.* I think they do.

*Q.* Is that your handwriting upon the back of that letter? (*shewing it to the witness.*)

*A.* It is.

*Q.* Was it written by you at the time you received it?

*A.* Yes.

*Lord Ellenborough.* What letter is that?

*A.* The letter of the Baron to Mr. Johnstone, of the 22d of February.

*Lord Ellenborough.* You wrote it on the same day?

*A.* I cannot say on the same day, but within a few days; when I doubled up the papers that lay on the table, with other documents.

*Mr. Scarlett.* Is it your habit, when you lay letters by, to endorse the date.

*A.* Yes, uniformly; but not on the day of receiving them; I let them lie till they accumulate unpleasantly.

*Lord Ellenborough.* If a man sends you letters enclosed from other persons, do you indorse the letters sent to you inclosed; that is no part of the correspondence with you?

*A.* No, it is not.

*Q.* Then I should apprehend, you would not usually do it?

*A.* I have done it differently; I have said "De Berenger to Johnstone."

*Q.* But you give it a date?

*A.* I have dated it above those words, as usual.

*Q.* When you receive a letter, you authenticate the period of receiving it, but not the date of a letter received by another.

*A.* I generally do; I enclose it in the letter to which it refers.

*Mr. Scarlett.* Was it so done in this instance?

*A.* It was.

*Lord Ellenborough.* Have you any letter-book?

*A.* I do not keep a letter-book; but I keep my letters very regularly tied up.

*Mr. Scarlett.* You have heard the contents of the letter from De Berenger to Mr. Johnstone read.

*A.* Yes.

*Q.* That refers to some documents in your hands, to serve as a security to Mr. Johnstone, in case he should require them?

*A.* Yes.

*Q.* Is it your usual practice, when letters of that sort are sent to you, to make the sort of endorsement you have done when you lay the letters by?

*A.* It is.

*Lord Ellenborough.* I only asked him as to the inclosure. If I received a letter, I should endorse the date of my receiving it as authenticating the fact; but I should not put the endorsement of the date upon the enclosure, for I know nothing of the date, whether it was received on that day or not; the gentlemen of the jury know whether that is the habit of business or not.

*A Juryman.* Is the date you have endorsed upon the enclosure, the date of your receiving it or the date of the letter?

*A.* The date of the letter.

*Lord Ellenborough.* Certainly it is not regular to authenticate the date of a letter, to which you are not privy; that is all my observation upon it.

*Mr. Scarlett.* Besides those plans you now produce, do you know whether there were other and subordinate plans drawn for the details of that same scheme?

*A.* Yes, there were.

[*Examined by Mr. Park.*]

*Q.* You have been a great while the attorney of Mr. De Berenger, and known to him?

*A.* Five or six years.

*Q.* Were you known to him before you were known to Mr. Cochrane Johnstone?

*A.* Yes.

*Q.* Did you become security for the Rules for this gentleman before you knew Mr. Cochrane Johnstone?

*A.* Some months.

*Q.* Then it was not at Mr. Cochrane Johnstone's desire that you became a surety for the Rules for this person?

*A.* Certainly not.

*Q.* Was Mr. Cochrane, who, I understand from Mr. Brushoft, was your co-surety, any relation of Mr. Cochrane Johnstone?

*A.* No.

*Lord Ellenborough.* That has been proved over and over again; nobody made an observation upon it.

*Mr. Park.* I beg your Lordship's pardon; there could be no other motive, I conceive, in calling Mr. Brushoft.

*Lord Ellenborough.* I understood him to be called to prove, that Mr. Tahourdin was a surety for the defendant; I never heard an observation made upon Mr. Cochrane, as being a relation.

*Mr. Park.* Are you acquainted with the hand-writing of your client, Mr. De Berenger?

*A.* Perfectly.

*Q.* That letter, or those letters lying before his Lordship, which have been proved, I think you say they are his hand-writing?

*A.* There is only one.

*Q.* Have you ever seen that letter before you saw it yesterday? (*handing to the witness the letter sent to Admiral Foley.*)

*A.* Never; I just saw it yesterday, and that was all.

*Q.* Upon the knowledge you have of the hand-writing of Mr. De Berenger, is that, in your judgment, the hand-writing of Mr. De Berenger or not?

*A.* Certainly not.

*Lord Ellenborough.* Be upon your guard.

*Mr. Park.* Be upon your guard, and look at it attentively. You have many times seen and read his letters?

*A.* A thousand times, and received a thousand letters from him.

*Q.* And you do not believe it to be his hand-writing?

*A.* I do not indeed; it is not his hand-writing.

*Lord Ellenborough.* That is the Dover letter?

*Mr. Park.* Yes it is, my Lord. If your Lordship will look at that and the other letter, you will see a marked difference.

[*The witness compared the two letters.*]

*Lord Ellenborough.* The gentleman may look at the two letters; but that furnishes no argument, for a person would certainly write a disguised hand at that time, if ever he did in his life. This gentleman does not go on belief that it is not, but he swears positively that it is not his hand-writing.

*Mr. Park.* Certainly, my Lord; and there is, on the other side, only Mr. Lavie. This gentleman having seen Mr. De Berenger write a thousand times, and received a thousand letters from him. Do you, in your judgment and conscience believe, that that is a disguised hand of Mr. De Berenger?

*A.* I do not.

*A Juryman.* Why did you take the two letters up to compare the two hand-writings, if you had no doubt in your mind?

*A.* I had no doubt at all of it.

*Lord Ellenborough.* Why did you compare the two then?

*A.* I wished to be circumspect; but if my life rested upon it, I should say, this is not his hand-writing, according to my belief and judgment.

*Mr. Park.* What has been, for the number of years you have known this person, his general character?

*A.* I have always considered him a man of strict honour and integrity.

*Q.* We have heard he has been in difficulties?

*A.* He has been.

*Q.* And he is a debtor of yours?

*A.* Yes, he is a very large one.

*Q.* To what amount have you trusted him?

*A.* To the extent, I believe, of about £.4,000, and upwards, besides my professional claim.

*Lord Ellenborough.* In money.

*A.* Yes, in money.

*Mr. Gurney.* I only want to ask Mr. Wood as to this road book. I believe it has been identified before.

*Lord Ellenborough.* That was put in yesterday.

*Mr. Jones.* I had it yesterday in my hands; it was put in by Mr. Wood.

*Mr. Gurney.* I wish to shew Mr. Tahourdin the hand-writing in that book.

*Lord Ellenborough.* The hand-writing in that road book certainly was as extremely like the Dover letter as ever I saw any thing in my life. [*The road book was handed to Mr. Tahourdin.*]

### Cross-examined by Mr. Gurney.

*A.* Have the goodness to look at that pencil-writing in that road book; do you believe it to be Mr. De Berenger's hand-writing.

*Lord Ellenborough.* Now be upon your guard.

*Mr. Gurney.* Look at both pages.

[*The witness examined it.*]

*A.* Some of it appears to be more like his hand-writing than the other part.

*Q.* Do not you believe it all to be his hand-writing?

*A.* No, I do not indeed.

*Q.* How much of it do you believe to be his hand-writing.

*Lord Ellenborough.* State the parts where you think the likeness ends, and where you think somebody else has taken up the pencil and written a part of it.

*A.* That looks more like his hand-writing [*pointing it out*] but it is not the general writing of Mr. De Berenger.

*Mr. Gurney.* How much of it do you believe to be his writing?

*A.* Some part of it looks more like his writing than other part.

*Q.* Is there any part which you believe is not?

*A.* The writing part is not at all like his writing.

*Q.* I ask you as to nothing but the writing part?

*A.* Some are figures.

*Q.* Looking at those two pages, you say it is not all his hand-writing?

*A.* No, I do not think I did.

*Q.* That was your first answer?

*Lord Ellenborough.* You said "There is some more like his hand-writing, but I do not believe it all is."

*Mr. Gurney.* How much is there of it that you do not believe to be his writing.

*A.* Some of the letters look like his hand-writing.

*Q.* How much or how little of it do you think to be his hand-writing?

*A.* The smaller parts look like his hand-writing.

*Q.* Now I ask you upon your oath, have you any doubt of the whole of those two pages having been written by the same hand?

*A.* Upon my word it is difficult to say.

*Q.* Not at all so; I have looked at it attentively, and I know it is not difficult to say; do not you believe it all written by the same hand?

[*The witness examined it again.*]

*Lord Ellenborough.* You can say whether you believe it to be De Berenger's hand-writing?

*A.* Upon my word, I really do not know what to say.

*Mr. Gurney.* I am quite content with that answer?

*Lord Ellenborough.* Mr. Park, would you like to look the Dover letter?

*Mr. Park.* I am no judge of hand-writing, my Lord.

*Lord Ellenborough.* That may be a concealed hand-writing, and I should think it extremely likely.

*Mr. Park.* I mean to call other witnesses to this; I have nothing to conceal in this case?

*Lord Ellenborough.* No; you announced to us that you flatly contradict the whole of the story as to Mr. De Berenger.

*Mr. Park.* Yes, I do my Lord; I observe this is all pencilling which has been shewn to you?

*A.* Yes, it is.

*Mr. Park.* Is this pencil writing in the same kind of character that a man writes when he writes with pen and ink; are you enabled to say from your knowledge of the hand-writing, whether it is or is not?

*A.* That it is which puzzles me more than any thing, its being in pencil.

*A Juryman.* We should like to see that road book.

*Mr. Park.* Does your Lordship think the jury have a right to see that; they cannot take it for the purpose of comparing with any thing else?

*Lord Ellenborough.* It is in evidence, being found in the desk of the defendant, they may look at each, if they please.

*General Campbell,* sworn.

*Examined by Mr. Brougham.*

*Q.* Do you know Mr. Cochrane Johnstone?

*A.* I do.

*Q.* Did you meet him in the month of September or October last, at a meeting or hunt in Scotland?

*A.* I met him the second week, I think in last October, at the Perth meeting.

*Q.* Did he at that time shew you some plans and prospectus of the new place of amusement, in the nature of a Ranelagh?

*A.* I saw in Mr. Cochrane Johnstone's hands, the prospectus of a new public place, he called it, to be erected in the Regent's Park, or the neighbourhood of the Regent's Park.

*Q.* Do you recollect the name he gave to it?

*A.* I think he called it Vittoria.

*Q.* Will you look at the prospectus, and see whether that is the same? [*The prospectus was shewn to the witness.*]

*A.* I believe this is a copy of the same that I saw.

*Q.* Look at the plan?

*A.* He did not shew me the plan.

*Q.* Did he shew this prospectus, and communicate to other persons at that meeting upon the subject of it, as well as you?

*A.* I cannot speak to that; he communicated to me in my own apartment or his own, I cannot recollect which.

[*Mr. Hopper was called, but did not answer.*]

*Mr. Serjeant Best.* This gentleman was taken very ill, being kept here last night; if he comes by and by, I trust your Lordship will permit him to be examined out of his turn.

*Lord Ellenborough.* Certainly, at any period.

*Mr. Serjeant Best.* That is the case of the three defendants for whom I appear.

*The Right Honourable the Earl of Yarmouth sworn.*

*Examined by Mr. Park.*

*Q.* You are I believe, or were, the Colonel of the Duke of Cumberland's sharp-shooters?

*A.* Lieutenant-colonel commandant.

*Q.* It is called the corps of sharp-shooters?

*A.* Yes.

*Q.* Captain De Berenger was adjutant of that regiment, was he not?

*A.* He was a non-commissioned officer, acting adjutant.

*Q.* How long have you known Mr. De Berenger?

*A.* Ever since a few days after I was elected to command that corps; that was in the beginning of the year 1811; I cannot fix the day, very early in that year I know it was.

*Q.* Has your Lordship had opportunities of seeing Mr. De Berenger write, or of receiving letters from him, and of acting upon those letters from him.

*A.* I have received a great many letters from him, and have seen him write occasionally.

*Q.* And you have seen him, probably, on the subject of the contents of those letters?

*A.* Very frequently; two or three times I have seen him alter the regimental orders, and have received very many letters from him.

*Q.* Are you, from that opportunity that you have described, in a capacity to state to his Lordship and the jury, whether you are acquainted with his character of hand-writing?

*A.* As well as I am with that of any other gentleman with whom I have been in the habit of correspondence.

*Q.* Then, not knowing what your Lordship's answer may be, I will trouble your Lordship to look at that.—[*The letter sent to Admiral Foley was handed to his Lordship.*]

*A.* I will read it through, if you please.—[*His lordship read the letter.*]

*Q.* Supposing you had heard none of the circumstances which this trial has brought to every body's ears, and of which your Lordship has heard so much yesterday; from the character of the hand-writing of Mr. De Berenger, should you have believed it to be his hand-writing?

*A.* Certainly not.

*Q.* Your lordship, I believe, knows that in the month of July, this gentleman was very urgent and solicitous to go out as a sharp-shooter to America, with Sir Alexander and afterwards with Lord Cochrane?

*A.* He mentioned to me one day, when he came to me on the business of the corps——

*Q.* Was that in January?

*A.* I think so; but I cannot swear to the date; he mentioned to me, that he had very nearly arranged to go out, to drill the crew and the marines on board of the Tonnant. I thought he mentioned it in a way to suggest, that he wished some little additional influence, and I got rid of the thing.

*Cross-examined by Mr. Gurney.*

*Q.* The writing of that is larger than Mr. De Berenger usually writes?

*A.* Certainly, it is longer.

*Q.* The character of the letters is longer?

*A.* Oh, certainly; it is a very round small hand he generally writes, and a very pretty hand.

*Q.* Will your lordship look at that letter, and tell me, whether you received that letter at or about the time that it bears date? (*shewing a letter to his lordship.*)

*A.* Yes; either the day it bears date, or the day immediately after it.

Mr. *Gurney.* I request Mr. Law will mark that letter; the date of it is March the 19th?

*A.* I believe I marked the cover.

*Q.* Will your lordship have the goodness to look at the hand-writing in that road book (*shewing it to his lordship*); that I believe is larger than Mr. De Berenger's usual writing, is it not?

*A.* I think it is; some part certainly does not look larger; it is less round—it is more angular.

*Q.* Does your lordship or not, believe that to be Mr. De Berenger's hand-writing?

*A.* I am not sufficiently conversant with hand-writing, to wish to swear to an opinion either way.

### Re-examined by Mr. Park.

*Q.* That is in pencil?

*A.* Yes.

*Q.* With respect to the letter in question, although it is of a larger description than Mr. De Berenger's usual writing, does it appear to your lordship to be at all a feigned hand, as disguising the real hand?

*A.* Another question to which I am not competent to give an answer; if I was to look through the letter—there is one letter which creates a suspicion, but I should never have suspected it on a cursory view of the letter; it is the letter R before Du Bourg, but that I should have never looked at or suspected; that looks more like his hand-writing than any other part; it looks like the way in which he makes the R of Random.

*Q.* Does your lordship mean the large capital R, or the little r?

*A.* The large capital R is the only letter I can see that looks in the least like his hand.

*Q.* Your judgment upon that letter, upon the whole inspection of it, is, that it is not his hand-writing?

*A.* I should never suspect it, except from that letter.

*Lord Ellenborough.* It is a larger character?

*A.* Yes, it is a fuller character.

*Q.* It is a stiffer character, and more upright?

*A.* It is less upright, I think, than his; it is more angular and longer.

*Lord Ellenborough.* That is his usual writing, is it not? (*shewing another letter to the witness.*)

*A.* Oh, yes; certainly, I am perfectly familiar with that.

*Lord Ellenborough.* You are certainly borne out in your observation upon the letter; look at that letter R again?

*A.* It struck me on reading the letter.

*Q.* In what manner an artificial letter may be written, so as to disable a person from saying whether it is the hand-writing of a certain person, you cannot say?

*A.* I am perfectly incompetent, as I informed your lordship and the jury before, to give any judgment upon that.

*Q.* What is the uniform of your corps?

*A.* The uniform is, the waistcoat green, with a crimson cape.

*Q.* A bottle green, is it not?

*A.* Some have got it a little darker than others, but it should be a deep bottle-green with a crimson collar; the great coat is a waistcoat with black fur round it, consequently no crimson collar.

*Q.* The body in your uniform is not red?

*A.* It is deep bottle green.

*A Juryman.* A jacket or coat?

*A.* It is a waistcoat, very like the light-horse uniform.

*Lord Ellenborough.* It is almost unnecessary to ask you, whether the members of your corps wear any decorations; a star or a cross?

*A.* When in uniform, some wear medals that they have gained as prizes given by the corps; they occasionally wear them hanging by a ribband.

*Q.* You wear no such decorations as this? (*shewing the star to his lordship.*)

*A.* No, certainly not.

*Q.* Supposing a gentleman appeared before you in an aid-de-camp's uniform, with that star upon his breast, and that other ornament appendant, should you consider that was a man exhibiting himself in the dress of your sharp-shooting corps?

*A.* Certainly not.

*Q.* If a sharp-shooter belonging to your corps presented himself to you in that dress, you would think it a very impertinent thing?

*A.* Certainly.

*Mr. Serjeant Best.* As Lord Yarmouth has been called by the defendant, De Berenger, and has given evidence which may affect Lord Cochrane, we conceive, we submit we have a right to make an observation upon it.

*A Juryman.* If Colonel De Berenger had appeared before your lordship in the uniform of his corps, would it have been any thing extraordinary?

*A.* Nothing extraordinary; it would have been more military that he should do so, though I never exacted it.

*Captain Sir John Poo Beresford, sworn.*

*Examined by Mr. Richardson.*

*Q.* Are you acquainted with Mr. De Berenger?

*A.* I have seen him twice in my life before yesterday.

*Q.* Have you had any occasion to see him write, or to be acquainted with the character of his hand-writing?

*A.* Never.

*Q.* Do you know at any time in the early part of this year, or the latter end of the last, of any applications he was making to go to America as a sharpshooter?

*A.* I will tell you the part I took in reference to that business. In the beginning of February, I paid my ship off; after that, I met Mr. Cochrane Johnstone in town, who told me Sir Alexander Cochrane was very anxious he should go out in the Tonnant, to teach the marines the rifle-exercise. I went to the Horse Guards to ask whether anything could be done; I was told it would be useless to apply to the Duke of York; and I told Mr. Cochrane Johnstone of it the day after. I was dressing before breakfast, and Mr. De Berenger sent up to say, that he was very much obliged to me for the part I had taken.

*Q.* At what time was this?

*A.* I think, the beginning of February; but before Sir Alexander Cochrane sailed, I met him at Mr. Cochrane Johnstone's, with Admiral Hope and some ladies; I think that was in January, or the latter end of December; there were, I think, fourteen of us, some of them ladies. This application was after he had sailed. When I went to Mr. Cochrane Johnstone's, I was to have met Sir Alexander Cochrane, but he went to dine somewhere else, and my Lord Cochrane came in after dinner; he did not dine there, but a great many of the family did.

*James Stokes sworn.*

*Examined by Mr. Park.*

*Q.* I understand you are a clerk of Mr. Tahourdin, the attorney.

*A.* Yes.

*Q.* How long have you been so?

*A.* Between three and four years.

*Q.* Have you, in the course of those three or four years, had frequent opportunities of seeing the hand-writing of Mr. De Berenger?

*A.* Daily.

*Q.* He has been a client of your master, and has been assisted very much by him?

*A.* Yes.

*Q.* Have you seen him write, as well as seeing letters purporting to come from him?

*A.* A great deal.

*Q.* Be so good as to look at that paper (*the Dover letter*), and tell his lordship and the jury, whether in your judgment and belief, that is the hand-writing of Mr. De Berenger?

*A.* Certainly not.

*Q.* Look at that, and say whether you think it is a feigned hand, but still the hand-writing of De Berenger?

*A.* It certainly is not.

*Q.* Of course, a man can only speak to belief and judgment when he does not see a thing written; do you believe, from your knowledge of his hand-writing, that that is his writing, either feigned or real?

*A.* Not a word of it.

*Lord Ellenborough.* Look at the letter R in the signature?

*A.* It is not like it at all.

*Mr. Park.* I mean the large R.

*A.* The capital R is nothing like it.

*Mr. Park.* It is a singular R certainly, it looks as if it had been intended for a P and made into an R.

*Lord Ellenborough.* It is not at all like that R, is it? [*shewing another letter to the witness.*]

*A.* No, I do not think it is any thing like that.

*William Smith sworn.*

*Examined by Mr. Richardson.*

*Q.* You are servant to Mr. De Berenger?

*A.* Yes.

*Q.* How long have you been his servant?

*A.* About three years and a half.

*Q.* Do you write yourself?

*A.* Yes.

*Q.* During the time you have been in his service, have you seen him write, and become acquainted with his hand-writing.

*A.* A great deal of it.

*Q.* Is he a gentleman who writes a good deal?

*A.* Yes.

*Q.* Are you well acquainted with the character of his hand-writing?

*A.* Yes.

*Q.* Have the goodness to look that over, and then I will ask you a question respecting it, and among other things look at the signature at the bottom, R. Du Bourg.—[*The letter sent to Admiral Foley was handed to the witness, and he examined it.*]

Mr. Park. Having examined that paper, is that, in your judgment and belief, the hand-writing of your master, Mr. De Berenger?

*A.* I really believe it is not.

*Q.* The whole, or any part of it.

*A.* None of it.

*Q.* Have you any doubt of that?

*A.* I am positively sure it is not his hand-writing.

*Q.* According to the best of your judgment and belief?

*A.* According to the best of my judgment and belief.

*Q.* You have been his servant three years and a half?

*A.* Yes.

*Q.* We understand he has lately lodged with a person of the name of Davidson, in a place called the Asylum Buildings.

*A.* Yes.

*Q.* Were you with him till he went away in the month of February?

*A.* Yes.

*Q.* That was on Sunday the 27th, was it not?

*A.* Yes.

*Q.* Do you remember, whether he was at home on the Sunday preceding that, that would be the 20th?

*A.* I perfectly remember it.

*Q.* Did he sleep at home on the Saturday night?

*A.* He did.

*Q.* Did he go out at any time on Sunday morning?

*A.* He did.

*Q.* Do you remember at what time?

*A.* About nine o'clock.

*Q.* Did he come in again after that?

*A.* Yes.

*Q.* And go out again?

*A.* Yes.

*Q.* About what time was that.

*A.* It was near eleven when he came home, and he went out immediately afterwards; he was not above a quarter of an hour or twenty minutes before he returned again.

*Q.* Did he return again after that?

*A.* Yes.

*Q.* How soon after?

*A.* About twenty minutes.

*Q.* Would that be after persons were gone to church that he returned?

*A.* Yes.

*Q.* How long did he stay at home then?

*A.* Till about four o'clock.

*Q.* He went out again about four o'clock?

*A.* Yes.

*Q.* Were you at home at the time he went out again, about four o'clock?

*A.* I was over the way.

*Q.* Did you see him?

*A.* Yes; I had the dogs out, and was leaning with my back against the rail when he came down.

*Q.* Your master's dogs?

*A.* Yes.

*Q.* He kept dogs, did he?

*A.* Only one; one was mine; I was with them opposite, on the other side of the road, leaning against the rail facing the door.


*Q.* What were you doing with the dogs?

*A.* I generally take them out for occasions.

*Q.* Did you see him go out about that time?

*A.* I did.

*Q.* Did you yourself go out soon after that?

*A.* Yes I did, and my wife.

*Q.* About what time did you return home that evening?

*A.* About eleven o'clock, within a few minutes of eleven.

*Q.* Was your master at home when you returned or not?

*A.* He was not at home.

*Q.* Did he come home afterwards?

*A.* Yes.

*Q.* About what time?

*A.* I had not been at home, I suppose five minutes, before my master came home.

*Q.* That would be a few minutes before or after eleven?

*A.* Yes.

*Q.* Did he sleep at home that night.

*A.* Yes.

*Q.* What means have you of knowing that?

*A.* The means I have were these; after I came home we were down in the kitchen taking our supper, my master was in the drawing-room before we had got to bed, I heard him going up stairs to his bed-room, he passed my room door; that was not above half past eleven.

*Q.* Did he breakfast at home the next morning, or not.

*A.* No, he did not.

*Q.* Did you see him the next morning early?

*A.* No.

*Q.* About what time did you see him the next day?

*A.* About three o'clock; I cannot speak to a minute or two.

*Q.* Did you hear or see him go out?

*A.* I did not.

*Q.* You saw him about three o'clock on the Monday?

*A.* Yes, I did.

*Q.* Who made his bed?

*A.* My wife.

*Cross-examined by Mr. Gurney.*

*Q.* Did you let him in?

*A.* Yes.

*Q.* You opened the door to him?

*A.* Yes.

*Q.* At a little after eleven, that night?

*A.* Yes, thereabouts, it might be a little before, or a little after.

*Q.* He gave a good loud knock at the door, in his usual way?

*A.* He rapped as usual.

*Q.* And his usual rap was a loud one?

*A.* Not over loud.

*Q.* Not very gentle?

*A.* Between.

*Q.* Between loud and gentle?

*A.* Yes.

*Q.* And he slept at home that night?

*A.* I cannot say that he slept, he went to his bed-room, and the bed when I went in the morning looked as if he had slept in it.

*Q.* Did you see him in bed the next morning?

*A.* No, I did not, I heard him go into the bed room.

*Q.* You did not see him the next day till three o'clock?

*A.* No.

*Q.* Did you write that letter to Lord Yarmouth? (*shewing a letter to the witness.*)

*A.* I did.

*Q.* Of your own head?

*A.* Yes.


*Q.* No body furnished you with any draught to write from?

*A.* No.

*Q.* Have you your master's military great coat here?

*A.* Yes.

*Q.* His military grey great coat?

*A.* Yes; not in this present place.

*Q.* It is at Guildhall?

*A.* Yes.

*Q.* Now attend to this question, have you not acknowledged that your master slept from home that night?

*A.* Never.

*Q.* Have you not acknowledged it to Mr. Murray?

*A.* Never.

*Q.* I give you notice he is here?

*A.* I know he is.

*Q.* Now I ask you, did you not on Monday the 21st, tell Mr. or Mrs. Davidson, or both, that coming home, and not finding your master at home, you had left the key for him at the usual place in the area, that he might let himself in?

*A.* I did not tell them so, upon my oath.

*Q.* Neither of them?

*A.* No, neither of them.

*Q.* Did you tell Mr. or Mrs. Davidson that on any other day; did you ever tell them so?

*A.* No, not to the best of my knowledge.

*Q.* To the best of your knowledge?

*A.* I never told them so.

*Q.* As you did not attend your master on the Monday morning, who attended him and brought him his shaving things, and gave him the usual attendance of a gentleman?

*A.* He never has any attendance; I never go to his bed room till about half past eight, and sometimes he is up, and sometimes not.

*Q.* Do you mean to say, he is a gentleman that wants no attendance?

*A.* Yes; he cleans his teeth, and washes himself and powders his hair, without my being in his bed room.

*Q.* He does not usually ring his bell in a morning, I suppose, doing without attendance?

*A.* Not before he comes down to breakfast.

*Q.* What time does he usually come down to breakfast?

*A.* At different hours.

*Q.* What is his usual hour?

*A.* Sometimes nine, sometimes ten, sometimes eight.

*Q.* Till he comes down, he does not ring for you?

*A.* Very seldom.

*Q.* He is a very quiet, a remarkably quiet man in his lodging?

*A.* I never knew him to be otherwise.

*Q.* Not a person walking about, or making a noise of any kind?

*A.* Not making any disturbance; he walks about very much.

*Q.* Your master finally left his lodgings on Sunday the 27th.

*A.* Yes.

*Q.* Do you remember your paying or changing a fifty-pound note with a Mr. Seeks?

*A.* I do.

*Q.* From whom did you receive that fifty-pound note?

*A.* Mr. De Berenger.

*Q.* On what day did you receive that?

*A.* On the 27th, I think it was.

*Q.* On the Sunday?

*A.* Yes; I think it was.

*Q.* The day he went away?

*A.* Yes; I think it was.


*Q.* When he went away, he took his things to the Angel Inn, St. Clements.

*A.* I took them for him.

*Q.* For him to go into the country?

*A.* Yes.

*Q.* Did you receive no more than fifty pounds from him; did you not also receive a twenty pound from him?

*A.* I did not; not the same day.

*Q.* What day did you receive that twenty pounds?

*A.* I cannot positively say.

*Q.* Was it a day or two before he went away?

*A.* Yes.

*Q.* Did you receive also a two pound from him?

*A.* I do not recollect.

*Q.* Did you receive and give to any person, of the name of Sophia, thirteen pounds from him?

*A.* No; I gave none to Sophia.

*Q.* Did you see him give her any thing?

*A.* No, I did not; if I was in the room I did not notice it.

*Q.* Do you know any person of the name of Hebden, or Heberdine?

*A.* No.

*Q.* Do you remember, the day before your master finally went away, Mr. Cochrane Johnstone calling with a letter?

*A.* I do not remember that; I was not at home.

*Q.* Upon your oath, did not a gentleman call there, who you told Mr. Davidson was Mr. Cochrane Johnstone?

*A.* Upon my oath I was not at home; she told me a gentleman called there, and giving a description of him, I said, most likely it was Mr. Cochrane Johnstone.

*Q.* You knew Mr. Cochrane Johnstone?

*A.* Very little.

*Q.* But you did know him?

*A.* I once saw him.

*Q.* Did you not tell her on the Sunday, that if your master had been at home on the Saturday, when Mr. Cochrane Johnstone brought that letter, he would have gone off on the Saturday night?

*A.* I did not.

*Q.* Did you not on the Saturday or the Sunday?

*A.* I did not.

*Q.* Was your master at home all that week, from the 20th to the 27th?

*A.* He was not always at home.

*Q.* He was at home every day?

*A.* Yes.

*Q.* Going out as usual?

*A.* Yes.

*Q.* On the 21st, for instance?

*A.* The 21st he went out to dine.

*Q.* Where did he go to?

*A.* I cannot positively say.

*Q.* Did he tell you where he was going to?

*A.* I do not recollect.

*Q.* Upon your oath, did he not tell you he had been to Mr. Cochrane Johnstone's?

*A.* No.

*Q.* You swear that?

*A.* Yes.

*Q.* Nor that he was going there?

*A.* No.

*Q.* When you came home on the Monday, did you see any black coat in the room?

*A.* I did.

*Q.* Was that your master's black coat, or a strange black coat?

*A.* A strange black coat.

*Q.* That black coat must have fitted your master vastly well?

*A.* I cannot say, I never saw it on.

*Q.* You brushed it, did not you?

*A.* Yes; but not on his back.

*Q.* You are used to brushing his coats?

*A.* Of course.

*Q.* Now, a servant used to brush his master's coat, must know the size pretty well; this would be rather a short coat upon him, would it not?

*A.* No; I do not think it would.

*Q.* Upon your oath, would it not have been a great deal too long; was not it the coat of a man six feet high?

*A.* I did not know who owned the coat.

*Q.* I did not ask you that; but was not that the coat of a gentleman six feet high?

*A.* I do not know.

*Q.* You are not competent to say what sized man that would fit?

*A.* That coat would fit me very well; it is rather wide.

*Q.* Not at all too long for you?

*A.* No, not at all.

*Q.* You have seen Lord Cochrane, have not you?

*A.* Never in my life, to my knowledge.

*Q.* You have sworn some affidavits, have you not?

*A.* I have.

*Q.* Did you draw them yourself?

*A.* I did.

*Q.* Without any assistance?

*A.* Without any assistance.

*Q.* Whom had you seen before you drew them?

*A.* I cannot say who I saw, thousands.

*Q.* Upon that business?

*A.* No body.

*Q.* Before you made that affidavit, you had not seen any body upon that business?

*A.* No.

*Q.* Not Lord Cochrane?

*A.* Never in my life.

*Q.* Nor Mr. Cochrane Johnstone?

*A.* No.

*Q.* Nor Mr. Tahourdin?

*A.* I saw Mr. Tahourdin, but he did not know of my making the affidavits; I told Mr. Tahourdin of my master's absence; I went to tell him.

*Q.* How soon was that after he left his lodgings?

*A.* I cannot positively say to a day.

*Lord Ellenborough.* What absence do you mean?

*A.* From the 27th.

*Mr. Gurney.* How soon after the 27th did you tell him?

*A.* About the 7th or 8th.

*Q.* Of March?

*A.* Yes.

*Q.* You swore your affidavit on the 24th of March?

*A.* Yes; but I drew it out before then.

*Q.* And that without any concert with any body whatever?

*A.* Yes.

*Q.* Merely for the vindication of your master's character?

*A.* Yes.

*Q.* And when you had done it, what did you do with the affidavit?

*A.* I sent it to have it published.

*Q.* To whom did you send it?

*A.* I took it to Mr. Cochrane Johnstone. I found my master a very injured gentleman.

*Q.* And therefore you took it to Mr. Cochrane Johnstone, to be published?

*A.* I did not take it to be published.

*Q.* You gave me those very words?

*A.* He did publish it.

*Q.* Did you not take it to be published?

*A.* I did not take it to the printer.

*Q.* Did you not take it to Mr. Cochrane Johnstone, that it might be published?

*A.* Yes.

*A Juryman.* Did your master breakfast at home on Monday the 21st of February?

*A.* No, he did not.

Re-examined by Mr. Richardson.

*Q.* When was it that you first saw this black coat?

*A.* On the 21st of February.

*Q.* That was the Monday?

*A.* Yes.

*Q.* That was after he came home, which you say was about three o'clock?

*A.* I came home about three o'clock.

*Q.* He was at home?

*A.* Yes.

*Q.* He might have been at home before that?

*A.* Yes, he might.

*Q.* Does your master play on any musical instrument?

*A.* He was used to do.

*Lord Ellenborough.* I will ask any question upon that subject for you, but there has been no question put on the cross-examination with reference to it?

*Mr. Park.* There was a question about his being still.

*Lord Ellenborough.* There was no allusion to musical instruments; you should have gone through it in your original examination, as it was to contradict their case. Does your master play on any musical instrument?

*A.* Yes; both the bugle-horn and violin.

*Q.* You say Mrs. Davidson described to you a person who called, and that you said it was most likely Mr. Cochrane Johnstone?

*A.* Yes.

*Q.* You had seen Mr. Cochrane Johnstone?

*A.* Yes; I had seen him but once.

*Q.* This was on Saturday the 26th?

*A.* Yes.

*Q.* Why did you say it was most likely Mr. Cochrane Johnstone?

*A.* Because she told me it was a tall gentleman, and his long hair very much powdered.

*Q.* Having seen him but once, and not being much acquainted with him, what led you to say most likely it was Mr. Cochrane Johnstone; had you any expectation that he would come that day?

*A.* No, not the least.

*Q.* But having seen him once, you thought it must be that tall man and powdered, whom you had seen but once in your life?

*Q.* I might have seen him oftener than that, but not to my recollection.

*Q.* What you said was, that you had seen him once?

*A.* I had seen him once, I know.

*Q.* Had you seen him oftener than that?

*A.* I cannot say; but I once saw him at his own house.

*Q.* I supposed you had never seen him but once from your answer?

*A.* I might have seen him oftener, but I do not know that I had.

*Q.* You are as sure as that you are existing, that your master went up at eleven o'clock, or sometime after eleven, on Sunday evening the 20th of February?

*A.* So help me God; I am sure he did.

*A Juryman.* Did you see him go up, or only hear him go up?

*A.* I heard him go up; I was in my bed room.

*Lord Ellenborough.* But you let him in?

*A.* Yes, I did.

*A Juryman.* You are sure that was on Sunday the 20th?

*A.* Yes.

*Q.* Did your master often breakfast out?

*A.* Sometimes.

*Q.* Not often.

*A.* Not very often.

*Ann Smith sworn.*

*Examined by Mr. Park.*

*Q.* Are you the wife of Charles Smith?

*A.* Of William Smith.

*Q.* Were you a servant, with your husband, of Mr. De Berenger, in February last?

*A.* Yes.

*Q.* Had you been so for any length of time?

*A.* Two years and a half.

*Q.* Do you recollect having seen him at home on Sunday the 20th of February?

*A.* Yes.

*Q.* In the forenoon?

*A.* Yes.

*Q.* Do you know what time he went out that morning?

*A.* About nine o'clock.

*Q.* When did he come in again?

*A.* Between ten and eleven o'clock.

*Q.* How long did he stay at home at that time?

*A.* Not a great while.

*Q.* He then went out again?

*A.* Yes.

*Q.* When did you see him again?

*A.* He did not stay long.

*Q.* When did you and your husband go out that day?

*A.* Between four and five, after my master was gone out.

*Q.* What time did he go out?

*A.* About four o'clock.

*Q.* And you and your husband went out between four and five o'clock.

*A.* Yes.

*Q.* At what time did you and your husband return home that night?

*A.* About eleven, as near as I can guess.

*Q.* Was your master come home before you, or did he not return till afterwards?

*A.* My husband came in a few minutes before my master, and went down to strike a light, and I stopped to bring him some beer.

*Q.* Did your husband and you come home together?

*A.* Yes; only that I called at the public house for some beer; my husband said he would go in, and strike a light.

*Q.* Did your master come in that evening?

*A.* Yes.

*Q.* Did you see him come in?

*A.* No, he was let in before I returned with the beer.

*Q.* You heard him up stairs?

*A.* Yes.

*Q.* Is it your custom yourself to see him in the evening; does he sup?

*A.* He takes a little supper, but I was never in the habit of carrying it up stairs.

*Q.* Your husband does that?

*A.* Yes.

*Q.* Did he carry it up that evening?

*A.* He had nothing but a bit of bread, and a glass of ale.

*Q.* You did not see him that night?

*A.* No.

*Q.* Was it your business, as the female servant of this gentleman, to make his bed?

*A.* Yes.

*Q.* At what time did you get up on the Monday morning?

*A.* About seven.

*Q.* Are you sure that the time we are speaking of, was the Sunday morning before he finally went off?

*A.* Yes.

*Q.* Did you usually get up about seven?

*A.* Yes.

*Q.* At what time did your master go out that morning?

*A.* He went out before breakfast.

*Q.* At what hour do you take that to be?

*A.* Before Smith went out; he went out about eight and my master went out a little before him.

*Lord Ellenborough.* Did you see him go out?

*A.* No.

*Mr. Park.* Did you hear him?

*A.* No, I did not know that he was out, till I let him in.

*Lord Ellenborough.* You did not know that he had been at all absent from home on Monday, till you let him in?

*A.* No.

*Mr. Park.* Had you made the bed on the Sunday, the day you saw him go out so many times in the morning?

*A.* Yes, I was up stairs making the bed, and he went out; I looked out of the window, and saw him go.

*Q.* Did you, or not, make his bed on the Monday?

*A.* I did.

*Q.* At what time of the day did you make his bed?

*A.* Not till after my master came home; my master came home, and when I found he had been out, I went up stairs immediately, and I made his bed.

*Q.* As you did not see your master on the Sunday night or Monday morning, what was the last time upon the Sunday that you did in fact see him; not that you believe him to be there, but that you saw him with your own eyes?

*A.* I am not certain whether I saw him go out on the Sunday at four o'clock, but I think I did.

*Q.* You say you made his bed after he came home on the Monday?

*A.* Yes.

*Q.* You let him in on the Monday, at twelve o'clock?

*A.* Yes.

*Q.* Was the bed the same as it was to all appearance on other days?

*A.* Yes.

*Lord Ellenborough.* It appeared like a bed that had been slept in?

*A.* Yes.

*Mr. Park.* Had he been constantly sleeping in his own bed for several months?

*A.* Yes.

*Q.* Did you sleep in that bed, that night?

*A.* No.

*Q.* I did not mean to ask you an improper question; but you did not sleep in that bed; I meant no such insinuation as might be supposed?

*A.* I did not sleep in it.

*Q.* Did your husband sleep in that bed, and you in your own?

*A.* No.

*Q.* Did you and your husband sleep together that night?

*A.* Yes.

*Q.* Are you quite sure that you made the bed on the Sunday, and again on the Monday?

*A.* I did; I am quite sure of that.

*Q.* Do you recollect how your master was dressed when he came home on the Monday?

*A.* I do; he had a black coat on.

*Q.* Had he any thing in his hand?

*A.* Yes.

*Q.* What was it?

*A.* A bundle.

*Q.* Did you happen to see, while either it was in his hand, or immediately on his laying it down, the contents of the bundle?

*A.* I saw a part of a coat where the bundle was open at the tie; a grey coat, just where the knot was tied?

*Q.* Had your master a grey great coat?

*A.* Yes, he had.

*Q.* Had he had one for some time?

*A.* Yes; about a month, I believe.

*Q.* Did your master continue after that Monday to sleep regularly at home, till he finally went away on the following Sunday?

*A.* Yes.

*Cross-examined by Mr. Bolland.*

*Q.* Your master had no other servant but you and your husband?

*A.* No.

*Q.* In what capacity did he serve him?

*A.* As man-servant; he used to wait upon him, and do any thing that was requisite to do.

*Q.* He waited upon him at dinner?

*A.* Yes; and at breakfast; he always used to carry it up; I never did that, except when he was out.

*Q.* You did not know till your master came home, that he had been out that morning?

*A.* No, I did not.

*Q.* Your husband went out about eight o'clock.

*A.* Yes.

*Q.* Was not Mr. De Berenger in the habit of ringing his bell in the morning for breakfast?

*A.* After he came down he used to ring the drawing-room bell, and then I used to carry it up, if my husband was out.

*Q.* Who supplied him in the morning with water, for the purpose of shaving?

*A.* He never used warm water; he had water in his room.

*Q.* He never rang for your husband to attend him?

*A.* Sometimes he did; but he knew my husband was going out that morning, and therefore he did not ring.

*Q.* Did it not appear to you extraordinary that morning, that there was no call for breakfast till that hour?

*A.* Yes; I supposed my master had breakfasted out, of course, when he came in.

*Q.* But you did not know of his going out?

*A.* No.

*Q.* Was not your surprize excited by his not ringing?

*A.* Yes; I was rather surprized that he had not rang.

*Q.* Do you recollect how he was dressed on the Sunday when he went out last; you do not mean to say that you saw him go out at four o'clock?

*A.* I do not recollect.

*Q.* The last time when you saw him go out on Sunday, how was he dressed?

*A.* He had on a black coat and waistcoat, and grey overalls.

*Q.* Of course, not seeing him on the Monday, you did not know in what dress he went out that morning?

*A.* No.

*Q.* But you say he returned home in a black coat?

*A.* Yes.

*Q.* Was that black coat his own?

*A.* That I cannot say.

*Q.* Was not that coat much too long for your master?

*A.* I did not observe it.

*Lord Ellenborough.* He did not come home in the same black coat he had gone out in on the Sunday?

*A.* That I cannot tell; I was not in the habit of brushing his coat.

*Mr. Bolland.* Did you ever see Lord Cochrane?

*A.* No.

*Q.* Was not the coat that he came home in, on the Monday, so long, that you recollect remarking it could not belong to him?

*A.* No, I did not remark that.

*Q.* Did you see the coat lie on the chair afterwards?

*A.* It might be there, but I did not observe it.

*Q.* What was in this bundle that he brought home?

*A.* I saw a part of a grey coat between the tie of the bundle.

*Q.* Did you make an affidavit upon this business?

*A.* Yes.

*Q.* When was that?

*A.* The 24th of March.

*Q.* Who suggested to you the necessity of making the affidavit?

*A.* No body but my husband; it was his wish to make his, and he said, therefore Ann do you make yours.

*Lord Ellenborough.* What did you see besides the grey coat in the bundle?

*A.* I saw nothing but that.

*Lord Ellenborough.* Recollect yourself, because you have sworn you saw a green uniform?

*A.* There might be a green uniform.

*Q.* Was there, or was there not?

*A.* Yes, there was a green uniform.

*Q.* Was it in the bundle or not?

*A.* Yes, it was in the bundle.

*Mr. Bolland.* Was there any thing extraordinary in your master going out in his green drill dress?

*A.* No; not that I know of.

*Q.* Was he in the habit of going out in it?

*A.* Yes.

*Q.* And of returning in it?

*A.* Yes.

*Q.* Did you ever know him go out in his green drill dress and come home in a black coat?

*A.* No.

*Q.* That morning he had his green drill dress in his bundle, with his great coat?

*A.* Yes.

*Q.* Your husband made an affidavit, and you made an affidavit as well yourself?

*A.* Yes.

*Q.* Had you seen any body on the subject of that affidavit?

*A.* No.

*Q.* Had you seen Mr. Tahourdin?

*A.* No.

*Q.* How soon after or before making that affidavit, did you see Mr. Tahourdin?

*A.* I saw Mr. Tahourdin a few days after.

*Q.* Did you know for what purpose your affidavit was made; how it was to be used?

*A.* No.

*Q.* Do you know to whom it was taken; what did your husband do with it; do you know of your own knowledge?

*A.* It was put in the papers, I know.

*Q.* Was it put in by him or by any body else?

*A.* I believe it was put in by him.

*Lord Ellenborough.* Did Mr. De Berenger ever wear whiskers?

*A.* Yes, sometimes he used.

*Q.* How long before the 20th of February had you seen him wear whiskers?

*A.* I do not know; I was so little in the habit of seeing my master, that I do not know whether he had whiskers or not.

*Q.* You saw him come in at the door, did not you?

*A.* On the Monday morning.

*Q.* At times you used to see him?

*A.* Yes.

*Q.* Were you so little acquainted with the countenance of the man in whose service you had lived two years and a half, that you did not know whether he was a whiskered man or an unwhiskered man?

*A.* I never attended the door when my husband was at home.

*Q.* You used to go backwards and forwards; just before you did not know whether there was a green coat in the bundle; and then when I put you in mind of what you had sworn, you say positively there was?

*A.* Yes, there was.

*Q.* And now you mean to say, you saw so little of your master, that you do not know whether he had whiskers?

*A.* No, I do not know.

*A Juryman.* You say you did not make your master's bed until his return on Monday?

*A.* No.

*Q.* Did you see it before his return on Monday?

*A.* No; but he was not up stairs, he was in the drawing room.

*Q.* You did not see the bed till after his return?

*A.* No, I did not.

John M'Guire, sworn;

*Examined by Mr. Richardson.*

*Q.* I believe you are ostler at Smith's livery stables, at the Cross Keys yard, Chelsea?

*A.* Yes.

*Q.* Were you acquainted with the person of Mr. De Berenger?

*A.* Yes.

*Q.* Was he in the habit of frequenting your master's stables, or that neighbourhood?

*A.* Yes.

*Q.* Were you well acquainted with his person in the month of February last?

*A.* Yes, I was.

*Q.* Do you remember seeing him upon the 20th of February?

*A.* Yes.

*Q.* On a Sunday?

*A.* Yes.

*Q.* What makes you remember the day?

*A.* I remember the day perfectly well, on the account that I knew him to be in the Rules of the King's Bench.

*Q.* How does that enable you to recollect the particular day?

*A.* Upon account, that I determined in my own mind, that I would ask his servant the next time I saw him, whether he was out of the Rules.

*Q.* Before that time had he ever lived at Chelsea?

*A.* Yes, he had.

*Q.* And so you became acquainted with his person?

*A.* Yes.

*Q.* On this 20th of February, at what time did you see him at Chelsea?

*A.* At a quarter past six.

*Q.* Where did you see him?

*A.* At Mr. Smith's stable-yard gateway.

*A Juryman.* A quarter past six in the morning or the evening?

*A.* The evening.

*Mr. Park.* Did any thing pass between you?

*A.* Yes; he asked me whether the coach was gone; I told him the six o'clock coach was gone, but the seven would be ready in three quarters of an hour.

*Q.* What further passed?

*A.* He made no more to do, but turned round and took his way to London.

*Q.* Did he say any thing more?

*A.* He said it would not do to wait for the seven o'clock coach.

*Q.* And he set out on foot for London?

*A.* He did.

*Q.* This was about a quarter past six, you say?

*A.* Yes.

*Q.* Are you confident as to the day?

*A.* I am.

*Q.* And as to his person, you have no doubt about it?

*A.* No, not the least.

*Q.* Did any circumstance occur to call this to your recollection?

*A.* Yes; I mentioned it to my wife, when I went home that night.

*Q.* What induced you to mention it to her?

*A.* That I had seen Mr. De Berenger on that evening, at a quarter past six.

*Lord Ellenborough.* You mentioned the time to her?

*A.* Yes.

*Q.* You mentioned particularly to her, that you had seen him at a quarter past six?

*A.* I did.

*Mr. Richardson.* What induced you to mention the circumstance to your wife?

*A.* Knowing that he was in the Rules of the Bench, and not having seen him that way, from the time that he was in the Rules before.

*Q.* Did he go from that lodging he had in Chelsea, to the Rules of the King's Bench?

*A.* Yes, he did.

*Cross-examined by Mr. Adolphus.*

*Q.* How long had you known Mr. De Berenger before this?

*A.* I had known him about three years and a half; I was living at Mr. Smith's yard at that time.

*Q.* And you had known him all that time?

*A.* I had.

*Q.* It was on the Sunday you saw him?

*A.* Yes.

*Q.* You knew him to be an officer in the corps of riflemen, did not you?

*A.* Yes, I did.

*Q.* Perhaps you thought he was out on Sunday on military duty, or something of that kind?

*A.* I did not know, but the answer my wife made, when I said that to her was, that she supposed it was the same as it was at Edinburgh, and that on the Sunday a person used to come and visit her aunt.

*Q.* I cannot see what makes you remember particularly that it was the 20th of February?

*A.* I had very good occasion for it.

*Lord Ellenborough.* Did you write it down?

*A.* No, I cannot write.

*Q.* Did your wife put it down?

*A.* No; she cannot write neither.

*Mr. Adolphus.* How do you know it was on the 20th of February?

*A.* I can swear that was the day; on that day fortnight I saw his servant, and that was the 6th of March, and I asked him, whether his master was out of the Rules of the Bench? and he said, he was not; and I said, I had seen him there; and he said, if he was there he did not know any thing of it, nor his master was not out of the Rules of the Bench.

*Q.* He said that he was at home, in the Bench, then?

*A.* No, that was not his meaning; that he was not got out of the Rules then, that he was not got clear of the Bench.

*Q.* The servant told you so on the 6th of March?

*A.* Yes.

*Q.* That he was not out of the Rules of the Bench?

*A.* Yes.

*Q.* That he was not on that day, the 6th of March?

*A.* Yes; that he did not know it if he was.

*Q.* He was quite surprised at hearing of it?

*A.* He did not seem in the least astonished, to me; I did not see him take any notice.

*Q.* He told you he was in the Rules of the Bench, and he did not see how he could come to Chelsea that day?

*A.* He told me he was not out of the Rules of the Bench, and if he came to Chelsea, he did not know it.

*Q.* It was by the conversation with the servant, you fix the date?

*A.* No, I knew the date.

*Q.* On what do you found your recollection that it was on that day?

*A.* I know that was the day.

*Q.* The 13th of February he was within the Rules of the Bench, and might have been at Chelsea?

*A.* No, it was not the 13th.

*Q.* How soon did you tell any body that you saw him on the 20th?

*A.* I told my wife that night.

*Q.* Your wife is here?

*A.* Yes, she is.

*Q.* How soon did you tell any body besides William Smith, the servant, any thing about him?

*A.* I told no body but William Smith, and my wife.

*Q.* Not to this moment?

*A.* Yes, I did, when I was sent for.

*Q.* When was that?

*A.* Last Monday week.

*Q.* Then you were seen by the attorney, and examined about this matter?

*A.* Yes.

*Q.* Was any body so particular as to ask you how this gentleman was dressed, when you saw him on this Sunday?

*A.* No.

*Q.* Now I am so particular; will you tell me how he was dressed?

*A.* He had a black coat, and black waistcoat, and grey pantaloons or overalls, but I will not say which.

*Q.* You have seen your old acquaintances, the two Smiths, here this morning?

*A.* I have seen one of them this morning.

*Q.* Which was that?

*A.* William, the servant.

*Q.* Had you any conversation with him about the dress on this Sunday?

*A.* No.

*Q.* You know Mr. De Berenger very well?

*A.* Yes.

*Q.* Did he wear whiskers on that Sunday?

*A.* No, he was close shaved upon that Sunday, I am certain.

Re-examined by Mr. Richardson.

*Q.* When you saw Mr. Smith, on the 6th of March, what question did you ask him?

*A.* I asked him, whether his master was out of the Rules of the Bench? that I had seen him on the Sunday fortnight, that he called at our yard, to know if the coach was gone; that I told him, the six o'clock coach was gone, but the seven o'clock coach would go in three quarters of an hour.

*Q.* You related the circumstance that had passed on the 20th of February, and then asked him, whether his master was out of the Rules of the King's Bench?

*A.* Yes.

*Q.* What did he answer?

*A.* That his master was not out of the Rules, and that if he was at Chelsea, it was more than he knew of.

*Lord Ellenborough.* You were struck with seeing him out of the Rules?

*A.* Yes.

*Q.* You thought it a very wrong thing of him?

*A.* Yes.

*Q.* And being shocked at it, you had a mind to enquire of his servant, whether he was within the Rules?

*A.* Yes.

*Q.* You did not say to him, Good God, Sir, how is it you are out of the Rules on this Sunday?

*A.* He did not stop to have any conversation.

*Q.* If he had stopped long enough, you would have told him so?

*A.* I do not know that I would.

*Q.* Where was he coming from, at a quarter past six?

*A.* He came up from the water-side; I cannot tell which way he came to the stable-yard gateway.

*Q.* And he seemed in a hurry to get home?

*A.* He did.

*Q.* How far is it from Asylum Place to Chelsea?

*A.* It is two miles from the bottom of our street to Buckingham-gate, and it is a mile from that to the middle arch of Westminster-bridge; I cannot tell how far it is from that to the Asylum.

*Q.* You did not see where he came from?

*A.* No.

*Q.* But he was in a hurry to get home?

*A.* Yes.

Mr. *Park.* It is three miles and a half, or four miles, my Lord.

A *Juryman.* Was it day-light or dark, when you saw him?

*A.* It was between the two lights; it was not very clear at that time.

Mr. *Park.* I will call this woman, and will put a question to her; I had not intended it, conceiving that what he said to his wife, could not be evidence.

Lord *Ellenborough.* You will call her, or not, as you see fit; I do not desire to have more persons called than is necessary.

Mr. *Park.* I must call her, as your Lordship has asked the question, what he told her?

*Mr. Brougham.* If your Lordship will permit us, we will examine Hopper now; he is extremely ill, I understand.

*Lord Ellenborough.* If you please.

*Mr. Thomas Hopper sworn.*

*Examined by Mr. Brougham.*

*Q.* What are you?

*A.* An architect.

*Q.* Do you know Mr. Cochrane Johnstone's premises at Allsop's buildings?

*A.* I saw them two nights ago.

*Q.* You saw a piece of ground that he possesses there?

*A.* I did.

*Q.* Will you look at that plan, which is lying there, for the laying out of the ground? (*the witness looked at it.*)

*A.* These plans I saw at the time.

*Lord Ellenborough.* That is two nights ago?

*A.* Yes, it is.

*Mr. Brougham.* Did you at the same time see the prospectus of the plan for laying out the place?

*A.* This, I believe, is a copy of it.

*Q.* What should you think is a reasonable compensation to the person who arranged that plan, and made that drawing, and the others connected with that plan, and the prospectus?

*A.* That it would be almost impossible for me to tell; that must be governed by the trouble that was attendant upon it, and of course of that I cannot be a judge.

*Lord Ellenborough.* It is a very well drawn plan?

*A.* Certainly it is.

*Mr. Brougham.* Are you aware, that a plan of that kind cannot be made out, without a survey of the ground?

*A.* Certainly.

*Q.* Are you aware, that in making a plan of that sort, there are various other plans previously made, before it comes into that state?

*A.* No doubt, there must be.

*Q.* Can you take upon you, from that, and from your understanding of the manner in which such plans are made, to say what would be a fair reasonable compensation for the trouble bestowed?

*A.* Mr. Cochrane Johnstone, whom I saw upon the premises, made a representation to me——

*Mr. Gurney.* We cannot hear that.

*Mr. Brougham.* From your own knowledge of the subject, and the ground, what should you take to be a reasonable compensation?

*A.* It is so governed by the trouble attending it, that I cannot say, with any precision; I should judge, from the calculation of the trouble that must attend it, that a compensation of from two to three hundred pounds, might not be excessive.

—— *M'Guire sworn.*

*Examined by Mr. Park.*

*Q.* Are you the wife of the person who has just been here now?

*A.* Yes.

*Q.* Did you know Mr. De Berenger, when he lived at Chelsea?

*A.* No.

*Q.* Did you know Smith, his servant?

*A.* Yes.

*Q.* Did your husband on any day, and if so, on what day, mention to you his having seen Mr. De Berenger, Smith's master?

*A.* Yes, he did on the 20th February, about ten o'clock at night.

*Q.* When he came home?

*A.* Yes.

*Q.* How do you happen to know it was the 20th of February, more than the 13th or the 6th?

*A.* It was the Sunday before Shrove-tuesday.

*Q.* What led you to recollect it so particularly?

*A.* It was my child's birth-day.

*Q.* Do you mean that Shrove-tuesday was your child's birth-day, or that Sunday?

*A.* The Sunday; the first child I ever had in my life.

*Q.* On that day he told you he had seen Mr. De Berenger at his master's yard?

*A.* Yes, he did.

*Lord Ellenborough.* Did he tell you at what o'clock he saw him?

*A.* Yes; at about a quarter past six.

*Q.* Did he tell you that he thought it was shocking he should be out of the Rules?

*A.* Yes, he did; that he wondered whether he had got his liberty or not.

*Q.* Did he say it was shocking he should be out of the Rules?

*A.* I cannot particularly say, whether he said it was shocking or not.

*Q.* Had you known these Smiths long?

*A.* About three years and seven months.

*Q.* You are in the habits of visiting them sometimes?

*A.* Smith came backwards and forwards to Chelsea, when his master lived at the end of the bridge.

*Q.* Have you kept up your acquaintance with them, since they lived in Chelsea?

*A.* Yes, I have.

*Q.* You are very well acquainted with them?

*A.* Yes, I am.

*Q.* Had you seen him that day, the 20th?

*A.* No; I saw him that day fortnight.

*Q.* Your husband did not stay at home to keep the birth-day of his child?

*A.* No; my husband is an ostler, and he cannot come and go at his own time.

*Q.* But he mentioned about the Rules to you, did he?

*A.* Yes, he did; he said he should enquire from Smith, the first time he saw him, whether his master had got his liberty or not.

*Q.* Had your husband an anxiety to know whether he had got his liberty or not?

*A.* No, I cannot say that he seemed anxious, but he said he wondered how he came down there.

*Henry Doyle Tragear sworn.*

*Examined by Mr. Richardson.*

*Q.* Do you remember being at Mr. Donithorne's house, in York-street, Westminster, in the month of February last?

*A.* Yes, I do.

*Q.* Were you staying at his house?

*A.* Yes, I was.

*Q.* Living and sleeping there?

*A.* Yes.

*Q.* When did you go there?

*A.* I went there on the 17th of February.

*Q.* On what occasion?

*A.* I let my house, No. 39, Little Queen-street, Holborn, where I had carried on the hatting business, and I went from thence to Donithorne's.

*Q.* Was it on the 17th you let your house, finally.

*A.* Yes, it was.

*Q.* Did you stay at Mr. Donithorne's until or after the Sunday following, the 20th of February?

*A.* Yes, and until this very time.

*Q.* Are you acquainted with the prisoner Mr. De Berenger?

*A.* Yes, I have seen him frequently previously to that, at Mr. Donithorne's house.

*Q.* Do you or not, remember having seen him on Sunday the 20th of February?

*A.* Yes, very particularly on that day.

*Q.* Did you see him more than once on that day?

*A.* Yes, I saw him twice on that day.

*Q.* When was the first time you saw him?

*A.* Between nine and ten in the morning.

*Q.* When was the last time you saw him?

*A.* Between eight and nine in the evening of the same day.

*Q.* Did he stay any time when you saw him the last time on that day?

*A.* Yes, he did.

*Q.* Both these times you saw him in Mr. Donithorne's house?

*A.* Yes.

*Q.* How long did he stay when he came in the evening?

*A.* It might be somewhere about half an hour; I cannot exactly say; it might be an hour, or it might be less.

*Q.* Was it thereabouts, as nearly as you can remember?

*A.* Yes; it was, as nearly as I can remember.

*Q.* You are sure it was somewhere thereabouts?

*A.* Yes.

*Q.* Was he a visitor of Mr. Donithorne's, or did he come on business?

*A.* I have seen him frequently talking to Mr. Donithorne, about drawings, designs of furniture, and things of that sort.

*Q.* What is Donithorne?

*A.* He is a cabinet maker.

*Q.* You had seen him before that time?

*A.* Yes; Mr. Donithorne has shewn him to me.

*Lord Ellenborough.* What are you yourself?

*A.* A hat manufacturer by trade.

*Q.* You have been out of business since that time?

*A.* Yes, I have; not entirely out of business; but I have not a house at the present moment; I went there to reside, till I saw a house that would suit my purpose.

*Q.* He was talking with Mr. Donithorne?

*A.* Yes, he was.

*Mr. Richardson.* Was any body else present?

*A.* Yes; there was my wife, Mr. Donithorne and Mrs. Donithorne; we were in the parlour in the evening, when he came.

*Q.* Did he sit down?

*A.* He said that he would not come into the parlour to disturb the company; Mr. Donithorne went to the back part of the house with him, into the garden.

*Q.* Did he come into the parlour?

*A.* Yes, he did just come into the parlour; but he said he would not disturb the company.

*Q.* Did he afterwards come in?

*A.* I do not know whether he came in afterwards or not.

*Q.* But you saw him there?

*A.* I saw him in the house.

*Q.* You are well acquainted with his person?

*A.* Yes; I had seen him repeatedly before that.

*Q.* You did not see him after that?

*A.* No, I did not.

*Cross-examined by Mr. Gurney.*

*Q.* Do you remember being struck with any alteration in his appearance that night?

*A.* No.

*Q.* How long before that time had he left off wearing the large whiskers he used to have?

*A.* I cannot say.

*Q.* He had not them on that night?

*A.* I cannot say that I saw any alteration.

*Q.* He had no whiskers on that night?

*A.* No.

*Q.* He had never been used to wear whiskers?

*A.* That I cannot say.

*Q.* You knew him well, and had seen him often?

*A.* Yes.

*Q.* And you mean to say, you do not remember whether he wore whiskers on not?

*A.* He might or might not, I do not look so particularly into a gentleman's face, as to see whether he has whiskers or not.

*Q.* I happen to look at your face, and I cannot help seeing that you have whiskers, and a man who has such, might look at those on another person's face; do you mean to say, that in viewing the countenance of a gentleman you were acquainted with, you did not look so as to see whether he had whiskers?

*A.* Not unless a person spoke to me about them.

*Q.* Unless a person said "whiskers," you would not look at them?

*A.* No.

*Q.* Mr. De Berenger had not whiskers that night, however?

*A.* No.

*Q.* You were a hatter, in business at one time, and are not now?

*A.* Yes; I sell a great many hats now, though I have no house.

*Q.* Perhaps though you do not take notice of a man's whiskers, you take notice of his coat; what coat had he on?

*A.* A black coat.

*Q.* That you did take notice of?

*A.* Yes.

*Q.* It was so remarkable he should wear a black coat, you took notice of that?

*A.* No; I do not know that it is remarkable; but I know he had a black coat.

*Q.* Was his head powdered?

*A.* I cannot say; I did not see his hat off.

*Q.* He staid half an hour with his hat on?

*A.* He went into the back part of the house.

*Q.* Do you mean to say, he staid half an hour in the house with his hat on?

*A.* I do not mean to say, he stopped the whole time in house; he went into the garden.

*Q.* On the 20th of February he went into the garden?

*A.* Yes.

Lord *Ellenborough.* Did he stand ancle-deep in the garden, or how?

*A.* I cannot say, indeed.

Mr. *Gurney.* Was not there a good deal of snow at that time on the ground?

*A.* I cannot say, indeed.

*Q.* At what time was this?

*A.* Between eight and nine in the evening.

*Q.* And they took a walk in the garden?

*A.* Yes; it was in consequence of some alteration they were going to make in the premises.

*Q.* So that they went at ten o'clock at night to survey this alteration in the premises?

*A.* No; it was between eight and nine.

*Q.* It is just as dark then as it is at ten o'clock; they went to make a survey in the morning, did they not?

*A.* They had made a survey in the morning, I saw them pacing the garden.

*Q.* You told me they went out in the evening, to make a survey of the premises?

*A.* I cannot say what they went for, but I know they went there.

*Q.* Do you happen to know, whether Mr. Donithorne is acquainted with Mr. Tahourdin, the attorney?

*A.* I do not know whether he is acquainted with him, or not.

*Q.* You swear that?

*A.* I swear that; I do not know that he is acquainted with him particularly.

*Q.* Upon your oath have you not seen them together?

*A.* Yes, I have.

*Q.* Had not you seen them together before that time?

*A.* No, I had not.

*Q.* How often have you seen them together since?

*A.* I never saw them together but once.

*Q.* When was that?

*A.* One day last week.

*Q.* Do you mean to swear, that you did not know that they were acquainted with each other before that time?

*A.* Yes, I do.

*Q.* What is Mr. Donithorne; a cabinet-maker?

*A.* Yes.

*Q.* This you say was about making alterations in the garden; are they made?

*A.* No, they are not.

*Q.* They are waiting till February perhaps, to survey this garden again?

*A.* I do not know, indeed.

*Q.* When were you first sent for to become a witness on this occasion?

*A.* I never was sent for.

*Q.* When did you go to any person upon the subject?

*A.* I never went to any place upon the subject, further than going myself to Mr. Tahourdin; but he did not send for me.

*Q.* You went to Mr. Tahourdin without being sent for?

*A.* I went with Mr. Donithorne.

*Q.* When was that?

*A.* I cannot exactly say, but I think it was some day last week.

*Q.* Did you know before last week that you were to be a witness?

*A.* No, I did not.

*Q.* Did you know before last week, that it was at all material that you should recollect the 20th of February?

*A.* No, I did not know it; but I can tell you one particular thing that makes me recollect it; I let my house, No. 39, Little Queen-street, Holborn, on the 17th of February, to Samuel Nicholson, and went to Mr. Donithorne's to live; and on that very morning, the 20th, the Sunday, Mr. Donithorne (I rather indulge myself with lying in bed on Sunday morning) came to my door and knocked, and told me Mr. De Berenger was come to look over the house, and that if I would get up he should be obliged to me.

*Mr. Gurney.* I congratulate you on the cure of your deafness[417:A].

*Lord Ellenborough.* You lay a-bed and were disturbed?

*A.* No, not particularly; only I lay a-bed on the Sunday till about nine o'clock.

*Lord Ellenborough.* Do you know Smith, De Berenger's servant?

*A.* I have seen him.

*Re-examined by Mr. Richardson.*

*Q.* You saw them in this piece of garden in the morning?

*A.* Yes.

*Q.* My learned friend has asked, whether the alterations are carried into effect, or not?

*A.* They are not.

*Q.* Do you know, whether Mr. De Berenger went away after that?

*A.* He stopped about half an hour.

*Q.* Has he been absent from a period soon after the 20th of February?

*A.* Yes; I never heard much about him till last week.

*Lord Ellenborough.* When they came to you, you immediately recollected the 20th of February?

*A.* When who came down to me?

*Q.* When you went to Mr. Tahourdin, you immediately recollected the 21st of February?

*A.* He asked me, whether I could recollect on what day I came to this house; and I told him I do not know that I can recollect exactly; but I can go to Mr. Nicholson, upon whom I drew a bill at two months, for half the money for the goods and fixtures of my house, and ask him whether it is correct.

*Q.* He asked you, whether you recollected the 20th of February?

*A.* Yes.

*Q.* Did you say you recollected it by being disturbed in the morning?

*A.* Yes, I did.

*Q.* There was no snow in the garden when they paced it in the way you have spoken of?

*A.* I cannot positively say; I did not charge my memory with that.

*Q.* Are you perfectly certain in your recollection, as to having had your sleep disturbed?

*A.* Yes, I am perfectly certain of that.

*Q.* You know De Berenger very well?

*A.* I have seen him several times at Mr. Donithorne's house?

*Q.* And you know Tahourdin?

*A.* I never saw him till last week.

*Q.* Do you know where Mr. De Berenger dined that day?

*A.* No, I do not.

*Q.* At what time did he come in the morning?

*A.* Between nine and ten.

*A Juryman.* That might be any other Sunday morning, as you were in the habit of indulging on a Sunday morning?

*A.* No, but I know the time; it was the Sunday after I let my house; I have it impressed upon my mind that it was on the 20th of February I saw him at this house in York-street, Westminster.

*A Juryman.* Then the lying in bed in the morning had nothing to do with it?

*A.* No.

*Lord Ellenborough.* Have you ever been bail?

*A.* Yes.

*Q.* Have you ever justified in any action?

*A.* Yes.

*Q.* What action was that?

*A.* A fifteen-pound action.

*Q.* How long was that ago?

*A.* Five or six months.

*Q.* Is that debt paid?

*A.* Yes.

*Q.* Did you ever justify in any other action?

*A.* Yes, I have.

*Q.* Is that satisfied?

*A.* Yes.

*Q.* You are clear as to that, that these debts are paid?

*A.* Yes.

*Q.* Were you never bail but twice?

*A.* I do not recollect that I was; I might be, but I do not recollect; but I have not been in the habit of being bail for people.

*Q.* You have not been in the habit, but you have been twice:—what was the other sum besides the fifteen pounds?

*A.* I do not exactly know what the money was; but the other was more than that, a good deal.

*Q.* That is only within a few months?

*A.* I dare say that is five months back.

*Lord Ellenborough.* You may go away, and let me advise you not to be either a bail or a witness again. If the master had been here with the book, I have no doubt you might have gone much further with him.

---

### FOOTNOTE:

[417:A] The Witness, at the commencement of the cross-examination, had affected not to hear; Mr. Gurney gradually sunk his voice, and at last spoke in a very low tone, and the Witness heard, notwithstanding.

---

*Mrs. Tragear sworn.*

*Examined by Mr. Park.*

*Q.* Are you the wife of the last witness, Mr. Doyle Tragear?

*A.* Yes.

*Q.* Do you know the Defendant, Mr. De Berenger?

*A.* Yes.

*Q.* Have you seen him often?

*A.* Yes, I have.

*Q.* Were you at Mr. Donithorne's house in the month of February last?

*A.* Yes.

*Q.* At what time did you and your husband go to stay there, after having given up your house?

*A.* The day we gave up our house was the 17th of February.

*Q.* And then you went down to Mr. Donithorne's?

*A.* Yes.

*Q.* What day of the month was it after you had gone there, that Mr. De Berenger called there?

*A.* On the Sunday.

*Q.* That would be on the 20th?

*A.* Yes.

*Q.* What time in the morning did he first call?

*A.* Between nine and ten.

*Q.* Do you remember, whether your husband was up or not, when he first came.

*A.* No, he was not.

*Q.* What is Mr. Donithorne?

*A.* He is in the cabinet business.

*Q.* Did you see Mr. De Berenger do any thing that morning?

*A.* Yes; Mrs. Donithorne came up (we were not up that morning) and desired us to get up and get our rooms ready, for that she had a gentleman to look over the house.

*Q.* In consequence of that you did get up?

*A.* Yes.

*Q.* Did you see Mr. De Berenger afterwards there, when you got up?

*A.* Yes; I saw him; I drew down the sash in the back room, and I saw him through the window; I saw him in the garden.

*Q.* Does the sash draw up or down?

*A.* Both.

*Q.* What was he doing in the garden?

*A.* He appeared to be measuring the ground, I believe.

*Q.* Had you any conversation with Mr. De Berenger at that time?

*A.* No.

*Q.* You are sure he was the man?

*A.* I am sure he was.

*Q.* Did you see him again that day at Mr. Donithorne's, and at what hour in the day?

*A.* I did; I saw him again in the evening.

*Q.* At what time?

*A.* Between nine and ten—I mean between eight and nine.

*Q.* Did he stay any time then?

*A.* I believe he did; we were in the parlour, along with Mr. and Mrs. Donithorne, and he came; and he (Mr. Donithorne) asked him to come in; and he said, he would not come in to disturb good company.

*Q.* Are you sure he was the man?

*A.* I am sure he was the man.

*Q.* How near was he to you?

*A.* We got up, of course, when the gentleman was coming in, and we saw the gentleman in the small parlour.

*Q.* What happened then, when you got up?

*A.* He went to speak with Mr. Donithorne, and they walked backwards into the garden.

*Q.* Did you see them go out of the door that leads into the garden?

*A.* Yes, I saw them go backwards.

*Q.* You did not go to look after what they were doing?

*A.* No.

*Q.* Did you afterwards see them again, after they came from the back part of the house?

*A.* No, I did not.

*Q.* You saw Mr. De Berenger no more?

*A.* No.

*Cross-examined by Mr. Bolland.*

*Q.* How long has your husband had the affliction of deafness?

*A.* He has, at times.

*Q.* So we have seen to-day; you were indulging that morning in bed, as well as your husband?

*A.* Yes.

*Q.* And Mrs. Donithorne came to wake you?

*A.* Yes.

*Q.* It was natural she should do it?

*A.* Yes.

*Q.* Mr. Donithorne did not wake you?

*A.* No.

*Q.* But Mrs. Donithorne came and waked you, and wished you to get up, because somebody was coming to see the house?

*A.* Yes.

*Q.* Do you mean to say, that Mr. De Berenger afterwards went through the house, so as to render that necessary.

*A.* He went up into the attics.

*Q.* Did he go into your room?

*A.* He did not.

*Q.* What occasion was there for your getting up to see him measure the garden?

*A.* There was no occasion for that; but we were getting up, and she thought the gentleman might come into our room.

*Q.* Was she in the habit of calling you?

*A.* Sometimes she has done it.

*Q.* Who was with Mr. De Berenger, besides Donithorne.

*A.* I do not remember seeing any other.

*Q.* Who carried the rod with which they measured; was it Mr. De Berenger or Donithorne?

*A.* I cannot say, indeed.

*Q.* You may recollect who held the paper, and put down the measurements; which of the two carried the paper, and which carried the measuring rod?

*A.* I cannot tell which of the two it was, they being at the top of the garden almost.

*Q.* It is only a small garden, we know the situation?

*A.* It is a long garden.

*Q.* Which of them was it?

*A.* I cannot say, indeed, which of them it was.

*Q.* But one of them did?

*A.* Yes.

*Q.* Was there snow on the ground then?

*A.* No, it was a wet morning, I think.

*Q.* Are you sure it was a wet morning?

*A.* I think it was a wet morning, but I did not take particular notice of the day.

Lord *Ellenborough.* It had rained a good deal, had it?

*A.* Yes, it had.

*Q.* There was a good deal of rain last February, was there?

*A.* I think that was a wet morning.

Mr. *Bolland.* Had the effect of the rain been such, as to give them a good view of the surface of the ground, so as to measure?

*A.* Yes, I think it had.

*Q.* The snow was melted?

*A.* I think it was.

*Q.* And you saw them lay the rule regularly, that they could take the measurement properly?

*A.* Yes.

*Lord Ellenborough.* Did your husband fail, when he gave up the hatting business?

*A.* Why, yes.

*Q.* There had been no commission of bankrupt against him?

*A.* No.

*Q.* And he gave up his business in that house, and you have been since living at Mr. Donithorne's house?

*A.* Yes.

*Q.* How long has he been in the bail line?

*A.* In the bail line!

*Q.* How long has he been bail for people?

*A.* That is unknown to me, if he has.

*Q.* You have never known of people coming after him to be bail?

*A.* No, I have not.

*Q.* He has told us he has been bail for two persons; you know nothing of that?

*A.* No.

*Q.* When did he fail?

*A.* On the 17th of February.

*Q.* Has there been an execution in the house you lived in since that?

*A.* No.

*Q.* Is Mr. Donithorne a creditor of your husband's; do you owe him money?

*A.* No.

*Q.* Is he a relation?

*A.* Yes; he is a cousin.

*Lord Ellenborough.* How far is York-street, Westminster, from the Asylum?

*Mr. Park.* I understand it is behind the barracks in Bird-cage Walk.

*Lord Ellenborough.* It is about a mile I should suppose then?

*Mr. Park.* From a mile to a mile and a half.

*Mr. Gurney.* Is Mr. Donithorne here?

*A.* I believe he is.

*Mr. Gurney.* Then I suppose we shall see him.

*Isaac Donithorne, sworn.*

*Examined by Mr. Richardson.*

*Q.* We understand you live in York-street, Westminster?

*A.* Yes.

*Q.* Do you remember Mr. Tragear coming to your house, after he had given up his house in Queen-street?

*A.* Yes.

*Q.* Do you remember what day it was?

*A.* I believe it was Thursday; I am positive it was.

*Q.* What day of the month?

*A.* The 17th, I think, or the 18th of February.

*Q.* Are you well acquainted with the person of Mr. De Berenger?

*A.* Very well; I have been for some time.

*Q.* You are a cabinet-maker?

*A.* I am.

*Q.* Had Mr. De Berenger furnished you with designs for furniture at any time?

*A.* Yes, he had.

*Q.* Do you or not remember seeing him on the Sunday after that time when Tragear came?

*A.* Yes.

*Q.* That would be the 20th?

*A.* Yes.

*Q.* At what time in the day did you first see him?

*A.* Between nine and ten in the morning.

*Q.* For what purpose did he come?

*A.* To look over the grounds. I was going to make some alterations in my little garden, and also about other work that I had in hand.

*Q.* What other work do you mean?

*A.* Work I had for Miss Johnstone, No. 18, Great Cumberland-street; work I had in hand; I furnished all her house.

*Lord Ellenborough.* Mr. Cochrane Johnstone?

*A.* Yes.

*Mr. Richardson.* You were furnishing Mr. Johnstone's house at that time?

*A.* A house for Miss Johnstone.

*Q.* Did you see him again in the course of that same day?

*A.* Between eight and nine in the evening.

*Q.* Did he call again at your house in York-street?

*A.* Yes.

*Q.* About what time was it?

*A.* It was between eight and nine; I did not take particular notice of the time, not expecting there would be any question about it; we were all sitting in the parlour, and Mr. De Berenger knocked at the door, and I let him in, and he walked in, and while I was handing a chair to him to sit down, he said I will not disturb your good company, and he said he would walk into the back; and he did, and he staid about a quarter of an hour or twenty minutes.

*Q.* Did you walk back together?

*A.* Only into the parlour; in the morning, we were, I dare say, an hour together in the garden.

*Q.* Did you go into the garden in the evening?

*A.* We did not.

*Q.* What was the purpose of his calling in the evening?

*A.* Merely to answer the purpose of the morning, we meant to do something in the garden; he said he would call if he came that way in the evening, to tell me when he would draw a plan for the work I was going to do in the garden; I was going to build a room there.

*Q.* He was to draw a plan?

*A.* Yes.

*Q.* In the evening he called about the same business?

*A.* Yes.

*Q.* Was any further answer to be given to him?

*A.* This was the business; I was going to turn the front part of my house into an inn, and to make the back part of my house into pleasure grounds.

*Q.* And you had consulted him about the mode of doing it?

*A.* Yes, I had; Mr. De Berenger told me he could make out a handsome plan for me.

*Lord Ellenborough.* Did he tell you what you were to pay for it?

*A.* That house was not his, I pay £.60 a year for it.

*Q.* He did not tell you, that from £.200 to £.300 would not be excessive for a good plan?

*A.* Not for that plan.

*Q.* What did you expect to pay for a good plan?

*A.* That depended upon what sort of plan it might be, they might make a good plan worth that.

*Q.* You would not scruple paying that for a good plan?

*A.* I think I should for that for I had not the money to pay it.

*Q.* He put down the measurements in the morning?

*A.* Yes, he paced it over, but he told me he would come again and measure it quite correct.

*Q.* He put down the figures?

*A.* I do not know precisely whether he did or not.

*Q.* He had his pencil?

*A.* Yes, and a ten-foot rod that he carried.

*Q.* Did he bring a ten-foot rod to walk with?

*A.* I have a ten-foot rod myself, as a cabinet maker, and Mr. De Berenger paced it over.

*Q.* What sort of a morning was this?

*A.* A damp cold morning, a kind of misty rain; very cold.

*Mr. Richardson.* He said he would call at a subsequent time?

*A.* Yes, he did; here are all the designs.

*Q.* Those are the designs of furniture?

*A.* Those are the designs of furniture that I made for Miss Johnstone, or the honourable Cochrane Johnstone, for furniture in Great Cumberland Street; I believe I have some notes respecting them.

*Cross-examined by Mr. Adolphus.*

*Q.* Mr. De Berenger came to you, as a friend of Mr. Cochrane Johnstone, to give you plans for Mr. Cochrane Johnstone?

*A.* That was the case.

*Q.* He never gave you plans for any body else's furniture?

*A.* Never.

*Q.* You never employed a draftsman of his class to give you plans?

*A.* No, I made up two pieces of furniture from his plans, to go into a library; that was the first thing.

*Q.* He came as a friend of Mr. Cochrane Johnstone's?

*A.* Yes, to look to the furniture.

*Q.* And then, out of friendship to you, knowing you had little alteration to make, he proposed to assist you?

*A.* Yes; I first proposed the business, and Mr. De Berenger approved of it.

*Q.* He was going to make a survey of the inside of your house that morning; was he not?

*A.* He did of that also.

*Q.* Particularly your lodgers bed-room; he was very anxious to see that?

*A.* And all my own.

*Q.* He was very anxious to see your lodgers bed-room?

*A.* Not that particularly.

*Q.* You went and knocked up Mr. Tragear?

*A.* Yes; I went up and desired them to rise, and to clear up their room, for that he was coming there.

*Q.* Did you desire them to rise yourself?

*A.* Yes, there is not a doubt of it, for I went up stairs.

*Lord Ellenborough.* Will you take upon you, upon your oath, to say, that you went into that bed-room out of which they had come?

*A.* Yes, twice over.

*Mr. Adolphus.* What is your christian name?

*A.* Isaac Donithorne.

*Q.* Do you know any thing about the Stock Exchange?

*A.* A little; something about it.

*Q.* Have you ever done business there?

*A.* Never in my life.

*Q.* Have you ever employed an attorney?

*A.* Yes.

*Q.* Who is your attorney?

*A.* That gentleman there.

*Q.* What is his name?

*A.* Mr. Tahourdin.


*Q.* In what particular business is Mr. Tahourdin your attorney?

*A.* By the desire of the honourable Cochrane Johnstone, who thinks himself very ill used by a set of villains.——

*Q.* After all that preamble, as to Mr. Cochrane Johnstone's being ill used by a set of villains, will you answer my question, what Mr. Tahourdin is doing for you?

*A.* Issuing some writs.

*Q.* What have you desired him to do?

*A.* To issue some writs.

*Q.* How many?

*A.* A hundred and thirty-five.

*Lord Ellenborough.* A hundred and thirty-five writs, of what kind?

*Mr. Park.* Qui tam actions, and that was the reason I did not propose calling him.

*Mr. Adolphus.* Are you to pay Mr. Tahourdin the costs of those actions, or Mr. Cochrane Johnstone?

*A.* Mr. Cochrane Johnstone most undoubtedly, I should think.

*Mr. Park.* I really think that ought not to be asked.

*Lord Ellenborough.* If a man at my instance issues a hundred and thirty-five writs, to be sure I must bear him harmless; how long has your neighbour Tragear failed?

*A.* Why he never failed, to my knowledge; he left his shop publicly, and came to my house.

*Q.* He does nothing in the bail way, by way of filling up his time, does he?

*A.* I know nothing about his private concerns.

*Lord Ellenborough.* You take upon yourself to say, that you know he has not failed; is not his wife likely to know, she has told us he did when he came to your house. You may go about your business.

*A Juryman.* Are you a journeyman or a master?

*A.* I am a master in a small way, sometimes I keep three or four men.


*Lord Ellenborough.* Whom else do you call?

*Mr. Park.* No more, my Lord.

*Lord Ellenborough.* Do not you prove where De Berenger dined that day?

*Mr. Park.* No, I have no means of doing that.

*Mr. Gurney.* I beg to call Mr. Murray, to put one question to him, in contradiction to Smith?

*Lord Ellenborough.* If that question occasions a reply that will throw us into the night; if you think this case of alibi requires a serious answer, you will of course give it; but I think you would disparage the Jury by doing so.

*Mr. Gurney.* I will not call him, my Lord.

*Lord Ellenborough.* Do not let me supersede your discretion, if you think there is any use in having your witness.

*Mr. Gurney.* No, my Lord, I am quite content with the case as it stands.

# REPLY.

Mr. GURNEY.

May it please your Lordship;

Gentlemen of the Jury,

It is now my duty to make a few observations in reply on this momentous cause; and, I assure you, that I rise to the discharge of that duty with feelings of no ordinary nature. It is a duty in which it is impossible to feel pleasure; for every gentleman must feel degraded in the degradation of a gentleman, and every Englishman must feel mortified in the disgrace of a man whose name is associated with the naval or military glories of his country. But we are here to try these defendants by their actions; and whatever their conduct may have been in other respects, by those actions must they stand or fall. By the actions of these defendants, as respecting the matters charged by this indictment, you are now called upon to pronounce upon all the evidence that you have heard, whether they are innocent or guilty.

Gentlemen, if in the outset of this case I addressed you with confidence, as to the result, I address you now with confidence, increased ten-fold, when I recollect the arguments by which these defendants have been defended; when I recollect the evidence which *has* been adduced in their defence, and when I recollect too the evidence which has *not* been adduced in their defence; the first, as it appears to me totally failing, in making out a case of innocence; and the two latter concluding to their guilt.

Gentlemen, as it is the smallest part of the case, I will take up that part upon which you were addressed last this morning, by my learned friend Mr. Serjeant Pell, which has been denominated in this transaction the underplot. My learned friend endeavoured, with great ability and ingenuity, to persuade you, that the transactions which have been brought before you, did not constitute one plot, consisting of two parts; but two separate and distinct plots, two conspiracies totally unconnected with each other. And my learned friend concluded very properly, that if he could convince you of that, he should entitle his own clients to an acquittal on this indictment.

Gentlemen, if there were two conspiracies, then miracles have not ceased; for unless you can believe, that a most extraordinary miracle has occurred, it is quite impossible to conceive that there were two plots. It is not necessary in a conspiracy, that every party should know every other party in the conspiracy; it is not requisite that he should be acquainted with all the dramatis personæ, and the character assigned to each; it is enough if they engage in the general plan to forward the same general end, and each takes the part which is assigned him to the furtherance of that end. Now, gentlemen, look at the whole of the case, and see whether it is possible to believe, that these persons who came in the second post-chaise from Northfleet to London, were not cognizant of part of the plan, at least, if they were not of the whole, and that they were not aiding in the general conspiracy, to give a temporary rise to the funds on the 21st of February. That they afforded very material assistance in the completion of that purpose, is proved to demonstration. Independent of the facts, we have their own testimony against themselves, which is quite conclusive. Ask M'Rae, whether the plot was one or whether it was two? M'Rae was ready to come forward, and to impeach *all* the parties who were concerned in the conspiracy. Did he not, therefore, know the *whole*? When Mr. Cochrane Johnstone proffered him as a person who should betray the *whole*, and inform against *all* the parties conspiring. Are we to be told, that Mr. Cochrane Johnstone thought he knew a *part* only instead of the *whole*? Was Mr. Cochrane Johnstone meditating a second fraud upon the Stock Exchange? Was he endeavouring to get another £.10,000 out of them, by tendering them a witness, under pretence of his disclosing the *whole*, when he had it in his power to disclose no more than they already knew?

Gentlemen, M'Rae has been surrendered by my learned friend Mr. Alley, who never deserts his client if he can render him any service. No advocate is more zealous for his clients; yet my learned friend felt the proof given so irresistible, that he should be disgracing himself, if he stood up to ask you to disbelieve that proof, or even to hesitate about it, and he surrendered his client at once. Mr. M'Rae then stands here confessedly guilty of this conspiracy. Mr. M'Rae, who on the 15th of February had been proposing to Vinn the same plot, which was executed by De Berenger on the 21st. You find his companions in the post chaise were Sandom and Lyte, and their employer, by his own acknowledgment, the defendant Holloway. What can you wish more to prove that they were all engaged in this transaction? Mr. Serjeant Pell says, you must take Holloway's confession altogether; and because he declares, that he was not concerned with the Cochranes and Butt, you are to take that to be the fact.—Gentlemen, I do not assent to that doctrine, that when a defendant makes a confession, you are to take all the circumstances he alleges in his own favor, at the same time that you take those which are against him. Mr. Holloway came to propitiate the Stock Exchange committee; he came to ask them not to prosecute him. He could not have asked for that forbearance, if he had confessed a participation with De Berenger and the Cochranes. The only chance he had, therefore, was to deny his having any part in that plot, which, he knew, they were most anxious to unravel. But taking the whole of the case together, I think that it is impossible for you to entertain the smallest doubt upon this part of the subject.

I come therefore, gentlemen, to the other part of the case, upon which, after the great length of time which you have employed upon this case, and the fatigue you have undergone, I will not trespass upon you long.

Gentlemen, this part of the case branches itself into three or four heads, upon each of which I must make a few observations.

My learned friend, Mr. Serjeant Best, addressed you at considerable length upon the subject of the stock transactions of his three clients, Lord Cochrane, Mr. Cochrane Johnstone, and Mr. Butt; and he argued, that because it appeared not by any accounts which he put in, in addition to mine, but by the accounts which I gave in evidence, that these parties had been large dealers in consols and omnium, and had had large balances previous to the 21st of February; that therefore you were to believe, that they had on that day no possible interest to commit this fraud. That because they had had on a former day a larger balance, they could have no possible inducement to the commission of this crime. Gentlemen, observe the amount of the balance on that day, it was in omnium and consols very nearly a million. Reduced to consols it amounts to £.1,600,000. Then attend to the evidence of Mr. Baily, who tells you that the fluctuation of one-eighth was a gain or loss of two thousand pounds. Though they had been both buying and selling, yet their purchases had been much larger than their sales, and their attempts to purchase larger than their actual purchases. On Saturday the 19th, Mr. Butt had endeavoured to purchase one hundred and fifty thousand, and actually purchased fifty thousand. On this Monday, the 21st, all the three have this immense quantity of stock upon their hands; they have no means of getting rid of it, for Mr. Baily has told you, that but for this fraudulent transaction, it would have been impossible to have got rid of it, but at a great loss. They had been buying as a person must do, to keep up the market, to redeem himself from loss; and on this memorable day, all this stock is sold, it is sold at a profit of upwards of ten thousand pounds; and if it had been sold without a profit of one single farthing, still the getting out without a great loss, was to them very great gain.

Recollect gentlemen, that just one month afterwards came the news of the rupture of the negotiation at Chatillon, when the premium on omnium fell from 28 to 12 per cent.; if that news had come instead of this false news, on the morning of the 21st of February, the loss of these three defendants, would have been upwards of one hundred and sixty thousand pounds. These persons, therefore, were so involved, that ruin stared them in the face, and when they were in this situation, they did as I allege, and as I maintain I have proved by evidence perfectly irresistible, engage in this conspiracy, to give this fraudulent rise to the funds by this false news; and the moment the object had been attained of the rise of the funds, that moment all the stock was sold, and sold to the profit that I have proved. So much for these several stock transactions, which supply the corrupt motive by which these defendants were instigated to the commission of this crime.

Then, Gentlemen, we come to that which is a very important part, and indeed a main part of this case, *the identity of Mr. De Berenger*; that identity, including the question of hand-writing. Upon this subject we have had, for the last two hours, the evidence which has nauseated every man in Court; the evidence of the alibi, which no man living can believe; in which no two witnesses agree; in which we have contradiction after contradiction from every one of them. My learned friend, Mr. Park, last night told us we should have the evidence of two watermen, who had rowed Mr. De Berenger across the Thames, who knew his person perfectly well, and who recollected the occurrence particularly, because it was the first Sunday after the frost had broken, and the river became navigable. I suppose the river is frozen again this morning as they are not here. Gentlemen, the interval of the night has made the advisers or manufacturers of this part of the case reflect upon it, and they have brought, instead of the two watermen from the river, the Irish ostler from Chelsea. Gentlemen, they who projected this alibi, did not attend to one circumstance, which cannot fail to have struck you long ago, namely; that this is a case perfectly unassailable by alibi. Let it be supposed, that I had not identified Mr. De Berenger by the persons who saw him at Dover; by the persons who saw him on the road; by those who saw him get out of the chaise at the Marsh Gate, and get into a hackney coach; that I had not identified his countenance by any one of them, still his identity is established beyond all contradiction, for knowing that an alibi would be attempted, I defeated it by anticipation. I take up De Berenger at Dover as I would a bale of goods—I have delivered him from hand to hand from Dover to London—I have delivered him into the house of Lord Cochrane—and I have Lord Cochrane's receipt acknowledging the delivery. You have, at the Ship at Dover, the person pretending to be Colonel Du Bourg, the aid de camp, in a grey military great coat, in a scarlet uniform embroidered with gold lace, and he has a star and a medallion. You have him traced from stage to stage, identified by the Napoleons with which he is rewarding his postillions; the first postillion delivers him to the second, the second to the third, and so on till he is landed in the house of Lord Cochrane. Who went into the house of Lord Cochrane? Ask Lord Cochrane. It was Mr. De Berenger, and it is not pretended that any other person entered that house in that dress, or any thing resembling it; and therefore if I had not any witness to speak to the identity of the countenance of Mr. De Berenger, I have proved such a case as no alibi can shake. But add to that the evidence of identity. I have had much experience in courts of justice, and much upon the subject of identity, and I declare, I never in my life knew a case of identity, by the view of countenance, so proved. The countenance of Mr. De Berenger is not a common one, a person who has observed it cannot have forgotten it. I do not call merely such persons as have seen him at the messenger's, or in the court of King's Bench, or anywhere else. I put the case to the severest test, calling witnesses who had not seen him since his apprehension, desiring them to survey the court, Mr. De Berenger sitting, as he has done, undistinguished from other persons, in no conspicuous situation, and you saw, how one after another, when their eyes glanced upon his face, recognised him in an instant as the person who had practised this fraud. Now, gentlemen, if this were not a case of misdemeanor, but a case in which the life of the party were to answer for the crime he had committed, I ask, whether many—many—many guilty men have not forfeited their lives upon infinitely less evidence than I have given as to the person of Mr. De Berenger?

Then if Mr. De Berenger was Colonel Du Bourg, what becomes of the question of hand-writing? The hand-writing of De Berenger to Du Bourg's letter, was spoken to by Mr. Lavie, who had made particular observation on his hand-writing, having seen him write at the messenger's. My learned friend, Mr. Park, says he should not know the hand-writing from an hour's observation; perhaps not; but this was more than an hour's observation; it was observation repeated more than once, and it was observation for the very purpose. The fact confirms the judgment of Mr. Lavie. I ask, who sent the letter to Admiral Foley? The answer is, Mr. De Berenger; whose hand writing is it? can you have any doubt that it is the hand-writing of the person who sent it? On this point, witnesses are called by De Berenger (one of them a most respectable witness, undoubtedly) to prove that this does not resemble his ordinary hand-writing. No, gentlemen, certainly not; he would not write in his usual hand. Lord Yarmouth says, the character is more angular than his usual hand. That would be the case, where a man is writing a feigned hand; but still that occurs here, which almost always does occur, a person so writing is very likely to betray himself just as he gets to the end, and when he comes to sign his name, the initials shall be so striking, as at once to excite the observation of such a man as Lord Yarmouth, and his lordship says, This R in the signature of R. Du Bourg certainly does very much resemble the R in the usual signature in C. R. De Berenger; but, taking the evidence of identity and that together, it is clear, that he was the person at Dover; that he was the person, therefore, who sent the letter to Admiral Foley; and the evidence of Mr. Lavie is therefore so strongly confirmed, as far to outweigh all the evidence you have had on the other side respecting his hand-writing.

Then, gentlemen, we come a little further; my learned friends last night addressed you at great length, and with great earnestness, upon Lord Cochrane's affidavit, and they requested you would not suppose Lord

Cochrane was capable of making a false affidavit. Gentlemen, that Lord Cochrane would have been incapable of deliberately engaging in any thing so wicked some time ago, I am sure I as earnestly hope as I am desirous to believe; but you must see in what circumstances men are placed, when they do these things; Lord Cochrane had first found his way to the Stock Exchange, he had dealt largely in these speculations, which my learned friends have so liberally branded with the appellation of *infamous*; he had involved himself so deeply, that there was no way, but by this fraud of getting out of them; he had then got out of them in this way, and then he found, as guilty people always do, that he was involved still deeper; he found the great agent of the plot traced into his house, and traced into his house in the dress in which he had perpetrated the fraud; he was called upon for an explanation upon the subject. Gentlemen, he was gone to perdition, if he did not do something to extricate himself from his difficulty; then it was that he ventured upon the rash step of making this affidavit, and swearing to the extraordinary circumstances upon which, as I commented so much at length in the morning of yesterday, I will not trespass upon your attention by making comments now.

My learned friends were properly anxious not to leave Lord Cochrane's affidavit to stand unsupported; they were desirous of giving it some confirmation, and they exhausted two or three precious hours this morning in calling witnesses to confirm it; but those witnesses were called to confirm the only part of the affidavit which wanted no confirmation; they were called to give Lord Cochrane confirmation about applications to the Admiralty, and applications to the War Office, and applications to the Colonial Office, by Sir Alexander Cochrane for De Berenger; and after they had called witness after witness to give this confirmation upon this insignificant and trifling point, they leave him without confirmation upon that important, that vital part of this case to my Lord Cochrane, *videlicet*: the dress which Mr. De Berenger wore at the time he came to that house, and had with him that interview. Lord Cochrane puts him on a grey military great coat, a *green* uniform, and a fur cap. I have proved, that the uniform he wore was *red*. My learned friend, Mr. Serjeant Best, felt the strength of the evidence for the prosecution upon that, and he endeavoured to answer it by a very strange observation. "Why," says he, "consider, Lord Cochrane had been accustomed to see Mr. De Berenger in *green*; he did not make his affidavit till nearly three weeks afterwards; and how very easily he might confound the *green*, in which he ordinarily saw him, with the *red*, in which he saw him on that day, and on that day only." Now, if I wanted to shew how it was impossible for a man to make a mistake, as to the colour of the coat in which he had seen another, I should select the instance in which he had seen that other in a peculiar dress but for once.

But, gentlemen, my learned friend had to account for more than the red coat. It is not a plain red coat, it is a scarlet military uniform, the uniform of an aid-de-camp; and on the breast, there is that star which you have seen; and suspended from his neck, there is the medallion. Lord Cochrane is a man of rank, not unacquainted with the distinction of a star. If he was not in the secret of De Berenger's dress, he must have had curiosity upon the subject; and I beg to ask, what is to be said for Lord Cochrane seeing De Berenger in that scarlet uniform, with that star on his breast, and that medallion suspended from his neck, swearing that the uniform was *green*, and that he lent De Berenger a black coat, because he could not wait on Lord Yarmouth in that *green* uniform, which you will recollect was the uniform of Lord Yarmouth's corps, in which, Lord Yarmouth has told you, it would have been more military to have waited upon him, than in any other dress.

Gentlemen, there is more than this. My friends call one of Lord Cochrane's servants, who received De Berenger when he came there, who told him in the hearing of the hackney coachman, that his master was gone to breakfast in Cumberland-street, who took the note which De Berenger wrote to Cumberland-street, who brought back the note, and upon that note Mr. De Berenger wrote two or three lines more. Then what becomes of Lord Cochrane's affidavit, who says the signature was so near the bottom of the paper, that he could not read it. The postscript is written after the signature, yet Lord Cochrane cannot read the note, because the signature is written so near the bottom; and then when my learned friends had that servant in the box, they did not venture to ask that servant what was the dress of Mr. De Berenger. After calling witnesses to confirm Lord Cochrane, as to applications to different offices by Sir Alexander Cochrane, they dare not ask Lord Cochrane's own servant as to the dress De Berenger wore, to try whether he could confirm Lord Cochrane's affidavit upon that subject. They then tell us, that another servant is gone abroad with some admiral, and I pray you, as he was here long after this business was afloat, how was it he was suffered to go, unless his absence was more wanted than his presence; but they have a maid-servant who also saw him, and she is not called; and my learned friends, though they were so anxious to confirm Lord Cochrane's affidavit, leave him without confirmation, utterly abandoned and hopeless.

*Mr. Brougham.* Davis had left.

*Mr. Gurney.* I say why was he suffered to go away. The maid-servant is still here, and she is not called. Gentlemen, I say so much for the affidavit of Lord Cochrane, which is a vital part of this subject, and upon which, I observe with great regret; but if I forbore the observations, I should desert the duty which I owe the public. Gentlemen, there is indeed but little more for me to trouble you with, I think; but there was an observation made by my learned friend, which is very important; they cross-examined Mr. Wright, whom I put up to prove the affidavit, by asking him, whether Lord Cochrane did not at the time he put that affidavit into his hands, observe, that now he had furnished the Stock Exchange Committee with the name of Mr. De Berenger, if he was the person who practised this fraud. Gentlemen, Mr. Serjeant Best laboured this point with you in the course of his address to you, and labored it with great ability; but my learned friend did not advert to one circumstance respecting that affidavit, which disposes of all his observations in an instant. *When* did Lord Cochrane furnish the name of De Berenger to the Committee of the Stock Exchange? *On the 11th of March*; Mr. De Berenger having quitted London on the 27th of February, twelve days before; and when my Lord Cochrane had no more doubt that he was out of the country, than that he was himself in existence; he was gone to the north, not gone to the south, to Portsmouth, to go on board the Tonnant; he had been gone twelve days, twice as long as was necessary to find his way to Amsterdam; it was believed he was safe there, and when it was thought he was quite safe, Lord Cochrane was extremely ready to furnish the Stock Exchange Committee with the name of the party, and so to get credit for his candour. "What can a man do more? I have given you the name of the party, only find him, and you will see whether he is Du Bourg, or not;" he did not expect that he would be found; he was, however, found, and the intentions of these parties were frustrated.

I come now, gentlemen, to another part of the case, which would have excited my astonishment, if it had not been for the management and machinery that I had seen in this case; still I could hardly have expected to have met with that which we have had to-day in evidence, I mean the mode which has been resorted to, of accounting for the bank notes which were found in the letter-case of De Berenger, and those that were paid away by him. Gentlemen, the Defendants knew this part of our case; in truth, there is no surprize upon them in any part, they knew it all. You have it in evidence, that they have inspected the notes in the letter-case; they knew the use that we were to make of them, and then we have that notable expedient, the fruit of Mr. Cochrane Johnstone's fertile brain, the mode of accounting for all these bank notes, by this extraordinary transaction of the drawings of a design for improving an acre of ground behind Mr. Cochrane Johnstone's house in Alsop's buildings.

Now, gentlemen, only have the goodness to look at it. The work was done, it is said, last September; £.50 was then paid on account, respecting which you might, from Mr. De Berenger's letter, have supposed that no voucher had been given, for it is mentioned carelessly in the postscript, "a-propos, you have paid me £.50 on account." On the contrary, you find that Mr. Cochrane Johnstone took a stamped receipt at the time; then we have the architect called, as in an action on a quantum meruit; and architects have most magnificent ideas of plans and money, and he tells you, that two or three hundred pounds would not have been too much for such a design as that. Gentlemen, I think we are all as well qualified to decide upon that, as an architect; you will, if you think proper, look at it, and form your own judgment. But how comes it that we have these strange accounts from Mr. Tahourdin, his verbal testimony contradicting his client's letter. Mr. Tahourdin says, "I did delicately, but I did by Mr. Berenger's desire, again and again hint to Mr. Cochrane Johnstone the subject of payment, to which I must do him the justice to say he was never averse. I had done this some time before February, but no money had come;" and then, as soon as these words were out of his mouth, he puts in Mr. De Berenger's letter to Mr. Cochrane Johnstone, who says, "You (Mr. Cochrane Johnstone) have been pressing me to take money, and now I will take it." Oh, gentlemen, when does this fit of money-paying and money-taking seize these two persons? *On the 22d of February!* The day speaks volumes. Added to all the extraordinary coincidences, which the Defendants wish you to believe were accidental, we now have the acknowledged payment of money by Mr. Cochrane Johnstone to Mr. De Berenger on the day after Mr. De Berenger had so rendered Mr. Cochrane Johnstone, Lord Cochrane, and Mr. Butt, the important service of raising the funds by the imposition that he had practised, of which they had so promptly and profitably availed themselves.

Then, gentlemen, we have the extraordinary evidence of Mr. Tahourdin, the attorney for Mr. Cochrane Johnstone and for De Berenger, from which it appears that they were all getting up the defence to the indictment by anticipation. Mr. Tahourdin is to give a contemporaneous existence to the transaction by the production of these letters and instruments, the receipt for two hundred pounds, and the promissory note for two hundred pounds more. From all this it is plain, that Mr. Cochrane Johnstone, at the very moment when he was settling with his agent his reward for the fraud he had committed, like a man of great foresight, looked forward to the possible consequence of the trial of this day, and he provided for it, as he thought, sufficiently:—"It may be thought, Mr. De Berenger, that this money which I am now giving you is for the business of yesterday, let us take care to prevent it; you write to me, I will write to Tahourdin; it is not absolutely necessary (perhaps, he added) to trust him with the secret, he will be an admirable witness hereafter; I will put into his hands the promissory note and the receipt, he will give them contemporaneous date, and then I shall be able to account for my giving you, on this 26th of February, four hundred pounds."

Persons who devise these contrivances, gentlemen, have not, as I observed to you yesterday, the skill to provide for all circumstances, and now and then the very things which they do to effect concealment, shall lead to detection.—Now mark:—Mr. Cochrane Johnstone is to pay and to lend to Mr. De Berenger four hundred pounds. As he was to give him four hundred pounds, why did he, or Mr. Butt (for they are one and the same) take so much trouble, and go through so much circuity in shifting and changing the bank notes? You observe, that the bank note for £.200 is sent to the bankers, and exchanged for two notes of £.100 each; and then the same agent is sent to the Bank of England to get two hundred notes of £.1 each; and that about the same time another agent is sent to the bank, to exchange the two other notes for £.100 each for two hundred more notes of £.1 each. Why, for the purpose of this payment and this loan, do they go through this operation of changing and changing again, to procure a vast number of notes for Mr. De Berenger, to enable him to take this long journey to the north? Why, gentlemen, it is because one pound notes are not traced so easily as notes for one hundred pounds; people take these small notes without writing upon them, but they do write upon such large notes as £.100 and £.200, and that they knew might afford means of immediate detection, but the device, when detected, makes the fact still stronger, and you have in proof, that sixty-seven of one hundred, and forty-nine of another hundred, were found at Leith in De Berenger's writing-desk. This affords a strong presumption, that he had the whole four hundred, besides which I have traced to him; a forty-pound note which he changed at Sunderland, and a fifty-pound note which he gave to his servant, Smith; and these, too, have been traced up to Mr. Butt. When all these turnings and windings are thus discovered, what measure of your understandings, gentlemen, must these Defendants have taken, to imagine that you could be imposed upon by such flimsy materials as these manufactured papers? The device is gross, palpable, and monstrous. What does all this prove?—Nothing *for* the defendants; but then it proves a great deal *against* them. Recollect too, gentlemen, that this £.400, which is shewn to come out of the hands of Mr. Cochrane Johnstone and Mr. Butt, after the 24th of February, is also shewn to have come originally out of the hands of Lord Cochrane himself on a prior day; and therefore you have the money coming out of the hands of all the three; the reward of the agent coming out of the hands of the persons who had been benefited by the fraudulent services of that agent.

Gentlemen, it is difficult to abstain from many more observations on this defence; but the case is too clear to require them, and I will no longer trespass upon your patience. It appears to me absolutely impossible to doubt respecting the guilt of the several defendants. De Berenger is Du Bourg. When De Berenger is Du Bourg, the rest all follows; he was the agent of others, unquestionably; he was not himself the principal. You have had a mass of perjury exhibited to-day to extricate him, and consequently his employers. That, like all falsehoods, when detected, only serves to make conviction more clear and more certain. With these observations I sit down, feeling most grateful for the patient attention I have received, both from his Lordship and from you, and perfectly sure that you will do justice to the Public.

# SUMMING UP.

Lord ELLENBOROUGH.

Gentlemen of the Jury,

You are now come to that period of the case in which your most important duty is to be discharged, as it respects the individuals who are the object of this indictment, and the public, whose interests are to be protected by the justice you are called upon to administer.

This is an indictment for an offence of great malignity and mischief; it is for the offence of conspiracy, which is charged to have been committed by the eight persons whose names are upon this indictment; and it is for you to consider upon the statement of the evidence I shall make to you, how far that offence is brought home to all or any of these Defendants.

The offence of conspiracy, gentlemen, is an offence consisting in a wicked concert, contrivance, and combination of individuals, to effect some public or private injury or mischief; that contrivance and that combination is not to be collected, nor is it practicable, in the course of human affairs, to collect it from the mouths of the parties assembled for the purpose of communication, but from the actings and conduct of the several parties as they may appear generally, to conspire and conduce to the same wicked end and purpose; and if it appears to you, from the actings and conduct of these parties, that they entertained the same common purpose of mischief, and that they have by their several actings combined and co-operated to the effecting that same wicked purpose, that is sufficient to bring home the imputation of the crime charged against the parties; therefore the prosecutor need not shew that they have met in common council, or even that they have seen one another before, if their acting shews they were influenced by one common purpose of mischief, and aimed at the production of the same malignant end and effect. Suppose persons jointly charged in an indictment with the breaking of an house, are found on different sides of the same house, besetting and endeavouring to enter it at the same time; you need not shew that they had actually met, and previously contrived the plan of this joint robbery; the unity of their conduct proves their joint contrivance and concert to accomplish the same end; though, indeed, this is a case where personal presence at the acts done, renders all intendment of the personal concert of the actors unnecessary. The same rules which apply to the offence of conspiracy as a misdemeanor, apply equally to all crimes committed by concert up to the crime of high treason, which is often established by evidence of the distinct actings of separate parties breathing the same purpose, and immediately conducing to the same end. The question, therefore, for you to consider upon the evidence (which I am sorry it will be necessary for me to state to you at a greater length, than, with regard to your ease and convenience, I could have wished) will be, whether the case is not brought home by satisfactory evidence to a great number, if not to all the Defendants.

The crime charged upon this indictment, in eight different charges or counts, is that of conspiring to raise the price of the public funds; in some of them it is charged to be with a view to corrupt gain upon the part of these persons or some of them, or at least to the *prejudice* of other *individuals*; for that is enough to constitute the offence, even if the individuals engaged in this conspiracy had not (as it is imputed to them that they had) any corrupt motive of personal advantage to all or any of themselves to answer; if the criminal artifice operated, or was in all probability likely to operate to the prejudice of the public, and was clearly so intended, we need not go further; when we know that a great amount in the funds is at certain periods bought for the public or large classes of individuals; and you find by the testimony of Mr. Steers, that on this very day the sum of £.15,957. 10. 8. was bought for the Accountant General, which would have been bought for less; and every person for whose use the Accountant General purchased, having to acquire by means of such purchase shares in the public securities, would of course have so much the less stock for his money, on account of this fraud, and would consequently receive a great pecuniary injury thereby; and no doubt, multitudes of persons besides those immediately alluded to, and whose cases are not brought individually under your view, must have been affected by it; for the dealings in the funds are, we know, every day carried on to a vast amount, and every person dealing on that particular day, as a purchaser, was prejudiced by the practices by which a false elevation of the funds was on that day occasioned.

Of the counts, one or two, I think, are not counts on which, properly, your verdict can be founded, because they state, that every one of these Defendants knew that a gain was to be acquired by Mr. Cochrane Johnstone, Lord Cochrane, and Mr. Butt; and it does not appear, with sufficient certainty, that they knew the relation in which these three persons stood to the funds, or their interest and speculations therein; I mean, that such persons as M'Rae, Holloway, and so on, might not know the precise situation in which the three stood; but if they all co-operated to the same end, and the Northfleet imposition, as I may call it, was intended to be auxiliary to the imposition intended to be effected by the way of Dover, and the parties knew that they were acting in the same fraud, and were respectively conscious instruments in producing the same effect, they are all guilty of the same conspiracy; and it has been admitted, by a learned counsel for some of the Defendants, that his clients, Holloway, Lyte, and Sandom, have been concerned in a conspiracy; but, he says, that the conspiracy in which they were concerned, was another and a different conspiracy, from the one in which the three first-mentioned of the Defendants were engaged; and that you cannot unite the two conspiracies together, and convict them all as guilty of one entire individual conspiracy; and it will be one material point for your consideration, whether, under the circumstances which have appeared in evidence, it is made out to your satisfaction, that they were all conspiring to effectuate the same purpose, pursuing similar, and with almost a servile imitation and resemblance, the same means, at the same time, in the accomplishment of the same end.

Now how has it been done? in both instances, by the adoption of disguises. Of what nature are the disguises? in both instances, military disguises; one, indeed, has gold lace round the cape, and the other has embroidery. Sarah Alexander says, those procured by M'Rae, were officers coats, with flowers of worsted, and that the hats were embroidered, the one having a brass plate, and a gold tassel, instead of the sort of ornaments that the superior actor in this conspiracy (if such you shall be of opinion he was) had. One was decorated with a star, and that silver ornament that you have seen; the other was in rather a plainer dress; but there was in each case the assumption of the character of officers; and the communication of false intelligence respecting the good news which was to accelerate peace, was common to both parts of the scheme. You will consider, upon the whole of the evidence, whether there is not a link or connection, between the upper and under plot, through the means of M'Rae, and perhaps of Mr. Cochrane Johnstone, and, whether the two conspiracies are not united through the means of that person, M'Rae; his conduct itself is extraordinary; by a most remarkable offer, on the part of Mr. Cochrane Johnstone, it is proposed that there should be the sum of £.10,000 given to this man; a man in a low and ordinary and desperate situation; and it is stated, that Lord Cochrane, Mr. Cochrane Johnstone, and Mr. Butt, would give £.3,000 among them. Why should they give that? If, indeed, they could thereby mislead and draw away the public attention, and divert it to the pursuit and hunting down of M'Rae, as the sole artificer and perpetrator of the fraud, and could thereby turn aside observation and suspicion from themselves (supposing them to be properly charged with this offence), £.3,000 would be well paid, and cheaply employed for such a purpose. It is for you to say, whether these letters which have been read to you, do not appear pregnant of this contrivance and device on the part of the writer.

The first question, gentlemen, will be, was the Defendant, De Berenger, the man who was found at Dover, about one o'clock on the morning of Monday the 21st of February, and who proceeded through the several stages to London, and ultimately to the mansion of Lord Cochrane himself, and was there received with that dress, whatever it was, that he wore; but the dress he wore, is proved by so many witnesses, that I will not fatigue you with stating it now, because I must, by and by, state the whole of the evidence to you.

A great deal of observation has been made about the character of handwriting, of what I call the Dover letter—the letter sent to Admiral Foley; the object of sending it to him cannot be doubtful, for it was intended that the Port Admiral should (as he would if he had believed the report) communicate that intelligence to Government, and which, if the day had been tolerably clear, might by telegraph have reached this town in much less than half an hour, I believe in a quarter of an hour; and having been sent off at this very early hour to Admiral Foley, who was called out of bed to receive it, it would have been in town early, and the stocks would have been up at the very moment, when under the peremptory order before given, £.50,000 would have been sold, as well as every other part of the stock, standing in the names of the Defendants.

Gentlemen, there has been great stress laid upon this letter, and whether it be or be not the hand-writing of De Berenger, I will not (for it is not my province) draw the conclusion which might be drawn from looking at that letter; it appears to me evidently an artificial, upright, stiff hand, as contrasted with the ordinary natural character of hand-writing of that gentleman. It is sometimes useful to look where the same words occur in different parts of the same letter; and when you come to look at the words, "I have the honour to be," in one part of the letter, and the words "have pledged my honour," &c. in the other; they present in the first instance, a more angular formation of letters than I have generally seen, and with reference to the idea thrown out of this being written in great haste, it is not impossible that this gentleman having meditated the whole contrivance before-hand, should have brought this letter down with him, ready written and directed from town, and that he had called for pen and ink merely to go through the appearance of writing a letter, and which he might fold up as if for the purpose of being sent; but that he might hand over to Wright, of Dover, the letter he had brought with him, not trusting to the hurry of the moment for the proper formation of one. I do not say that such is the fact; but it is clear that the letter produced, is the one he actually sent; for he says afterwards to the witness, Shilling, that he had sent a letter to Admiral Foley, in order to apprize him that the telegraph might work; the Dover express-boy proves that he carried the letter given to him, to Admiral Foley, and what letter can that be, if it is not this, which is proved to have been delivered to Admiral Foley? This letter was calculated to impress the Admiral with the belief, that the allies had obtained a decisive victory, that Bonaparte was killed, that the allies were in Paris, and that peace was likely to take place immediately. After the calamity of the long war we have had, ending as indeed it has ended, in the fulness of glory; we all feel that we have had an abundant measure of glory, though painfully earned; every body recollects the sort of electric effect produced upon this town the moment the news now under consideration arrived; the funds were raised preternaturally; one cannot indeed on looking back, account for it, how the omnium should have been up to twenty-eight at that time; there was a considerable elevation beyond that price during the course of that day; it rose to thirty and a fraction.

Gentlemen, the prosecutors allege that the Defendant, De Berenger, having forwarded this letter, pursued his course, coming to town in the manner stated, and that he ultimately came to Lord Cochrane's house, upon which I shall hereafter comment. You will not, I think, have any doubt that De Berenger was the man who appeared under the name of Du Bourg; but in order to obviate or remove that impression from your minds, the learned counsel for the Defendant, De Berenger, did adventure or rather was forced upon an attempt, which I own it seemed to me to require the utmost firmness to attempt to execute; for there never was evidence given since I have been present in a court of justice, which carried to my mind such entire conviction of the truth and authenticity of that part of the story; you were yourselves witnesses to the manner in which the witnesses, who spoke to the person of De Berenger, were put upon the investigation; they were told to look round the court, and they accordingly threw their eyes about the court in every direction, before they found the person whom they said they had so taken notice of; you saw them look behind them, look down, and on every side of them, and then suddenly, as if they were struck by a sort of electricity, conviction flashed upon their minds the instant their eyes glanced upon him; this occurred in every instance I think but one, where the witness not having his eyes conducted that way, did not discover him. The learned counsel having such abundance of proof on this head, did not resort to a means usually adopted on occasions of this sort, and to which it is perfectly allowable to resort, namely, that of shewing the person to the witness, and asking him whether such person was the man; when a man stands for his life at the bar of the Old Bailey, the witness is frequently bid to look at the prisoner at the bar, and to say whether he remembers him, and whether he is the person, or one of the persons (as the case may be) who robbed him; and he pronounces whether according to his recollection, he is the person or not. So multiplied a quantity of testimony, so clear, and so consistent, was, I think hardly ever presented in the course of any criminal trial; differing in no circumstance respecting his person and dress, excepting in some trifles, which amidst the general accordance of all material circumstances, rather confirmed by this minute diversity, than weakened, the general credit of the whole, and gave it the advantage which belongs to an artless and unartificial tale. Some saying his cap was a little flat, as it might be owing to its being drawn over his face; one saying that it was brown; another I think, that it was of a fawn colour; and one who spoke with the utmost certainty in other particulars, that it was nearly the colour of his pepper and salt great coat; but in all the other substantial particulars, they concur in their accounts most exactly; and these minute variances exclude the idea of any uniform contrivance and design in the variation; for where it is an artificial and prepared story, the parties agree in the minutest facts, as well as the most important; and indeed, gentlemen, so abundant, so uniform, and so powerful is the evidence as to one point, viz. the identity of Berenger, that it strikes me, that if these witnesses are not to be fully believed as to this point, then almost every man who has been convicted at the Old Bailey upon so much weaker proof of his being the person who committed the particular crime with which he is charged, (and which has been the case in almost *every instance* I have known), may be considered as victims unjustly sacrificed in a course of trial, to the rash credulity of their judges and juries. If the evidence produced is not sufficient to establish this point, I am at a loss to say by what description and quantity of testimony, such a point can be satisfactorily made out in a course of trial.

When the learned counsel addressed himself to prove an alibi, I could not foresee how it would be satisfactorily accomplished; I cannot say I believed he would accomplish it, but I believed it would be attempted by better evidence than that which has been adduced; you recollect the prior testimony of the Davidsons; the servants had gone out at two, instead of four; Mr. De Berenger, according to the evidence he has adduced, is found three miles and a half off; where he had dined, is not shewn, he is in a hurry to get back; according to the next set of alibi witnesses, he is found at Mr. Donithorne's between eight and nine, having been found there in the morning, to measure the garden, at not a very convenient time, with the snow upon the ground; and who are the people who speak to this? a man who has been in the habit, which some of us are, of examining the countenances and demeanor of men brought forward to speak to guilty untruths, becomes in a degree familiar with the modes of behaviour which such persons adopt. From something in the manner of one of the witnesses, which suggested to me that such a question might not be improperly addressed to him, I asked him, whether he had not been used to be bail? (thinking that he might possibly be one of those hired bail, who are the disgrace of our courts of justice). What does he answer? why, he had been bail once, and then he had been bail another time, and the amount he did not know; and I think he said he did not know whether he had not been bail oftener; a man who is in the habit of being bail, must swear to the amount, and he must swear he is an housekeeper; and this man had no house over his head of his own, but was living in the house of another; I thought, too, the man might have failed, and been obliged to quit his house on that account; and it so appears, that he was undone in his circumstances, and that he was a man occasionally presenting himself to swear to his possession of property, warranting his becoming bail for others.

Then what becomes of Donithorne; he is an inferior cabinet-maker, employed by Mr. Cochrane Johnstone, and has brought a great number of penal actions for him; at every turn of the case, he doubles in upon us, and you will presently have to say, whether he and others, and which others, are not affected by this case.

Gentlemen, the evidence begins with that of John Marsh, who keeps the packet-boat public house at Dover, he says, "Upon that 21st of February, I heard a knocking at Mr. Wright's fore door of the Ship Inn, between one and a quarter after one o'clock; I went out upon hearing that, and, on going out, I found a gentleman there, who had on a grey great coat, and an uniform coat under it. I called for a person at my house to bring two lights across; when I had the two lights, the gentleman had got into the passage; he had a star on his red coat, under the great coat; it is similar to this star." Now, it is said these persons saw him in the dark, but candles were brought over, and you may see a man's countenance by the light of two candles placed near him, almost as well as you could in the day-light we have at present; it would certainly be sufficient for the purposes of observation; if it were not so, half at least of the injuries done at night would be very imperfectly proved, if proved at all. He says, "I do not recollect that he had any other ornament; he was very anxious for a post-chaise and four; the porter at the Ship came down to him; he wanted an express horse, and a man to send to the Admiral at Deal;" then it is highly probable, as he wanted an express horse, that he did send this letter by that express; the witnesses swear they saw him writing a letter. "I asked him where he came from, and he told me, he was the bearer of the most important dispatches that had been brought to this country for twenty years; I asked him where he came from? he told me, from France. I asked him, where he landed? he told me, on the beach; and he begged of me to get a post-chaise and four for him; and then I went and called Mr. Wright, of the Ship Inn; then he wanted pen, ink, and paper. I had shewn him into a room; as soon as Mr. Wright came down stairs, Mr. Wright gave me a sheet of paper, and pens and ink, which I carried into the room; I gave it to him, and he began to write upon it; he called for a bottle of Madeira, and something to eat." That circumstance of his having wine, is afterwards confirmed, for when he is going up Shooter's hill, he is giving it away to some of the postillions. "I asked him, whether I should call the collector of the port? telling him, that it was his business to see such people when they landed; he made answer to me, that his business did not lie with the collectors; then Mr. Wright came, and I had no more conversation with him; two candles were placed, one on each side of him, and I could see him; *that is the gentleman*; (pointing him out.) A gentleman of the name of Gourley was there, and another of the name of Edis, was also there." Then he says, "I went to get horses with all possible dispatch; he told the two postillions he would give them a Napoleon each;" and that description of coin attends him throughout, nor does it quit him to the last, for in the very desk when he is taken up in Scotland, there were found Napoleons tallying with these; therefore the proof in this particular is dovetailed and closed in, beyond any thing I almost ever saw in a court of justice. Then he says, "he had a German cap on, and gold fringe, as I thought;" and it turns out, upon an exhibit we had made to us of a similar cap, that De Berenger had such a cap; those that are shewn, were made in the resemblance of what, from the evidence, they collected the articles to be. They are not the originals; the coat, it appears, was cut to pieces, and got out of the Thames, but the actual cap is not produced; "this is all that I heard and saw."

Upon his cross examination, he says, "I am not in the least connected with the Ship Inn, but on hearing this knocking, I went across to see who the gentleman was out of mere curiosity; I did not observe whether it was moonlight, foggy, or star-light." It does not signify which it was, for he saw him by candle-light. "The boots let him in; I was with him about five minutes altogether, but I cannot speak to a minute; he was in great haste to get away; I should think he was not more than twenty minutes at Mr. Wright's altogether. I held the candle while the boots unlocked the parlour door, and I went and put them on the table; he wished me to quit the room, and I did not go in any more." Then he is asked about a large company in the inn, he says, "I do not know that there had been any; I never saw him before nor yet since, till to-day, but I can take upon me confidently to swear, *that this is the man.*" He made a very strong observation upon him, and he pointed him out in the manner you saw. "I never was examined upon this subject before, only by Mr. Stow, the collector."

On his re-examination, he says, "he told me before I sent for the lights what his business was, and that he had landed on the beach. I was in the passage with him till the lights came; my attention was called to him as a stranger of importance. I saw the person when I was by myself in the hall, and knew him the instant I saw him; I have not the least doubt that he is the same man."

One of the other persons who saw him, of the name of Gourley, a hatter at Dover, speaks to the same thing—"I was at Mr. Marsh's, the packet-boat, on the morning of the 21st of February; Mr. Marsh went over and called for lights; I took two candles and went across with them to the Ship, where I perceived a gentleman in a pepper and salt coloured coat, similar to that which is shewn to me. Mr. Marsh asked me to go and call the ostler up, and to tell him to get a post-chaise and four immediately. I did so; and after some time, when I had got the ostler up, I returned back again and found the stranger in the parlour; there were lights in the room; there were two candles upon the table; the gentleman was walking about in a red uniform trimmed with gold lace, with a star upon his breast, and he had a cap on similar to that, with gold lace on it. I asked him, what news; having heard them say he was a messenger. He said messengers were sworn to secrecy, but that he had got glorious news; the best that ever was known for this country. He rang the bell and called for pen, ink and paper, to write a letter, to send off to the Admiral at Deal." So that he professes, as the first witness says, to write a letter; and here he speaks of sending it off to the Admiral at Deal:—"that was brought to him, and he continued writing some little time while I was there. I took leave of him before he had finished the letter; the candles were sufficiently near him to observe him; that is the gentleman, and I have not the least doubt that it is him."

On his cross examination, he says, "I came over when I was called by Mr. Marsh to bring candles; I went and called the ostler, and waited till I waked the ostler; I left the candles in the passage; I saw him write on the paper when it was brought; I was sitting with Mr. Marsh when he arrived; I had not dined at the packet-boat." I suppose the question pointed to whether this man was likely to have been sober or drunk at that time: I do not know that there is any thing extraordinary in a man's sitting up till twelve or one o'clock; but that has been the subject of the observation.

Upon his re-examination, he says, "perhaps I might be in the room, so as to have an opportunity of observing him three or four minutes; my attention was called to him particularly; he had a cap on sometimes, and sometimes not; *I have no doubt that is the man.*"

Eliot Edis, a person who you recollect was rather deaf, says, "I am a cooper in the victualling yard at Dover, I was at the packet boat on the morning of the 21st of February, Gourley was there with me; my attention was called to a messenger who had arrived. I saw the messenger first at the Ship, he was in a room at the time, walking up and down the room. I observed his dress; he had a grey great coat and regimentals, scarlet trimmed with gold; I did not particularly notice any other ornament; he had a cap with a gold band, that was the colour of the coat, it was a slouched cap;" upon that there has been much observation; "the cap appeared to be made of a kind of rough beaver, I do not know whether it was black or brown;" by that light you would not know very distinctly whether it was black or brown; "it was rather flat all round, and had no rim like a hat. I saw him sit down and write. I did not hear him say whom he was writing to. I could hear him talk; but not to understand him, being rather deaf; his cap was on while I was there." He is desired to look round, and to point out the gentleman, and he says, "that is the gentleman," pointing to him. "I have no doubt that is he; I had never seen him before that night, nor since;" and yet as you saw him, looking round, he instantly found him out among so many as there were then round him, it is not probable that if they had not seen him before, and had not his picture engraved upon their minds, they would have known him again so well; and it would be very remarkable that they should all pitch upon the same person.

"I might see him perhaps for five or six minutes; the cap was rather slouched; it had no brim to it; it was drawn over his forehead; the round part of it was drawn over his forehead. I was not in court when Marsh was examined." It was suggested that he might have picked up his story from Marsh; but a man who was deaf could not have heard him, if he had been in court.

Mr. William St. John is next called; he speaks in the same manner; it is unnecessary to go through the whole of it. He says, "he wore a scarlet coat with long skirts, buttoned across, with a red silk sash, grey pantaloons, and a grey military great coat, and I think it was a seal-skin cap;" now with that light he might very easily mistake; I believe it is very common to have seal-skin caps for travelling.

*Mr. Gurney.* This is seal-skin, my Lord.

*Lord Ellenborough.* I did not know that; "he had, I think, a seal-skin cap on his head, of a fawn colour," and it is a fawn colour, certainly; "there were some ornaments on his uniform, but I do not know what they were, something of a star on his military dress; he was talking up and down the room in a very good pace; I asked him, whether he knew anything of the coming of one Johnson," a messenger whom the witness expected; "he said he knew nothing at all about him, and begged I would leave him to himself, as he was extremely ill;" this gentleman appears too inquisitive, and he did not seem to like him. "On my leaving the room, he requested that they would send in paper, and pen and ink; I immediately retired, and met the landlord, Mr. Wright, coming into the room, I believe, with the paper, pens and ink; in a few seconds afterwards I returned into the room, and he was writing, I did not hear him say any thing about the paper he was writing. I left the room immediately. I saw him again at the door in the street. When he was stepping into the carriage, I asked him what the news was; he told me it was as good as I could possibly wish; I did not see what he did with the paper he was writing upon, nor did I hear him say what he was writing about, he went away the first of us."

Now this man has been made a good deal the subject of comment; for it appears that he had gone down to Dover, and was, in some respect, waiting for news; there was a kind of reluctance in him to acknowledge that, in respect of which there need not have been any, for there is nothing whatever objectionable in his sending up paragraphs for the Traveller newspaper. I believe the publishers of these papers mostly have some persons stationed at the out-ports, to obtain intelligence of important events, and particularly so critical and anxious a moment as that was they would naturally have such persons at the port of Dover; there was nothing he should not avow; and if it was with the view to purchase in the funds, in consequence of the intelligence he should receive; if a man purchases funds upon public intelligence fairly and honestly come by, when every body has an equal opportunity of acquiring it and the intelligence is genuine, it is like buying any other article in the market, upon fair knowledge of the circumstances connected with its value; it is as allowable to deal in that article as in any other, upon equal terms; but the objection here is to a dealing which resembles the playing with loaded dice; if one plays with secret means of advantage over another, it is not fair-playing—it is a cheat: I own I have been much shocked with this sort of fraudulent practice, called three times over, in the letter of Cochrane Johnstone, *a hoax*; I cannot apply a term which imports a joke to that, which if the Defendants are guilty of, is a gross fraud upon public and private property; and unless every species of depredation and robbery is to be regarded as a species of pleasantry, I think the name of hoax, which has been given to it, is very ill applied to a transaction of so dishonest and base a description.

Then Mr. St. John says, "I went to Dover, by desire of a friend of mine; his name is Farrell; he is a merchant in the city, and is a proprietor of the Traveller." Then being asked, where that gentleman lived, he says, "In Austin Friars: I was to communicate to Mr. Farrell or to Mr. Quin." Then he says, "certainly the arrival of news at such a time would have an effect upon the funds."

Then William Ions, the express-boy, being shewn to the last witness, St. John, he says, "this is the boy whom I saw sent with one of the two expresses that was sent that night; this lad went with the express to the Port-admiral at Deal, I believe; it was the express that Mr. Wright gave him from the gentleman who was there; *from that gentleman*."

William Ions says, "In February last I was in the service of Mr. Wright, of Dover; I was called up when the officer arrived there, and was sent with an express to Admiral Foley; I took the letter I received to Admiral Foley; Mr. Wright gave me the letter whilst I was upon my pony; he came out to the door with it; and that letter which I received, I delivered to the Admiral's servant at Deal. She took it up stairs to the Admiral, and I saw the Admiral before I left Deal, after the letter was delivered to the servant, who took it up stairs." Therefore, whatever he received at Dover he delivered to the Admiral, and what the Admiral received we have here; there is an interruption in the proof certainly, in consequence of Wright, of Dover, not being well enough to be here as a witness; and therefore it did not appear by his testimony, that that which he, Wright, had received, Wright had delivered to his express-boy, to go over to Deal with; but that is supplied by the circumstance of De Berenger, if he was the person, telling Shilling, the Dartford driver, that he had sent off such an express; therefore it must be presumed that he had sent that letter which contained an express to the Admiral; and that which the Admiral received he shews you.

To supply that defect in the evidence, Mr. Lavie was called to say, that he believed it to be De Berenger's hand-writing; and though this does not appear to be the ordinary undisguised hand of this Defendant, yet after Lord Yarmouth, who had given his evidence that he did not consider it his hand-writing, referred to the letter R, the initial letter of Random de Berenger's christian name, he considered *that* as resembling his hand-writing, and you would observe, whether there was not such a resemblance as Lord Yarmouth mentions, if it were at all material; but it ceases entirely to be material, when he tells Shilling, as he does, that he had actually sent such a letter to the Admiral.

Admiral Foley is next called; he says, "The letter was brought to me, that that boy brought to the house; I was a-bed; I read the letter in bed; I did not mark it; I enclosed it in a letter to Mr. Croker, the Secretary to the Admiralty; that is the letter; I sent it enclosed in this letter to Mr. Croker; I arose immediately, and sent for the boy into my dressing-room; I questioned the boy a good deal; I did not telegraph the Admiralty, because the weather was too thick; when I sent for the boy up, I had the letter in my hand; it was then three o'clock, and dark; the telegraph would not work; I had a candle, of course; I am not certain I should have telegraphed the Admiralty," and if he had seen reason to doubt, he would have acted very properly in abstaining from so doing; he could not communicate all that would excite the doubts he might himself entertain; he could only send a few words, indicating the most important particulars of the story which the letter contained, and therefore he might very properly hesitate about communicating any part, if he thought the whole contained doubtful, still more if untrue intelligence.

The evidence of Mr. Lavie is only that he believed this to be De Berenger's hand-writing; that he had seen him several times in the custody of the messenger in the month of April, and in the course of those interviews, he saw him write a considerable deal; he saw a whole letter which he handed across to him when he had written it, and it was given back and copied again, and for about an hour he was writing different things, and handing them backwards and forwards. He says, "I also saw his papers in his writing-desk, and I verily believe that to be his hand-writing, from what I saw him write." This is the evidence, and much less than this evidence, is what we receive every day in proof of bonds, notes, and bills of exchange; a person says, I have seen such an one write, and I belief that to be his hand-writing; and that is sufficient to launch it in evidence as primâ facie proof, leaving it to the other side to resist such proof, if they can.

Gentlemen, now we put this person in motion from Dover. Thomas Dennis is next called, who says, "I am a driver of a post-chaise in the service of Mr.

Wright, at the Ship, at Dover. Early on the morning of the 21st of February, I drove the chaise from thence to Canterbury to the Fountain Inn; I drove only one person, it was a man; it was too dark to see how he was dressed; I had the leaders; he gave me and the other lad a Napoleon a-piece." He could not see the person; and there is identity only by the sort of specie in which he deals. "I sold it for a one pound note. I know the lads at Canterbury, who took him after me, Broad, and Thomas Daly; I saw Broad and Daly set off. There is nothing extraordinary in persons travelling day or night into Canterbury. I cannot say whether it might be the 20th or 22d; persons do not often give us Napoleons for driving them, I never had one given me before." No immaterial circumstance to induce a recollection of this particular traveller, nor (connected with similar evidence from other witnesses) to establish his identity.

Edward Broad, a driver of a chaise at the Fountain at Canterbury, says, "I remember the last witness coming to our house with a fare, early in the morning in February, I do not remember the day of the month, nor the day of the week; it was one gentleman came from the Ship at Dover; I drove the leaders—I drove to the Rose at Sittingbourn; the chaise went forward with four horses—he did not get out. Michael Finnis and James Wakefield drove him from thence; I did not receive any money from him, the other boy received the money, I had a Napoleon for my share." Till the day-light breaks, we have nothing to identify him in the course of his conveyance, but the Napoleons.

Then Broad, upon his cross-examination, says, "I have long lived at the Fountain, and have known Thomas Dennis some years; I do not know that I ever drove a fare that he brought before; I might; there are a great many boys from that inn at Dover; I have driven a single gentleman before, and sometimes a chaise and four." But upon re-examination, he says, "I never before received a Napoleon for it."

Michael Finnis, the driver of a chaise at Sittingbourn, says, "I remember the last witness bringing a gentleman in a chaise and four to our house, I did not take particular account of the time, it was early in the morning, it might be between four and five o'clock; I did not take particular notice, for I had no watch with me—it was dark; I drove him to the Crown at Rochester, Mr. Wright's house; I cannot say what time it was when we got there, we were not above an hour and ten minutes in going. The Gentleman got out there, and gave me two Napoleons, one for myself, and one for my fellow-servant; I took no particular notice of him; he had a pepper and salt coat on, and a red coat under that, I perceived, and a cap." So that this man took no particular notice of his countenance, but speaks to his dress and his appearance, as the other witnesses do.

Mr. Wright, who keeps the Crown Inn at Rochester, who saw him in the house, speaks with much more particularity; he says, "I remember a chaise and four from Sittingbourn arriving at my house on the morning of the 21st of February, I remember that was the day; it was a tall person, rather thin than otherwise, who came in the chaise; he had a pepper and salt great coat, with a military scarlet coat under it; the upper coat was nearer the colour of that coat, than any thing I could state (*pointing to the coat on the table*); the scarlet military coat he had under that, was very much trimmed with gold lace down the front, as it appeared by candle light, and a military cap with broad gold lace round it; it appeared to me to be cloth or fur, it appeared to be nearly the colour of the great coat." The cap does not appear to have any resemblance to the great coat, but in all other respects his description seems to be right. "On the military coat, there was a star, and something suspended, either from the neck or the button, I do not know which, something which he told me was some honour of a military order of Russia;" it turned out to be a masonry order. He is shewn the star, and he says, "it had very much the appearance of that sort of thing. I suppose I was in conversation with him about ten minutes; it was about half past five when the chaise drove into the yard; during those ten minutes I was getting some chicken for him, in our bar parlour. I was called up by the post-boy of my brother at Dover, I went into the yard, and found a gentleman looking out at the front window of the chaise, and he said, he was very hungry, could he get any thing to eat? that he had ate nothing since he left Calais; I asked him, if he would have a sandwich, as I supposed he would not get out of the chaise; he said he would get out, and he did get out, and I took him into our bar parlour; when he got there I said, I am led to suppose, that you are the bearer of some very good news to this country;"—a very natural overture to conversation on the part of an innkeeper, and to extract a little intelligence from him; "he said, he was, that the business was all done—that the thing was settled; I asked him, if I might be allowed to ask him what was the nature of his dispatches? he said, he is dead; I said, who? he said, the tyrant Bonaparte, or words to that effect, I believe these were the exact words; I said, is that really true, Sir." Upon which this gentlemen seems to have been piqued at having his veracity questioned, and said, "if you doubt my word, you had better not ask me any more questions;" in answer to which, Wright, not being willing to have his curiosity unsatisfied, said, "I made an apology for doubting the veracity of his story, and asked him, what were the dispatches? he said, there had been a very general battle between the French and the whole of the allied powers, commanded by Schwartzenberg in person; that the French had been completely defeated, and Bonaparte had fled for safety; that he had been overtaken by the cossacks, at a village which I think was called Rushaw, six leagues from Paris; that the cossacks had there come up with him, and had literally torn him in pieces; that he had come from the field of battle from the emperor Alexander himself, and that he either was an aide-de-camp of the emperor, or of one of his principal generals." Now the account he gives, tallies almost in terms with the letter which had been sent off to Deal; so that there is another proof of the identity of this person, and a connexion of him with this letter sent to Admiral Foley. Then he adds, "He told me, that the allies were invited by the Parisians to Paris, and the Bourbons to the throne of France. That was pretty well all the conversation that passed; he ate very little, if he did any thing—he said he was very cold; I asked him, if he would take any brandy? he said, no, he would not, for he had some wine in the carriage;" it turned out that it was so. "He enquired what he had to pay? I told him, what he had had, had been so uncomfortable, I did not wish to take any thing for it; he did not accept of that, he threw a Napoleon on the table, and desired me to take that for what he had himself taken, and wished me to give the servants something out of it, he meant the whole of the servants, for when he got into the chaise, the ostler asked for something; and he told him, that he had left something with his master, out of which he might be paid. He went away in the same chaise that brought him, with four horses. James Overy and Thomas Todd, were the persons who drove him." Mr. Wright had proceeded thus far, and then he looked round the court, and fixing upon De Berenger, said, "I believe that is the person; I have no doubt—it is certainly the gentleman; I had never seen him before, or since." This undoubted identification of person, is almost peculiar to this case; I never saw a case in which so many persons turned into the court at large, recollected a man at once, and with so much certainty.

Upon his cross-examination, he says, "I never saw the gentlemen before nor since till to-day; he wore a large cockade, very dirty, as if it had been worn a long time;" then he produced the Napoleon; and he says, "upon looking at him, I am sure he is the same person."

James Overy, who was the postillion, says, "I took up a person at my master's house at Rochester, on a Monday; I do not remember the day of the month. I drove him to Dartford, to the Granby; he had on a grey mixture coat; a red coat like an aid-de-camp, adorned with a star, very full indeed, something about his neck hanging down, and a cap, and a bit of white ribbon about the cap, such as officers wear, with a gold lace band round it. When I came to Dartford, it was ten minutes before seven; it was day-light two miles before we came to Dartford. I am not sure I should know the person again; he gave me two Napoleons, and he paid me five £.1. notes, and a shilling for mine and the Dartford horses, and the turnpikes; he gave us a Napoleon a-piece. Thomas Shilling and Broad took him from Dartford."

On cross-examination, he says, "the cap was such a cap as officers wear in a morning, slouched down, I think the top of the cap a little turned down; I did not observe the colour."

William Tozer, the next witness, says, "I keep the Crown and Anchor at Dartford; I remember Jem Overy bringing a fare to a house in our town on a Monday about the 21st of February, and the person I took notice of was sitting in the chaise. I made my obedience to the gentleman in the chaise, hoping that he had brought us good news; he said he had, and that it was all over; that the allies had actually entered Paris; that Bonaparte was dead, destroyed by the cossacks, and literally torn to pieces." Here again is the same account in effect which is contained in the letter to Deal, given by word of mouth, "and that we might expect a speedy peace. During the conversation, I saw him give Overy two gold pieces, which afterwards proved to be French pieces; I had them in my hand. I saw enough of the person in the chaise, to be positive I should know him if I saw him again." This was the witness, who looking round, did not find the Defendant; to be sure, the Counsel might have asked him whether that was the person; but from delicacy that was not done, which was certainly an unnecessary delicacy upon such a subject.

Thomas Shilling, the chaise-driver from Dartford, says, "I remember taking up a gentleman who came in a chaise and four to Dartford, I believe it was on the 21st of February, it was on a Monday. I had the wheel-horses. On our road to London, he discoursed with me a good deal; the waiter at Dartford, at the Granby, first spoke to him, asking him whether he brought any good news; the gentleman said, yes, it was all over; Bonaparte was torn in a thousand pieces; the cossacks fought for a share of him all the same as if they had been fighting for sharing out gold; and the allies were in Paris. We were ordered to go on; we had gone to Bexley before the gentleman spoke; the gentleman then told me not to hurry my horses, for his business was not so particular now, since the telegraph could not work. I told him, I thought the telegraphs could not work, for I knew almost every telegraph between Deal and London. He then said, "postboy, do not takes any notice of the news as you go along;" I told him I would not, unless he wished me to do so; he said, I might tell any of my friends as I returned, for he durst to say they would be glad to hear it; he said he had sent a letter to the Port Admiral at Deal, for he was obliged to do so;" therefore you have him, unless this be a premeditated falsehood in the evidence of this man, Shilling, authenticating the fact of the letter from Dover; "he said that he had walked two miles when he came ashore at Dover, before he got to the Ship Inn; that the Frenchmen were afraid of coming any nigher to Dover, for fear of being stopped." Where he got into Dover, or how, we do not hear; of the points of the outward voyage we know nothing; of the homeward we have a pretty good account of all the places where he touched, &c. "then we drove on till we came to Shooters Hill; when I got there, my fellow-servant and I alighted, and the gentleman gave us part of a bottle of wine; he said we might drink, because he was afraid the bottle would break; he gave us some round cakes also. I chucked the bottle away, and handed the glass again into the chaise; he told me that I might have it; he then said, "postboy, you have had a great deal of snow;" I said, "we have;" he said, "here is a delightful morning, postboy; I have not seen old England a long while before;" then he asked me which was the nearest coach stand; I told him at the Bricklayers Arms; he told me that would not do, it was too public, he was afraid somebody would cast some reflections, and he should not like it." It was bringing him very nearly within the vicinity of the King's Bench, where it should seem his countenance was better known than he liked it to be. "I told him I did not think anybody would do that, they would be too glad to hear of the news; he asked if there was not a hackney-coach stand in Lambeth; I said "yes," he said "drive me there.""

Now it has been observed he points his direction towards Lambeth, and the other express, it seems, that went through the city, which has been called the Northfleet expedition, is ordered not to go Lambeth, but to Lambeth Marsh. The learned Counsel has remarked, that they are not ordered to the same point at first, and that it would have been a strong confirmatory point, if they had been so; but there is to a great degree an identity of direction, an identity of object, and something like an identity of disguise in military uniform; "he said, drive me there, postboy, for your chaise will go faster than a hackney-coach will. I drove him to the Three Stags in the Lambeth road; there was no hackney-coach there. I ordered my fellow-servant to stop, and looked back, and told the gentleman there was no coach there; but that there was a coach stand at the Marsh Gate." So that the Marsh Gate arose incidentally, and was not his original plan; "and if he liked to get in there, I dared say nobody would take any notice of him; I think he pulled up the side blind, that had been down before all the way; when I got there, I pulled up along side to a hackney-coach; I called the coachman, and the waterman opened the coach door, and I opened the chaise door; the gentleman stepped out of the chaise into the coach without going on the ground;" the question which produced this answer was put with a view to something adverted to, as published upon the subject, in which some evidence was supposed capable of being opposed to the story of the driver, in this particular, who, however, relates it plainly and naturally, and is confirmed by the waterman, who was there at the time; "he then gave me two Napoleons; he did not say one was for my fellow-servant, and the other for myself, but I concluded that it was so; I have got them here," and he produces them; so that it does not appear that he has distributed this gentleman's bounty, but he is still a trustee for his fellow-servant. "I did not," he says, "hear him tell the coachman where to drive to. The name of the coachman is Crane. I know the person of the waterman very well. The gentleman was dressed with a dark fur round cap, and with white lace, and some gold round it; whether it was gold or silver I cannot say; he had a red coat on underneath his outer coat; I think his outer coat was a kind of a brown coat, but I will not swear to that; I saw a red coat underneath it, down as far as the waist; I did not see the skirts of it; I think it was turned up with yellow, but I should not like to swear that; it had some sort of a star upon it. I think upon his outer coat there was a kind of white fur; but I should not like to swear to that. I should know him in a moment. I have seen him and knew him again; that is the gentleman (*pointing to him*); I have no doubt. I saw him once before in King-street, Westminster, in a room; I knew him then the moment I saw him; I never had the least doubt about him; the moment I saw him I knew him."

Upon his cross-examination, he says, "I was not told this morning in what part of the court he sat; I looked round the court when I came in, and saw him immediately; I never saw him before February." He is asked about a reward that was offered by the Stock Exchange, he says, "I heard of it the day it was printed, two or three days after this transaction happened. I remember a club at Dartford, called the hat club; I was there;" and then there is some foolish story about his laying a wager there; but as there is no evidence brought to impeach his testimony upon the grounds to which the cross-examination went, it is unnecessary to pursue that part of the examination further; he says "Lambeth Marsh is not far from the Asylum. I went there for the purpose of getting a coach; *that he says* (pointing to Bartholomew) *is the waterman.*"

Then William Bartholomew the waterman is called; he says "I am a waterman attending the stand of coaches at the Marsh Gate; I know Shilling by seeing him come up with post chaises; he is a Dartford chaise-boy. I remember his coming with a chaise on the 21st of February; there were four horses, and there was a gentleman in it; it was between nine and half past nine in the morning; there was only one coach on the stand; one Crane drove the coach; I saw the gentleman get out of the chaise into the coach, he stepped out of the one into the other; I opened the door, and let down the step for him; he had a brown cap on, a dark drab military great coat, and a scarlet coat under it; I only took notice of the lace under it. The gentleman ordered the coach to drive up to Grosvenor-square; I do not remember that he told me the street in Grosvenor-square. I really think that is the gentleman, it is like him; dress makes such an alteration, that I cannot with certainty say."

Then Mr. Richard Barwick says, "I am a clerk to Messrs. Paxtons and Co. bankers, in Pall Mall. I remember passing by Marsh Gate on the morning of Monday the 21st of February. I observed a post-chaise with four horses, it had galloped at a great rate; the horses were exceedingly hot, and I saw a man getting into a hackney coach; I followed it, and saw it as far as the Little Theatre in the Haymarket; I wanted to know what the news was." Being a banker's clerk, it was natural he should wish to know what the public news was. "I observed the coach passed the public offices in the way." It appears, that he was a little surprized at this person not stopping to communicate his news at those offices. Whether he suspected him or not, he does not say; but observing that he stopped at none, and it being time for him to go to the banker's shop, he did not think it worth while to pursue him any further. This was about nine o'clock, as he supposes, that he left him in the Haymarket. Then he says, the gentleman had a cap on with a gold band, such as German cavalry use at evening parade; this appears to me something like it.

Then William Crane, the coachman, says, "I remember on Monday morning the 21st of February, taking up a fare at Marsh Gate from a post-chaise and four from Dartford. I was directed to drive to Grosvenor-square; I drove into Grosvenor-square; the gentleman then put down the front glass, and told me to drive to N° 13, Green-street; the gentleman got out there, and asked for a colonel or a captain somebody; I did not hear the name, and they said he was gone to breakfast in Cumberland-street; the gentleman asked if he could write a note; he then went into the parlour; the gentleman gave me 4*s.*; I asked him for another." Hearing that Napoleons had been distributed to drivers, he thought that a hackney-coachman might ask for a little more of his bounty than he at first received. "He took a portmanteau that he had, and a sword, went in and came out again, and gave me another shilling. The portmanteau was a small black leather one; I saw that gentleman in King-street, Westminster, at the messenger's house. I think this is the gentleman here; when I saw him in King-street, as I came down stairs, he looked very hard at me; I knew him then, though he had altered himself a great deal in his dress."

Upon his cross examination, he says, "I went to Mr. Wood's, the messenger of the Alien Office, for the purpose of seeing him; I walked down stairs, and met the gentleman coming up stairs, and I thought he was something like the gentleman I had carried; I do not know every person I carry in my hackney-coach; this person, when I got to Green-street, I saw had a red coat underneath; the waterman opened the coach-door for him to get in." So that he was within view of the waterman. "He had on a brown grey great coat, with brown fur cap."

Now, gentlemen, he is brought to the house of Lord Cochrane; further evidence arises afterwards upon the subject of his being there.

We will at present follow the dress to its conclusion. George Odell, a fisherman, says, "In the month of March, just above Old Swan stairs, off against the Iron Wharfs, when I was dredging for coals I picked up a bundle, which was tied up with either a piece of chimney line or window line, in the cover of a chair bottom; there were two slips of a coat, embroidery, a star, and a piece of silver, with two figures upon it; it had been sunk with three pieces of lead and some bits of coal; I gave that which I found to Mr. Wade, the secretary of the Stock Exchange; it was picked up on the Wednesday, and carried there on the Saturday. I picked this up on the 24th of March." You have before had the animal hunted home, and now you have his skin, found and produced as it was taken out of the river, cut to pieces; the sinking it could have been with no other view than that of suppressing this piece of evidence, and preventing the discovery which it might otherwise occasion; this makes it the more material to attend to the stripping off the clothes which took place in Lord Cochrane's house. When he pulled off his great coat there, what must he have displayed to his Lordships eyes, if present at the time? Did he display the uniform of the rifle corps? The uniform of the rifle corps is of a bottle-green colour, made to resemble the colour of trees, that those who wear it may hide themselves in woods, and escape discovery there; that is, I presume, the reason of their wearing that species of uniform, and as to the idea suggested in Lord Cochrane's affidavit, that his exhibiting himself in that uniform would be deemed disrespectful to Lord Yarmouth. Lord Yarmouth has told us, that on the contrary he should have thought it a matter of respect to him, and proper as his officer, to have appeared before him in that very dress.

The account that is given of this man's pulling off his dress, as contained in the affidavit of Lord Cochrane, is highly deserving of your attention. It is a rule of law, when evidence is given of what a party has said or sworn, all of it is evidence (subject to your consideration, however, as to its truth) coming as it does, in one entire form before you; but you may still judge to what parts of this whole you can give your credit; and also, whether that part, which appears to confirm and fix the charge, does not outweigh that which contains the exculpation. Now I will state to you, what is Lord Cochrane's affidavit; it may as well come in now in this period, as in the later period in the cause; it was produced in the pamphlet published by Mr. Butt, and is prefaced by Lord Cochrane thus, "Having obtained leave of absence to come to town, in consequence of scandalous paragraphs in the public papers, and in consequence of having learnt that hand bills had been affixed in the streets, in which I have since seen it is asserted, that a person came to my house at No. 13, Green Street, on the 21st day of February, in open day, and in the dress in which he had committed a fraud; I feel it due to myself to make the following deposition, that the public may know the truth relative to the only person seen by me in military uniform at my house on that day." Now it is material to observe, this affidavit first introduced the name of De Berenger in any public document; whether it was known privately at any earlier period we are not informed, the date of it is the 11th of March. The Davidsons have informed you, that the day he finally disappeared was the 27th of February, (Mr. Cochrane Johnstone having called and left a letter, for what purpose we know not, on the 26th,) he appears to have very soon got to Sunderland, and might, on the 11th of March, the date of this affidavit, be reasonably supposed to have been out of the kingdom.

It is in evidence, that when De Berenger was taken, there was found in his writing-desk part of the produce of the exchange at the bank of four £.100 notes, two of the bank notes of £.200 being changed first into two £.100 notes, and then into ones; the whole are identified by the clerks of the bank; sixty-seven the produce of one £.100; forty-nine identified as the produce of another, and seven the produce also of one of those; there are traced to him likewise a £.50 and a £.40; the £.50, traced by the evidence of Smith to-day, the evidence upon that subject being deficient yesterday, I stopped them short, because I thought that the entry of the mere initials W. S. and £.50, did not afford distinct and sufficient proof that the person meant by those initials was William Smith, and that the £.50 was a sum which had passed between Wm. Smith, Mr. De Berenger's servant, and him, and that the evidence was deficient in that respect. The principal part of these are the produce of the draft of £.470, and a fraction, which was changed as will appear in the evidence, when that part of it is stated to you. Originally the £.470 draft had been laid down before and paid to Lord Cochrane; it had afterwards got into the hands of Mr. Cochrane Johnstone and of Mr. Butt, for there appeared to be such a communication between the parties, that you cannot say from whom ultimately it proceeded, but it had been in some sort in the hands of all, and the produce of this check, originally paid to Lord Cochrane, is found in the desk of this man.

I have been led aside by reading the affidavit to these observations on the dates. To return, the affidavit was, as I have already stated, sworn March 11th 1814, by which time it might well be supposed that De Berenger, if he made proper speed, had got out of the kingdom. The affidavit proceeds thus; "I, Sir Thomas Cochrane, commonly called Lord Cochrane, having been appointed by the Lords Commissioners of the Admiralty to active service, (at the request, I believe, of Sir Alexander Cochrane) when I had no expectation of being called on, I obtained leave of absence to settle my private affairs, previous to quitting this country, and chiefly with a view to lodge a specification to a patent," there is no doubt that patent exists, and that there is a true transaction as to the patent; but whether it be introduced here as a colour, and to draw off your attention from other matters is another point. "That in pursuance of my daily practice of superintending work that was executing for me, and knowing that my uncle, Mr. Cochrane Johnstone, went to the city every morning in a coach, I do swear, on the morning of the 21st of February, (which day was impressed on my mind by circumstances which afterwards occurred) I breakfasted with him at his residence in Cumberland Street, about half past eight o'clock, and I was put down by him (and Mr. Butt was in the coach) on Snowhill, about ten o'clock," therefore these three gentlemen who had so much to do on that day, were brought together, and had an opportunity of communicating together at least at this time. They go on to the city together, after having, it may be supposed had so much of communication together as was necessary for the current business of the day, whatever that business was. "I had been about three quarters of an hour at Mr. King's manufactory, at No. 1, Cock Lane, when I received a few lines on a small bit of paper, requesting me to come immediately to my house, the name affixed, from being Written close to the bottom, I could not read;" that was certainly a very pointed observation which was lately addressed to you, by the learned counsel for the prosecution, that the name which he says he could not read, would not in all probability have been written at the bottom, for he had finished the note once, and when it was sent back to him there was space enough still left for him to write something more; for the servant says, he added something more afterwards, therefore it was not from its being crowded at the bottom, unless it be, that he had not signed any name till quite the last, and after he had written the addition which Lord Cochrane mentions, "the servant told me, it was from an army officer, and concluding that he might be an officer from Spain, and that some accident had befallen to my brother, I hastened back, and I found Captain De Berenger." Now certainly, his anxiety about his brother, if true, was a very good motive for his returning, but I addressed some questions to the witness on this subject; I thought it very likely if that was the motive which induced Lord Cochrane to return, that he should have disclosed that motive to the person who brought the note, especially as he was a servant who had been seventeen years in the family; nothing could be more natural than to say, "Thomas, I hope there is no bad news from my brother, your old master;" no such thing passes, but—"Well, Thomas, I will return," is all that he says to him; he does not mention any thing about any apprehension as to his brother. His brother, as appears by the returns which have come home, had been wounded, or was upon the sick list; but it does not appear that he had then actually received any communication upon that subject; and which, if he had received any such, might have been expected to be proved, and might easily have been so. That his brother was in fact upon the sick list appears, but not that he then knew him to be so; nor did he intimate to the servant that came, one word of apprehension about his brother, or any mention of his health or of him, but came back immediately on receiving this note. Now, with the acquaintance he had with De Berenger, no doubt such application had been made to get him appointed as is proved; and he must have been, one would suppose, familiar with his hand-writing; and *if so*, he could have had no doubt who was the person from whom he received this note, and whom he was to meet when he should get home; but he says, "I found Captain De Berenger, who, in great seeming uneasiness, made many apologies for the freedom he had used, which nothing but the distressed state of his mind, arising from difficulties, could have induced him to do; all his prospects, he said, had failed, and his last hope had vanished of obtaining an appointment in America. He was unpleasantly circumstanced on account of a sum which he could not pay; and if he could, that others would fall upon him for full £.8,000. He had no hope of benefitting his creditors in his present situation, or of assisting himself. That if I would take him with me, he would immediately go on board and exercise the sharp-shooters (which plan I knew Sir Alexander Cochrane had approved of;)" and there is no doubt that Sir Alexander Cochrane had, on some application of Mr. Cochrane Johnstone or Lord Cochrane, applied for him, but that for reasons not communicated to us, such application had not been successful, and it had not been thought fit to appoint him.

Then he says, "That he had left his lodgings, and prepared himself in the best way his means allowed. He had brought the sword with him which had been his father's; and to that and to Sir Alexander, he would trust for obtaining an honourable appointment. I felt very uneasy at the distress he was in, and knowing him to be a man of great talent and science, I told him I would do every thing in my power to relieve him; but as to his going immediately to the Tonnant, with any comfort to himself, it was quite impossible; my cabin was without furniture; I had not even a servant on board. He said he would willingly mess anywhere; I told him that the ward-room was already crowded; and besides, I could not with propriety take him, he being a foreigner, without leave of the Admiralty. He seemed greatly hurt at this, and recalled to my recollection certificates which he had formerly shewn me from persons in official situations; Lord Yarmouth, General Jenkinson and Mr. Reeves, I think, were amongst the number; I recommended him to use his endeavour to get them or any other friends to exert their influence, for I had none; adding, that when the Tonnant went to Portsmouth, I should be happy to receive him; and I knew from Sir Alexander Cochrane, that he would be pleased if he accomplished that object; Captain Berenger said, that not anticipating," now this is very material, "any objection on my part, from the conversation he had formerly had with me; he had come away with intention to go on board and make himself useful in his military capacity; he could not go to Lord Yarmouth, or to any other *of his friends in this dress*;" what is the dress that Lord Cochrane represents as then belonging to him? a green dress? had he a green dress? he must have had that dress with him whatever it was in which he had come in the coach; he says that would excite suspicion; why, if he had really a green uniform, that would not have excited observation or suspicion; it was the very uniform he ought to have worn; but if it was that in which he had got out of the coach, and it does not appear that he had any means of shifting himself; if he had on an aid-de-camp's uniform with a star, and so presented himself to Lord Cochrane, how could Lord Cochrane reconcile it to the duties he owed to society, and to Government, and to his character as a gentleman and an officer, to give him the means of exchanging it; it must be put on for some dishonest purpose; this red coat and star, and all this equipment, must have appeared most extraordinary, and must have struck Lord Cochrane most forcibly, if he was not aware of the purpose for which it was used; "that he could not go to Lord Yarmouth, or to any other of his friends in this dress, or return to his lodgings, where it would excite suspicion (he was at that time in the Rules of the King's Bench); but that if I refused to let him join the ship now, he would do so at Portsmouth; under present circumstances, however, he must use a great liberty, and request the favour of me to lend him a hat to wear instead of his military cap. I gave him one which was in a back room, with some things that had not been packed up; and having tried it on, *his uniform appeared under his great coat*; I therefore offered him a black coat that was laying on a chair, and which I did not intend to take with me. He put his uniform *in a towel*, and shortly afterwards went away." If he put that uniform in a towel, he must have pulled it off his back, for it was on his back before, and then Lord Cochrane, one would think, must have seen him do it; what business had this man with a red aid-de-camp's uniform? he had no business to wear any such garb, he was almost as much out of his proper character, as I should be if I appeared habited in the particular dress and professional habits of an officer or a clergyman; but it does not rest there, for he himself lends to this person the immediate means of his concealment, he lets him have a hat instead of his *laced cap*; and what had such a cap to do with a sharpshooter's uniform? upon seeing him appear habited as all the witnesses represent him to have been in his way from Dover to Green-street, Grosvenor-square, would not any one who had known him before have immediately exclaimed, where have you been, and what mischief have you been doing in this masquerade dress. It is for you, gentlemen, to say whether it is possible he should not know, that a man coming so disguised and so habited if he appeared before him so habited, came upon some dishonest errand, and whether it is to be conceived a person should so present himself to a person who did not know what that dishonest errand was, and that it was the very dishonest errand upon which he had been so recently engaged, and which he is found to be executing in the spreading of false intelligence, for the purpose of elevating the funds, if he actually appeared to Lord Cochrane stripped of his great coat, and with that red coat and aid-de-camp's uniform, star and order, which have been represented to you, he appeared before him rather in the habit of a mountebank than in his proper uniform of a sharpshooter.

He says, "he went away in the hackney coach I came in, which I had forgotten to discharge in the haste I was in. The above conversation is the substance of all that passed with Captain De Berenger, which, from the circumstances attending it, was strongly impressed upon my mind; I most positively swear that I never saw any person at my house resembling the description, and in the dress stated in the printed advertisement;" which I suppose will be read, "of the members of the Stock Exchange; I further aver, that I had no concern directly or indirectly in the late imposition, and that the above is all that I know relative to any person who came to my house in uniform, on the 21st day of February before alluded to, Captain De Berenger wore a grey coat, a green uniform, and a military cap;" now did he wear a green uniform? They are at issue upon the dress then worn by him; if he had not this dress on, what other had he? And if he had the green one on, what true or probable reason existed for the change of that? the unfitness of appearing in it before his commanding officer, Lord Yarmouth, is negatived by Lord Yarmouth himself; supposing him to have appeared in any disguise, it is the conduct of an accomplice, to assist him in getting rid of his disguise, to let a man pull off at his house, the dress in which (if all these witnesses do not tell you falsely) he had been committing this offence, and which had been worn down to the moment of his entering the house, namely, the star, a red coat and appendant order of masonry, seems wholly inconsistent with the conduct of an innocent and honest man, for if he appeared in such an habit, he must have appeared to any rational person, fully blazoned in the costume of that or of some other crime, which was to be effected under an assumed dress, and by means of fraud and imposition; this circumstance is therefore very important for your consideration; the judgment to be formed upon it must rest with you, and you will no doubt consider, whether supposing him to have appeared before Lord Cochrane, dressed as the witnesses represent him to have antecedently been, the circumstance of his so appearing in a dress proper for the commission of such a fraud, as appears to have been committed on that day, by attracting a false belief of the person being a messenger bringing great public news, coupled with the fact of his afterwards walking off with that dress in a bundle, instead of having that dress upon his back, and also with the evidence given in order to prove a connexion with the notes afterwards found in De Berenger's desk, you are not satisfied that he was privy to and assisted in the scheme of effecting a deception upon the public.

Gentlemen, I have taken this subject a little out of its place in adverting to it here. To return—

Mr. Lavie says, "I received the parcel, *(that produced by Odell)*, in the Stock Exchange room, in which Mr. Baily and Mr. Wade were present."

Mr. Wade says, "I am Secretary to the Stock Exchange, in company with other gentlemen, I received from Odell a bundle, said to be found in the river, which was given to Mr. Lavie; the star was then in two pieces, and was afterwards sewn together, for the purpose of being exhibited."

Then Solomons, who originally sold the dress, is called; he says, "I am a military accoutrement-maker; we have a shop at Charing Cross, and another at New Street, Covent Garden. On Saturday the 19th of February," the very day before this is put into execution, with the intervention of the Sunday; "a military dress was purchased at my house; a military great coat and foraging cap made of dark fur, with a pale gold border; I have since had a cap and a coat made exactly resembling them, as nearly as I could possibly recollect." He had them made I suppose in order to exhibit them. "The person purchased at our house in New Street, something which came to Charing Cross shop, as being ordered at New Street, and the person came to Charing Cross and took it away; there was a military great coat, a military staff coat, such as persons on the staff wear, the uniform of an aid-de-camp. I have examined the fragments, the star and the badge, I believe those to be the same, we had the very fellow-star to that; except those two, I do not know that I ever saw any star like them, the badge I did not take much notice of;" that is the silver masonry ornament, "I have examined these fragments, and they appear to be part of the same materials, the same description of embroidery, the same description of coat; I had a conversation with respect to the great coat, and also the cap; he observed that they were wanted for a person who was to *perform the character of a foreign officer*, they were to be sent into the country that evening, he took them away with him in a coach, he had a small portmanteau with him;" you remember there is a leather portmanteau spoken of; "he did not beat me down in the prices, or make any observations about money, but merely paid for them, I was conversing with him for a short time, I have been since introduced to a person at the Parliament-street coffee house; I cannot undertake to say it was the person, in point of appearance he resembles him, except that the person I served had whiskers." Now if you recollect the history of the whiskers, it is established that he had worn whiskers, though the woman who endeavoured to make us believe that he slept at home on the Sunday night, said she had not so much as observed (though she had been his servant two years and a half) whether he had any whiskers. It appears to me that is a circumstance in the countenance of a person which one would very much observe; he says, "the person I saw in Parliament-street had not whiskers;" he then looked at Mr. De Berenger, and said, "this is the person I was introduced to at the coffee house in Parliament-street; I really cannot undertake to swear that he is the person, the gentleman that represented himself to be Mr. Wilson, was dressed in a different manner, he had black whiskers, and from that circumstance I could not possibly undertake to swear it was the same person, it resembles the person, except that the person I served had whiskers, I cannot say that I believe it is the person, or that it is not."

Mrs. Abigail Davidson, the woman with whom Mr. De Berenger lodged, is then called; she says, "In the month of February last I resided in the Asylum

Buildings, near to the Asylum; the house is within the Rules of the King's Bench. Mr. De Berenger lodged with me; he finally quitted my house on the 27th of February, on a Sunday. I do not remember where he was on the Sunday before that, I did not see him on the morning of that Sunday; I cannot say whether he slept at home that night, we never attended to the door; I usually heard him in the morning, I did not hear him as usual on the morning of the 21st; I used to hear the bell ring for the servant, more than once; he occupied the whole of the upper part of the house, I and my husband had the two parlours. I heard him also occasionally playing the violin and trumpet, and he used to walk about; he then wore whiskers. I generally heard his bell; I did not see him come home on the Monday; I saw him in the evening, about half past five; I had heard him in the afternoon. He quitted my house on the Sunday after; I remember a gentleman calling on the Saturday night, the day before he quitted, with a letter; I have since seen that gentleman again, I saw him at the Temple; Mr. Lavie was then present. I cannot say that I positively knew the gentleman, but I think it was the same that I had seen deliver the letter on the 26th of February. Mr. De Berenger had two servants of the name of William Smith, and his wife; when he dined at home, his servants attended him; on Sunday the 20th, I cannot say whether he dined at home; his usual dinner hour was about four. I think his servants went out about two or half past on that Sunday." If you remember, Smith and his wife swear to De Berenger's going out about four on that Sunday, and Smith says, that he and his wife went out soon after; this woman swears, that they went out at two or half past. "There was a private place where the key always hung, for the accommodation of Mr. De Berenger, and as the key was always under the care of Smith, I did not see where the key was put that evening."

On her cross-examination she is asked, what Sunday it was that these servants went out to dinner at two or half past? she says, "On Sunday the 20th, about eleven o'clock, I heard my husband observe, De Berenger was gone out; I cannot say whether he slept from his bed on Sunday the 20th; I sleep in the back parlour. I have heard him trumpet by nine o'clock, not by seven. I had no call to look after him on any morning."

Upon her re-examination she says, "My husband observed to me, our lodger is gone out with a new great coat on." So that he is, for the first time, observed by them in that great coat on that Sunday.

Mr. Lavie says, the person Mrs. Davidson saw at the Temple getting out of the hackney coach, was Mr. Cochrane Johnstone, that she said she believed that the person who was striking the Jury, and who was Mr. Cochrane Johnstone, was the person who brought the letter on the Saturday.

Mrs. Davidson, on being called again, and further cross-examined, says, Mr. Lavie desired me to attend to see a gentleman; I was told Mr. Cochrane Johnstone was to be there; I will not swear that the person who left the letter was Mr. Johnstone. I had a conversation about the person with Smith, Mr. De Berenger's servant.

Then Mr. Launcelot Davidson, the husband of the last witness, is called; he says, "Mr. De Berenger lodged in my house; he quitted my house finally on Sunday the 27th of February. The Sunday before that, I saw him go out before eleven (that was on Sunday the 20th); I had been out before; I was waiting to hear the Asylum clock strike eleven; I saw him go out, I had seen him come in ten minutes before; when he came in, he had a plaid cloak on, which he had worn the winter; when he went out, he had a great coat of that colour (pointing to the grey coat produced by Solomon); as he went, I observed to my wife, there goes our lodger, he has a new great coat on; he did not come home again at all during that day, that I saw or heard; I did not see or hear him the next morning before nine; I go out at nine. I generally used to hear him before that time walking about, or ringing for his servant. I made an observation upon his servants going out on the Sunday at two; I do not think they were at home *at four o'clock*, which was Mr. De Berenger's usual dinner hour; the man servant always attended him when he dined, and the woman dressed his dinner; he did not dine at home on that Sunday. A conversation took place with the Smiths afterwards, respecting that Sunday night." Now to be sure it is a most obvious thing, that if he had been in town at that time, nothing could be so easy as to have proved where he dined; and probably those who might have been called to prove that fact, would have been persons of a better description than Donithorne, Tragear, and the other persons called, to give an account of him on that day.

On cross-examination he says, "I had nothing to do with his domestic life. He made a loud rap at the door, and had few visitors. I am a broker, and clerk of a broker, and out a considerable part of the day."

Gentlemen, the next evidence applies to the Northfleet part of the transaction.

Mr. Vinn says, (and to be sure it is an odd story he tells); "in consequence of a note left at my house, dated the 14th of February last, I went to the Carolina coffee-house on the 15th, where I met Mr. M'Rae, in company with an elderly gentleman; he desired me to sit down. I had known M'Rae before for some years, he was standing near the door, and in about seven or ten minutes, he came and joined me; he told me he had known me a long time, and that he thought he had now an opportunity of making my fortune; that he knew from the knowledge I had of languages, I should have an opportunity of benefiting others and myself; I asked him what the object was; he said not to travel abroad, but probably at home, and that almost immediately; that it was a scheme that he had in contemplation, to be employed by men of affluence and consequence, and that no man was more competent than myself; he said there was no moral turpitude in the business, but that it was practised daily by men of the first consequence." What M'Rae says, is, you will observe, evidence criminally only as against himself; because what he *confesses*, is not evidence to affect others. What he *does*, may affect others as parties to the conspiracy; but what he *says* cannot affect others; "that it was only biting the biters, or in other words, a hoax upon the Stock Exchange; and that by going down to Dartford, Folkestone or Dover, I should receive instructions." So that in his communications, Dover is mixed with Dartford, as the probable destination to which the parties to this business might be sent; "that it was necessary to have for himself and me, two dresses of French officers;" so that dresses similar to that in which the Dover plan was executed, were in his contemplation. "I there stopped him, and asked him whether he really meant to be employed in this transaction; to which he replied, certainly; and that I should be in the first place remunerated, and ultimately have a fortune made me: I replied with indignation, that I would as soon be concerned in a highway robbery; that I thought he had known me better; I expressed myself rather loudly, as offended at it; he endeavoured to hush me, saying, hush! that we might be overheard. He took me up Cornhill, where I left him; I told him if he would go with me to another coffee-house, I would introduce him to a person who, though I would not undertake the business, might do it. I took him there; it was the Jamaica coffee-house; there was a young man there, to whom I was about to introduce him; but he turned round suddenly, and I did not: upon M'Rae returning, he asked me whether I would not give him in writing some French sentences, sentences such as Vive le Roi, Vive les Bourbons, Vive Louis Dix huit; I gave him those terms in writing;" so that he might play off those terms, to assist in the prosecution of this business. A letter is then shewn to the witness; he says "this is the letter I received from M'Rae; it is his hand writing." The letter is in these terms, "Mr. Vinn, Please to meet me at the Carolina coffee-house, about eleven to-morrow, upon very particular business, yours," so and so.

On his cross-examination, he says, "I am an accountant; I have been acquainted with M'Rae five years and a half. I never bought and sold as a broker; I had been in business myself; there was no person to hear the conversation I have stated. I communicated this at the Stock Exchange to Mr. Rothery, and mentioned it publickly on the 15th, and that I had refused it; my object was not to get another person really to undertake the business, but to furnish myself with a confirmatory witness."

Sarah Alexander is called, and she proves very material circumstances as to the preparation for this North-fleet expedition, to take place at the same period of time as that from Dover. She says, "I live at Fetter-lane; I have lived there ever since last September. I know Mr. M'Rae; he lodged on the same floor that I did; he is a married man; his wife lived with him; on Saturday the 19th of February, he came to my room." The other military uniform, you will recollect, was purchased on this very same day for the Dover scheme: "He brought a small parcel, and gave it to his wife; he said it was of value, and bade her take care of it. He went out on Sunday the 20th; he went out between ten and eleven, and returned before twelve, and brought with him two coats and two opera hats; they were inclosed in a bundle; I saw the coats; they were very dark blue, done with braiding; they were officers coats; the flowers were of worsted embroidery; they were flat hats; one coat was lined with white silk; one coat and one hat was better than the other; the one had a brass plate and gold tassel; he put them on, and walked about, and asked whether he did not look like an officer." So that he was representing and playing this character before-hand: "He went out again, and came home before one, and brought some ribbon with him; he wanted two cockades to be made round; he applied to his wife; his wife asked what he was going to do with them; he said, to deceive the flats." So that he not only exhibits the materials by which he was to effect the fraud, but avows the object, "to deceive the *flats*;" that is, I suppose, *credulous persons*. "He put the cockades into his pocket, and the hats and coats in a bundle, and went out, saying he must be at Billingsgate, to start at two by the Gravesend hoy. The next day, I met him a quarter before two in Cursitor-street; he was dressed the same as he went out, in his own clothes; he had apparently the same bundle; he brought home one coat and one hat; the best coat and hat were in the bundle; he said he had slept at North-fleet, but he had the appearance of not having been a-bed at all; he brought home the cockades in his pocket; he appeared very tired: His wife unripped the cockades, and took the white lining out of the coat, and carried it to the dyers to be dyed black." Then she says, "From December to February we lodged together; we kept but one fire, and lived a good deal together; he was in a state of great indigence, and never had any money except a shilling or an eighteen-penny piece now and then; after the North-fleet expedition, he had a £.10 and a £.1 note, and the day before he finally left his lodgings, he had three £.2 notes; he finally left his lodgings on the 2d or 3d of March. On Sunday the 27th of February, he bought a new coat and a new hat; on Monday the 28th, he said he was to have £.50 for what he had done; he wished when he went away finally, for nobody to know where he was going; and I wished not to know." On the 2d or 3d of March this gentleman disappears as the other De Berenger had done on the 27th; such were the nearly contemporaneous and similar actings of these parties. Both of them on Saturday are making preparations for a scheme which is to operate on London at the same period; you will consider whether there was not a communion of purpose in these persons, whether they did not conspire to produce a common end, though they might not particularly know how the others were co-operating with them at that time; in short, whether there might not be one master workman, who played the puppets in both directions. Then you have the course of the Northfleet people.

Philip Foxall, (the next witness), says, "I keep the Rose Inn at Dartford;" a letter was shewn to him, he says, "I received that letter from Mr. Sandom, I knew him by his frequently having chaises from my house." That note is one in pencil, ordering a chaise, "please to send me over immediately, a chaise and pair to bring back to Dartford, and have four good horses ready to go on to London with all expedition." "I sent a chaise over to Northfleet, and had horses ready, as the letter advised me; the chaise on its return drove furiously into my yard, with Mr. Sandom and two gentlemen with white cockades, and large flat hats, quite plain, except white ribbon or paper, and blue clothes, I cannot say whether they were plain. I forwarded them with four horses. I asked Mr. Sandom whether they would breakfast; he said no, they have breakfasted at my house, they have been out in an open boat all night, and are very much fatigued; I asked who are they? Sandom said he did not know, but they had news of the utmost consequence, and begged I would let them have good horses; they ordered a chaise and horses for Westminster."

On his cross-examination he says, "I think I must have received the note about seven o'clock in the morning; the chaise with Sandom and the other gentlemen came back in about an hour. I was surprised to see it in so short a time. I only know Sandom by his having chaises at my house to Northfleet. I understood he lived there; he had been in the habit for nine months before that, of occasionally having horses from my house." This evidence introduces Mr. Sandom in this chaise, with these persons in this assumed garb, and presents him therefore as acting in this purpose.

Foxall Baldry is next called; he says, "I am a post-boy at the Rose at Dartford; on the morning of the 21st, I recollect a chaise coming from Northfleet to our house; I have seen one of the gentlemen since; I did not know Mr. Sandom personally at the time; he was one of those persons; I did not know the other two; I drove the leaders. Just as we were coming to Shooters Hill, Mr. Sandom got out of the chaise, and said, give your horses their wind, and when you get up the hill, make the best of your way; I will give you twelve shillings a-piece for driving; my fellow servant ordered me to go over London Bridge, down Lombard-street, along Cheapside, over Blackfriars Bridge, down the New Cut, and when I was in sight of the Marsh Gate, I was to stop." That was the line they were to take, they were to come through the town with these laurels and white cockades, which would attract attention; and it appears that this chaise came about two hours after the other, so that when the rumour began to be languid, this would revive and also strengthen it, the same report reaching London through two channels that morning. "I took that course; Mr. Sandom had on a brown coat, and the other two were in blue coats I think; the horses had laurels upon them; when I was in sight of the Marsh Gate I pulled up, the parties took off their cocked hats, put them into their handkerchiefs, put their round hats on, and they walked away." It had answered their purpose, they had exhibited themselves in the city, and they then resumed their usual habits. "I got to the Marsh Gate about eleven o'clock I should think; Mr. Sandom did not give us any thing at that time, nor pay for the chaise; he asked what house we stopped at; I told him the Bull, Kent-street end, and he came to us there, and gave my fellow servant a £.1 note and the rest in silver; the chaise he did not pay for." Whether it is yet paid for, nobody has informed us.

Mr. Baily is then called again, and he says, "In consequence of inquiries that had been made, Mr. Holloway and Lyte attended the committee of the Stock Exchange. Holloway denied any knowledge of the transaction, after which he came and confessed that he had planned that plot or participated in it; he said that he had done it with view to obtain money by a rise in the public funds; and Lyte said that he had been employed by Mr. M'Rae, at Mr. Holloway's solicitation. Lyte stated, that he and Sandom, and M'Rae, rode in the post chaise from Northfleet to Dartford, and afterwards from Dartford to London; there were present at this time, Mr. Wakefield, Mr. Lavie, and Mr. Chaumette. Holloway and Lyte came together, and what Lyte stated, was in the presence of Holloway; he (Holloway) stated, that he was not aware of the serious turn it would take; but finding that it had taken so serious a turn, he had come forward and confessed it, in the hope that the Stock Exchange would not pursue it to extremities. He was asked, whether he had any connexion with Lord Cochrane, Mr. Cochrane Johnstone, or Mr. Butt, and he denied that he had;" and certainly, if his denial was complete evidence of the fact, it would be proper for your consideration in that respect; but what he admits is to be taken as against himself, subject to your discreet consideration of the whole of the circumstances; and you will, upon the whole, determine, whether these defendants conspired with the rest in the promotion of the same end, accomplished by the same or similar means, about the very same period. Mr. Baily adds, that nothing he supposes, but the publicity of the measures, induced Holloway to come forward; and that he believes Holloway stated, that he would communicate all he knew of the business, because M'Rae had offered, for a large sum of money (I believe that sum was mentioned to be ten thousand pounds) to come forward; he denied also any connexion with De Berenger.

Several Brokers are then called. Mr. Robert Hichens, one of them, says; I have known Mr. Cochrane Johnstone for several years, I have never done business for him till the present year; from the 8th of February to the 19th, I made various purchases for him, the balance was £.250,000 omnium, at the leaving off of the business on Saturday; I furnished Mr. Baily with an account of the purchases and sales on Monday the 21st; I met Mr. Cochrane Johnstone as I was coming out of the Stock Exchange, about a quarter before eleven o'clock; I received an order from him on the Saturday to sell £.50,000 at one per cent. profit on the Monday, and that I sold before I saw him on Monday; now it does appear very probable, that the communication this person had made at Dover, might have reached town before De Berenger, for it appears by the evidence of Wright of Rochester, that he had been called up by a post-boy of his brother's at Dover, who had probably brought before De Berenger's arrival at Rochester, some of the news which De Berenger had announced at Dover, for Wright of Rochester addresses him as a person whom he was "*led to suppose*" was the bearer of some very good news; some such cause appears to have operated, so that the stocks were at 29 early in the morning; on the Saturday he ordered me to sell a certain quantity at an eighth per cent. more; I sold the whole of it that day by his directions, at 29, 29-1/8, 29-1/2, 30-3/4 and 30-7/8. I disposed of the whole which Mr. Cochrane Johnstone held at one or other of those prices.

Then on cross-examination, he states Mr. Cochrane Johnstone's balance on this and different days, and it appears that they had been dealing in the funds, with a view to this particular day; for a length of time they all had their hands full of omnium and consols; and the omnium having obtained a price which would allow of a profit, all was sold, and the object appears to have been as much to raise the price a little, so as to get out without present loss, as to gain a profit; this is the substance of the evidence of the different brokers, who all prove the quantities of stock, and that they were both buyers and sellers; the persons who were interested to prevent a depression, must feed the market occasionally as a buyer, I should imagine, though I am not very conversant in these things.

Mr. Baily then states in substance, what from an inspection of the accounts, with which he states himself to have been furnished by the several brokers, Hichens, Fearn, Smallbone, and Richardson, it turns out had been the balances of the three persons, Mr. Cochrane Johnstone, Lord Cochrane, and Mr. Butt, in the different speculation they had, which had lasted for a considerable time; from the month of November, according to Mr. Fearn, down to that day, and particularly from the 8th to the 21st of February (the particulars of which are specified in this paper) they appear to have had a larger balance, at least Mr. Cochrane Johnstone appears to have had on an antecedent day, than he had on the 21st of February; but it appears as if they not only were speculating on what they were buying, but they were speculating to such an amount, that unless they got rid of it, every one of them might be ruined; and they had determined, it should seem, on getting a profit of about one per cent. to sell the whole. It turns out, that on the 21st of February, as appears by this paper, £.420,000 of omnium, and £.100,000 of consols, belonged to Mr. Cochrane Johnstone; £.139,000, of omnium to Lord Cochrane; and to Mr. Butt, £.200,000 omnium, and £.178,000 consols. It appears that he sold on that day, £.24,000 more of omnium than he had; and £.10,000 of consols short of what he had; and with those differences merely, they, on that day, evacuate themselves of the whole; and, by Mr. Baily's account, you will see there was a profit upon the whole. The gross amount of the balances of all three, was £.759,000 omnium, and £.278,000 consols, which would make, he says, if the whole amount were reduced to consols and calculated as consols, £.1,611,430, £.3. per cents. Of that quantity of stock they were holders on the 21st of February. When I have stated the total amount as being £.1,611,430, 3 per cents., that is supposing the omnium was calculated in terms of consols; he says, the fluctuation of only *an eighth*, would, upon this large amount, have been a profit of above £.2,000. The profit upon the sales of that day, was, he says, £.10,450. Lord Cochrane's share of this profit was, as he computes, £.2,470.; Mr. Cochrane Johnstone's, £.4,931. 5.; and Mr. Butt's, £.3,048. 15.; he says, "If no news had arrived on the 21st, no person could have sold this large quantity of omnium and consols, without very much depressing the market;" therefore, it was necessary, it should seem, that there should be good news to keep up the market, that great holders of stock might get out of the adventure without loss. "I should think the news arrived in about half an hour after ten; business begins at ten; the news had a gradual effect, as the report was believed, the first decline was about the middle of the day;" he says, "the recovery of the funds was generally attributed to the chaise passing through the city;" therefore one chaise was, in point of effect, a good auxiliary to the other, and the blue coats and the worsted embroidery, aided, it should seem, the effect of the red coat and gold lace; and you will consider whether it was not all part of the same transaction. I think, he says, the chaise through the city carried it to its highest amount; I should think, he says, the accounts were time bargains, from the magnitude of the sums, and it should seem, they were so; but though the gain which these parties made, might not be a legitimate gain arising on legitimate bargains, the evil of this to the fair dealer is palpable, and the argument of its invalidity is a sword with a double edge; its operation, at any rate, is to cut very deeply into the interest of innocent dealers in the funds.

Mr. Wetenall then speaks to the different prices of the stock on that day; he says, "I collect the prices at different times of the day, and furnish the bank with these papers. Omnium left off at 26-3/4, that was the money price; the time price is generally one per cent higher. It commenced on Monday at 26-1/2. On news arriving, it rose to 30-1/4; fell back to 30, and afterwards to

28. After the stocks had begun to fall; on a report of a chaise having come through the city, they rose again."

Pilliner, who was a stock-broker, says; "before the 21st of February I had made purchases for Holloway to the amount of £.20,000 omnium, and £.20,000 consols. I sold for him £.20,000 omnium, and £.14,000 consols. I saw Holloway on the morning of the 21st;" he declines answering whether they were time bargains, or for money; "he desired me to sell his stock, to sell all about the middle of the day. I had acted as broker for him two years."

Then Mr. Steers says, "I am broker to the Accountant General of the Court of Chancery. On Monday the 21st of February I made purchases, as broker for the Court of Chancery, to the amount of fifteen thousand and odd; I bought at 71-5/8 consols; that was the price about eleven o'clock, when the funds had considerably risen; that was all that I did that day for the Accountant General. I can speak to nothing else that day. I purchased £.6,894. 11*s*. 4*d*. consols for the Accountant General, on Saturday, at 70;" therefore the difference between 71-5/8 and 70, seems to have been occasioned by the operation I have before stated to you.

Mr. Wright is next called; he appears to have printed this affidavit by Lord Cochrane's direction, on slips for the newspapers; he says, "In a conversation with Lord Cochrane, when he was giving me directions, he said, I once saw captain De Berenger at dinner at Mr. Basil Cochrane's. I have no reason to think that captain De Berenger is capable of so base a transaction;" giving his own name to the transaction; "but if he is, I have given the committee of the Stock Exchange the best clue to find him out;" he had given them a clue, by giving his name in the manner he has done in his affidavit; but it would have been very ineffectual if De Berenger had carried away his own person previous to that; but it was by accident that he was found at Leith.

Mr. Le Marchant is next called; there is a great deal, he says, which is no evidence against any body but the person who relates it; viz. captain De Berenger, and I do not think it at all necessary to state it; he does himself no credit, and he is a person on the statement of the letters which have been read, whom Government might do very well in letting ride at anchor here without going abroad. He says, however, "I became acquainted with captain De Berenger about eighteen months ago, our acquaintance continued until the 16th of February; from the 10th to the 16th of January he spent his evenings with me occasionally; I learnt that he was connected with Lord Cochrane and Mr. Cochrane Johnstone; he stated that he was about to go to America, under the command of Lord Cochrane; upon his mentioning this, I put the question to him, how he could possibly do it under the embarrassments that he lay under, upon which he answered that all was settled on that score; this conversation passed about the 14th of February;

he said, that for the services he had rendered to Lord Cochrane and Mr. Cochrane Johnstone, whereby his lordship could realize a large sum of money, by means of the funds or stocks. His lordship was his friend, and had told him a few days before, that he had kept unknown to him till that period, a private purse for him De Berenger, he frequently mentioned particular intimacy of dining, breakfasting, and supping with his lordship; he said, in this purse he had deposited a certain per centage out of the profits which his lordship had made by his stock suggestion." This is only what De Berenger says, and the declarations of persons are evidence only against the parties themselves who make them, and do not prove the fact as against any body else. "I afterwards heard of the events of the 21st of February, and made known my suspicions, that captain De Berenger had been active in them, to captain Wright of the East India Company's service, and lieutenant Taylor of the 22d infantry;" he said the per centages were for the benefit of his (De Berenger's) ideas he had given to Lord Cochrane and Mr. Cochrane Johnstone as to stock transactions; it applied to both.

Upon his cross-examination, he says, "I have been corresponding with Lord Cochrane, I am not now a prisoner in the King's Bench, I have never had any communication with Lord Cochrane but in writing; my promotion is not suspended, I hold the situation of Secretary and Register to the Court of Antigua and Montserrat: I have been prevented from going out in consequence of being compelled to give my evidence either at this court or some other court, and only for that purpose; this is my hand-writing; most undoubtedly I must have been compelled to give this evidence upon oath if called upon in a court of justice; I do not give my evidence from resentment, or from any refusal to lend me money; I know one Palfreyman," *he* is not called. "I am persuaded I never represented myself as having any resentment against Lord Cochrane to Mr. Palfreyman, nor said to him, that I would be Lord Cochrane's ruin;" and it is not proved that he did. "I never told him that I would assist the Stock Exchange; I have a very slight acquaintance with Mr. Palfreyman. The conversation with De Berenger was about the 14th of February; he mentioned to me, that he had expectations of getting some employment in America, to serve under Lord Cochrane; he particularly wished to be employed, that he might be useful in drilling the sharp-shooters, and said other things of that sort; I had a very high opinion of him, as being acquainted with the service; he was adjutant for a number of years in the Duke of Cumberland's sharp shooters. I do not know of his making preparation to go to America at that time, if he should be successful in procuring the appointment he was soliciting."

Upon his re-examination, he says, "The Stock Exchange applied to me to give them information, and sent me a subpœna after Lord Cochrane's publication."

The honourable Alexander Murray is called; he says, "I am not at present an officer in His Majesty's service, I am now in the King's Bench. I have been acquainted with captain De Berenger a year and a half; I was introduced to him by Mr. Tahourdin, who is my solicitor, and likewise Mr. De Berenger's; we were frequently together; when I first went over to the Rules of the Bench, I lodged with Mr. De Berenger in the same house, for about one month; towards the end of January, or beginning of February, I had a conversation with him about a pamphlet that Mr. Harrison was writing, respecting the trial between Mr. Basil Cochrane and Mr. Harrison; Captain De Berenger was, I knew from himself, employed in planning out a small piece of ground for Mr. Cochrane Johnstone; he said that he had a plan in view, with Lord Cochrane and Mr. Cochrane Johnstone, which if it succeeded," this is what De Berenger said, "would put many thousand pounds in their pocket; I asked, is that the plan with regard to Ranelagh, which it was proposed to build on Mr. Cochrane Johnstone's land; and he said no, it is not; it is a far better plan. I knew there was a very particular intimacy between Mr. De Berenger and Mr. Cochrane Johnstone; I understood Lord Cochrane was a more recent acquaintance, but that there was some acquaintance; I understood that there was a great acquaintance between him and Mr. Cochrane Johnstone, and that he was with him almost every day."

Upon his cross examination, he says, I have known Mr. De Berenger a long while; he is a man of considerable science and attainments; he had been for a considerable time before employed in drawing plans for the Ranelagh. Mr. Cochrane Johnstone has a house in Alsop's Buildings, and about an acre of land behind it, which was to be converted into something upon the plan of the old Ranelagh. As far as I have seen, I believe Mr. De Berenger to be a man of honour and integrity; I saw nothing but the most perfect gentleman during the time I lodged under the same roof.

William Carling says, "I am servant to the Honourable Basil Cochrane. Mr. Cochrane Johnstone and Lord Cochrane visited at my master's house, in company with Baron De Berenger, the gentleman there," pointing to him. "De Berenger came there to dine as a visitor; he was invited by my master. Lord Cochrane and Mr. Cochrane Johnstone dined there with him once, did not the second time; they appeared to be acquainted with him."

Then, on cross-examination, he is asked, when this took place, he says, "In January the first time, and the next in February. I cannot say the precise day; there was a dinner party, four or five there. Sir Alex. Cochrane and his Lady there the first time; an indiscriminate mixture of company, De Berenger was one of them. I did not learn that Mr. De Berenger was going to serve in America."

Barnard Broochooft, Clerk to the Marshal of the King's Bench, is next called. He says, "I know Captain De Berenger. He has been a prisoner in the King's Bench prison from the latter end of the year 1812, to within a month or six weeks of the present time; he had the Rules. I missed him for some months. Mr. Cochrane, a bookseller in Fleet-street; and Mr. Tahourdin the solicitor, were his securities for the Rules: they entered into this surety nearly two years ago. I cannot recollect seeing him on the morning of the 21st of February. The security was under £.400; they generally take £.100 beyond the amount of the debt and costs." So that it appears he was not very heavily charged in debt at that time; however, his debts might be, as supposed by Lord Cochrane, £.8,000.

Joseph Wood, the Messenger of the Alien Office says; "I left London on the 4th of April, in order to find De Berenger. I found him at Leith, on the 8th of April; I found him in possession of a writing desk, containing papers and bank notes; before I parted with any of them I marked them before the Grand Jury; there were guineas and half guineas, and two Napoleons in the pocket book." He produced two packets, and a pocket-book containing a £.50 bank note, four £.5 notes, and two Napoleons in a pocket-book. He also produced a memorandum-book, and a paper of memorandums, and a road-book. A memorandum is shewn to Mr. Lavie, which he says he believes to be Mr. De Berenger's hand writing.

Mr. Wood says, on his cross examination, "I carried the box and the papers before the Grand Jury, by orders of the Secretary of State. I was subpœnaed to bring it before the Grand Jury; the seals put on at Edinburgh, were taken off by order of the Secretary of State, before I went before the Grand Jury; it has been in my possession ever since I took it at Edinburgh. When I went to Holland, in my absence, Mr. Tahourdin wished to see it, and Mr. Musgrave opened it for him; the seals had been opened before that time. I was absent about a week or ten days. I was present all the time it was before the Grand Jury; it was locked up with all its contents; when I went out I locked it, and left it upon the jury table; I had the key; I was present when Mr. Lavie and Mr. Wakefield, and another gentleman of the Stock Exchange were with Mr. De Berenger the day he arrived. I was present the greatest part of the time. Mr. Wakefield went very close to Mr. De Berenger, and I declare I do not recollect any particular words; he put some questions respecting the Stock Exchange. I did not hear any names mentioned. I remember the word information, that they wanted information, but that is all I recollect. Mr. De Berenger said he was unwell, and exhausted by his journey. Mr. Wakefield conversed with him about ten minutes; I put my marks upon these things before I went to Holland." So that his going to Holland is immaterial, for his marks put upon them before he parted with them, identify the bank notes, and the bank clerks say they gave them in exchange for other notes.

Mr. Fearn is shewn a check of the 5th of February; he says, "I gave that check to Mr. Butt on the day of its date." That was afterwards attempted to be proved, but it came, I think, to nothing.

Mr. Smallbone says, "On the 10th of February I drew that check, which was a check for £.470. 19. 4. I drew it for Lord Cochrane; I gave it him on some stock account; I think Mr. Butt was in the office at the time; I feel satisfied I gave it to Lord Cochrane, and not to Mr. Butt; I did not see him hand it to Mr. Butt; I presented it to him on the table, that he might see it." The check is then read, it is upon Messrs. Jones, Loyd & Company, dated the 19th of February, very shortly, that is on the Friday before the Sunday on which this person must have departed from town, it is payable to No. 119 or bearer, and is signed William Smallbone.

Then Edward Wharmby says, "I am a clerk to Jones, Loyd & Company. I paid that check on the 19th of February, in one £.200 note, two of £.100 each, and a £.50.; the £.200 note was No. 634, the £.100 notes were, one No. 18,468, and the other 16,601, and the £.50 note was No. 7,375."

Then to shew that Lord Cochrane dealt with the produce of this check as his own, Thomas Parker, the coal-merchant of Lord Cochrane, says, "I received in payment a bank note of £.50 from Lord Cochrane, which is this very note, the number of which is 7,375; I wrote on the back of the note, and that is my hand-writing." Therefore it appears that this check, which was drawn for Lord Cochrane, was in the first instance for his benefit; for £.50 of it went to his coal merchant, and the other notes appear to have come to him, or to Mr. Butt, and the produce is afterwards found at a very critical period in the hands of this person, De Berenger, seized after he had gone from London. The check itself is the 19th of February; the money is found in this desk after he had gone off.

Then the bank notes of £.100 each are shewn to Mr. Lance; he says, "On the 24th February I went to the bank to change some bank notes for smaller notes, by the desire of Mr. Butt;" the notes were shewn to him, and he says, "those are the notes," I received two hundred notes of £.1 each for them.

Upon his cross examination, he says, "I remember on the 15th of February Mr. Butt lending Lord Cochrane £.200;" but on examination, it turns out that he only heard it, and did not see it lent. "I went with this check to get the money to Jones and Loyd's, I gave the notes of £.100 each to Lord Cochrane, I was not present when Lord Cochrane paid those notes back to Mr. Butt, I received those notes from Mr. Butt afterwards, and it was by Mr. Butt's desire I changed them for small notes at the bank." Then he says, "I advanced £.450 to Lord Cochrane, as clerk to Mr. Smallbone; when he had got this check for

£.450 he wanted £.200 more; Mr. Butt was not present. I do not know when Lord Cochrane gave these two £.100 notes to Mr. Butt, which by Mr. Butt's desire I took to the bank."

John Bilson and Thomas Northover, who are clerks in the bank, are shewn the two notes of £.100 each; Bilson says, these two notes were sent for payment in the bank on the 24th of February: I have the book here in my own hand-writing, they were paid in £.1 notes, and he specifies the number of each; we have looked over the notes in De Berenger's trunk before the grand jury; here are forty-nine, part of the two hundred.

Thomas Christmas says, "I am clerk to Mr. Fearn; I remember being sent on the 24th of February to change a note for £.200; I went to Messrs. Bond and Co's.; that is the note I gave; I received two notes of £.100 each; I then took those two notes to the bank, and changed them for two hundred notes of £.1 each; I gave them to Mr. Fearn; I did not see what Mr. Fearn did with them; I put Mr. Fearn's name upon the two £.100 notes before I gave them in at the bank." Mr. Miller, a bank clerk, produced the two £.100 notes, and Christmas says, "Those are the notes."

Mr. Fearn says, "On the 24th of February I received from Christmas two hundred notes of £.1 each; I gave them to Mr. Butt, and he gave them to Mr. Cochrane Johnstone."

Bilson and Northover, the bank clerks, say, "That on the 24th of February they paid to Fearn two hundred £.1 notes, for two notes of £.100 each." Then they are shewn sixty-seven of the notes of £.1 each, found in De Berenger's writing desk, and they say those are part of the notes they paid to Fearn on the 24th of February.

Then Wood produces a box and two watches.

Bishop Bramley is called; he says, "I am a watchmaker and silversmith living at Hull," (*the watches were shewn to him*); "I never sold this watch or that, but I sold a watch to the gentleman who sits there for £.30. 19*s*. 6*d.* on the 4th of March, and he paid me in £.1 bank notes; I put my own initials upon them, I should know them again;" [*Miller having produced some notes to the witness*], "all those seven notes I received of the person I sold the watch to; I put my initials and the date upon them; we took no other Bank of England notes on that day; I received twenty in the forenoon, and the other eleven in the afternoon; and I marked them, and paid them away the same afternoon."

Bilson and Northover are shewn the seven notes; they say those seven notes were part of the two hundred notes we paid to Fearn, on the 24th of February.

Lance says, "On the 26th of February, I gave Mr. Butt a check on Prescott & Co. for £.98. 2s. 6d. that is the check."

Isherwood, a clerk to Prescott & Co. says, "I paid that check, I think on the date of it, the 26th of February 1814," just before the time when De Berenger went off, "in a £.50 bank note, No. 13,396, and a £.40 note, No. 6,268." A £.40 note and a £.50 are shewn to him, to each of them he says, "that is the note."

John Seeks is shewn a cancelled bank note of £.50; he says, "I gave change for it, I cannot exactly recollect the day; here are some letters on the back that I know it by; I gave change for it to Mr. De Berenger's servant, Smith."

Now there we stopped last night, upon that note, because it could not be proved that Smith, De Berenger's servant, paid it for his master; this morning it is proved by Smith, that he did pay that £.50 bank note to Seeks, by desire of Mr. De Berenger, therefore that £.50 is fixed upon him as drawn from the same source, namely, the bank note which had come from Mr. Butt.

A memorandum in Mr. De Berenger's book, written in pencil, was referred to by the counsel, "W.S. £.50." Mr. Lavie says, "I never saw any writing in pencil of Mr. De Berenger's, but I believe this to be his writing, it is exactly the same sort of character as the other."

Benjamin Bray is called, he says, "I live at Sunderland;" he is shewn a £.40 note, he says, "I received it from the waiter of the Bridge Inn, at Sunderland; I had seen Mr. De Berenger at Sunderland, previous to that; I gave the waiter six £.5 notes, and ten £.1 notes for it, of the Durham Bank. Mr. De Berenger came shortly after to my house, to take his leave of me: I am a druggist, and agent to the Durham Bank. From the 17th to the 21st of March, I had known of his being at Sunderland; the waiter had come requesting bank paper. I made an apology to Mr. De Berenger for not sending him more bank paper in change, and he acknowledged having received the whole of the notes I had sent from the waiter; he went by the name of Major Burne."

Then, on cross-examination, he says, "I know that £.40. note, by the copy I made of it in my waste-book"—he had not the waste-book here, but he says, "I know it also *from my initials on the back* of the note, made a day or two afterwards, when it was fresh in my recollection. I did not keep it distinct from my other notes, but I marked it between the 31st of March and the 4th of April; but" (what is more material) "I generally do not put my initials on bank notes, but I did on this; I had no other £.40. note at the time, and have had no other since;" so that that £.40. bank note is proved likewise.

Mr. Pattesall says, "I am a partner in the house of Bond & Co. I did not pay that check of Mr. Fearn's, it was paid by Mr. Evans, a clerk of ours." That person of the name of Evans never came, and was called on his subpœna.

They then produced two Napoleons, found in the pocket-book of De Berenger, and with that they closed the evidence on the part of the prosecution.

On the part of the defendant, they first read the letters of Le Marchant, which, as I have before observed, certainly reflect very much upon himself.

They then call Lord Melville, who says, "I am acquainted with Sir Alexander Cochrane; I recollect Sir Alexander more than once applying to me, that Mr. De Berenger might be allowed to accompany him, and to remain with him on the North American station, to which Sir Alexander Cochrane was appointed; it was shortly before Sir Alexander sailed upon the command; I think it was five or six months ago. Sir Alexander was desirous that he should accompany him, for the purpose of instructing either a corps to be raised in that part of the world, or the Royal Marines, in the rifle exercise; and afterwards, when Sir Alexander wished that an officer of engineers should accompany him, and when I suggested that it would be difficult to give him that assistance, from the small number of engineer officers that could be procured, Sir Alexander mentioned, that as an engineer officer, he would be quite satisfied with Mr. De Berenger. I think there was some rank necessary to accompany such an appointment. I said I could not agree to the appointment, as far as the naval service was concerned, but I advised him to apply to the Secretary of State, or to the Commander in Chief; stating, that if they agreed to it, I should have no objection to let him accompany Sir Alexander. Lord Cochrane was appointed to the Tonnant, about the time Sir Alexander Cochrane sailed. I have no personal knowledge of Mr. De Berenger."

Colonel Torrens, who is secretary to the Commander in Chief, says, "I remember an application being made on behalf of Captain De Berenger in the latter end of December, or the beginning of January, by Sir Alexander Cochrane, to urge the appointment of De Berenger to go to America, for the purpose of applying his talents in the light infantry drill, that is, the rifle service; he says, there were great difficulties started to this application; and in consequence of those difficulties the appointment did not take place. It was under consideration, however, at the Commander in Chief's office. I do not know personally the character of Mr. De Berenger."

Then Mr. Goulburn, Under Secretary of State for the Colonial Department, says, "there was an application made by Sir Alexander Cochrane, on behalf of De Berenger;" but he gives no further account.

William Robert Wale King says, "I am a tinplate worker. I was employed by Lord Cochrane, in making signal lanthorns and lamps. I made him a new sort of lamp, for which he had a patent. He came frequently, nearly every day, to my manufactory; he was there the 21st of February. He came between ten and eleven in the morning, that was about the time he usually came. I perfectly recollect the circumstance of a note being brought to him by his servant. I was present when the note was delivered. He immediately opened it, and retired into the passage; and he came into the workshop again, and shortly after went away. His Lordship had been about a quarter of an hour there, that is a mile and a half from Grosvenor Square; his Lordship only said 'very well, Thomas,' not making any observation expressive of anxiety as to his brother."

Mr. Bowering says, "I am clerk in the Adjutant General's Office. Major Cochrane, the brother of Lord Cochrane, was returned as with the army in the South of France, "sick," on the 25th of January. The returns ran from the 24th of December to the 24th of January."

Then Thomas Dewman says, "I am a servant to Lord Cochrane, and have been seventeen years in the family. I carried a note to Lord Cochrane at Mr. King's manufactory; I remember the gentleman coming to Lord Cochrane's in a hackney coach; I do not know that I have seen him before or since. He first asked, where Lord Cochrane was gone to? and I told him he was gone to Cumberland-street to breakfast, because his Lordship told me he was going there to his uncle's; I went there after him, and not finding him, I returned to the gentleman; his Lordship had told me to follow him with some globe glass to Mr. King's. I had been there on Saturday; I supposed he might be there; I told the gentleman that I most likely should find him there; I should however have gone, if the gentleman had not sent me; he took the note from me, and said, I will add two or three more lines. I took the note to his Lordship at Mr. King's; his Lordship read the note in my presence; I left him at Mr. King's; his Lordship had no man in Green-street but me; the other servant was in the country; he had been there two or three months before that; his Lordship had given Davis warning on his appointment to the Tonnant. Davis was not in his Lordship's service at that time, but he happened to be in the kitchen when the gentleman came; Davis is gone." This, it should seem, is only to account for not calling Davis. "Davis is gone with Admiral Fleming to the West Indies. It was a little past ten when the gentleman arrived. I was engaged to Lord Cochrane since Christmas; I had been in the family of Lord Dundonald; I do not know Holloway or Lyte. When I gave the note to Lord Cochrane, he said, 'Well, Thomas, I will return.' I waited on Major Cochrane when he first went into the army; I saw Lord Cochrane leave the place, that is Mr. King's."

Then it is admitted, that Lord Cochrane has a patent for the invention of a lamp, dated the 28th of February last.

Mr. Gabriel Tahourdin says, "I have known Mr. De Berenger five or six years; I introduced him to Mr. Cochrane Johnstone, in May 1813. Mr.

Cochrane Johnstone was in possession of a place at Paddington, named Vittoria, which he was desirous of improving. I introduced De Berenger to Cochrane Johnstone by mere chance; De Berenger afterwards employed himself in preparing a plan, and had nearly completed it. Shortly before Mr. Cochrane Johnstone went to Scotland, in September, he made him one payment on account of it. Besides the plan, De Berenger prepared a prospectus; Mr. Johnstone had got a number of that prospectus printed, early in October, to take to Scotland with him. I conveyed a letter from De Berenger, and I spoke several times to Mr. Johnstone, upon the subject of paying for those plans, but no price was fixed upon till February last; I made repeated applications to Mr. Johnstone, in a delicate way, to pay him, and on the 22d of February." That is a very remarkable time, immediately after the transaction on the 21st; if the gentleman knew any thing of De Berenger's conduct, on the previous day, it may deserve consideration, whether that was the most likely time, in point of delicacy, to have made the application. "Mr. Johnstone sent me a letter on the 22d of February 1814, enclosing a letter from Mr. De Berenger to Mr. Cochrane Johnstone." Now these letters, if you wish them to be read, I will read.

*Foreman of the Jury.* We think there is no necessity, my Lord.

*Lord Ellenborough.* They relate to other work he was doing for him; there was that plan, I should have thought from two to three hundred pounds very excessive compensation for it; but still there was some claim affording a ground for money transactions to pass between them. As to the dates, there is one circumstance of Mr. Tahourdin dating the letter of De Berenger to Cochrane Johnstone, enclosed in the letter of Cochrane Johnstone to himself, which appears not very usual in the course of business; the letters shew other transactions between them. Whether they were pretended or not, or if existing, then artificially brought forward or not, may be a question; but the letters certainly are dated at a most critical time, namely, on the 22d of February. Then he says, "There is a reference in the letter, to an assignment of some property, which De Berenger had, which assignment was prepared at my office: I do not know whether Mr. Cochrane Johnstone answered De Berenger's letters." He is shewn a letter, and he says, "That is my answer to the letter of Mr. Cochrane Johnstone; I wrote it on the 23d of February."

There was a business to settle with Lady Mary Crawford Lindsay. There is a great deal of business certainly introduced into these letters, so much almost as to induce one to think there is an artificial introduction of business, to give the appearance of reality to the letters; however, Mr. Tahourdin certainly swears that there were such transactions at that period. But one cannot help recollecting that Mr. Tahourdin, towards the close of the case, appears to have been in communication with the two last witnesses, Donithorne and Tragear, on whose evidence I shall have to observe. He says, "I saw a very few days after their date, a receipt for £.50. dated 20th September 1813, received of C. Johnstone by hands of G. Tahourdin, on account of large plans;" there is a receipt for £.200. dated the 26th of February: "Received £.200. on account of plans and prospectus delivered, C. R. De Berenger;" and a note of hand for £.200. more, De Berenger to C. Johnstone, dated the 26th of February; I saw it two or three days afterwards. So that, just after the extraordinary transaction which had such an effect upon the funds, a communication that had taken place between them, and these letters are produced, and which are conceived to be material, with reference to the question now before you. He says, "there were subordinate plans for the details of that same place." Then he says, "I had become security for the Rules for De Berenger, some months before I knew Mr. Cochrane Johnstone." Then he is shewn the letter, which has been described as the Dover letter; he says, "this certainly is not the hand-writing of De Berenger; I have received a thousand letters from him, and this is not his hand-writing; I do not believe it is a disguised hand of Mr. De Berenger; I have always considered De Berenger as a man of strict honour and integrity; I have trusted him to the extent of about £.4,000. in money, besides my professional claims on him." Some writing in a road-book found in De Berenger's desk, is then shewn to him; and how any person should have writing by him like that, purporting to be his own, and it should still not be his own hand-writing, one cannot conceive. But he says, "some of it is more like his hand-writing than others, but I do not believe," he says, "that all the writing is his; some of the letters" he says, (on being shewn the pencil-writing in the book found in De Berenger's desk) "look like his writing; the smaller parts look like his hand-writing." He is asked, "whether he does not believe the whole of it to be his hand-writing?" and he says, "I do not know what to say, this pencil is not like what he writes in general; it being in pencil puzzles me more than any thing else."

Then General Campbell is called, who says, "I know Mr. Cochrane Johnstone; I met him the second week in October last, I think at the Perth meeting; he shewed me a prospectus of a new public building to be erected in the Regent's Park, or in the neighbourhood of it, I think he called it Vittoria." He is shewn the prospectus, and he says, "I believe this is a copy of the same that he communicated to me in his or my own apartment."

Then on the part of Mr. De Berenger, Lord Yarmouth is called; he says, "I am lieutenant colonel commandant of the regiment of Sharp-shooters. Captain De Berenger was acting adjutant, a non-commissioned officer. I have known him since 1811; very early in that year. I cannot recollect the day. I have received letters from him, and have seen him occasionally write, and have seen him frequently on the subject of the contents of those letters, and am acquainted with his character of hand-writing." Then that letter sent to Admiral Foley is shewn to him; he says, "If I had heard none of the circumstances, I should not have believed it was his hand-writing. He solicited to go out in the month of January last. Some time back he told me, that he had very nearly arranged to go out to drill the men on board the Tonnant."

Upon his cross-examination, he says, "the hand-writing of this is much larger than Mr. De Berenger's; he generally writes a round and neater hand." He is shewn another letter; and he says, "I received that letter on the day it bears date, or the day immediately after." He is then shewn the writing in the road book; and he says, "It is larger than De Berenger's usual writing; some part of it is not larger, it is less round; it is more angular. I am not sufficient conversant with hand-writing, to swear either way to this." Then he looks again at the letter sent from Dover to Admiral Foley; he says, "the letter R looks very much like his hand-writing in the R of Random, before De Berenger, Random being his second name." Then being asked, what he should think of this gentleman coming to him in his bottle-green coat of uniform; he says, "It would have been more military that he should come so, though I never exacted it of him. I should not have been angry at it, but should have thought it the regular dress for him to appear in. If he had appeared before me in an aid-de-camp's scarlet uniform, and with a star, I should have been indeed surprised to see him present himself before me in that dress."

Sir John Beresford is then called; he says, "I have seen Captain De Berenger twice before yesterday. I never saw him write; I know of his application to go to America, as a sharp-shooter. In the beginning of February I paid my ship off, and met Mr. Cochrane Johnstone in town, who told me, Sir Alexander Cochrane was very anxious he should go out in the Tonnant, to teach the marines the rifle exercise. I went to the Horse Guards, to ask whether any thing could be done; I was told it would be useless to apply to the Duke of York, and told Mr. Cochrane Johnstone of it; this was before Sir Alexander Cochrane sailed in January or December. I met him at dinner at Mr. Cochrane Johnstone's. I was there to meet Sir Alexander Cochrane, but he did not come."

Mr. James Stokes says, "I am a clerk of Mr. Tahourdin; I have been so between three and four years, and during that time have frequently seen the hand-writing of De Berenger; he has been a client of my master's, and has been assisted very much by him. I have seen a great deal of his writing; this is certainly not his writing, not a word of it; and the letter 'R.' (which Lord Yarmouth had spoken to) is not at all like it."

Then they call witnesses, who at last come to swear, that captain De Berenger slept in his own apartments on the Sunday night, the 20th of February; of course, if he did so, he could not have been on the 21st at Dover, at the time sworn to by the witnesses.

William Smith is called; he says, "I was servant to Mr. De Berenger, I was so about three years and a half; I have seen him write frequently." Then he is shewn the Dover letter, and he says "I do not believe that is his hand-writing; the signature there, Du Bourg, I really believe is not his hand-writing, no part of the letter; I am positively sure it is not. He has lately lodged with a person of the name of Davidson, in Asylum Buildings. I was with him on Sunday the 27th of February, when he went away; I perfectly remember he was at home on Sunday the 20th; he slept at home on the Saturday night the 19th, and went out about nine o'clock on Sunday morning; he came in afterwards at nearly eleven o'clock, and went out again immediately afterwards; he stayed out only about twenty minutes, and returned again when people were gone to Church, and stayed at home till about four o'clock, he then went out again. I was not at home then, I was over the way with my master's dog, leaning with my back against the rail, when he came down on the opposite side of the road facing the door. I went out with my wife soon after, and returned in the evening about eleven or a few minutes afterwards; he was not at home then, he came home afterwards, in five minutes after I got home, that was a few minutes after eleven; he slept at home that night. I and my wife were down in the kitchen taking our suppers, and my master was in the drawing room; before we got to bed, I heard him pass my room door to go to his bed-room, that might be about half-past eleven. He did not breakfast at home the next morning; I did not see him the next morning; I saw him about three o'clock in the afternoon of Monday; my wife made his bed."

Then he says, on cross-examination, "I let him in at a little after eleven at night. He rapped at the door in his usual way; his usual rap was not over loud, between loud and gentle; he went to his bed-room that night; I did not see him in bed the next morning, I heard him go into the bed-room." Then he is shewn a letter, which he says, "I wrote to Lord Yarmouth," (but that is not given in evidence) "I have my master's military grey great coat here at Guildhall; I never acknowledged that my master slept from home that night, to Mr. Murray; I never told either Mr. or Mrs. Davidson, that coming home and not finding my master at home, I had left the key for him at the usual place in the area, that he might let himself in; I never told them so, either on Monday the 21st or any other day, to the best of my knowledge. He has no attendance in the morning, he does every thing for himself, he does not usually ring his bell of a morning before he comes down to breakfast; he is a very quiet man, I never knew him otherwise, he never makes a disturbance, he walks about very much. My master finally left his lodgings on Sunday the 27th; I remember changing a £.50 note with Seeks," (that is the £.50. I have mentioned to you) "received it from Mr. De Berenger, I received it on the

27th, the day he went away; I took his things to the Angel Inn behind Saint Clement's; a day or two before he left to go into the country he gave me £.20. I never saw him give Sophia £.13. if I was in the room, I did not notice it. I do not remember, after my master finally went away, Mr. Cochrane Johnstone's calling with a letter; I never told Mrs. Davidson, that a gentleman who called there was Mr. Cochrane Johnstone. I was not at home; she told me a gentleman had called there, and described him; I said, most likely it was Mr. Cochrane Johnstone." Upon his examination I thought he had said, that he had seen him only once, but then he said, at last, that it was only once at his house. "I did not tell her on the Sunday, that if my master had been at home on the Saturday, when Mr. Cochrane Johnstone brought that letter, he would have gone off on the Saturday night; I did not tell her so either on the Saturday or the Sunday. My master was at home every day from the 20th to the 27th, going out as usual. On the 21st, he went out to dine; he did not tell me where he was going to, or when he came back where he had been to, that I recollect; he did not tell me he had been to Mr. Cochrane Johnstone's, when he came home, nor before he went out, that he was going there. When I came home on the Monday, I saw a strange black coat; I cannot tell whether the coat fitted my master; I never saw it on; I brushed it; I am used to brushing coats; I did not know whose coat it was; I cannot tell whether it was the coat of a man six feet high. I swore an affidavit; I drew that affidavit myself; I told Mr. Tahourdin of his absence on the 7th or 8th of March; I drew out the affidavit before that time, and did it without any sort of concert with any body whatever, merely for the vindication of my master's character. I sent the affidavit to be published; I found my master a very injured gentleman; I took it to Mr. Cochrane Johnstone, and he published it." And then he says, "I let him in," that is, De Berenger his master, "on Sunday the 20th."

Ann Smith, the wife of William Smith, says, "I was a servant with my husband to Mr. De Berenger, in February last, and had been so two years and a half. I saw my master at home on the 20th of February; he went out about nine o'clock in the morning, and came in again between ten and eleven; he did not stay at home long then, before he went out again. My husband and I went out between four and five, after my master was gone out; he went out about four o'clock. My husband and I returned home about eleven, a few minutes before my master; my husband got in a little before me. My master came in that evening; he was let in by my husband, and I heard him above stairs; he had a bit of bread and a glass of ale that night for supper. I did not see him that night; it was my business to make his bed. I got up on the Monday morning about seven, that was the Sunday and Monday before he finally went off, I am sure; I usually get up about seven. My master went out that morning before breakfast; my husband went out about eight, and my master went out a little before him; I did not see him go out nor hear him; I did not know he was out till I let him in; I made his bed on the Sunday morning; I was up stairs making his bed, and he went out, I looked out of the window and saw him go; I made his bed on Monday, but that was not till after he came home, which was about twelve o'clock; when I found he had been out, I went up stairs immediately to make his bed." You will consider whether there is any room for believing she might be correct, and that he might have lain down upon his bed before she made it. "The bed appeared as usual, as if it had been slept in on Sunday night; I and my husband slept in our bed, and I made his bed on Monday as well as on Sunday. I remember how my master was dressed on the Monday when he came home; he had a black coat on; he had a bundle in his hand; I saw a part of a coat where the bundle was open, a grey coat just where the knot was tied; my master continued to sleep regularly at home til he finally went away."

Upon her cross-examination she says, "my master had no other man servant but my husband; he used to wait upon him, and do any thing he was requested to do. I used to carry up breakfast when he rang, if my husband was out; he did not ring for my husband to attend him in the morning to dress. I supposed my master had breakfasted out when he came in; I was rather surprised that he had not rung. On the Sunday, when he went out, he had on his black coat and waistcoat, and grey overalls; I did not remark that the coat was too long for him; I do not know how he was dressed when he went out on the Monday; he came home in a black coat; I cannot tell whether it was the black coat in which he went out on Sunday. I never saw Lord Cochrane. I never observed the black coat at all in the bundle; I saw part of a grey coat, and the green uniform coat was in the bundle. There was nothing extraordinary in my master's going out in green, it was his drill dress; he was in the habit of going out in it, and returning in it; I never knew of his going out in a green drill dress, and returning with a black coat before. I made an affidavit; I saw nobody on the subject of that affidavit; I saw Mr. Tahourdin a few days after making the affidavit. Mr. De Berenger wore whiskers sometimes; I do not know whether he wore whiskers then or not, I did not see much of him. I had not seen the bed on Monday morning till after his return."

Then the ostler at Chelsea, and his wife, are called to prove, that he was at a late hour in town. John M'Guire says, "I am the ostler at Smith's livery-stables, at the Cross-keys yard, Chelsea. I am acquainted with the person of Mr. De Berenger; I remember seeing him on the 20th of February; it was on a Sunday. I remember it perfectly well, because I knew he was within the Rules of the King's Bench; and I determined to ask his servant, how he was out of the Rules. He had lived at Chelsea before. It was a quarter past six in the evening that I saw him at Smith's stable-yard gate; he asked me if the coach to London was gone; I told him the six o'clock coach was gone, but the seven would be ready in three quarters of an hour; he said, it would not do to wait for the seven o'clock coach, and he turned round and took his way to London. When I went home that night, I mentioned to my wife, that I had seen Mr. De Berenger at a quarter past six. I was induced to mention it, from knowing he was in the Rules of the Bench, and not having seen him that way for some time before; he went from the lodgings he had at Chelsea, to the King's Bench."

Upon cross-examination, he says, "I have known him three years and a half, I knew him to be an officer in a corps of Riflemen; that day fortnight I saw his servant, on the 6th of March, and he said, he was not clear of the Bench then. Last Monday week I was examined by the attorney. He had on, when I saw him, a black coat, a black waistcoat, and grey overalls or pantaloons. I have seen William Smith this morning. De Berenger wore whiskers when I knew him before, but when I saw him on this Sunday he was close shaved, he had none then; it was three miles and a half from the Asylum." Now it appears, that De Berenger was three miles and a half from the Asylum at a quarter past six, where he had dined; if he had dined any where, we have not heard. He says, "he thought it was wrong to be out of the Rules, and he was shocked at it."

Then Mr. Hopper says, "I am an architect. I saw Mr. Cochrane Johnstone's premises at Alsop's Buildings two nights ago." He is shewn the plan and prospectus, and he says, "From the trouble that must attend it, a compensation of from, £.200 to £.300. might not be excessive." I have mis-stated it, therefore before; he does not say, it would not be excessive, but it *might* not be so.

Then Mrs. M'Guire says, "I am the wife of M'Guire, the ostler. I did not know Mr. De Berenger, when he lived at Chelsea, I knew Smith his servant. My husband mentioned to me on the 20th of February, his having seen Mr. De Berenger, Smith's master; he mentioned it to me at ten at night; it was the Sunday before Shrove Tuesday, it was my child's birth-day, and therefore I remember it. My husband told me, he had seen him at about a quarter past six; he said, he wondered whether he had got his liberty yet or not; I cannot particularly say whether he said it was shocking or not; he said, he wondered whether he had got his liberty."

How this should have excited the curiosity of this man, one cannot well conceive; but one cannot comment upon that which one cannot read and believe.

Then Henry Doyle Tragear is called; he says, "I was at Mr. Donithorne's house in York-street, Westminster, in the month of February last. I was staying there; I went there upon the occasion of my leaving my house, No.

39, Little Queen-street, Holborn, where I had carried on the hatting business. I left my house finally on the 17th, and went to Donithorne's; I remain at his house still. I had seen Mr. De Berenger frequently previous to that, at Mr. Donithorne's house. I particularly remember having seen him there on Sunday the 20th of February; I saw him twice that day; I saw him between nine and ten in the morning, and again between eight and nine in the evening; I saw him at Donithorne's house both these times; he might stop about half an hour, more or less. I have seen him frequently talking with Mr. Donithorne about some drawings, designs for pieces of furniture, and things of that sort. Donithorne is a cabinet maker. Donithorne has shewn me these things before. I am a hat manufacturer; I am not entirely out of business but I have not a house at the present moment; I went there to reside till I could get a house to suit myself, to start in business again." According to the wife, it did not appear as if he was likely to go into business again. "My wife, Mrs. Donithorne and Mr. Donithorne were there in the evening. When he came, Mr. Donithorne went into the garden with him; he said he would not come into the parlour to disturb the company; I had seen him repeatedly before."

Then upon cross examination, he says, "I was not struck with any alteration in his appearance that night; he had no whiskers on that night; I do not know whether he had ever worn whiskers before; he had a black coat on that day; he had his hat on. It was between eight and nine when they took a walk in the garden. I cannot say whether his hair was powdered; they went out to take a survey of the premises in the morning. I have seen Mr. Donithorne and Mr. Tahourdin together one day last week. I will swear, that I did not know they were acquainted together before that time; I never was sent for to become a witness upon this occasion; I went myself; Tahourdin did not send for me; I went to Tahourdin I think one day last week. I did not know that I was to be a witness till last week, or that it was material I should recollect the 20th of February. I let my house on the 17th of February to Samuel Nicholson; and on the Sunday morning following Mr. Donithorne came to my room, and told me a gentleman was come to look over the house, and if I would get up he should be obliged to me. I have seen Smith, the servant." He then says, "I have been bail twice, once for fifteen pounds, that I believe is settled; I have been bail again, but I do not quite know whether that has been settled, nor the amount. I don't recollect if I have been bail oftener."

Then Mrs. Tragear, the wife of the last witness, is called; she says, "I know the defendant De Berenger; I have seen him often. I and my husband went to stay at Donithorne's when we gave up our house; the day we gave up our house was the 17th of February. Mr. De Berenger called at Donithorne's on Sunday the 20th, between nine and ten in the morning; we were not up then. Mr. Donithorne was in the cabinet business. He came up and said, he was anxious we should get up, as a gentleman was come to look over the house.

When I got up, I threw down the sash, and saw Mr. De Berenger; he was measuring the ground in the garden. I am sure it was he; I saw him again in the evening between eight and nine; we were in the parlour along with Mr. and Mrs. Donithorne; asked him to come in; and he said he would not disturb the company; he wanted to speak with Mr. Donithorne; they walked backwards into the garden, and I saw him no more."

Then, on cross-examination, she says, "my husband is deaf at times; Mrs. Donithorne came to call us; Mr. De Berenger went into the attics; he did not go into our room." It is afterwards said by Donithorne, that he went two or three times into it. "I do not remember seeing any one in the garden with De Berenger and Donithorne; one of them held the measuring rod and the other, took the figures down. There was no snow; I think it was a wet morning, and the rain had cleared the snow away. My husband failed on the 17th of February; he then came to Mr. Donithorne's, who is a cousin."

Then Donithorne is called; he says, "I live in York-street, Westminster. Mr. and Mrs. Tragear came to live at my house, on Thursday the 17th of February. I had known De Berenger a long while; I am very well acquainted with his person; I am a cabinet-maker; De Berenger had furnished me with designs for furniture. I remember seeing him on the Sunday morning, after Tragear came to my house, which would be the 20th of February, between nine and ten in the morning; he came to look over my ground, as I was going to make some alterations in my little garden, and also some designs for cabinet work. I furnished Mr. Cochrane Johnstone's house in Cumberland-street, for Miss Johnstone. I saw him again between eight and nine in the evening; I let him in, and asked him to walk into the parlour where we were sitting; he said he would walk into the back-parlour; he stayed about a quarter of an hour or twenty minutes; he did not go into the garden. In the morning, we were I dare say, an hour together in the garden; he called in the evening, to give me an answer when he was to draw a plan for me." (This does not appear to be business of sufficient consequence to have led this man twice there in the course of that day.) "I was going to convert the front part of my house into an inn, and the back part into pleasure-ground; it was a misty rainy morning, and very cold."

On his cross-examination, he says, "he came as the friend of Mr. Cochrane Johnstone, to give me plans for furniture; I proposed to him surveying my house, with a view to the improvements I intended to make. I went and called Mr. and Mrs. Tragear, and desired them to get up; I have no doubt of it, I went twice." He is then asked as to some writs against persons in the Stock Exchange; he says, "I employed the attorney, Mr. Tahourdin, by desire of Mr. Cochrane Johnstone, to issue 135 writs; Mr. Cochrane Johnstone is to pay for them;" it appears that these writs are against persons for stock-jobbing transactions. "Tragear never failed, to my knowledge."

Gentlemen—This is the whole of the evidence on each side. I have made my observations upon it, as it has proceeded. You have heard from me already, that this is a case in which both the individuals and the public are deeply concerned. It is important that public justice should be vindicated by the conviction of the defendants, if they are guilty; and that justice should likewise be done to the defendants, by exempting them from punishment, if they have committed no crime. You will consider upon the whole of the evidence, whether these several parties were connected in one common plan, and were using their several endeavours and means to raise the Funds for corrupt advantage, by false contrivances, and the circulation of false intelligence—if you believe that all of them were concerned in it, you will find them all guilty—if you believe that any of them are exempt from a share in this Conspiracy, you will acquit them.—You will now consider of your Verdict.

*Mr. Richardson.* Your Lordship stated, that there were some Counts upon which they ought not to be found guilty.

*Lord Ellenborough.* Yes; Gentlemen, you will find the defendants not guilty upon the first and second Counts of the Indictment, as those allege facts and motives, in which they cannot all be supposed to be joined.

*A Juryman.* They are guilty or not guilty of a Conspiracy.

*Lord Ellenborough.* Yes; a Conspiracy, which is a crime that cannot be committed by one; it must be committed by more than one.

*The Jury retired at ten minutes after six o'clock, and returned at twenty minutes before nine with their Verdict, finding all the Defendants—GUILTY.*

# Court of King's Bench.

*Tuesday, 14 June 1814.*

LORD COCHRANE.

My Lords, scarcely recovered as I am from the shock, which I experienced on hearing of the verdict pronounced against me at the late trial, I must crave your utmost indulgence, not only on that account, but also because I am unacquainted with the proceedings and forms in Courts of Law. I feel it essentially necessary, and I trust I shall make it evident to the minds of your Lordships, that it is essentially necessary to the cause of justice, that there should be a revision of the proceedings that have been lately had, and that a new trial should take place, at least as far as I am concerned and implicated in that transaction.

It has been my misfortune to suffer from an intimacy, or rather an acquaintance, with men, over whose conduct I could have no control whatever. I have been informed, that it is not competent for my counsel to rise up on the present occasion to ask your Lordships to grant me a new trial, and therefore it is necessary I should address you myself.

*Lord Ellenborough.* Your Lordship must have been misinformed on the subject; any application you wish to address to the Court may be addressed to them by counsel, and perhaps with more convenience to yourself.

*Lord Cochrane.* I understood there was the case of a conspiracy, in which it had been held that a revision of the case, and a new trial could not be moved for, unless all the defendants appeared in Court.

*Lord Ellenborough.* That would be the same, whether the application was made by counsel or by yourself.

*Lord Cochrane.* It is only for the purpose of preventing my counsel from trespassing on the rules of the Court, that I have adopted this mode of proceeding, and I trust—

*Lord Ellenborough.* I am afraid, my Lord, we cannot hear you, unless all the parties are present in Court. That is the rule of the Court, and we have acted on it so lately as this very morning.

*Lord Cochrane.* I have to complain, that evidence was not brought forward on the late trial, which was extremely material to shew my innocence. If your Lordships will permit me to read the evidence to which I allude—

*Lord Ellenborough.* It will answer no beneficial purpose, because we cannot advert to what you are now stating, unless the other parties convicted are now in Court.

*Lord Cochrane.* If your Lordships will grant me permission to read the statement, you will be better able to judge of the propriety or impropriety of granting my application.

*Mr. Justice Dampier.* By the rules of the Court it cannot be; your Lordship has been informed of the practice of the Court, and from that practice, the Court has no power to depart.

*Lord Ellenborough.* The practice of the Court is exceedingly beneficial, and must be adhered to by us.

*Lord Cochrane.* My Lords, I have now in my hands several affidavits that will prove my innocence, if the Court will hear them. They are very short.

*Lord Ellenborough.* We have announced to your Lordship the rule of practice, and we are extremely unwilling to give you any pain, but we cannot forego the regular practice of the Court. We could not do it on the application of Counsel, and no more can we do it upon your application.


*Lord Cochrane.* I shall be exceedingly brief. The facts, which I shall prove by these affidavits, will sufficiently justify me; and it will redound to the honour of the judges of this land, to suffer me in this instance, though contrary to the practice of the Court, to shew my innocence; when those who are guilty of this transaction, and over whose conduct I have no control, dare not appear in the place where I now stand.

*Lord Ellenborough.* We must abide by the rules of the Court. If we give way to the importunity of one, we must give way to the importunity of all; we must administer the same justice to all, without distinction of persons.

*Lord Cochrane.* I beg only to state——

*Lord Ellenborough.* It would be idle to announce to your Lordship, that there is such a rule of practice as that which I have mentioned, unless we meant to abide by it; the rule is, that no application can be made for a new trial, unless all the persons convicted are here: we have acted on that rule this day; and if we were now to adopt a different rule, it might very properly be said, there was one rule for the poor and another for the rich.

*Lord Cochrane.* My Lords, I have briefly to state these facts, that before the late trial, so conscious was I of my innocence, that I did not think it necessary to instruct counsel, as several gentlemen in court know. I never read over the brief on the subject, till after the trial, when I found a very gross error had crept into it, with regard to the dress of the stranger who called at my house; and my servant is in consequence represented as having admitted that he was dressed in a red coat. The fact was, that being questioned as to the colour of the coat, he stated that he appeared to be an army officer, to which he very naturally attached the idea of a red coat, for the servants did not see it.

# Court of King's Bench.

Monday, *20 June 1814.*

*Mr. Gurney.* I move your Lordships for the Judgment of the Court in the case of the King *v.* De Berenger, and others.

[*The Officer called the Defendants, who appeared, excepting the Honourable Andrew Cochrane Johnstone, and Alexander M'Rae.*]

*Mr. Serjeant Best.* Upon this occasion I appear only as Counsel for Mr. Butt; and before I make the motion which I feel myself called upon, under the circumstances of this case to make, I take the liberty to suggest to your Lordships, that if I should not succeed in my motion in arrest of judgment, there is a fact which was not proved at the trial, but which it was necessary to prove for the purpose of convicting these defendants upon any count of the indictment, in which it forms a material averment, namely, that there was war between England, and the Allies of England, and France.

*Lord Ellenborough.* I am afraid there are too many statutes which speak of war with France, for the Judges to allow themselves not to have cognizance of that objection.

*Mr. Serjeant Best.* But there is none, my Lord, which refers to any war between England, and the Allies of England, and France. Unfortunately it has been only of late that we have had Allies. I make this application on the part of Mr. Butt only, and I submit to your Lordships upon the counts on which this defendant has been convicted——

*Lord Ellenborough.* You appear now only for Mr. Butt?

*Mr. Serjeant Best.* I do, my Lord.

*Lord Ellenborough.* I have made a minute, that on the trial you told me you were Counsel for the second, third, and fourth, defendants, Lord Cochrane, Mr. Cochrane Johnstone, and Mr. Butt.

*Mr. Serjeant Best.* I am not now Counsel for Lord Cochrane, I am moving merely for Mr. Butt.

*Lord Ellenborough.* That is a new proceeding, that Counsel shall renounce some clients, in order to serve others.

*Mr. Serjeant Best.* My Lord, Lord Cochrane has desired me not to move on his behalf; and I may state so much for him, that he has no intention to move in arrest of judgment. My other client, Mr. Cochrane Johnstone, is not here.

*Lord Ellenborough.* If you move in arrest of judgment for one, all have the benefit of it.

*Mr. Serjeant Best.* My objections are three; first, taking the third count as it stands, (and the objections apply to every successive count in the indictment) that there is no body of crime alleged, no offence known to the law, the raising the price of the public funds not being necessarily a crime; In the second place, that if there be any crime, which is alleged, the persons who are to be affected by that crime are not particularized; My third objection is, that it is stated, that the object of the conspiracy was, to raise the price of the public funds of *this kingdom*: this kingdom being now the United Kingdom of Great Britain and Ireland, I conceive there is no kingdom of England, but that the kingdom of England is merged in the United Kingdom of Great Britain and Ireland, and I humbly conceive, nothing that is here charged has reference to any funds and government-securities, except the funds and government-securities of that part of the United Kingdom of Great Britain and Ireland, called England.

My Lords, I am aware of the extent to which the decisions pronounced on this subject have carried the doctrine, with respect to conspiracy; but I conceive it will not be found there is any adjudged case which goes so far as to reach this transaction, taking it as an abstract proposition, that the conspiracy was, to raise the price of the government funds of this country. Unless your Lordships can pronounce that the raising the price of the government funds of this country is a crime of itself, a conspiracy to raise the price of those funds cannot be a crime by itself; but in order to make it a crime, it is necessary to state some particular circumstance which gives it a criminal character.—I conceive nobody will be found to argue, that the raising the price of the public funds, without some side object, must be mischievous to the country, and therefore a crime; so far from that being the case, I conceive the higher the prices at which the government funds can be kept, except in particular cases, the better for the country, because it is upholding the credit of the country.

*Mr. Justice Le Blanc.* It is stated, that they were to be raised on a particular day.

*Lord Ellenborough.* By false reports and rumours.

*Mr. Serjeant Best.* An intention of doing that on a particular day, may be either a meritorious or a criminal action; but what I submit to your Lordships, is, that of itself, it is neither the one nor the other; it is therefore necessary to put on the record something which shall bring the fact within the purview of the law. It is not stated upon this record, that the defendants were possessed of any funds, that they were desirous of selling those funds, and that therefore they meditated a fraud on the particular persons to whom they should sell their funds, by raising the price;—it is merely stated, that the object was to raise the price of the funds, which I submit to your Lordships may be commendable or criminal.

One can conceive many circumstances in which this might be stated to be a public mischief, and some such circumstances were stated by my learned friend, who very ably opened this prosecution upon the trial. If the public funds were raised in price on a day on which the commissioners for reducing the national debt would make purchases, that would be an injury to the country, by the commissioners being enabled to purchase a smaller amount of stock for the same amount of money; but there is no allegation of the kind upon this indictment, and in no other way, do I conceive, could the public be injured. If the public had been injured, it was enough to have stated, that what was done, was done with a view to the injury of the public; but all that I find stated upon the record, is, that the defendants conspired and agreed together to raise the price of the public funds upon a given day; and the prosecutors knew there was no purchase made by the commissioners for reducing the national debt on that day; because, as I understand the fact to be, they never purchase on a Monday;—however, all that is material to me is, that the transaction is not so charged upon the face of the indictment. If I am right in this, I am persuaded your Lordships will be of opinion, that this is not an indictable offence.

If I am to be told, there is a distinction made between conspiracy and other offences, I submit to your Lordships, no distinction which has ever been made goes to a length which reaches the present case. I am aware many acts are made criminal, being accomplished by conspiracy, which accomplished by an individual only, would not be the subject of judicial animadversion; but I can find no case (and I have very carefully looked into all of them) which carries the principle on which the doctrine relating to conspiracy is founded further than this; that in conspiracy, though the means may be lawful, yet the end must be unlawful, either as it is mischievous to the public or to individuals; and I can state no case, in which parties have been held guilty of conspiracy, where the end they have had in view has not been either mischievous to the public, or at least to a specified class of individuals.

Looking back to the earlier statutes and cases on the subject of the law regarding conspiracy, your Lordships must collect, that neither the legislature nor the judges of the land had the least idea of embracing such a transaction as this, within their view of conspiracy. The older cases, in which the doctrine upon conspiracy has been applied, have been cases described by the statute of 21st Edward I. of persons who have conspired to instigate a criminal prosecution against an innocent individual, and of persons who, for the purpose of supporting their unlawful enterprises, have kept retainers in the country. In modern times, the decisions have come nearer to the present case; but I think I can satisfy your Lordships, there is none that reaches it.

The case in which the doctrine relating to conspiracy has travelled on, if I may so say, embracing a larger compass of acts, is that of the King *v.* Edwards, 8 Modern Reports, 320. In that case the doctrine laid down is, that a conspiracy to do a lawful act for effecting an unlawful end, is a crime. If the end be unlawful in this case, undoubtedly the endeavour to accomplish it was a crime. But I submit to your Lordships, as the act is stated upon the Record, the end is not unlawful, and that no case can be found which shews, that the end which these parties had in view was an unlawful end. Upon the principle of the case which I have mentioned, which goes far beyond the former cases on this subject, if I am right in stating, that *per se* there is nothing criminal in raising the price of the public funds, something must be added upon the record to make that act a crime.

Another case is that of The King *v.* Starling, 1 Siderfin, p. 174. It was an indictment for a conspiracy to depress what was called the gallon-trade, (that is, the practice of selling beer by the gallon) and thereby to cause the poor to mutiny, and to injure the farmers of excise; that was stated as the object of the conspirators. They were acquitted of that part of the charge which alleged an intention to cause the poor to mutiny; but found guilty of a design to injure the farmers of excise. The reporter says, after many debates it was adjudged, not that a conspiracy to injure the farmers of excise, speaking of them generally, was a crime—but, that the verdict relates to the information, the information relates to the excise, which is part of the revenue of the king; and to impoverish the farmers of excise would make them less able to pay the king his dues. And so the Court, in giving judgment, say, we must look at the record, to see if we can find out that what is charged upon the defendants be that which must necessarily produce a public mischief; and they say it does in this way; that the verdict relates to the information, and the information to the excise, which is part of the revenue of the country; and, as to impoverish the farmers of excise, would render them less able to pay the king his dues, there appears a public mischief on the face of the record itself. This I take to be a strong authority in my favour; for if the Court, after many debates as it is stated, and having given the subject every possible attention, came to the conclusion, that they were obliged to look at the record, to see whether the case stated on the record was one which necessarily connected the act done with some public mischief, we must necessarily infer from this, that the Court would have been of opinion, that unless that necessary connexion was established by the statement on the record, the judgment ought to be different. If I am not correct in this position, the Court had no occasion to look to the verdict and see whether it related to the information, and to the information, to see whether it had a relation to the revenue: the Court would have said, we must give judgment against the defendants, because it is stated upon this record, that the object of the defendants was, to impoverish the farmers of excise. It is by tracing back the thing itself, by shewing that the farmers of excise are thus made less able to pay their debts to the government, and therefore that the government was to be injured, that the act is constituted an offence.

There is another case, in Salkeld, 174, The King *v.* Best. The judgment of the Court in that case is, that several persons may lawfully meet and consult to prosecute a guilty person; otherwise, to charge a person who is innocent, right or wrong, would be indictable. The inference is, that upon a charge of conspiracy to do an act which in itself is perfectly innocent, which is not indictable, you must state something upon the face of the record, shewing a mischief connected with it, to make it indictable. I submit to your Lordships, there is nothing upon the face of this record, which does shew any mischief connected with the act which is made the subject of charge. In conspiracy as in every other offence, the means may be lawful; but in conspiracy, the end must be unlawful. It is this which constitutes the only distinction between cases of conspiracy and of any other crime; that although the means may be lawful, the end must necessarily be unlawful and mischievous. I say, it is impossible for your Lordships to collect from any part of this record, that the end sought to be obtained by these defendants was unlawful, as against any Act of Parliament or the positive decision of any Court; or unlawful, as generally mischievous to the public.

It is stated indeed upon these counts, that the act was mischievous to certain individuals; and if the individuals had been named, that would have answered my objection. But I submit to your Lordships, in support of the second proposition which I stated, that this offence, if it be any, is alleged in too general a way to convict any of the defendants. It would have been otherwise, if it had appeared that they were actuated by any malicious motive against those individuals, or had any clear intention of benefiting themselves at the expense of those individuals; and I may with safety to my client concede this, though I am not driven to it. On the contrary, I beg to state, it does not appear on this record, that the defendants could possibly gain any thing by what they are accused of having done; for it is not stated upon any of the counts, nor is it the fact, that they possessed one sixpenny worth of stock from the sale of which they could derive an advantage: they were therefore doing mischief without any purpose to answer by it.

*Lord Ellenborough.* Brother Best, was it possible to state that their purpose was to injure certain individual persons who should purchase stock, when by no possibility could they know who the persons were that would become purchasers? If that could have been stated, can you suggest any name which in any way might have been inserted?

*Mr. Serjeant Best.* I submit to your Lordship it might have been stated; and the evidence in the cause helps me to suggest an answer to your Lordship's question. Your Lordship will remember, that evidence was given of the accountant-general of the Court of Chancery having made purchases of stock on this day; it might have been stated on the face of this record, that it was known the accountant-general of the Court of Chancery would purchase stock on the day in question, for he purchased most days, and that the offence was committed with a view to injure the said accountant-general, or the persons in whose behalf he purchases.

*Lord Ellenborough.* I do not know, that in the course of his office he is directed to purchase on account of certain named individuals, on a given day; if he is not, even so the allegation could not be precise.

*Mr. Serjeant Best.* The stock is purchased, my Lord, to the credit of a particular cause, the accountant-general being the agent in the transaction for the suitors in that cause. Therefore the allegation might have been, that it was to injure the accountant-general, in his character of agent for those persons on whose behalf he purchased stock on the particular day. And this brings us to the true character of conspiracy. I submit to your Lordship, this act could only be made conspiracy, by shewing that the defendants possessed stock, and by stating on the indictment, that possessing stock, they conspired to raise the price of the funds on a particular day, and that when raised, they sold their stock to certain persons specified. Suppose they knew of persons who were going to purchase on this day, and with a view to make those persons pay more than they otherwise would, they did that which is charged upon this indictment; that would clearly be an indictable offence. It is not the difficulty of bringing the case within the law that furnishes an answer to the objection; if the law is defective, your Lordship would recommend it to the Legislature to remedy the defect, by making a new law.

*Lord Ellenborough.* Impossibility is some answer in point of law.

*Mr. Serjeant Best.* Your Lordships may be protecting gamblers as infamous as any of these defendants; you may be giving your support to prosecutions instituted by one set of gamblers against another, if this indictment is supported. A fair holder of stock could have no difficulty in coming by indictment, and stating, I was compelled by circumstances to lay out a sum of money in the public funds on a given day, the day on which this transaction took place, and I paid so much per cent. more for what I bought.

If it is necessary to constitute conspiracy, that the intent be to injure that person who in the event is injured, then it is impossible to support this indictment. I put it most strongly against my clients when I say, they meditated a fraud upon all who should purchase stock on this day; but to use the criminal law of this country, for the protection of those who honestly purchase stock, and not to support a prosecution brought by one set of gamblers against another, your Lordships will require it to be stated on the face of the indictment, who they were that were injured.

*Mr. Justice Bayley.* Suppose the conspiracy had been stated in the way it is, but the allegation had gone on; that by reason of the said conspiracy, A. B. and C. who on that day were obliged to purchase stock, were obliged to pay a larger sum than they otherwise would have paid?

*Mr. Serjeant Best.* That would have answered my objection, and that is the way in which it should have been stated; because then your Lordships would see, you were raising the arm of criminal justice to protect those who were the objects of its protection.

*Lord Ellenborough.* Your argument goes upon this supposition, that the description of persons to be affected by a criminal act, may lessen its criminality, which it does not.

*Mr. Serjeant Best.* But I submit to your Lordship, there must be something to be gained on the part of the actors, moving them to injure those who are capable of being injured by the act which is done. No such thing is stated upon any part of the indictment. A conspiracy may be complete without any act, but there must be an intention. I say, the intention here, is too generally stated; strike out all but the words, "conspired to raise the price of the public funds," and I ask your Lordships whether it would be possible to pronounce any judgment upon it.

*Mr. Justice Dampier.* How could the object have been stated with more particularity, with reference to a future event, than that it was to raise the price of the public funds?

*Mr. Serjeant Best.* I do not state it to be necessary that any damage should actually follow, but damage must be meditated by the conspirators, either a damage which aims at the public at large, or at some individual. It could not have been stated, nor is it stated, that any damage was aimed at the public at large; was any meditated against a part of the public? they must be individuals.

*Mr. Justice Dampier.* All the public could not be named; and individuals could not be named, because of the impossibility of knowing the individuals.

*Mr. Serjeant Best.* I submit to your Lordship there could be no difficulty in that. If the indictment had been preferred before the 21st February, your

Lordship's observation would be unanswerable; but after that period, the prosecutors could have no difficulty in obtaining the names of individual purchasers from the books of the Stock Exchange.

*Mr. Justice Dampier.* The crime was complete before the 21st of February.

*Mr. Justice Le Blanc.* If the conspiracy was, by false rumours to raise the price of the public funds on a certain day, with a view to oblige persons who should purchase into the funds on that day to pay an increased price, the crime would be complete if the funds were raised on that day, though no person should purchase a halfpenny-worth of stock; in like manner as conspiring to raise the price of commodities in a market, though no person should purchase, would still be a crime.

*Mr. Serjeant Best.* The commodities in a market are articles of necessity, which, I apprehend, makes a distinction.

*Lord Ellenborough.* Whether it be an article of necessity, or if universal sale, comes to the same thing. Besides, as to not stating the multitude, one would think we had forgotten the number of cases which have been decided on charges which are in their nature multitudinous; as for instance in barratry, or the inciting persons to institute and maintain suits; in those instances you need not state the individuals injured.

*Mr. Serjeant Best.* The instances of barratry and of common scolds, I believe, are the only exceptions.

*Lord Ellenborough.* By no means; I remember a case in which it was held, that where the circumstances cannot be conveniently specified upon the record, the necessity forms the exception.

*Mr. Serjeant Best.* But in all those cases your Lordship will find the excuse is stated upon the record; as ignotum, where an unknown person has been murdered.

*Lord Ellenborough.* In this case the nature and reason of the thing suggest the excuse, or one must reject one's common sense. The nature and reason of the thing form an exception, if it could be necessary to state the name of an individual, as having suffered from an act of this kind; but it is the tendency of the act, not the success of it, that constitutes the crime. If there had been an apprehension of pestilence or commotion, which made it unsafe to resort to the Stock Exchange on the day on which the fraud was practised, the crime would have been as complete by the conspiracy, as it was by the damage sustained by individuals who suffered under it.

*Mr. Serjeant Best.* In whatever way your Lordships dispose of these objections, I shall be satisfied. I am sure your Lordships will excuse my mentioning, in a case of this sort, The King v. Robe, 2d Strange, p. 999, though it is not a case of conspiracy.

*Lord Ellenborough.* No doubt they ought in that case to have specified the persons, they had the means of stating every one of them. The offence did not consist in the combination, but in doing the very act they combined to do.

*Mr. Serjeant Best.* Another objection which applies to all the counts is, that it is stated, the intention was to produce a great rise in the Government funds of this kingdom. It appears clearly on the face of this record that the intention was very different; in fact there are no general Government funds belonging to the United Kingdom of Great Britain and Ireland.

*Mr. Justice Bayley.* But there are British and Irish funds?

*Mr. Serjeant Best.* Certainly, but that is not the allegation; the allegation is, that it was with a view to raise the funds of this kingdom, which supposes there are general funds of Great Britain and Ireland; whereas the funds of each are entirely distinct, and of that your Lordships will take notice, because there are Acts of Parliament which speak of the British and Irish funds separately. Therefore I submit to your Lordships, it is impossible those defendants could contemplate the mischief with which the count concludes.

*Lord Ellenborough.* In a large sense, the Irish funds are funds of this kingdom, and so are the British; they are each a part of the resources and means of the United Kingdom.

*Mr. Serjeant Best.* It is impossible they should have had in view the Irish funds.

*Lord Ellenborough.* Why not? I believe the Irish funds are saleable upon the Stock Exchange as well as the British. The interest is payable in this country, and the great money-market is here; and I believe full as much is done in the Irish funds here as in Ireland.

*Mr. Serjeant Best.* I am unacquainted with the fact; still I insist, that those funds could not be called the funds of this kingdom?

*Lord Ellenborough.* I think they could not be correctly called otherwise; they are funds of the kingdom in a large sense.

*Mr. Serjeant Best.* A very large part of the Irish funds were not raised by the United Parliament; and they have been kept distinct ever since the Union.

*Lord Ellenborough.* They may be distinctly arranged, and the application of them may have been in different ways; but still they are a part of one whole, they are a part of the stock and revenues of the United Kingdom.

MR. PARK,

My Lords, I am counsel for Mr. De Berenger alone. The first two general grounds of objection, my learned friend has argued very fully, and I shall not trouble your Lordships upon them; but I confess there seems to me to be a great deal of weight in the last objection. Your Lordship will recollect, the beginning of this indictment states His Majesty to be (as the Act of Parliament requires he shall be stated) the King of the United Kingdom of Great Britain and Ireland. The very first article of Union requires, that after a day specified, the kingdoms of Great Britain and Ireland shall be called the United Kingdom of Great Britain and Ireland. Throughout this indictment, in all the counts except the last, the offence charged is stated to have been committed for the purpose of creating a rise in price of the funds of *this kingdom*. Now your Lordships perhaps may not be aware, that in the seventh article of Union it is expressly provided, that the funds of the United Kingdom, forming the separate funds of the two kingdoms, shall continue to be kept distinct. But after the indictment has stated His Majesty as King of this kingdom, which can only mean of the United Kingdom, then what is stated of the funds of this kingdom, can only relate to funds of the United Kingdom; not in the large sense in which your Lordship considers them, as forming a part of the funds of the United Kingdom, but in the same sense the general funds of the United Kingdom, as His Majesty is stated to be the King of this kingdom; whereas by the articles of Union, the funds of the United Kingdom are to be considered two distinct funds.

*Mr. Justice Dampier.* Then the statement relates to a fund, which, by law, can have no existence.

*Mr. Park.* That may be, my Lord.

*Mr. Justice Dampier.* If it could by possibility relate to no other fund, the objection might be a good one; but there is a sense in which it does relate to the funds of the United Kingdom, distributively considered.

*Lord Ellenborough.* It is a description applicable to a new state of society, namely, to the aggregate kingdoms of Great Britain and Ireland; and the funds of the Kingdom are the funds of the United Kingdom.

*Mr. Park.* I only mention this to draw your Lordship's attention to the statute, in addition to the observations which my learned friend has made. Before I sit down, your Lordship will give me leave to suggest to the Court, upon the motion for a new trial, in addition to what the learned Serjeant threw out, an observation founded upon the Russian cases, where an Order of Council was stated, which your Lordships decided you could not take judicial notice of, that there was no proof of the falsehood of the rumours by which, they say, the price of the funds was to be raised.

*Lord Ellenborough.* But there was proof of the fabrication of them.

*Mr. Serjeant Pell.* On the part of Mr. Holloway, Mr. Random, and Mr. Lyte, I am not disposed to trouble your lordships with any observations in arrest of judgment.

*Lord Ellenborough.* Does Lord Cochrane wish to address any thing to the Court?

*Lord Cochrane.* My Lord, I am desirous, previously to your passing judgment upon this matter, that I should have an opportunity of explaining those things which I deem essential to be brought under your consideration.

*Lord Ellenborough.* If you mean to offer any observations in arrest of judgment, this is the proper time; we will afterwards hear, as a distinct thing, whatever may occur to you as fit to be presented to the Court, to induce them to grant a new trial; that is probably your object.

*Lord Cochrane.* I do not move in arrest of judgment.

LORD ELLENBOROUGH,

I am perfectly clear there is no ground for the motion in arrest of judgment, and that a public mischief is stated as being the object of this conspiracy. The conspiracy is, by false rumours to raise the price of the public funds and securities; that crime is committed in the act of conspiracy, concert, and combination, to effect the purpose, and the offence would have been completed even if it had not been pursued to its consequences, or from circumstances the conspirators had not been able to effect it. And the purpose is in its nature mischievous; it is one which strikes at the value of a vendable article in the market, and if it gives a fictitious value, by means of false rumours, it is a fraud on all who may by possibility have to do with that article; it is a fraud on all the public who may have to do with the funds on the day to which the conspiracy applies.

It seems to me quite unnecessary to specify the persons who became purchasers of stock, for without the gift of prophecy how could the defendants know who would be purchasers on a succeeding day? The impossibility is the excuse; besides if it were possible, the multitude is an excuse in point of law. But such a statement is wholly unnecessary, the conspiracy being complete independently of any persons becoming purchasers.

Mr. Justice Le Blanc,

The motion in arrest of judgment has been made upon three grounds; the first, that it is no crime in itself to raise the price of the public funds, and that we are to look to the indictment to see what is the mischief charged. The charge in the indictment is a conspiracy by false rumours to raise the price of the public funds on a particular day. I admit that the simple fact of raising or lowering the public funds is no crime. A man having a necessary occasion to sell a large sum out of the stocks, though it may have the effect of depressing the funds on that day; or to purchase a large sum, though he thereby raises the funds, commits no offence. But if a number of persons conspire to raise the funds on a particular day by spreading false rumours, that is an offence, and the offence consists in raising the funds by false rumours on that day, not in the simple act of raising the funds.

The next objection is, that the indictment states a purpose to defraud, without naming the persons who were to be defrauded. From the nature of the case, persons could not be named; the offence was a conspiracy on a previous day, to raise the price of the funds upon a future day. It was therefore uncertain who would be the purchasers; but the object was, that the price of the funds should be raised to all who should become purchasers on that day, and could not be aimed at particular individuals. The offence was general, in the same manner as if a false rumour were spread previous to a market-day, to raise the price of some commodity which should be brought to market.

A further objection is, that the indictment refers to the funds of *this kingdom*, and that since the Union, this kingdom can only mean the United Kingdom of Great Britain and Ireland. But although particular sums may be applied to the particular service of one or the other part of the United Kingdom, yet the public funds of either part are funds of the United Kingdom, and go in furtherance of the general service of the United Kingdom. It appears to me there is no reason why this judgment should be arrested.

Mr. Justice Bayley,

If the question admitted of any doubt, I should be desirous of giving the defendants the advantage of that doubt; but it seems to me perfectly clear, that there is no foundation for any one of the objections that have been made. To raise the funds may be an innocent thing; but a conspiracy to raise the funds by illegal means, and with an illegal view, is, as it seems to me, a crime; a crime which might perhaps affect the public in its aggregate capacity; but which, if it take effect, will certainly prejudice a class of His Majesty's subjects; and it is not necessary to constitute a crime, that it should be prejudicial to the public in its aggregate character, or to all of His Majesty's subjects, it is sufficient if it be prejudicial to a class of His Majesty's subjects.

Here is not only a conspiracy for an illegal end, but a conspiracy to effect that end by illegal means; because when it is endeavoured to raise the funds by false rumours, the means are illegal, then is the end illegal. The object is to produce a temporary rise in the funds without any foundation; and the necessary consequence of that is, all those who purchase on the day, and during the period of time that rise affects the funds, will necessarily be prejudiced.

Another objection is, that the indictment does not state by name the persons whom the defendants intended to defraud; but it is said, the indictment would have been good if it had stated, that by means of this conspiracy certain persons, naming them, had been prejudiced. As to that, the conspiracy constitutes the crime, and it is sufficient to state the crime upon the indictment in the way it existed at the moment when the crime was complete. It might have happened from circumstances coming to light, that the plot should be detected before the mischief had been effected; yet the offence would not have been less, because the parties had done all in their power, and every thing that was necessary to constitute the crime, when they had formed the conspiracy, and used the illegal means for an illegal purpose. It depended not on them how far their crime would be prejudicial to others; but their criminality must depend on their own act, not upon the consequences of that act.

The other objection is, that the indictment describes the funds to be raised as the funds of *this kingdom*. It is true, that since the Union the funds which are raised must be raised in certain proportions upon one part of the kingdom and upon the other: but when those funds are raised, they become respectively the funds of the kingdom, they are raised by the Legislature of the kingdom, and are applied by the Government of the kingdom to such purposes as Parliament say they are to be applied to. But if you can properly predicate of them, that they are funds, in part only applicable to England, and in part to Ireland, still it is true that those two funds do constitute the funds of this kingdom; and when it can only be said, that the funds of this kingdom are distinguishable into British and Irish funds, then when you speak of the funds of this kingdom, you mean both the British and Irish funds.

MR. JUSTICE DAMPIER,

The charge upon this indictment is, that the defendants, by false rumours, conspired to create a temporary rise in the funds of the kingdom, in order to defraud those who should purchase into the funds on a particular day. I cannot raise any doubt in my mind, but that this is, according to any definition of the act of conspiracy, a complete crime of conspiracy. The means are wrong, they are false rumours; the object is wrong, for it is to give a false value to a commodity in a public market; and the consequences are injurious to all who have to purchase that commodity. This disposes of the first objection.

The second objection is, that the persons defrauded ought to have been named. The first answer to that is, the crime of conspiracy is complete when the concert to bring about an object with a mischievous intent is complete; it is not at all necessary for the perfection of the crime that its object should be attained. Therefore, the first answer is, there need be no person injured. The next answer is the impossibility of the defendants knowing before-hand who would be defrauded. It is said, the indictment was preferred after the mischief had taken effect, therefore the persons injured might have been named; but to require such a statement we must hold, that the consequential damage created by this crime is necessary to constitute the crime itself.

The third objection is, that there are no such funds as the funds of *this kingdom*; that there are no funds raised at the common charge of both parts of the United Kingdom. But every fund that is raised from either part becomes, when it is raised, a fund of the kingdom at large, and is strictly a part of the funds and government securities of the United Kingdom; the United Kingdom is answerable for them, and for the service of the United Kingdom, whether applied to England or Ireland, it is that they are raised. I think the description is better than any other which might be framed. For these reasons I am of opinion, there is no ground to arrest the judgment, nor any doubt to require a rule for a further discussion.

*Lord Ellenborough read the report of the evidence.*

LORD COCHRANE,

Your Lordships having listened to those who had any thing to offer which they considered material for their defence, emboldens me to trust that your Lordships, though I do not address you by Counsel, will grant me a similar indulgence, and even that you will extend that indulgence further to me on account of my not appearing by Counsel, for the reasons which I had the honour to state to you upon a former occasion. In order that those feelings which must agitate me on the present occasion, may as little as possible enter into what I have now to state, I have judged it proper to reduce it to writing; and in order to give the Court as little trouble as possible, to make my statement as short as the circumstances of the case appear to me to admit of.

It has been my very great misfortune to be apparently implicated in the guilt of others with whom I never had any connexion, except in transactions, so far as I was apprised of them, entirely blameless. I had met Mr. De Berenger in public company, but was on no terms of intimacy with him. With Mr. Cochrane Johnstone I had the intercourse natural between such near relatives. Mr. Butt had voluntarily offered, without any reward, to carry on stock transactions, in which thousands, as well as myself were engaged, in the face of day without the smallest imputation of any thing incorrect. The other four defendants were wholly unknown to me, nor have I ever, directly or indirectly, held any communication with them. Of Mr. De Berenger's concern in the fraud, I have no information, except such as arises out of the late trial. With regard to Mr. Johnstone and Mr. Butt, I am willing to hope that they are guiltless. They repeatedly protested to me their innocence. They did not dare to communicate any such plan to me, if such was projected by them, or either of them. Be they guilty, then, or be they, one or both, erroneously convicted, I have only to lament, that, without the most remote suspicion of their proceedings, if they, or either of them, were concerned in the fraud, I have, through my blameless intercourse with them, been subject to imputations which might, with equal justice, have been cast upon any man who now hears me. Circumstanced as I am, I must keep myself wholly unconnected with those whose innocence cannot be so clear to me as my own. Well had it been for me if I had made this distinction sooner.

I do not stand here to commend myself—unhappily, I must seek only for exculpation; but I cannot exist under the load of dishonour which even an unjust judgment has flung upon me. My life has been too often in jeopardy to make me think much about it; but my honour was never yet breathed upon; and I now hold my existence only in the determination to remove an imputation, as groundless, as it is intolerable.

The evidence which I now tender to your Lordship, will aid me in performing this duty towards myself, my rank, and my profession. I first offer the affidavit, which I have repeated at a risk which I formerly had no opportunity of encountering. I have been told, that I then incurred the moral guilt of perjury, without exposing myself to the legal penalties. I know nothing of such distinctions. I have repeated the statement upon oath—and I am now answerable to the laws if I have falsely sworn. The affidavits of three persons who saw De Berenger at my house on the 21st of February, fully confirm my statement, and I have only been prevented from bringing forward a fourth, by his sailing to a distant situation, before I could possibly stop him for this purpose.

The grounds upon which I have been convicted are these:—That notes were found in De Berenger's possession which had been changed for others, that had once been in mine. That De Berenger came to my house after returning from his expedition; and that my account of what passed at this visit is contradicted by evidence.

The first ground has been clearly explained away; it amounts to nothing more than that which may happen to any man who has money transactions. Mr.

Butt voluntarily made purchases and sales of stock for me, and having received a small loan of money from him, I repaid him with bank notes which he used for his own purposes. He says that he exchanged these notes, and that a part of the notes which he received in exchange he paid to Mr. Cochrane Johnstone, who states, that he gave them to De Berenger in payment of some drawings; but with this story, whether true or false, I have no manner of concern, and consequently no wish to discuss it. In what way soever the notes which were received in exchange for mine reached De Berenger, I can only say, that mine were given to Mr. Butt in discharge of a *bonâ fide* debt; and I have no knowledge whatever of the uses to which he applied them.

De Berenger's coming to my house, I before accounted for upon the supposition of his being unconcerned in the fraud; but is it not obvious that he might have come there to facilitate his escape, by going immediately on board of my ship, with the additional prospect of obtaining employment in America? It has been said that there was a suspicious degree of familiarity in his treatment of me and my house. I can only observe, that over his conduct I had no controul. But he knew, it seems, of my change of abode, which had occurred within a few days. I trust it will be recollected, that he is proved to have left town three days after such change, and that though not intimate with me, he had the means of knowing where I resided, even if he should not have enquired at my former lodgings, where my address was left. Indeed, if taking refuge in my ship, in order to facilitate his escape, was part of his scheme, it was very likely that he would have ascertained the precise place of my abode, previous to his quitting London. Again, I am said to have left the tinman's, (where I think I should hardly have gone had I expected such a messenger) as soon as I heard of the officer's arrival. I was in apprehensions of fatal news respecting my brother then in France, from whom I had received a letter but three days before, with the intelligence of his being dangerously ill; and I now tender you his affidavit, with the surgeon's certificate, dated the 12th of February, which he brought home with him. And therefore, on receiving the note from De Berenger, whose name I was unable to decypher, and as that note announced that the writer, whom I learnt from my servant had the appearance of an officer in the army, who was desirous of seeing me, I hastened to learn intelligence so anxiously expected; nor had I the least doubt that it related to my brother. When, however, I found that the person was De Berenger, and that he had only to speak of his own private affairs, the apparent distress he was in, and the relief it gave my mind to know that he was not the bearer of the news I dreaded, prevented me from feeling that displeasure which I might otherwise have felt at the liberty he had taken or the interruption it had occasioned. Comments have been made on my saying so little to the servant who brought that note; but the fact is, I did ask him several questions, as appears by his affidavit.

That I did not learn the name of the writer from the note itself, I have truly accounted for, by its being written so close to the bottom of the paper that I could not read it. This assertion is said to be contradicted by the circumstance of the writer having found room to add a postscript, as if there was only one side to the paper. Of the postscript I have no recollection, but it might have been written even opposite the signature. That I did not collect from the hand-writing, that it was addressed to me by De Berenger, is nothing extraordinary; my acquaintance with that person was extremely slight; and till that day I had never received more than one or two notes from him, which related to a drawing of a lamp. I was too deeply impressed with the idea that the note was addressed to me by an officer who had come with intelligence of my brother, to apprehend that it was written by De Berenger, from whom I expected no communication, and with whose hand-writing I was not familiar. All that I could afterwards recollect of the note, more than what is stated in my affidavit is, that he had something to communicate which would affect my feeling mind, or words to that effect, which confirmed my apprehensions that the writer was the messenger of fatal news of my brother.

If De Berenger had really been my agent in this nefarious transaction, how I should have acted or where I should have chosen to receive him, it is impossible for me to say: but I humbly apprehend that my own house was not the place I should have selected for that purpose. The pretended Du Bourg, if I had chosen him for my instrument, instead of his making me his convenience, should have terminated his expedition and have found a change of dress elsewhere. He should not have come immediately and in open day to my house. I should not so rashly have invited detection and its concomitant ruin.

But this is not the only extravagance of which I am accused. What supposition short of my absolute insanity will account for my having voluntarily made the affidavit which has been so much canvassed, if I really knew the plot in which De Berenger appears to have been engaged? Let me entreat your Lordships consideration of the situation in which I stood at the moment in which that affidavit was made; I was suspected of being connected with the pretended Du Bourg; if I had known that De Berenger was the person who had assumed that name, could I possibly have betrayed him, and consequently myself, more completely than by publishing such a detail to the world? The name of De Berenger was never mentioned till brought forward in my affidavit; which affidavit was made, as sworn by Mr. Wright, a witness on the trial, with the circumstance present to me, and remarked by me at the time I delivered it to him to be printed, that if De Berenger should happen to be Du Bourg, I had furnished a clue to his detection. The circumstance of his obtaining a change of dress at my house, never could have been known if I had not voluntarily discovered it; and thus

I am represented as having brought him publicly to my own house, of being the first to disclose his name, and of mentioning a circumstance, which, of all others, it was the most easy to conceal, and, if divulged, the most certain to excite suspicion! Is it not next to impossible, that a man, conscious of guilt, should have been so careless of his most imminent danger?

My adversaries dwell upon some particulars of this affidavit, which they pretend to find contradicted in the evidence. The principle one is my assertion that Berenger wore a green coat. I have repeated this assertion upon oath, under all the risks of the law; and I also solemnly affirm, upon my honour, which I regard as an obligation no less sacred, that I only saw him in that dress. The witnesses on the part of the prosecution have asserted, that he wore a red coat when he arrived in town. Granted. But may he not have changed it in the coach, on his way to Green-street? Where was the difficulty, and for what purpose was the portmanteau? My own fixed opinion is, that he changed his dress in the coach, because I believe that he dared not run the risk of appearing in my presence till he had so changed it. I tender affidavits of those who saw him, as I did, in his green coat, at my house. That he should have changed his dress before I saw him is most natural, upon the supposition of his wishing to conceal from me the work he had been about; but it is like many other confirmations of my innocence, fated to excite no attention in the minds of those who only seek food for their suspicions. Much is said of the star and other ornaments, as if any proof had been given of his wearing them in my presence. He took especial care, I doubt not, to lay them aside on his way, when he had divested himself of his official capacity, long before I saw him. The small portmanteau before-mentioned, which it is admitted he brought with him, in all probability furnished him with the green coat, and received the red coat and its ornaments, and very possibly for this reason no remark has been made upon it. A good deal of observation has been bestowed upon De Berenger's unwillingness to appear before Lord Yarmouth in uniform, and the inference was, that this uniform could not have been the green dress of his corps, otherwise he must have felt the reverse of uneasy at being seen in it by his Colonel. Does any volunteer officer go out of a morning to make calls in his regimentals? Could so unusual a circumstance have failed to excite remark from Lord Yarmouth? To me, indeed, he had explained himself—he had of necessity told me his nearly desperate state, in asking me to receive him on board my ship; but is there any thing so very incredible in the statement that he was unwilling to tell his whole case to every body? It may now doubtless be perceived, that he might have had other reasons for disliking to go out in a green dress.

Let it, however, be recollected, that my statement was, that he only asked me for a hat in lieu of his military cap, and that the black coat was my own voluntary offer. The idea of his applying to Lord Yarmouth, or to any other of his friends, originated with me, and I proposed it in consequence of his calling to my recollection the certificates he had received from them. I then had no suspicion awake, and I believed what he told me. In what manner the disguise was ultimately disposed of I can only conjecture, as any one else might, from the evidence given on the trial. He presented himself to me in a grey great coat, and a green under coat; and if the persons whose affidavits I now tender had been examined on the trial, and they did attend for that purpose, I do feel persuaded that a very different impression would have been made on the jury and the world at large, than that which they appear to entertain; and that your Lordships might have been disposed to take an opposite view of the case as it affected me. Those witnesses would have corroborated the particulars of my affidavit relative to De Berenger's dress, when I first saw him at my house, namely, a grey great coat, and a green under coat and jacket. Unfortunately, through some mistake or misconception, not on my part, they were left unnoticed, and, of course, were not examined. I have now to offer their several affidavits to your Lordships.

I would further submit to your Lordships, that my affidavit was made at the impulse of the moment, as soon as I heard that placards had been posted, stating that the pretended colonel Du Bourg had gone to my house; and in the conscious rectitude of my own conduct, I not only introduced the name of the only officer I saw at my house on the day stated, but narrated every occurrence that took place, and all the conversation that took place at the interview, to the best of my recollection. If I am censured for having been too ingenuous in my communication, I trust it will be admitted, that as ingenuousness disclaims all connexion with guilt, it is indicative only of my innocence.

If your Lordships will be pleased to reflect on all that I have offered respecting De Berenger, and to bear in mind the avowed intercourse which I had with two other defendants, respecting whose conduct I have been compelled to speak at last upon a supposition of their guilt, I am confident you will perceive how easily any man living so circumstanced might have been placed in the very situation. But waiving the supposition of De Berenger acting under the direction of either of the other defendants, I do still contend, that any man who had stock concerns, and was slightly known to De Berenger, ran the same risk with me, of being driven into the ruin, which undeservedly, as I am still willing to hope, has befallen the others.

The artifices which have been used to excite so much prejudice against me, I unfeignedly despise, in spite of the injury they have done me. I know it must subside, and I look forward to justice being rendered my character sooner or later: It will come most speedily, as well as most gratefully, if I shall receive it at your Lordship's hands. I am not unused to injury; of late I have known persecution: the indignity of compassion I am not yet able to bear.

To escape what is vulgarly called punishment, would have been an easy thing; but I must have belied my feelings by acting as if I were conscious of dishonour. There are ways, even of removing beyond the reach of ignominy, but I cannot feel disgraced while I know that I am guiltless. Under the influence of this sentiment, I persist in the defence of my character. I have often been in situations where I had an opportunity of showing it. This is the first time, thank God, that I was ever called upon to defend it.

---

The following Affidavits, handed in by Lord Cochrane, were read.

"In the King's Bench.

"The King *against* Charles Random De Berenger, & others.

"Sir Thomas Cochrane, commonly called Lord Cochrane, one of the above named defendants, maketh oath and saith, That the several facts and circumstances stated in his affidavit, sworn on the eleventh day of March last, before Mr. Graham, the Magistrate, are true; and this deponent further saith, that in addition to the several facts and circumstances stated in his said affidavit, he deposeth as follows, (that is to say); That he had not directly nor indirectly any concern whatever in the formation, or any knowledge of the existence of an intention to form the plot charged in the indictment, or any other scheme or design for affecting the public funds. That the sale of the pretended omnium on the twenty-first day of February, was made in pursuance of orders given to his broker at the time of the purchase thereof, on or about the fourteenth of that month, to sell the same whenever a profit of one per cent. could be realized; and that those directions were given, and the sale thereof took place without any knowledge, information, hint or surmise on the part of this deponent, of any concern or attempt whatever to alter the price of the funds; and the said sale on the twenty-first took place entirely without this deponent's knowledge. That when this deponent returned home from Mr. King's manufactory, on the twenty-first of February, which he did directly after the receipt of a note, he fully expected to have met an officer from abroad, with intelligence of his brother, who had by letter to this deponent received on the Friday before, communicated his being confined to his bed, and severely afflicted by a dangerous illness, and about whom this deponent was extremely anxious; but this deponent found Captain De Berenger at his house, in a grey great coat, and a green jacket. That this deponent never saw the defendants, Ralph Sandom, Alexander M'Rae, John Peter Holloway, and Henry Lyte, or any or either of them, nor ever had any communication or correspondence with them, or any or either of them, directly or indirectly; that this deponent, in pursuance of directions from the Admiralty, proceeded to Chatham to join his Majesty's ship "The Tonnant," to which he had been appointed on the eighth day of February last; that the ship was then lying at Chatham; that previous to the eighth day of February, this deponent applied to the Admiralty for leave of absence, which was refused until this deponent had joined the said ship, and had removed her down to Long Reach; that this deponent in pursuance of those directions removed the said ship from Chatham to Long Reach; and after that was done, viz. on Saturday the twelfth day of the said month, this deponent wrote to the Admiralty, to apply for leave of absence for a fortnight, for the purpose of lodging a specification for a patent, as had been previously communicated by this deponent to their Lordships; that leave of absence was accordingly granted for fourteen days, commencing on the fourteenth of the said month; that this deponent was engaged in London respecting the said specification, till the twenty-eighth of the said month, when the said specification was completed; and this deponent left town about one o'clock on the morning of the first day of March, and arrived at Chatham about day-light on the same morning; that on the eighth or ninth of the same month of March, this deponent received an intimation, that placards were affixed in several of the streets, stating that a pretended Colonel Du Bourg had gone to this deponent's house in Green-street; that he was on board the said ship at Long Reach, and in consequence went to Admiral Surrage, the Port Admiral at Chatham, to obtain leave of absence, which was granted previous to the receipt of the leave forwarded by the Lords Commissioners of the Admiralty; this deponent arrived in London on the tenth of that month, to the best of his belief; and that after his arrival, he himself, conscious of his own innocence, and fearing no consequences from a developement of every part of his own conduct, and desiring only to rescue his character from erroneous impressions made by misrepresentations in the public prints, he without any communication whatsoever with any other person, and without any assistance, on the impulse of the moment prepared the before-mentioned affidavit, which he swore before Mr. Graham, the magistrate, on the eleventh; that at the time he swore such affidavit, he had not seen or heard the contents of the report published by the Committee of the Stock Exchange, except partial extracts in the newspapers; that when this deponent understood that a prosecution was to be instituted against him, he wrote to Admiral Fleming, in whose service Isaac Davis, formerly this deponent's servant, then was, under cover to Admiral Bickerton, at Portsmouth, and that Admiral Bickerton returned the letter, saying, that Admiral Fleming had sailed for Gibraltar; that this deponent sent his servants, Thomas Dewman, Elizabeth Busk, and Mary Turpin, on the trial of this indictment, to prove that an officer came to this deponent's house on the morning of the said twenty-first of February, and to prove the dress that he came in, but that the said Thomas Dewman only was called; and as this deponent has been informed, he was not interrogated as to the dress in which the said officer came to his house; and this deponent further saith, that had the said witnesses been examined, according to the directions of this deponent, and who were in attendance on the Court for that express purpose, they would, as he verily believes, have removed every unfavourable conclusion respecting this deponent's conduct, drawn from the supposed dress in which the said De Berenger appeared before this deponent on the twenty-first of February, and on which circumstance much stress was laid in the charge to the Jury, the said De Berenger's dress being exactly as stated in this deponent's former affidavit hereinbefore-mentioned; and this deponent solemnly and positively denies, that he ever saw the said De Berenger in a scarlet uniform, decorated by medal, or other insignia, and he had not the least suspicion of the said De Berenger being engaged in any plot respecting the funds, but merely believed he wished, for the reasons stated in this deponent's former affidavit, to go on board this deponent's ship, with a view to obtain some military appointment in America; and this deponent declined complying with his request to send him on board his ship, without permission or an order from the Lords of the Admiralty; and this deponent further saith, that he was in no degree intimate with the said De Berenger; that he had no personal knowledge of his private or public character; that he never asked the said De Berenger to his house, nor did he ever breakfast or dine with this deponent therein on any occasion whatsoever; and further, this deponent saith, that he hath been informed, and verily believes, that the Jury who tried the said indictment, and the Counsel for the defence, were so completely exhausted and worn out by extreme fatigue, owing to the Court having continued the trial without intermission for many hours beyond that time which nature is capable of sustaining herself without reflection and repose, that justice could not be done to this deponent.

*Cochrane.*"

Sworn in Court the
14th June 1814.

"In the King's Bench.

"The King *against* Charles Random De Berenger, & others.

"Thomas Dewman, servant to Lord Cochrane, maketh Oath and saith,——
"

*Lord Ellenborough.* This was a person called as a witness on the trial; if the affidavit goes beyond what he then stated, or in contradiction to what he stated, it cannot be received.

*Lord Cochrane.* Would your Lordship permit me to explain the reason why he was not interrogated?

*Mr. Justice Bayley.* It is a settled rule, not to allow the affidavits of persons who might have been called upon the trial, much less of persons who were called.

*Lord Ellenborough.* And if any were not called, they were not called under the discretion of your Lordship. It would be a very dangerous thing, if persons whose evidence may have been discreetly kept back, should afterwards be admitted to come forward as witnesses.

*Mr. Dealtry.* The next is the affidavit of Sarah Busk.

*Lord Cochrane.* My humble hope is, that you will be pleased to grant a new trial, in order that these persons may have the opportunity of being examined: they were not called from an error in the brief, which (so little was I conscious of any participation in the fraud) I had not even read.

*Mr. Gurney.* My Lord, the Counsel for the defendant were not uninstructed, as to the evidence which these persons could give; because, annexed to the affidavit which your Lordship has stated, of Lord Cochrane, were the affidavits of all the servants, of the one who is not now in England, as well as of the three who are in England. They are all printed together in Mr. Butt's pamphlet, which was produced at the trial. Therefore the Counsel for the defendant were informed of every circumstance, and they might, if they had thought it would serve their client, have called all those persons as witnesses.

*Mr. Justice Le Blanc.* There is no rule better established, than that after trial we cannot receive the affidavits of persons who were called, or who might have been called as witnesses. Whatever might be the reason for keeping back their testimony, that the Court cannot hear.

*[The following Affidavit was read.]*

"In the King's Bench.

"The King *against* Charles Random De Berenger & others.

"The Honourable William Erskine Cochrane, Major in the fifteenth regiment of dragoons, now residing in Portman-square in the county of Middlesex, on his oath saith, That he was seized with a violent and alarming illness on the first of January one thousand eight hundred and fourteen, at Cambo in the south of France; and that this deponent remained in a state of dangerous illness until the eighteenth of the following month. That early in February last he wrote to his brother Lord Cochrane, to acquaint his Lordship with this deponent's situation, as deponent had then very little hope of recovery, and telling him that he had received a notification that he would be ordered to England, where he should proceed, if ever able to undertake the journey. And this deponent further saith, that the annexed certificate was given to him for the purpose of being laid officially before a board of medical officers at Saint Jean de Luz, by the surgeon of this deponent's regiment, and is in the said surgeon's hand-writing.

*W. E. Cochrane.*"

Sworn in Court,
this 14th day of June 1814.
By the Court.

"Statement of Major the Honourable William Cochrane's Complaint.
Monday, February 12, 1814.

"Was seized with the usual symptoms of fever on the 1st of January, which was continued for the first three days; then the remittent character developed itself. The evening paroxism was severe every day, and he was all through much worse on the third day than on the two preceding days. The treatment consisted in keeping the bowels perfectly free and the skin moist, and this was generally obtained by calomel and antimonial powder combined, in the proportion of two grains, and three every third hour, and an occasional purge of neutral salts. When the bowels were well emptied, I frequently gave saline draughts, which kept the skin moist and favourable for the exhibition of bark, the use of which was commenced the 16th day. On the 23d he had a crisis, and went on very well till the 1st of February, when he suffered a relapse, attended with rather alarming symptoms. There was great determination to the head, the eyes were suffused, great drowsiness, and a tendency to comæ; however, these symptoms gave way in six hours, in which time he was actively purged, the skin was made moist, and a profuse perspiration kept up for twelve hours, which left him perfectly tranquil and free from fever. From this term I continued to give him small doses of calomel, till his mouth was very slightly affected. He continued free from fever from the morning of the 2d till the 7th; his appetite good, his strength increasing, and every sign of health. On that morning he had a second relapse, but by no means so violent, though more embarrassing; he has not been well since, and has suffered very much indeed. The treatment latterly has been attention to the state of his bowels and diet. He has not taken bark since his first relapse. I hope the change of air and objects will serve him.

*Tho. Cartan,*
Surgeon, 15th Hussars."

*Lord Ellenborough.* This affidavit is not even material to shew, that Lord Cochrane was in possession of his brother's letter previous to the morning of the 21st of February, so as to account for a connexion existing in his mind between the note he on that morning received, and the state of his brother's health, which should induce him immediately on the receipt of it, to return home?

*Lord Cochrane.* I was not present at the trial, or those witnesses would have been examined.

*Lord Ellenborough.* But those witnesses would not have gone to this point, and your mind must have been drawn to it at the time you made your affidavit, when you came to mention your brother's illness?

*Lord Cochrane.* My brother's affidavit states, that he wrote to me early in the month, and I received his letter on the Friday previous to the fraud.

*Lord Ellenborough.* That was capable of being most distinctly verified.

*Mr. Justice Bayley.* The original letter is not annexed to the affidavit?

*Lord Cochrane.* It is not; I had no idea of bringing the letter of my brother before a court of justice.

[*The following Affidavit was read.*]

"In the King's Bench.

"The King *against* Charles Random De Berenger, & others.

"Charles Random De Berenger, the above-named defendant, (having been found guilty of certain counts, but acquitted of the two first contained in this indictment,) maketh oath and saith, That he, this deponent, has zealously and loyally served His Majesty and this country as a volunteer, during a period of sixteen years, without ever receiving pay, remuneration, or reward of any kind, although by a most punctual and uninterrupted discharge of his various duties, his pecuniary interests and views were consequently greatly injured, but more especially during the time he acted as Adjutant, being for a period of near seven years, when his time was daily occupied more or less by the duties of that situation; and instead of drawing permanent pay, as is the usual custom of volunteer adjutants, he even put himself to considerable annual expences, to further the views of that service. And this deponent further saith, That the testimonials now produced in Court, as proofs of his energetic and loyal services, are of the proper hand-writing of the parties whose names are thereunto respectively subscribed. And this deponent further saith, That he has lost his paternal fortune, exceeding the sum of thirty-three thousand pounds, solely owing to his father's loyal adherence to the crown of Great Britain, during the American revolution; and that no indemnity of any kind has ever been given for such loss, either to his late father or to himself. That perfectly unprejudiced by such hard fate, this deponent constantly and without fee, or even condition for reward, has since, not only tendered his loyal assistance to this country to the utmost of his power, and in a variety of ways, but has actually given several important suggestions and communications, which although made use of by the offices of Government, still continue unrewarded. And this deponent further saith, that he lately lost a considerable fortune from the failure of an expensive and spirited endeavour on his part, having the formation of a national fund for the succour of artists, and the relief of their widows and orphans, for its object, whereby he was ruined a second time, and deprived, in consequence, of his liberty: that although distressed himself, and having numerous debts on his books due to him from Englishmen unable to pay, he has always been merciful to them. And this deponent further saith, That he has already suffered a painful imprisonment, ever since the eighth of April last, by which his means of defence were not only decidedly impeded, but his strength and health most materially injured; that in this particular, as also in the mode of seizing his papers and property, he has suffered considerable hardships, while his slender pecuniary resources, from the aforesaid causes, and by the heavy expences of his confinement and trial, are totally destroyed; and that on these accounts his sufferings have been greater than those of any of the other defendants. And this deponent also saith, that any further degradation must ruin his prospects in life for ever, and bring anguish and despair upon him, who has already suffered so severely from his attachment to this country; and he respectfully hopes, that his severe losses and ruined circumstances, his general exemplary conduct, his uninterrupted loyalty, and his many unrequited services, will have due weight with this honourable Court, in mitigation of punishment; he also relies that considerations additionally stimulating to forgiveness, will animate his judges, when it is stated, that deponent to this moment has received no recompence whatever, for his many patriotic exertions and ruinous sacrifices; and above all, that in consequence of his not having succeeded in obtaining a respite of the judgment for a short time, he has been prevented from experiencing the benefit of important affidavits, which he anxiously expected from other persons.

*Charles Random De Berenger.*"

*Mr. Topping.* I was of Counsel with Mr. Serjeant Best on the trial; I am not furnished with any affidavit on the part of Mr. Butt.

*Mr. Butt.* I came into Court, my Lord, expecting the privilege of asking for a new trial, upon certain facts which I have put down in my pocket-book.

*Lord Ellenborough.* You are not in time to move for a new trial.

*Mr. Butt.* I know I am not, my Lord; I was merely going to explain——

*Mr. Justice Le Blanc.* If you appear by Counsel, your Counsel had better state what you have to suggest.

*Mr. Topping.* I have no instructions on the subject.

*Mr. Butt.* I hope you will forgive my importunity in begging for a few moments to address you, having never been before in a court of justice, either as plaintiff or defendant; that I trust will plead my apology. If you will hear me, I shall be much obliged to you.

My Lords; I have been tried for conspiring with other persons, to raise the price of the public Government funds, and also for promoting assistance to those measures, by the changing of notes, and various other circumstances. I beg to assure your Lordships, that I do not address you on the idea or wish of a mitigation of any punishment you may think proper to inflict upon me; it is merely to express to you, that my sole wish and desire is to claim the indulgence of the Court, in permitting me to have a new and distinct trial, that I may clear my character from the cloud with which it is now depressed, and which had previously been without a blemish; as I am confident, if my case was separated from other persons in the indictment, it would be the means of my acquittal. It was my intention to have appeared in Court some days since, to have made the same request which I now do of your Lordships, had it not been for my Counsel informing me, that I should have been committed directly I entered the Court; and that the defendants should all appear before the Court could grant my request. This I found impossible to accomplish; and I declare, that the defendants, Sandom, Lyte, Holloway, and M'Rae, are all perfectly unknown to me; that I never directly or indirectly had any knowledge or communication or ever saw them in my life, neither did I ever see Mr. De Berenger more than two or three times. I beg also to acquaint your Lordships, that the bank notes which have been stated to have passed through my hands must, unavoidably so have done, as I permitted, without thinking it any crime, at the solicitation of my friends, that all drafts connected with the Stock Exchange business should be paid in my name, whether I was in London or not; and I did at any time change notes, or lend Mr. Johnstone money, as a temporary accommodation, when he wished it; and yet it is a fact, that I had never seen Mr. Johnstone till the 2d of January last. But it is impossible for me, and certainly a case of hardship, that I should be answerable for the manner in which those notes might be disposed of afterwards. There appears no one witness on the trial, that can give any extraordinary reason for my having paid the notes alluded to by Mr. Johnstone; for I might, hundreds of times, have paid notes to an equal amount to him, or to any other man.

My own conscience clears me of the offence laid to my charge, and so far was I from avoiding investigation, that I courted it, and instructed my Counsel not to take advantage of any flaw, should there appear one in the indictment, but to force the trial to issue.

I can only, my Lords, accuse myself of one fault, if it can be so called, that of being too generous and unguarded upon money affairs. I shall not intrude myself any further upon your Lordship's time, only assuring you, that the magnitude of my concerns in the funds, upon which so much stress has been laid, was not, according to my calculation, any thing extraordinary, neither was the sum I held on the 21st February, an act of premeditation, my concerns being as extensive before that period as at that time, and my profit upon that day, which has been so much exaggerated, was only £.1,300, instead of £.3,000, as stated by the counsel for the prosecution. Whatever your Lordships decision may be respecting myself, I shall bow with submission, feeling conscious of my innocence of the charge upon which I have been found guilty.

MR. PARK,

My Lord, I am of Counsel for Mr. De Berenger, and it does not very often fall to my lot to be Counsel for a defendant in the situation he is in. When we are so, we are always placed in a most painful situation; because it does not become the defendants themselves, much less does it become us, to offer any thing to your Lordships that may go in contradiction to the verdict. Undoubtedly, Mr. De Berenger is convicted, and he must abide the consequences of that conviction. His affidavit, I have seen only this morning; it seems to me to contain no exceptionable matter in it, which is not always the case; that certainly is a circumstance which one may fairly press upon the Court in favour of a defendant. He states to your Lordships what was to a certain degree confirmed by a noble lord upon the trial. If I recollect rightly, your Lordship has reported, that Lord Yarmouth stated in evidence, that this gentleman had conducted himself as adjutant to the volunteer corps of which he was commander, in a most exemplary manner. That was a character in which he received no remuneration; and he states to your Lordships also, that himself and his family were American loyalists, who suffered very considerably during the American war, in consequence of their attachment to this country; those are all circumstances which will meet with attention in your Lordships minds. In addition to this he has stated, what the circumstances of the case alone would convince your Lordships of without any affidavit, that being a defendant, under so expensive a prosecution, has occasioned him an enormous expence. That will be taken into consideration; and it will not be forgotten, although this gentleman cannot be said to have been imprisoned on this charge, it being of a nature to admit of bail, yet he has been upwards of two months in actual custody in the jail of Newgate;

that is a circumstance which does not apply to any other of the defendants, and the Court will take it also into consideration in passing sentence. I am quite aware he was taken up under a warrant of the Secretary of State, under the Alien Act; but his imprisonment had its origin in this charge, and to a certain degree it has deprived him of those advantages for his defence which the other defendants have enjoyed; I am not aware that I can better serve this gentleman, than by drawing your Lordship's attention to the circumstances which are contained in this affidavit; and I trust I have not said any thing calculated to increase the severity of his punishment.

*Lord Ellenborough.* Lord Yarmouth only speaks to the time during which he had known him to be acting as Adjutant; he states that he had known him since the year 1811.

*Mr. Park.* I do not know that Lord Yarmouth's statement went beyond that, I thought he had added something of approbation; but I submit to your Lordship, it is of itself sufficient proof of his good conduct, that he was so long continued in the situation.

MR. RICHARDSON.

My Lord; I am also of counsel for this unfortunate foreigner. I have no observation to make, except merely to call your Lordship's attention to this;—it is confirmed by Lord Yarmouth, that the defendant was a voluntary servant to the interests of this country, his services were therefore praiseworthy, and he appears by his affidavit to have been a material sufferer by the loyalty of his ancestors. These circumstances, I hope, will be taken into consideration by the Court. Your lordships also see, that he was a person in an extremely distressed situation, and at the time was suffering imprisonment, in consequence of the ruin of his fortunes, which he has mentioned.

*Lord. Ellenborough.* Is he in custody now under this charge?

*Mr. Park.* He is in custody in Newgate, my Lord, under the Alien Act.

*Lord Ellenborough.* There was no application made to put off the trial; a day was mentioned to the Court, and the counsel on both sides, stated their wish that it should come on; no impediment therefore existed in the way of the defence.

MR. SERJEANT PELL.

I appear, my Lords, on behalf of the three last defendants, Holloway, Sandom, and Lyte, men in a very different situation from the noble, but unfortunate person who first addressed your Lordships, upon the present painful occasion. The office I had to perform for these three defendants appeared to me on the trial to be a very difficult one; because with regard to them there was a direct confession, that they were in part guilty of that which was imputed to them. Holloway and Sandom, voluntarily confessed themselves guilty of all that part of the transaction, which related to the Northfleet affair.

*Mr. Justice Le Blanc.* There was a confession by two of them.

*Mr. Serjeant Pell.* But though they were the only persons who made a direct confession, yet I, upon the trial as counsel for Mr. Sandom, had no scruple in saying, that Mr. Sandom concurred in the confession which they had made. In this situation, it not being possible for me to contend, that those for whom I appeared, were not guilty of that part of the transaction; the only point which I could enforce at the trial was, that they were unacquainted with the other part. It is not for me to contend now (against the verdict of the Jury) that they were not also guilty of the other part; though, if I might be permitted to state my own feelings, I cannot but think there was a considerable defect of proof on that part of the case. The only circumstance that connected the one transaction with the other, independently of their taking place at the same period of time—and we must be aware that history furnishes many examples of conspiracies, having the same object, formed at the same time, yet totally unconnected with each other—the only link that connected the first of these transactions with the last, was the letter of Mr. Cochrane Johnstone, in which he mentions M'Rae as a person, who, for £.10,000, was willing to explain the whole of the transaction of the 21st February. Unquestionably that letter was no evidence against Mr. Holloway, Mr. Sandom, and Mr. Lyte. There was but one other circumstance appearing on the trial that connected them together; it was, that the chaise which took Mr. De Berenger, went to the same place where the chaise went which carried the three others. But it appeared upon the evidence, with respect to that part of the case, that Mr. De Berenger went to the Marsh-gate at Lambeth, not in consequence of design, but of an intimation which he received from the driver who drove the last stage, that there was no hackney-coach to be procured at the first place where they would stop; in consequence of which, Mr. De Berenger directed the man to drive him to another.

I am not disposed to-day to go into that part of the case, and to argue the matter as I did before the jury. That there was evidence on which the verdict of the jury may be supported, I cannot for a moment dispute; but I am sure your Lordships will excuse me for just begging your attention to that part of the case, because, I think, when compared and considered, together with what Mr. Holloway did when he made the communication to the Stock-Exchange, it does furnish an additional ground, which may fairly be urged in mitigation of punishment.

Let us attend to the circumstances under which Mr. Holloway made this confession. M'Rae, of whom I know nothing, is absent, and I have no means of tracing who he is; but he, finding there was a strong disposition on the part of the Stock Exchange, upon any terms to obtain evidence of the transaction of this day, hastens to Mr. Cochrane Johnstone, and then this extravagant offer is made by Mr. Johnstone on his behalf, to communicate all the information he is possessed of for the sum of £.10,000. This reaches the ears of Mr. Holloway. Mr. Holloway, knowing he had been guilty of acts on that day, which certainly would subject him, if discovered, to a criminal prosecution, but having reason to believe that M'Rae knew nothing of the transaction in which De Berenger acted, with a view to save the gentlemen of the Stock Exchange from paying money for a communication which would be of no value, came forward and made the confession, which appears upon your lordship's notes. Were it not for that confession voluntarily made by Mr. Holloway, there is no evidence against him, to shew that he was guilty of any part of the charge; nor any evidence against Lyte, to shew that he was guilty; but he was present when Holloway made the confession, and permitted him to make it. Therefore the whole evidence against them is their own confession, made with a view to save the gentlemen of the Stock Exchange a useless loss of money. I think I may be permitted to say, particularly as it regards Mr. Holloway and Mr. Lyte, that they stand in a situation which at least entitles them to the consideration of your lordships. I will not presume to say, the confession of Mr. Holloway and Mr. Lyte was made under any promise from the gentlemen of the Stock Exchange that it should not be used against them; but I think I may be permitted to suggest, that could they have supposed, the only evidence to be used against them would be their own confession, they would rather have hesitated about making a confession which alone places them this day before your lordships. It must likewise be taken as part of that confession, that Holloway and Lyte denied any concurrence with the noble lord and the other defendants; and I think I may press upon your lordships attention, in confirmation of this, what Lord Cochrane has himself stated, that he had no knowledge of them.

My Lords, it is true these persons have been guilty of a great misdemeanor, and it is not for me to say a word in their favour, in the way of palliating the immorality of the act. All I could submit to the jury was, that there was not evidence to connect them, with the other part of transaction; all I can now submit to your Lordships, is that they have done all they could do, after having been led into the commission of so scandalous and mischievous an offence, to save the prosecutors further loss and trouble. I have not troubled the Court with affidavits to character, I am well aware that such a transaction as this must stand by itself, I pursue the same line of conduct which I did at the trial; I propose not to offer any thing in arrest of judgment, I produce no affidavits in mitigation of punishment; but I do submit to your Lordships upon the whole of the case, as it respects these three defendants, that they do stand in a different situation from the other defendants; and though it is not to be forgotten that they were parties in a most scandalous transaction, yet that their ready confession does entitle them to as much consideration, as your Lordships can give in such a case.

MR. C. F. WILLIAMS.

My Lord, I am also counsel for these three defendants; the grounds of indulgence have been so fully gone over by Mr. Serj. Pell, that I think it unnecessary to make any observations.

MR. DENMAN.

My Lord, I am with the two learned gentlemen who have preceded me; and I would merely observe, that the affidavits which we might have been expected to offer upon this occasion, in support of the line of defence which we pursued, and which the learned serjeant has stated, could not properly be addressed to the court, because they must have gone in contravention to the verdict of the jury. At the same time I may be permitted to say, it is extremely singular, that in the two plans to affect this mischief, in each of which so many persons were concerned, and where so much assiduity has been employed, no one circumstance of connection between them has been discovered but that which was stated by the learned serjeant. What M'Rae might communicate was no evidence against these defendants; no doubt Mr. Cochrane Johnstone gave his sanction to that communication, by offering to contribute to the reward for which M'Rae stipulated; but Mr. Johnstone's acts are no evidence against these defendants. It is most unfortunate for them, that M'Rae, who appears to have been connected with Mr. Johnstone in one part of the affair, has appeared to be connected with them in the other part. It will perhaps occur to your Lordships to enquire why I state these things, seeing there is an admission of something criminal. I state them, because I think they do afford an argument in mitigation of punishment; because I think they will lead to the conclusion in your Lordships minds, that had these defendants been aware of the whole extent of mischief which was to be carried into effect, they probably would not have joined in it. Your Lordship put it to the jury, at the trial, that it was not necessary all the actors in the drama should know the part assigned to each,—that it was enough they had each contributed to the general object.

*Lord Ellenborough.* That they were parties to the general object, and co-operating to effect it.

*Mr. Denman.* But your Lordship particularly stated, it was not necessary that the jury should arrive at the precise degree of participation and extent of criminality. I humbly conceive, the extent of criminality, as affecting these defendants, is, in comparison with the others, very small; and I trust your Lordships, considering their degree of guilt, will proportionably moderate the degree of their punishment. In the case of conspiracy, the law itself inflicts a most severe and heavy judgment; and in pronouncing that sentence which must come from your Lordship's lips, I have no doubt, the considerations which attach themselves to it, will not be overlooked.

MR. GURNEY.

My Lord; my learned friend Mr. Serjeant Pell has alluded to the different situations of the several defendants who now stand upon the floor for your Lordships Judgment. It is, my Lords, a lamentable spectacle, but it will not, I trust, be an unprofitable lesson to mankind, that conspiracy, like "misery, acquaints a man with strange bedfellows." The conspiracy of the 21st February was, for all the defendants to act in concert, each man to perform his part toward the accomplishment of their common purpose;—one to travel from Dover, others to travel from Northfleet, and others to be on the spot at the Stock Exchange, to avail themselves of the rise in the funds produced by these operations. But the conspiracy on the day of trial, and the conspiracy of this day, is, for each, to be distinct and separate, and, as much as possible, unknown to the others.

I am willing to concede to my learned friends who have last addressed your Lordships, that some of these defendants do stand in a very different situation from the others. Of Holloway and Lyte, it is fairly to be observed, that by their confession they did manifest a degree of contrition; it must, however, be recollected respecting Holloway, that the purpose which he conceived, was a fraud for his own personal advantage: It is in evidence that his fraud took effect; and he has not ventured to state to your Lordships, by affidavit, to what extent that fraud was successful and profitable.

With regard to Sandom, the other defendant of this class, his part in this transaction was a very prominent and important part; and he was proved to be guilty by the evidence of others, not by his own;—he cannot plead the merit of a confession. It may, however, fairly be urged for all these three defendants, Sandom, Holloway and Lyte, that they did not aggravate their case at the trial, in the manner in which the other defendants aggravated theirs.

As to the defendant De Berenger, it appears that he was the hired and paid agent of Lord Cochrane, Mr. Cochrane Johnstone, and Mr. Butt; and having received his wages, he was attempting clandestinely to quit the country: If he had effected that purpose, he would have escaped punishment himself, and would probably have defeated justice with regard to the others. But, my Lords, his case has been greatly aggravated, as indeed have the cases of Lord Cochrane and Mr. Cochrane Johnstone, by attempts to defeat public justice, as absurd as they were wicked; for all the swearing before the trial, all the swearing at the trial, and all the swearing of to-day, has proceeded on the presumption, that if men will have the hardihood to swear, there will be found those who will have the credulity to believe.

Your Lordship has reported to the Court to-day, the evidence that was given on the part of Mr. Cochrane Johnstone and Mr. De Berenger, the letters which were stated by Mr. Tahourdin to have been written by Mr. Cochrane Johnstone and Mr. De Berenger, on the 22d February, the day after this fraud had been perpetrated. Whether Mr. Tahourdin deposed to that which was correctly true, or not, appears to me to make no difference. If the letters were written at a period subsequent to their dates, they were fabricated for the purpose of constituting an artificial defence. If they were written at the time they bear date, then they were equally fabricated for an artificial defence; and at the very moment of the commission of the crime, the parties were providing the means of a false defence, in case they should be detected.

There was a flat contradiction between Mr. Tahourdin and the letter which Mr. Tahourdin produced; whether the evidence of the witness were true, or the statement in the letter were true, matters not; the contradiction, independent of all other circumstances, shews that the whole of this transaction was one premeditated scheme of fraud.

There was still more evidence respecting De Berenger; a number of witnesses were called to swear, that at the time when he was proved to have been at Dover, he was actually in London, or at least in London so short a time before, that he could not by possibility have been at Dover. The persons who formed this scheme totally forgot the sort of case they had to meet: they were endeavouring to meet a case of recognition of the human countenance, by witnesses who might be mistaken in that recognition; and they forgot, that to a recognition of the countenance, a recognition however which surpassed every thing that ever fell under my observation, though put to the severest test to which such testimony was ever exposed—De Berenger, seated among a number of persons, nothing distinguishing him, nothing to attract the attention of the witnesses, yet witness after witness, with but a single exception, on looking round the Court, recognized his person the moment he cast his eyes upon his countenance.—I say, my Lord, that they who contrived this false and perjured defence, forgot that, in addition to this, there was the delivery of De Berenger from hand to hand, from Dover into the house of Lord Cochrane; and into the house of Lord Cochrane it was never pretended that any other person but De Berenger entered.

Then, my Lords, we have the affidavit of Lord Cochrane, to which he has added the affidavit of to-day, respecting the dress which De Berenger wore upon that occasion. It is singular that a servant of Lord Cochrane's should have been called upon the trial, examined upon other points to the confirmation of his master's affidavit, and that my learned friends, who were of counsel for Lord Cochrane, whose ability, whose discretion, and whose zeal, no man who knows them can question, did not venture to put to that servant a question as to the colour of De Berenger's coat; and that they did not venture to call the two other servants, one of whom at least was in attendance, and if the other had been wanted, it would not have been difficult for Lord Cochrane to have detained him in England, that he too might have been examined. No man can doubt that the reason why my friends abstained from asking that question, and going into that examination, was, that after the evidence which had been given by all the witnesses for the prosecution, as to his dress, continued up to the last moment by the driver of the hackney-coach, who swore to De Berenger's entering the house in a *scarlet* coat; if all the servants in Lord Cochrane's house had been called to swear that the colour of De Berenger's coat was *green*, no man alive could have believed them.

Your Lordships have before you the whole extent of this gigantic Conspiracy and Fraud; you have seen the stock account of these persons, and you find that on the morning of this day Lord Cochrane, Mr. Cochrane Johnstone, and Mr. Butt, were possessed of as much in Consols and Omnium, as, reduced to Consols alone, would amount to £.1,600,000; on which sum, the fluctuation of only one-eighth per cent. would produce a loss or gain of £.2,000; and although these defendants have not profited to the extent they anticipated, first, because the telegraph did not work,—no thanks to them that it did not;—and next, because the fruit of their fraud was intercepted,— the stolen goods were stopped in transitu,—still it appears from the evidence of Mr. Baily, that they have been materially enriched by their fraud, for they were enabled to get rid of this immense amount of Consols and Omnium, without loss, which, but for the operation of this fraud, they could not have done.

At the trial, Mr. Serjeant Best pressed very eloquently upon your Lordship and the jury, the former services of Lord Cochrane: I must observe, my Lord, that those services had neither been forgotten nor unrewarded by his Sovereign or his Country:—by his Sovereign, he had been raised to a high rank in his profession, and was in the path to the highest; he had also been invested with a most honourable personal distinction, which adds lustre even to nobility itself; which, at the same time that it was a reward for the past, ought to have been an incentive for the future:—He had been raised by a grateful Country to the proud and enviable station of representative in Parliament for the city in which your Lordships are now sitting; which, at the same time that it imposed on him the duty of watching, and if necessary, of animadverting on the conduct of others, especially bound him to guard the purity of his own. For all this, what return has he made?—he has engaged in a conspiracy to perpetrate a fraud, by producing an undue effect on the public funds of the Country, of which funds he was an appointed guardian, and to perpetrate that fraud by falsehood: He attempted to palm that falsehood upon that very Board of Government, under the orders of which he was then fitting out, on an important public service; and still more, as if to dishonour the profession of which he was a member, he attempted to make a brother officer the organ of that falsehood.

This offence, my Lord, does not proceed from the infirmity of a noble mind, from the impetuosity of youthful passion, from the excess of any generous feeling;—it is cold, calculating fraud, scarcely capable of aggravation; but, if it be capable of aggravation, it has received this great aggravation, that when threatened with detection, he endeavoured to avert it by the deliberate commission of a crime which, I repeat, has all the moral turpitude of Perjury, without its legal responsibility. I have to add one observation only, which applies equally to Lord Cochrane and Mr. Butt, that they stand before your Lordship, though convicted, unrepenting.

The Prosecutors in this case have, through many difficulties, conducted this Prosecution to its termination: they have sought an honourable end by honourable means: they have sought for justice, and justice only; and to your Lordships justice they commit these Defendants.

*Lord Ellenborough.* Let all the Defendants stand committed, and be brought up to-morrow morning to receive the Judgment of the Court.

# Court of King's Bench.

*Tuesday, June 21, 1814.*

*Charles Random De Berenger, Lord Cochrane, Richard Gathorne Butt, Ralph Sandom, John Peter Holloway, and Henry Lyte were brought up pursuant to the order of the Court to receive judgment.*

MR. JUSTICE LE BLANC.

The six defendants, whose names have been now called, are to receive the judgment of the court, in consequence of a conviction upon an indictment for a conspiracy; that indictment, and the evidence which had been given upon the trial, on which trial the jury pronounced the several defendants guilty, was more particularly stated to the court yesterday, in the course of the discussion which took place. The sum of the offence charged in the indictment was, that these six defendants, together with two other persons, who do not now appear to abide the judgment of the law, had conspired together, by spreading false rumours and reports in different places, to occasion a rise in the price of the public funds of this country, on a particular day, and thereby to injure all those subjects who might purchase stock on that particular day; that was the sum of the charge contained in the several counts of the indictment on which the defendants were found guilty.

I will shortly advert to the circumstances of the case as they appeared in evidence. From that evidence it appeared, that some of the defendants had been, for a short time previous to the time when this conspiracy was put into execution, (namely the 21st of February,) largely speculating in the public funds of the country, and that at that time three of the defendants who now appear before the court, together with one of the defendants who does not appear, were either holders of stock, or persons who had contracted for the purchase of stock, to a very considerable amount. It appears, that on the 19th of February, which was on a Saturday, a person, not expressly spoken to by the witness, had purchased of a military accoutrement-maker in this town the dress, or at least part of the dress, and accoutrements, of a foreign officer, stating at that time, that it was designed for a person who was to appear in the character of a foreign officer, and that on the same day another person who was concerned in another part of the plot, had produced a small parcel at home which had been given to his wife, and the next morning (Sunday) had brought home two coats and two hats, evidently intended to fit out two persons with the appearance of foreign officers. Those are the first circumstances that appear previous to the day when this plan was to be put in execution.

The next period to be adverted to was the morning of Monday, the 21st of February, and on that morning, about a quarter after one o'clock in the morning, one of the defendants, Charles Random de Berenger, makes his appearance at the door of the Ship Inn at Dover, wearing the dress of a foreign officer, as described by four witnesses, who saw him at Dover with the scarlet uniform of a military officer under a grey great coat, and a military cap, the cap worn by military officers, applying to be furnished immediately with a chaise and four to proceed on his journey to town, holding himself out as a person who had just landed from a vessel come from the coast of France, and bringing very important intelligence of the success of engagements in that country, in which the Ruler of France had been defeated, with other circumstances not particularly necessary to be adverted to, and that the consequences would be in a very short time a peace between that country and this. He is expressly recognized and pointed out as being one of the defendants, Charles Random De Berenger, by four different persons who saw him at that time in the morning at the Ship Inn, where he continued for some time, while horses were preparing, having called for pen, ink and paper, to write a letter, as he professed, to be sent off to Admiral Foley, the Admiral commanding the ships stationed in the Downs, and while there actually dispatching a messenger with such letter to Admiral Foley, which is proved to be afterwards received by the Admiral, affecting to communicate this intelligence, and signing this by the affected name of De Bourg, as aid-de-camp, to what appears to be intended for Lord Cathcart.

From thence he is traced distinctly through the various stages where he changed horses, at Canterbury, Sittingbourn and Rochester, where he stopped and took some refreshment, and had some conversation with the landlord of the Crown Inn, who speaks to his dress at the time of the communication which he there made, similar to that which I have adverted to as having been made upon his first application for a chaise and horses at Dover. From thence he proceeds to Dartford, and from Dartford in like manner, the last stage, into London. The post-boy who drove him the last stage into town, besides speaking to his person, and all of them having picked out and fixed upon Charles Random De Berenger, whom they afterwards saw in court, as the person who had so travelled from Dover to London, having had opportunities, during the last stage, of seeing him while he was out of the carriage and walking up a hill, and while he conversed with them directing them to the place to which he should be driven. He inquired where he could first be set down, and could meet with a hackney coach; one place proposed by the postboy did not meet his approbation, he stating that it was attended with too much publicity, and he then directed himself to be driven to Lambeth where a hackney coach might be procured, and at the Marsh-gate turnpike at Lambeth he was ultimately set down, and stepped from the post-chaise into a hackney coach, and at that period he is spoken to positively, not only by the postboy who had driven him to that spot, but by the waterman who opened the door and put down the step of the hackney coach; he swears distinctly to his person and to his dress, that he had then a scarlet coat under a grey great-coat, with a military cap. From thence he directs himself to be driven to Grosvenor-square. Those are the orders given to the coachman when he gets into the coach, and then he directs the coachman to a particular house and number in Green-street, which was the house of one of the other defendants, Lord Cochrane, and into which house the coachman proves his having seen him enter in that dress first described by the witnesses at Dover, and confirmed by all the witnesses on his passage during his journey, namely, a red uniform coat under a grey great-coat. So much for that part of the transaction which relates to the spreading of false rumours and reports respecting what had happened in France, and the prospect of peace in the way from Dover to the place where he was last set down, the house of Lord Cochrane in Green-street on that same morning.

The other part of the plot or conspiracy was put in execution at somewhat a later date, by the efforts of some of the other defendants, namely, Holloway, M'Rae, Sandom, and Lyte, on that same Monday morning. The innkeeper at Dartford receives a note from Sandom, ordering a chaise to be sent to Northfleet, at a particular hour, to bring persons to Dartford, and to have four horses ready to convey them to London. Accordingly three persons, two of them, I think, described as wearing a military dress, and white cockades in their hats, come in that chaise to Dartford, from whence, with another chaise and four horses, the horses ornamented with laurel, and the men inside with white cockades in their hats, they drive at a quick pace to London, through some of the principal streets of London, over Blackfriars Bridge, and there directing to be set down at the same place, the Marsh-gate at Lambeth, they get into a hackney coach, and no more is heard of them. This seems to have been a counterpart—another branch of the plot, which was put into execution about two hours after the first chaise had arrived with the defendant De Berenger, and in that these persons are proved to have been concerned whom I have stated.

Immediately upon the arrival of De Berenger at the house of Lord Cochrane in Green-street, dressed as I have described, in the dress in which he was first observed at Dover, he appears to have dispatched a note to Lord Cochrane, who was not then at home, and that note is delivered to my Lord Cochrane at a place somewhere near Snowhill, where Lord Cochrane was at the time. What the contents of that note were, as the note has not itself been produced, we have no evidence. Upon that my Lord Cochrane immediately returns home in a coach. There is no doubt but the defendant De Berenger was then at the house of my Lord Cochrane, and there, before he leaves the house, with the privity and in the presence of my Lord Cochrane, he changes the uniform which he wore at the time, and in which he is proved to have entered clothed, and puts on a black coat of Lord Cochrane's; he exchanges his military cap for a round hat of Lord Cochrane's likewise, in the house, and then he gets into the hackney coach which had brought Lord Cochrane, and goes away in that dress, and in that coach, and on that same day, which is Monday the 21st of February, the whole of this property in the funds, or these contracts for stock in the funds (of which it is not now necessary to state the particular sums) which was held by Lord Cochrane, by Mr. Cochrane Johnstone, by Mr. Butt, and by Mr. Holloway, is sold by those persons at an advance which advance had been occasioned by that which had taken place in the course of the early part of that day.

The additional circumstances which are proved in evidence, and which I will only now shortly advert to, are those stated by the broker Fearn, who had been the purchaser and the seller of a considerable part of this stock for particularly three of the persons, Lord Cochrane, Mr. Cochrane Johnstone, and Mr. Butt; he was introduced by Mr. Butt to my Lord Cochrane and Mr. Cochrane Johnstone, and had managed, or appears to have had considerable hand in managing, these speculations in the funds.

In addition to that, it appears, that afterwards, I think, on the 27th of February, De Berenger disappears, and is some short time afterwards, the particular day was not, I believe, mentioned in evidence, apprehended, passing under a feigned name, at a distant part of the country, with considerable property at that time in his possession, having been before, up to the 21st of February, living as an insolvent within the rules of the King's Bench prison.

The question which is next material to be adverted to is, how far any of these circumstances implicate the defendants who are found guilty on this record. I have stated the circumstances with respect to the minor actors in this conspiracy. De Berenger, who was the actor and the propagator of the false rumours from Dover to London, and the other persons who were the propagators of these false rumours from Northfleet to London. It is singular that De Berenger should instantly drive, in the dress in which he travelled from Dover to London, to the house of my Lord Cochrane; should instantly send and have an interview with my Lord Cochrane; and that in the presence and with the knowledge of my Lord Cochrane, before he left his house, he should change that dress in which he had arrived, and should go away in a dress of my Lord Cochrane's: those are things which could not happen by accident; and the court see that they have not been accounted for in any satisfactory manner; and they certainly were not accounted for in a satisfactory manner to the minds of the jury, who have drawn the conclusion of guilt, by any explanation which was then given, either by word or upon oath. The manner in which it is attempted to be accounted for is, that De

Berenger, who was but slightly known to my Lord Cochrane, had come at that time to him upon some other business; that as to the note which he sent to my Lord Cochrane, and which has not been produced, my Lord Cochrane at the time did not clearly perceive by whom it was signed, or from whom it came, and that he went home immediately upon receiving it, in expectation that it might be from an officer coming from abroad, bringing him an account of the health of a brother, who at that time, or shortly before, had been labouring under a dangerous illness; that note which was sent has not been produced, and no satisfactory evidence has been stated, either before the jury or since, upon the application which was made to the court for a new trial, to fix precisely the time when any account had been received by my Lord Cochrane of the illness of this brother, or holding out to him any expectation at what time, and by what means, he was likely to hear further accounts of him. If any such letter had been received, if it had come by a private hand, the person who brought it might have been called to show the information which he had received; if it had been brought by a ship, or by post, the mark on the direction and the envelope of that letter, would have given some explanation of it, but no such explanation has been held out either to the jury at the trial, or to the court since, on the opportunity which was afforded my Lord Cochrane yesterday of stating the grounds upon which he wished to have a new trial.

There is another circumstance in evidence which I have not yet adverted to, and it is this, it was proved in evidence, and I will not go through the particulars, that shortly before this 21st of February, namely, on the 16th of February, a broker, of the name of Smallbone, had drawn a bill on Jones, Loyd, and Co. in London, for the sum of 470*l.* 19*s.* 4*d.* payable to a number, upon which nothing arises, or to bearer; but that this bill, or check, was given to Lord Cochrane, so that it was in his hands; the money received for this check at the bankers, was proved in evidence to consist of particular bank notes; those bank notes were afterwards changed, and appear to have been changed industriously for other notes, by a person employed, I think by the defendant Butt, and part of the produce of this check had been employed by Lord Cochrane himself in the payment of a bill of a coal merchant of his, and a number of the small notes that had been produced by the change of some of the larger notes for which the check was changed, were traced to the hands of De Berenger himself; and many of them actually found in his possession, and in his trunk at the time he was shortly afterwards apprehended in a distant part of this kingdom; now this is a coincidence of circumstances which requires very satisfactorily to be accounted for, in order to raise a doubt in the mind of any one that there was a connection with respect to this transaction, and an intimate connection between the parties charged upon this indictment, I mean particularly the defendant, my Lord Cochrane, the defendant Butt, and the defendant De Berenger. Where we find that it is to the house of my Lord Cochrane that he comes immediately after having acted this part in spreading this rumour between Dover and London, and where the very notes that are found upon the person of De Berenger, before in insolvent circumstances, are part of the produce of that very draft which had actually been traced to the hand of Lord Cochrane, and by the intervention of another of the defendants, Butt, had likewise, I think, been through the hands of Mr. Cochrane Johnstone paid to this very De Berenger, and found in his possession when he had absconded, and was going by another name in a distant part of this country.

With respect to the other part of the transaction, when we find who were the persons who benefited by this plan, which has been so put into execution; that the persons who were connected together in speculating in the funds up to the very period of the 21st, and were then the holders of very considerable sums, or contracts for those sums, down to the morning of the 21st, got rid of all of them in the course of the 21st, and when those circumstances of connection which I have adverted to have been so clearly made out, and no satisfactory account given, nor any reason given to expect that a satisfactory account would be given, if a further opportunity of investigating it should have been afforded, how can the court come to any other conclusion if they have to exercise their judgment upon the fact, but the conclusion to which the jury have come, namely, that the defendants are guilty; that it was a conspiracy ingeniously and cunningly devised, extensive in its operation, most mischievous in its effect, and contrived for the wicked and the fraudulent purpose of enriching some few individuals at the expense of others, who might be induced to sell, and to buy property on that day, or who might be in a situation to be obliged to do it, which was the case with the suitors of the court of Chancery.

The offence of conspiracy is in itself always viewed in the eye of the law as a heinous offence; and where a number of persons connect themselves together in order to carry into execution a plan which one alone cannot carry into execution, and where that is done with the evident intention of fraud, to put money into the pockets of certain persons, and by that means to defraud others, such an offence is and always has been considered in the eye of the law as an infamous offence, and calling upon the court who are to administer the justice of the country for a punishment, as far as they can inflict it, proportionate to the infamy of the crime.

It is with pain that the court in passing sentence upon the defendants have to advert to those circumstances, which, applying to particular persons, appear to aggravate the guilt of the offence of which they have been convicted; it is painful for the court to observe, that among those who stand for judgment there should be any person whose situation from rank, connections, education, and every thing held honourable among mankind, ought to have felt himself so far above being connected with persons of the description with whom he has been connected, and mixing in traffic with which he has been mixed, which independently of the crime of which he has been convicted is disgraceful and disreputable to any man, I mean gambling in the funds to the amount and to the extent to which it is proved; it is painful for the court to have to animadvert upon such an offence in such a subject; and more painful to feel, that in the exercise of their duty they are bound to say, that the greater opportunity which a defendant had of knowing his duty, and the higher he felt in rank and in situation, and the less temptation he ought to have felt to have offended the laws of his country, in this respect the heavier falls the weight of guilt upon him.

Another observation which one cannot fail to make in the present instance, is, that in the course of this inquiry, certainly with respect to the defence made by the defendant De Berenger, one cannot find any circumstances of which the court can lay hold, as a ground upon which they can mitigate the offence which the law calls for to be inflicted upon that defendant, because after a weight of evidence not depending upon the testimony of two, three, four or six persons, as to the identity of the man and his clothes, an attempt was made at the trial to delude the jury and the court, by inducing them to believe that he was at another place at the time, and that it was not De Berenger who had appeared at Dover; that it was not De Berenger who had travelled from Dover to London in the way described; and that it was not De Berenger who had been landed at last in the house of Lord Cochrane.

Though the court could not consistently with its rules hear the application for a new trial made by my Lord Cochrane within the first four days of the term, yet still it was willing to afford the opportunity at any time to state circumstances which might operate upon the mind of the court to show that the verdict had been improperly come to, and that the evidence did not justify it: but what was the attempt upon the part of that defendant, my Lord Cochrane, to show that he ought to have had a new trial?—that certain witnesses who were present at the time of the trial had not been examined; and that some of those who had been examined had not been examined to facts which it was wished they should be examined to; and what were those facts? why they went to show that at the time De Berenger was at the house of my Lord Cochrane he appeared, not in a red uniform, as was described by so many witnesses, and among others, the person who landed him at that house, but that he had on the green uniform, in which, from the situation he had been in, in a rifle volunteer corps he had been in the habit of appearing. It was probably a very prudent exercise of discretion in those who had the conduct of the case of that defendant at the trial, not to attempt to call servants at the house for the purpose of disproving a fact which had been proved by so many witnesses; and it is impossible to conceive that any change of dress could have taken place during that short interval, from the time at which he had got out of the coach, to the period when he had appeared before Lord Cochrane; or what could be the motive for changing his dress, if he then had on the uniform of any corps of volunteers in this town.

These are the observations which naturally present themselves as arising out of the detail of the evidence which has been read. It cannot be necessary to expatiate at all upon the nature of the offence. It is a conspiracy of the greatest magnitude, and of the most prejudicial effect to the community; it is conceived in mischief, and a great deal of deliberation practised previously to its being put into execution. In this respect an offence of this description differs from most of the offences which come under the cognizance of a court of criminal jurisdiction. In many cases offenders have been led to transgress the law by a suggestion of the moment; by a temptation, which, as it has been urged sometimes at the bar, human nature could not resist; but in the present instance it has been deliberately undertaken; great contrivance, and great previous consideration, have been used for the purpose of laying the plan and procuring the actors who were to bear their different parts of it; and the whole object of it founded in avarice on the part of some, and the hope of gain for acting that part which the others took in this transaction, not for their own immediate emolument, except so far as they were to receive the wages of their iniquity.

The court has deliberated upon the case, and the court cannot, in this instance, feel itself justified in measuring out justice to one by a different measure from that in which justice would be measured out to others; the sentence therefore of the court upon you, the several defendants now upon the floor, is, That you, Sir Thomas Cochrane, otherwise called Lord Cochrane, and you Richard Gathorne Butt, do severally pay to the King a fine of one thousand pounds each; that you, John Peter Holloway, the third person who was to be benefited by this conspiracy, do pay to the King a fine of five hundred pounds; that all you the six several defendants, Charles Random De Berenger, Sir Thomas Cochrane, commonly called Lord Cochrane, Richard Gathorne Butt, Ralph Sandom, John Peter Holloway, and Henry Lyte, be severally imprisoned in the custody of the Marshal of the Marshalsea of our Lord the King for twelve calendar months; and that during that period you, Charles Random Be Berenger, you, Sir Thomas Cochrane, otherwise called Lord Cochrane, and you, Richard Gathorne Butt, be severally set in and upon the pillory, opposite the Royal Exchange in the City of London, for one hour, between the hours of twelve at noon and two in the afternoon; and that you be now severally committed to the custody of the Marshal of the Marshalsea, in execution of this sentence, and be further imprisoned until your several fines be paid.

Milton Keynes UK
Ingram Content Group UK Ltd.
UKHW040833071024
449371UK00007B/789